Routledge Revivals

Microeconomic Analysis

First published in 1981, this book brings together a collection of essays on microeconomics and development presented at the conference of the Association of University Teachers of Economics. Topics covered include the intergenerational transfer of economic inequality, a review of the recent development in the theory of equity in the economy's distribution and production process, labour and unemployment, market structure and international trade, taxation and the public sector, Third World industrialisation and Indian agriculture. This book will be of interest to students of Economics and Development Studies.

Microeconomic Analysis

Essays in Microeconomics and Economic Development

Edited by
David Currie, David Peel and Will Peters

Routledge
Taylor & Francis Group

First published in 1981
by Croom Helm

This edition first published in 2016 by Routledge
2 Park Square, Milton Park, Abingdon, Oxon, OX14 4RN
and by Routledge
711 Third Avenue, New York, NY 10017

Routledge is an imprint of the Taylor & Francis Group, an informa business

Publisher's Note
The publisher has gone to great lengths to ensure the quality of this reprint but points out that some imperfections in the original copies may be apparent.

Disclaimer
The publisher has made every effort to trace copyright holders and welcomes correspondence from those they have been unable to contact.

A Library of Congress record exists under LC control number: 81157488

ISBN 13: 978-1-138-66561-3 (hbk)
ISBN 13: 978-1-315-61975-0 (ebk)

MICROECONOMIC ANALYSIS:

ESSAYS IN MICROECONOMICS AND ECONOMIC DEVELOPMENT

Edited by
D. Currie, D. Peel and W. Peters

CROOM HELM LONDON

Croom Helm Ltd, 2-10 St John's Road, London SW11

British Library Cataloguing in Publication Data

Microeconomic analysis.
1. Microeconomics
I. Currie, D. II. Peel, D.
III. Peters, W.
338.5 HB171.5

ISBN 0-7099-0709-4

Printed and bound in Great Britain

Contents

LIST OF CONTRIBUTORS

R. Allard	Queen Mary College, London
W.J. Baumol	Princeton University & New York University
G.S. Becker	University of Chicago and National Bureau of Economic Research
D. Bosworth	University of Loughborough
P. Dawkins	University of Loughborough
G.D. Fraser	University of Warwick
G.M. Folie	University of New South Wales, Sydney
P.A. Geroski	University of Southampton
T. Hazledine	Economic Council of Canada
J.D. Hey	University of York
D.M.W.N. Hitchens	N.I.E.S.R.
D.G. Leslie	University of Manchester
B.J. Loasby	University of Stirling
M. Jones-Lee	University of York
P.N. Junankar	University of Essex
S.M. Kanbur	University of Cambridge
B. Lyons	University of Cambridge
P. Madden	University of Manchester
J. Mirrlees	Nuffield College, Oxford
D.M.G. Newbery	Churchill College, Cambridge
A. Parikh	University of East Anglia
I. Papps	University of Durham
C.A. Pissarides	London School of Economics
A.F. Shorrocks	London School of Economics
A. Silberston	Imperial College, London
A. Singh	Cambridge University

P.K. Trivedi	Australian National University
N. Topham	University of Salford
A.M. Ulph	University of Southampton
D. Ulph	University College, London
T. Westway	University of Loughborough

EDITORS' INTRODUCTION

The proceedings of the 1979 and 1980 annual conferences of the Association of University Teachers of Economics, have been brought together here, and in a companion volume of essays in contemporary economic analysis. These annual meetings provide an important, and indeed the only well-established annual forum for professional economists in the United Kingdom. The activities of the Association, date back to the 1920's, and include amongst its past participants and officers such economic luminaries as John Maynard Keynes and Sir William Beveridge. That the Association meetings now represent a thoroughly professional conference venue is in no small measure due to the efforts and endeavours of Frank Paish and the late Harry G. Johnson. In partial tribute, the two keynote lectures of the meetings are named after them.

An A.U.T.E. conference is not drawn upon narrowly defined subjects, and previous conference volumes have not, therefore reflected any specific themes. The simultaneous publication of the 1979 and 1980 papers has offered the editors the opportunity to bring together papers in the general areas of micro-economics and development, (vol.1), and macro-economics and econometrics (vol.2).

The programme committee endeavours to invite contributions for the main keynote lectures from distinguished scholars actively pursuing research in areas which seem important and promising. This volume includes the Harry G. Johnson lectures for 1979 and 1980, which were delivered by Gary Becker and William Baumol of the Universities of Chicago and Princeton respectively.

Becker takes up the question of the transmission of economic inequality through succeeding generations. A first approximation to a long-run theory of inequality might argue that equilibrium results from a balance of two forces: a less than complete transmission of extremes of wealth or ability from parents to children (tending to reduce the dispersion of economic status) and an uneven incidence of luck (tending to increase the dispersion). Becker shows that these elements are indeed important, but that the transmission of inequality need not be modelled in a mechanical way; rather, it can be represented as the outcome of rational decisions by parents, weighing their own consumption against benefits for their offspring.

Equity issues in the context of policy problems are clearly of importance. Baumol's paper is a lucid review and interpretation of the recent development in the theory of equity in the economy's distribution and production process which will allow analysis of such policy problems. In particular he shows how the superfairness criterion can be applied to the important issue of the appropriate choice among rationing techniques.

The other essays in this volume deal with a variety of topics in micro-economic analysis and economic development. As may be expected of the conference sessions which are organized along seminar lines with one and a half hours for presentation, the papers elicited a considerable amount of discussion from the floor. We are grateful to the participants, formal discussants and referees for their helpful and critical comments. Particular thanks are due to Naomi Canter, Jeane Ashton, Simon Blackman and David Baum for efficient secretarial and editorial help.

The Editors.

THE HARRY G. JOHNSON MEMORIAL LECTURES

AN EQUILIBRIUM THEORY OF THE DISTRIBUTION OF INCOME AND INTERGENERATIONAL MOBILITY

Gary S. Becker.

APPLICATION OF THE THEORY OF SUPERFAIRNESS

William J. Baumol.

1. AN EQUILIBRIUM THEORY OF THE DISTRIBUTION OF INCOME AND INTERGENERATIONAL MOBILITY

Gary S. Becker

It is a privilege to be invited to address your Association, and a special privilege to give this lecture that honors Harry Johnson, a colleague for many years at the University of Chicago. The economics profession acclaims Harry Johnson for his outstanding contributions to economic science, especially to trade theory and macro-economics. I developed enormous admiration also for Harry's courage. I refer partly to his courage in coping with debilitating physical afflications during the last few years of his life. Harry continued writing, editing, teaching, travelling, and his other hectic activities to the end.

I refer also to his mental courage: Harry did not trim his views to court popularity. Whether in Britain, the United States, Canada, or elsewhere, Harry wrote and said bluntly what he believed, no matter how many people were annoyed or uncomfortable. Mental courage is a scarce resource in all endeavours and certainly has been of great value in the progress of economics.

My subject tonight is the distribution of income. Harry Johnson wrote wisely on this subject as on so many others. Since he stressed the importance of parents in determining the opportunities of their children, I would like to believe that he would approve of the theme of this paper, which is the influence of the family on the distribution of income.

I. Introduction[1]

More than a decade ago, one of us wrote

> How does one explain then that in spite of the rapid accumulation of empirical information and the persisting and even increasing interest in [the distribution of income],....economists have somewhat neglected the study of personal

> income distribution during the past generation? In my judgment the fundamental reason is the absence, despite ingenious and valiant efforts, of a theory that both articulates with general economic theory and is useful in explaining actual differences among regions, countries, and time periods. [Becker 1967, p. 1]

Although the "just" distribution of income has since received an enormous amount of attention (see, for example, Rawls 1971 and Okun 1975), a satisfactory theory of the actual distribution has not been developed.

A full analysis of the distribution of income should include both the inequality in income between different generations of the same family - what is usually called intergenerational "social" mobility - and the inequality in income between different families in the same generation. Sociologists have been mainly concerned with intergenerational mobility and economists with inequality within a generation because they have held divergent views about the forces generating inequality. Sociologists have emphasized the role of an individual's forebears in the determination of his "socioeconomic" status through their influence on his background, class, or caste (see Boudon 1974 or Blau-Duncan 1967). On the other hand, most models of inequality by economists have neglected the transmission of inequality through the family because they have assumed that stochastic processes largely determine inequality through distributions of luck and abilities (see Champernowne 1953 or Roy 1950).

Two recent analytical developments suggest that a unified approach to inter-generational mobility and inequality is possible. The human capital model shows that inequality can result from maximizing behavior without major reliance on luck and other stochastic forces.[2] The economic approach to social interactions (Becker 1974, Becker-Tomes 1976, Tomes 1978) views an individual not in isolation but as part of a family whose members span several generations. Members contribute to the production of family income and to the care of children who continue the family into the future.

The central decision-makers in this essay are infinitely long-lived families with mortal members in each generation.

The current generation can increase their consumption at the expense of future generations, but are discouraged from doing do by their concern for the interests of their children and perhaps of other future family members. This link between generations of the same family is buttressed by family "endowments" transferred from parents to children, including a family's caste, religion, race, "culture", genes, and reputation for honesty and reliability.

Our theory incorporated the human capital approach to inequality because parents maximize their utility by choosing optimal investments in the human and non-human capital of children and other members. Moreover, the theory recognizes that endowments and market rewards depend on luck, so that incomes are partly determined by the interaction between luck and maximizing behavior.

We show that the inequality in family incomes and inter-generational mobility over time approach equilibrium levels that depend on luck and various family parameters, especially the "inheritability" of endowments and the propensity to invest in children. They also depend, sometimes in surprising ways, on the rate of economic growth, taxes and subsidies, foresight about the incidence of "disturbances", discrimination against minorities, and family reputations. For example, even a progressive tax-subsidy system might raise the inequality in *disposable* incomes, and discrimination against blacks has raised their inter-generational mobility and reduced their incomes.

The theory developed in this essay is an outgrowth of our work on interactions and investments within a family (see Becker 1967, Becker 1974, Becker-Tomes 1976, Tomes 1978). It is related to some other recent approaches to inequality that also focus on the family (especially Loury 1979, but also see Conlisk 1974, Blinder 1973, 1976, and Parsons 1977). However, many results appear to be new because our treatment of endowments and inheritability, the propensity to invest, family income, and some other aspects of the family is new.

II. A Single Family

The utility function of a parent is assumed to depend not only on his own consumption, but also on the number of his children and various characteristics of each child. If all his children are identical, this utility function can be written as

$$U_t = U_t(Z_t, \psi_{t+1}, n), \tag{1}$$

where Z_t is the parent's consumption, n the number of children, ψ_{t+1} the relevant characteristics of each child, and t refers to the tth generation. These children are born in and accumulate human and non-human capital in the tth generation, and work, consume, and produce their own children in the $t+1$st generation.

To simplify the presentation, we assume that a parent only cares about his own consumption and the total characteristics of all his children, $n\psi$, and that $\psi_{t+1} = I'_{t+1}$, where I'_{t+1} equals the adult wealth of each child. This last assumption would be appropriate if parents only cared about the "quality" or economic success of their children (see the formulation in Becker-Tomes 1976). The utility function in equation (1) can then be written as

$$U_t = U_t(Z_t, I_{t+1}), \tag{2}$$

where $I_{t+1} = nI'_{t+1}$ is the aggregate wealth of children. Some readers may prefer the assumption that parents are altruists who care about the welfare or utility of their children. Although caring about quality is by no means the same as caring about welfare, they turn out to have quite similar implications for the distribution of income (Becker-Tomes 1979, section X). Therefore, since the analytic development is much easier for quality, we feel justified in assuming during this essay that parents care about quality, as measured by the wealth of children.

A parent can change the wealth of his children by investing in their human and non-human capital. Initially, all capital is assumed to be homogeneous, and y_t is the total amount invested in children, measured in physical units. If Π_t is the cost in foregone consumption of each unit of y_t, the budget equation of parents can be written as

$$Z_t + \Pi_t y_t = I_t, \tag{3}$$

where I_t is their wealth. If the value to children of each unit of capital equals w_{t+1}, the rate of return on these investments is defined by the equation

$$\Pi_t \; y_t = \frac{w_{t+1} \; y_t}{1+r_t}, \tag{4}$$

where r_t is the rate of return per generation, which may encompass 20 years.

The total wealth of children equals the sum of their wealth from the capital invested in them, from their endowed capital, e_{t+1}, and from the "capital gain" due to luck in the market for income, u_{t+1}:

$$I_{t+1} = w_{t+1} \; y_t + w_{t+1} \; e_{t+1} + w_{t+1} \; u_{t+1}. \tag{5}$$

The government sector is ignored (see, however, Becker-Tomes 1979, section VII), so no distinction need be made yet between before- and after-tax wealth. Since wealth can be converted into "permanent" income streams, we will treat Z_t and I_t as referring to flows of consumption and income within a generation,[3] although the basic analysis applies more directly to wealth and present values of flows.

If equations (4) and (5) are substituted into (3), the parent's budget constraint can be written in terms of the variables that enter his utility function:

$$Z_t + \frac{I_{t+1}}{1+r_t} = I_t + \frac{w_{t+1} \; e_{t+1}}{1+r_t} + \frac{w_{t+1} \; u_{t+1}}{1+r_t} = S_t. \tag{6}$$

Own consumption and the income of children are determined not by own income alone, but also by the value of the endowment and luck of children, discounted to the parent's generation. The sum of these values, denoted by S_t, will be called "family income".[4]

Parents maximize their utility with respect to Z_t and I_{t+1} subject to their expectations about family income. If they correctly anticipate both the endowment and market luck of their children, the equilibrium conditions are given by equation (6) and

$$\frac{\partial U}{\partial Z_t} \Big/ \frac{\partial U}{\partial I_{t+1}} = 1 + r_t. \tag{7}$$

If the utility function is assumed to be homothetic so that Z_t and I_{t+1} both have unitary family income elasticities, these equilibrium conditions determine linear demand functions for Z_t, I_{t+1}, and y_t that can be written as

$$\left.\begin{aligned} \frac{I_{t+1}}{1+r_t} &= \alpha(\gamma, 1+r)\, S_t \\ Z_t &= (1-\alpha)\, S_t \\ \frac{1}{1+r_t}\, w_{t+1}\, y_t &= \alpha\, S_t - \frac{1}{1+r_t}\, w_{t+1}\, e_{t+1} - \frac{1}{1+r_t}\, w_{t+1}\, u_{t+1} \end{aligned}\right\} \tag{8}$$

The parameter γ measures the preference for the income of children relative to own consumption, where $\partial\alpha/\partial\gamma > 0$, and $\partial\alpha/\partial(1+r) \gtreqless 0$ as the elasticity of substitution between Z_t and I_{t+1} in the utility function exceeds, equals, or falls short of unity.

The equilibrium condition given by equation (7) assumes that the rate of return is independent of the amount invested in children, and that parents can consume more than their own income by creating a debt to be repaid by their children. Both assumptions are maintained in the formal development of the analysis, but the distinction between human and non-human capital can be explicitly considered (Becker-Tomes 1979, section VIIIb).

By substituting the definition of family income into (8), the demand function for the income of children can be written as

$$I_{t+1} = \alpha(1+r_t)\, I_t + \alpha\, w_{t+1}\, e_{t+1} + \alpha\, w_{t+1}\, u_{t+1}$$

$$= \beta_t\, I_t + \alpha\, w_{t+1}\, e_{t+1} + \alpha\, w_{t+1}\, u_{t+1} \qquad (9)$$

where $\beta_t = \alpha(1+r_t)$.

Also

$$w_{t+1}\, y_t = \beta_t\, I_t - (1-\alpha)w_{t+1}\, e_{t+1} - (1-\alpha)w_{t+1}\, u_{t+1}.$$

If parents correctly anticipate their children's luck and endowment, an increase in either would not add an equal amount to the income of children because part of the increase would be spent on the parents' own consumption through reduced investment in their children; this can be seen from the negative relation between y_t and e_{t+1} (or u_{t+1}). Equation (9) shows that the equilibrium relation between I_{t+1} and e_{t+1} (and u_{t+1}) depends on α, the fraction of S_t that is spent on children. This equation also shows that I_{t+1} is related to I_t through β_t, which can be called the propensity to invest in children. This propensity links the incomes of parents and children, and is one of the important building blocks in our analysis of inequality and inter-generational mobility.

The concept of the endowment is also a fundamental part of our analysis. Children are assumed to receive endowments of capital that are determined by the reputation and "connections" of their families, the contribution to the ability, race, and other characteristics of children from the genetic constitutions of their families, and the learning, skills, goals, and other "family commodities" acquired through belonging to a particular family "culture". Obviously, endowments depend on many characteristics of parents, grandparents, and other family members, and may also be "culturally" influenced by other families.

To simplify the analysis, the expected endowment is assumed to depend only on the endowments of parents and the average endowment in society. No significant generality for present purposes is lost by neglecting non-endowed incomes or the endowments of grandparents and more distant relatives (a more general formulation can be found in Becker 1980). A simple linear endowment-generating equation can be written as

$$e_{t+1} = (1-h+f)\bar{e}_t + h\, e_t + v_{t+1}\,, \tag{10}$$

where e_t is the endowment of parents, h is a constant that measures the fraction of e_t transmitted to ("inherited by") children, $\bar{e}_t$ is the average endowment in generation t, f is the rate of growth of $\bar{e}_t$, and the term $(1-h+f)\bar{e}_t$ is a simple way of incorporating the influence of the "culture" or "social capital" of other families (for a formulation of "cultural" transmission along these lines, see Cavalli-Sforza and Feldman 1973). The difference between actual and expected endowment, v_{t+1}, measures the exogenous component in the endowment of children.

If equation (10) is substituted for e_{t+1} in the demand functions in equation (9), the income of and investments in children would depend on parents' income and endowment, children's market and endowed "luck", and the average endowment in the parents' generation:

$$\left.\begin{aligned} I_{t+1} &= \alpha\, w_{t+1}\,(1-h+f)\bar{e}_t + \beta_t\, I_t + \alpha\, h\, w_{t+1}\, e_t \\ &\quad + \alpha\, w_{t+1}\, v_{t+1} + \alpha\, w_{t+1}\, u_{t+1} \\ &\text{and} \\ w_{t+1}\, y_t &= \beta_t\, I_t - (1-\alpha)\, w_{t+1}\,(1-h+f)\bar{e}_t - (1-\alpha)h\, w_{t+1}\, e_t \\ &\quad - (1-\alpha)\, w_{t+1}\, v_{t+1} - (1-\alpha)\, w_{t+1}\, u_{t+1}\,. \end{aligned}\right\} \tag{11}$$

Each dollar of endowed luck also raises the equilibrium income of children only by α dollars because the rest is spent on parents' consumption through their reduced investments in children.

Equation (11) shows that each dollar's worth of parent

endowment directly raises the income of children by less than h dollars, the amount "inherited" by children, because some of the latter's endowment is "spent" on parents' consumption through reduced investment. However, an increase in the parent endowment also directly raises their own income, which increases their investment in children. The total effect of a change in parent endowment on the income of children is the sum of these effects:

$$\frac{dI_{t+1}}{d\omega_{t+1}e_t} = \alpha\, h + \beta_t \frac{dI_t}{d\omega_{t+1}e_t} = \alpha\, h + \beta_t\, \alpha \frac{w_t}{w_{t+1}}$$

$$= \alpha(h+\beta_t \frac{w_t}{w_{t+1}}). \qquad (12)$$

The total effect would exceed the degree of inheritability if the fraction of family income spent on children and the propensity to invest were large relative to the degree of inheritability. Indeed, if they were sufficiently large, the total effect would exceed the change in the parent endowment.

Clearly, the income of children is affected differently by the endowment and other income of parents because their endowment not only raises their income but also directly raises the income of children through the transmission of endowments. Consequently, the income of children depends on the division of their parents' income between endowment and other sources.

Parents may be able to anticipate fully the endowment luck of their children because unusual ability, motivation, or handicaps are often revealed prior to the time when most investments in children are committed. The market luck of children, however, is determined by fluctuations in production possibilities and the prices of goods and factors of production that are often revealed only after children have received their education and much of their other training, and entered the labor force (although usually prior to their "inheritance" of some non-human capital). Therefore, parents may have to commit most of their investments before they know a great deal about their children's market luck.

If parents can fully anticipate the endowed luck but

cannot anticipate the market luck of children, and if parents are risk neutral[5] and maximize utility subject to expected family income, the demand function for the expected income of children would be

$$E_t I_{t+1} = \beta_t E_t S_t \;, \tag{13}$$

where E_t represents expectations taken on the basis of information available at time t. If the incidence of u_{t+1} cannot be anticipated,

$$E_t S_t = I_t + \frac{w_{t+1} e_{t+1}}{1+r_t} \;;$$

hence

$$\left.\begin{aligned} I_{t+1} &= E_t I_{t+1} + w_{t+1} u_{t+1} = \alpha\, w_{t+1} (1-h+f)\bar{e}_t + \beta_t I_t \\ &\quad + \alpha\, h\, w_{t+1} e_t + \alpha\, w_{t+1} v_{t+1} + w_{t+1} u_{t+1} \,, \\ &\text{and} \\ w_{t+1} y_t &= \beta_t I_t - (1-\alpha)\, w_{t+1} (1-h+f)\bar{e}_t - (1-\alpha)\, h\, w_{t+1} e_t \\ &\quad - (1-\alpha)\, w_{t+1} v_{t+1} \,. \end{aligned}\right\} \tag{11'}$$

The only difference between equations (11) and (11') is in the coefficient of market luck. Increased investment cannot partially offset bad luck and reduced investment cannot partially nullify good luck if luck cannot be anticipated. Hence the coefficient of market luck is raised from α in the equation for I_{t+1} in (11) to unity in (11'), and from $-(1-\alpha)$ in the equation for y_t in (11) to zero in (11').

III. *The Equilibrium Inequality in Income*

Even if all families were basically identical, incomes would be unequally distributed because of the unequal incidence of endowment and market luck. The income inequality in any generation depends, of course, on the inequality of luck in that generation, but also in a decisive way on the luck in previous generations. Since lucky parents invest more in their children, the increase in the children's incomes would, in turn, induce them to invest more in their own children in the succeeding generation, and so on until all descendants benefit from the initial luck. Since investments depend on the parameters β and h that measure the propensity to invest in children and the degree of inheritability of endowments, the effect of luck in previous generations on the income inequality in a given generation must also depend on these parameters.

The exact relation between the income inequality in any generation, the incidence of luck in that and in previous generations, and β and h can be derived from equations (11) or (11'). To separate the effect of differences among families from the incidence of luck, we assume that all families have the same utility function, degree of inheritability, and rate of return (this assumption is dropped in Becker-Tomes 1979, section VI). We also avoid any discussion of factor market equilibrium by assuming that r_t and w_t are independent of the aggregate accumulation of capital, and are given to the community as well as to each family. These parameters and the average endowment are assumed to be stationary over time (see, however, Becker-Tomes 1979, section VIIIa), so that $r_t = r$, $w_t = 1$ by the choice of units, and $f = 0$. The income of children of the ith family in the $t+1$st generation can then be expressed as

$$\left.\begin{aligned} &I^i_{t+1} = \alpha\, a + \beta\, I^i_t + \alpha\, h\, e^i_t + \alpha\, v^i_{t+1} + \alpha\, u^i_{t+1} \\ &\text{where} \quad a = \bar{e}(1-h). \end{aligned}\right\}^{6} \qquad (14)$$

We assume that children have the same utility function as their parents and are produced by perfect assortative mating: each person, in effect, then mates with his own image. A given family then maintains its identity indefinitely, and its fortunes could be followed over as many generations as desired.

Since all families are assumed to be identical, they would have the same income in any generation if they had had the same luck in that and in all previous generations. Therefore, the income inequality in any generation would depend on the distribution of luck in all previous generations. This can be shown explicitly by repeatedly substituting equations (10) and (14) into (14) to relate the income of the ith family in the $t+1$st generation to its income and endowment in the $m+1$st generation, and to its luck in all intervening generations:

$$\left.\begin{aligned} I^i_{t+1} &= \alpha a \sum_{j=0}^{m} \beta^j \sum_{k=0}^{m-j} h^k + \beta^{m+1} I^i_{t-m} \\ &\quad + \alpha h \left[\sum_{j=0}^{m} \beta^{m-j} h^j\right] e^i_{t-m} + \alpha \sum_{j=0}^{m} \beta^j u^i_{t+1-j} \\ &\quad + \alpha \sum_{k=0}^{m} \sum_{j=0}^{k} \beta^j h^{k-j} v^i_{t+1-k} . \end{aligned}\right\} \quad (15)$$

Presumably, $0 < h < 1$, some but only part of the parent's endowment passes to his children. The rate of return, r, has the units of percent per generation, and even a modest percent per year implies a sizable percent per generation because human generations are separated by 20 or perhaps more years. So r would exceed 0.5 and might well be above unity. Therefore, $\beta = \alpha(1+r)$ also might exceed unity because α, the fraction of family income spent on children, is far from negligible.

If, however, we assume that β as well as h are less than unity ($\beta > 1$ is considered in Becker-Tomes 1979, section VIIIa), the coefficients of both I^i_{t-m} and e^i_{t-m} approach zero as m becomes larger and larger, and the coefficient of αa approaches a constant. Since

$$\sum_{j=0}^{k} \beta^j h^{k-j} = \begin{cases} \dfrac{\beta^{k+1} - h^{k+1}}{\beta - h} & \text{for } \beta \neq h \\ \beta^k (k+1) & \text{for } \beta = h , \end{cases}$$

equation (15) could be extended back through infinitely many generations and written as (for $\beta \neq h$)

$$I^{i}_{t+1} = \frac{\alpha a}{(1-\beta)(1-h)} + \alpha \sum_{k=0}^{\infty} {}^{k} u^{i}_{t+1-k} + \alpha \sum_{k=0}^{\infty} \left| \frac{\beta^{k+1} - h^{k+1}}{\beta - h} \right| v^{i}_{t+1-k} \tag{16}$$

The income of the ith family in any generation is expressed solely in terms of its luck in this and all previous generations, the family parameters α, β and h, and the "social" parameter a. Starting from *any* initial distribution of income and endowment, the distribution of income would change over time and eventually approach the right hand side of equation (16).

If the u_t and the v_t were identically distributed random variables with finite variances, the variance of income must approach a stationary level without any additional restrictions on the properties of u_t and v_t or on the utility function. If u_t and v_t were also independently distributed, the stationary variance can be simply written as[7]

$$\sigma^2_I = \frac{\alpha^2}{1-\beta^2} \sigma^2_u + \frac{\alpha^2 (1+h\beta)\sigma^2_v}{(1-h^2)(1-\beta^2)(1-h\beta)} \tag{17}$$

where σ^2_I, σ^2_u, and σ^2_v are the variances of I, u, and v respectively.

Since the expected value of both endowed and market luck equals zero, equation (16) shows that expected or average income in any generation must approach the stationary level

$$\bar{I} = \frac{\alpha a}{(1-\beta)(1-h)} = \frac{\alpha \bar{e}}{1-\beta} \text{ since } a = \bar{e}(1-h) \tag{18}$$

(steady state growth is discussed in Becker-Tomes 1979, section VIIIa). $\bar{I}$ is a simple function of the family parameters α and β and the social parameter $\bar{e}$, and is independent of the inheritability of endowments. The fraction of $\bar{I}$ contributed by investments is given by

$$d = 1 - \frac{\bar{e}}{\bar{I}} = 1 - \frac{1-\beta}{\alpha} = 2 + r - \frac{1}{\alpha} \; ; \tag{19}$$

not surprisingly, this fraction is positively related to the rate of return on investments and to the fraction of family income invested in children.

Writers on social "justice" and on the political process have usually been interested in relative measures of inequality, such as the Gini coefficient or the coefficient of variation. If the expression in equation (17) is divided by the square of the expression in (18), the square of the equilibrium coefficient of variation in income can be written as

$$\begin{aligned} CV_I^2 &= \frac{1-\beta}{1+\beta}\, CV_u^2 + \frac{(1+h\beta)(1-\beta)}{(1-h^2)(1-h\beta)(1+\beta)}\, CV_v^2 \\ &= \frac{1-\beta}{1+\beta}\, CV_u^2 + \frac{(1+h\beta)(1-\beta)}{(1-h\beta)(1+\beta)}\, CV_e^2 \, , \end{aligned} \tag{20}$$

since $\sigma_v^2 = (1-h^2)\, \sigma_e^2$ (see footnote 6),

where the inequality in both market and endowment luck has been measured relative to the average endowment since both u and v are assumed to have zero means

$$CV_u = \frac{\sigma u}{\bar{e}} \text{ and } CV_v = \frac{\sigma v}{\bar{e}} \, .$$

Of course, the equilibrium inequality in income depends on, and indeed is proportional to, the inequality in market and endowed luck. The factors of proportionality, however, are determined by families through the inheritability of endowments and the propensity to invest in children. Since $\beta < 1$, the coefficient of market luck must be less than unity, probably less than one-third because β almost certainly exceeds one-half. Therefore, the effect of market luck on inequality is greatly attenuated by the reactions of parents to its anticipated incidence.

The coefficient of endowed luck exceeds that of market luck, and the difference is large when both h and β are large; for example, the coefficient of CV_v^2 would be about 2.5 times and the coefficient of CV_e^2 would be about twice that of CV_u^2 when $\beta = 0.6$ and $h = 0.5$. Endowed luck has a much greater effect on income inequality because it is automatically inherited by children. This also explains why endowed luck has a larger effect on income inequality when h is greater.

Not only does the coefficient of endowed luck exceed the coefficient of market luck but also the inequality in endowed luck probably exceeds the inequality in market luck. Since variations within a life cycle are ignored, the income concept is close to "permanent" income (see the dicussion after equation (5)). Endowed luck is determined by genetic inheritance and childhood experiences, and tends to last throughout a lifetime, whereas market luck is more transitory and fluctuates from year to year. Therefore, the inequality in lifetime endowed luck would be considerably greater than the inequality in lifetime market luck if the annual inequality in market and endowed luck were about the same. The inequality in both endowed and market luck could be estimated from information on the permanent incomes of different generations (see Becker-Tomes 1979, section V).

An increase in the rate of return raises the propensity to invest $\beta = \alpha(1+r)$, which according to equation (17), would raise the equilibrium variance of income. An increase in β also raises the equilibrium level of average income (see equation (18)); indeed, the percentage increase in the latter exceeds the percentage increase in the variance, so that an increase in the rate of return and the propensity to invest lowers the coefficient of variation in income in equation (20). A well-known result from human capital theory states the contrary, that an increase in the rate of return on human capital raises inequality, but this result only considers the *impact* of a change in the rate of return on income inequality, and neglects longer-run effects on the level of income.[8]

An increase in h raises income inequality by raising the coefficient of endowments. An increase in β, on the other hand, lowers income inequality by lowering the coefficients of endowments and market luck. Although an increase in β raises the standard deviation of income (see equation (17)), it lowers the coefficient of variation because average income (equation (18)) is raised by an even larger percent than the standard deviation.

Perhaps the most interesting property of equation (20) is that h and β do not enter additively but multiplicatively: the effect of an increase in h on income inequality is greater when β is greater. This interaction reflects the interaction in the model between inheritability and investment in children. β and h interact through the covariance between income and endowment in any generation (see footnote 6).

The effect of utility maximization on this interaction between inheritability and investment as well as on other properties of the equation generating income inequality ((20)) can be determined from a comparison with the equation generating inequality when families do not maximize. If the amount invested in children were independent of rates of return, family income, endowments, and luck, the interaction between inheritability and investment would be eliminated, and the contribution of endowment inequality to income inequality would be greatly reduced.[9] For example, if $h = 0.5$ and $\beta = 0.6$, the coefficient of endowment inequality would be twice that of market luck with utility maximization, and only the same as that of market luck without maximization. Therefore, "mechanical" models of the inter-generational transmission of inequality that do not incorporate optimizing responses of parents to their own or to their children's circumstances greatly understate the contribution of endowments, and thereby understate the influence of family background on inequality.

If parents could not anticipate their children's market luck but were risk neutral and had unbiased expectations, the coefficient of CV_u^2 in equation (20) would simply be multiplied by $1/\alpha^2$. Since α is below unity, imperfectly anticipated "disturbances" increase the variability in individual incomes as well as the cyclical variability in aggregate incomes (on the latter, see Sargent-Wallace 1975). Moreover, the coefficient of market luck might then exceed the coefficient of endowed luck because parents could not offset the bad or good market luck of their children with larger or smaller investments.

IV. Intergenerational Mobility

Variation in the income and status of a given family in different generations has usually been discussed under the heading of intergenerational mobility, the "circulation of elites" (Pareto 1935), or equality of opportunity. Considerable inequality among different families in the same generation is consistent with a highly stable ranking of a given family in different generations, or an unstable ranking is consistent with only moderate inequality in the same generation. An enormous literature discusses each type of inequality, yet they have rarely been brought together through a common analytic framework. This section analyzes intergenerational mobility with the same framework used in the previous section for intragenerational inequality, and shows that the propensity to invest in children and the degree of inheritability also are important determinants of intergenerational mobility.

The influence of the family on the income of children can be measured by the correlation between their incomes and those of their parents or grandparents. If the degree of inheritability, h, were negligible, the equilibrium correlation coefficient between the incomes of children and parents would equal β, the propensity to invest in children, regardless of the inequality in market and endowed luck.[10] If h were not negligible, the equilibrium multiple correlation coefficient between the income of children and the income *and* endowment of parents would exceed β by an amount that depends only on β and h if the inequality in market luck were small relative to the inequality in endowments[11] (see the discussion of luck in the previous section).

We will spend the rest of this section on a different and in some ways more revealing measure of intergenerational mobility: the sequence of changes in the incomes of parents, children, grandchildren, and later descendants. If the degree of inheritability were negligible, an increase in the income of parents by δI_t because of market or endowed luck, would increase the income of children by $\beta\delta I_t$, the income of grandchildren by $\beta^2 \delta I_t$, and the income of the *m*th generation of descendants by

$$\delta I_{t+m} = \beta^m \delta I_t, \; m = 1, 2, \ldots, \quad \text{when } h = 0 \text{ (see equation (15))}. \tag{21}$$

These increases decline monotonically as long as $\beta < 1$, and are close to zero after a few generations if $\beta < 0.8$: "from shirtsleeves to shirtsleeves in four generations". Consequently, utility maximization without inheritability of endowments implies considerable intergenerational mobility unless β is close to unity; that is, unless an increase in the income of parents increases their investment in children by almost an equal amount.

If investments did not depend on income or other variables and were simply given to each family, an increase in the endowment of parents by δv_t would increase the income of their children by $h\delta v_t$, the income of grandchildren by $h^2 \delta v_t$, and the income of the *m*th generation of descendants by

$$\delta I_{t+m} = h^m \delta v_t, \; m = 1, 2, \ldots, \quad \text{when } y_t \text{ is exogenous} \tag{22}$$

These increases also decline monotonically if $h < 1$, and would be close to zero after a few generations because usually $h < 0.75$. Consequently, cultural and biological inheritance with exogenous parental investments implies considerable intergenerational mobility except where the degree of inheritability is close to unity.

If investments in children depended on family circumstances, and if the degree of inheritability were not negligible, an increase in the income of parents would not simply raise the incomes of their descendants by the sum of the increases given in equations (21) and (22) because inheritances and investments interact. In particular, the incomes of descendants could continue to rise for several generations even though h and β were both less than unity, and many generations might elapse before the increases were below 25 percent of the initial increase. Consequently, the interaction between investments and inheritances can sharply reduce the degree of intergenerational mobility so that incomes in any generation become more dependent on the incomes and endowments of ancestors.

Consider, for example, an increase in the endowment luck of the ith family in the tth generation that is compensated by a decline in market luck so that own income, I_t^i, remains the same. Since family income, S_t^i, increases because the endowment of children increases by $h\delta v_t^i$, parents want to increase their own consumption and reduce their investment in children. Consequently, the own income of children, I_{t+1}^i, would increase only by the fraction α of their increased endowment because the rest is spent by parents on their own consumption. The own income of grandchildren, I_{t+2}^i, would also increase partly because the own income of their parents increased and partly because they inherit some of the increased endowment of their parents. The total increase in the income of grandchildren would be

$$\left.\begin{aligned} \delta I_{t+2}^i &= \beta\delta I_{t+1}^i + \alpha\delta e_{t+2}^i = \alpha h\beta\delta v_t^i + \alpha h^2\delta v_t^i \\ &= \alpha h(\beta+h)\delta v_t^i = (\beta+h)\delta I_{t+1}^i \end{aligned}\right\} \quad (23)$$

Therefore, if $\beta + h > 1$, if the sum of the degree of inheritability and the propensity to invest in children exceeded unity, a compensated increase in the endowment of parents would increase the income of grandchildren by *more* than the income of children.

The effects on the incomes of great-grandchildren, great-great-grandchildren, and still more distant descendants can be derived in the same way. The increase in the income of say great-great-grandchildren would also exceed that of children if $\beta + h$ were *sufficiently* greater than unity. A general formula relating the change in the income of the mth generation of descendants to a compensated change in the endowment of parents is given by the coefficient of e_{t-m}^i in equation (15). This coefficient can be measured relative to the equilibrium level of average income and written as

$$\frac{\delta I^{i}_{t+m}}{\bar{I}} = h(1-\beta) \sum_{j=0}^{m-1} \beta^{m-1-j} h^{j} \frac{\delta e^{i}_{t}}{\bar{e}}$$

$$= \begin{cases} h(1-\beta) \dfrac{\beta^{m}-h^{m}}{\beta-h} \dfrac{\delta e^{i}_{t}}{\bar{e}} = h(1-\beta)g_{m} \dfrac{\delta e^{i}_{t}}{\bar{e}} & \text{for } \beta \neq h \\ h(1-\beta)m\, \beta^{m-1} \dfrac{\delta e^{i}_{t}}{\bar{e}} & \text{for } \beta = h \end{cases} \quad (24)$$

The term g_m is a symmetric polynomial in β and h that has a maximum at the initial generation when $\beta + h < 1$, and rises to a peak and then declines monotonically when $\beta + h > 1$, where the peak is later the larger $\beta + h$ is.[12] The figure plots the path of g_m for three sets of values of β and h. In curve A both are "low", $h = 0.2$ and $\beta = 0.45$, and by the fourth generation g_m is only 16 percent of its initial value; in curve B, $h = 0.3$ and $\beta = 0.8$, and g_m rises for one generation and then declines to less than 25 percent of the initial value by the tenth generation; in curve C, $h = 0.7$ and $\beta = 0.9$, and g_m rises for five generations, then slowly declines and does not reach its initial value until the 15th generation, and is less than 25 percent of the initial value only after the 29th generation.

The income of a given family can be well above or below average for several consecutive generations because of a run of very good or bad luck; that is, because the u^i and v^i in equation (15) have the same sign and are not negligible for several consecutive generations. Since these random variables are assumed to be independently distributed, the probability is low that more than two consecutive generations have unusually good or bad luck. However, the income of a family with unusual luck in only one generation and average luck in all subsequent generations would also

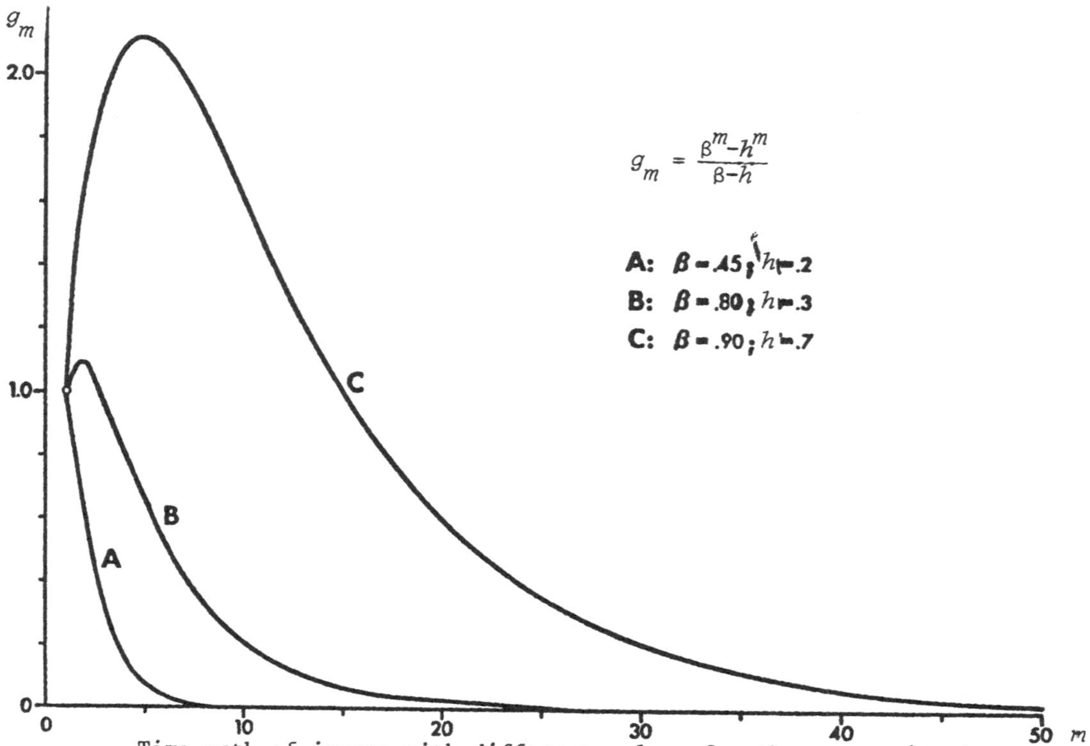

Time path of income with different values for the propensity to invest and the degree of inheritability.

be well above or below average for several consecutive generations if the degree of inheritability and the propensity to invest in children were substantial.

Consequently, the welfare of several consecutive generations of the same family would be closely linked whenever inheritability and investments were substantial. The degree of inheritability is not rigidly determined by the biology of human inheritance but is greatly influenced by social organization. Some socities, which can be called pre-modern or "closed", rely heavily on family reputation in assessing various characteristics of individuals because such societies do not have accurate methods of assessing these characteristics directly. Families then have an incentive to maintain and enhance their reputations by controlling and guiding the characteristics of their members (see the fuller discussion in Becker 1980). As a result of these efforts, members of the same family become more similar in closed than in modern "open" societies where the behaviour and development of children are less controlled by their families.

In terms of the concepts used in this essay, the endowments of children would be more similar to those of parents and other family members in closed than in open societies - that is, the inheritability of endowments would be greater in closed societies. We have shown that intergenerational mobility is smaller when endowments are more inheritable, and that the degree of inheritability interacts with the propensity to invest in children. Therefore, the income of children would be more similar to the incomes of their parents, grandparents, and other relatives in closed than in open societies - which is a different way to state that mobility would be smaller - because the interaction among cousins, uncles, nephews, grandparents, grandchildren, and other family members is greater in closed societies. Of course, this assumes that propensities to invest in children are not much less in closed than in open societies.

Since a run of successes or failures in the same family is more likely in closed than in open societies because inheritability is greater, perhaps the Adams family in the United States has received so much attention precisely because many generations of accomplishment is unusual in this open society. Successful families are presumably more common and less worthy of attention in closed societies like traditional India or China.

V. Summary and Conclusions

The crucial assumption in the theory of inequality and intergenerational mobility presented in this essay is that each family maximizes a utility function spanning several generations. Utility depends on the consumption of parents and on the quantity and quality of their children. The quality of children is measured by their income when they are adults, although the implications are similar when quality is measured by their utility when they are adults.

The income of children is raised when they receive more human and non-human capital from their parents. Their income is also raised by their "endowment" of genetically determined race, ability, and other characteristics, family reputation and "connections", and knowledge, skills, and goals provided by their family environment. The fortunes of children are linked to their parents not only through investments but also through these endowments acquired from parents (and other family members).

In addition, the income of children depends on stochastic terms measuring their luck in the endowment "lottery" and in the market for income. The distribution of luck is the foundation of many models of the distribution of income that ignore utility maximization. Both luck and utility maximization are important in our analysis; indeed, they interact because the optimal investment in children depends on their market and endowed luck.

Parents maximize their utility subject to their own income, the "inherited" endowments of children, and any anticipated endowed and market luck of children. The optimal investment in children depends on the propensity to invest in children, an important parameter in our analysis. This propensity is positively related to the fraction of family income spent on children and to rates of return on investments in children, and is negatively related to the rate of growth in income.

The equilibrium income of children is determined by their market and endowed luck, the own income and endowment of parents, and the two parameters, the degree of inheritability and the propensity to invest in children. If these parameters were both less than unity, the distribution of income between families would approach a stationary distribution. The stationary coefficient of variation would be greater, the larger the inequality in the distribution of market and endowed luck, the larger the degree of inheritability, and the smaller the propensity to invest in children. In particular, income inequality would increase if the rate of growth in average income increased or if rates of return on investments decreased.

Intergenerational mobility measures the effect of a family on the well-being of their children. We have shown that the family is more important when the degree of inheritability and the propensity to invest are larger. If both these parameters are less than unity, an increase in family income in one generation has negligible effects on the incomes of much later descendants. However, the incomes of children, grandchildren, and other early descendants could be significantly increased; indeed, if the sum of these parameters exceeded unity, the changes in income would rise for several generations before falling, and the maximum increase in income could exceed the initial increase. Moreover, these parameters do not have independent effects: an increase say in the degree of inheritability raises the effect on the incomes of descendants of a change in the propensity to invest.

We believe that the analysis in this essay firmly demonstrates that a theory of the distribution of income need not be a mixture of Pareto distributions, ad hoc probability mechanisms, and arbitrary assumptions about inheritance, but can be based on the same principles of maximizing behavior and equilibrium that form the core of microeconomics. At the same time, however, our theory does incorporate the effects of luck, family background, and cultural, biological, and financial inheritance on the distribution of income. Our theory also demonstrates that inequality within a generation and inequality across generations (intergenerational mobility) do not require separate "economic" and "sociological" approaches, for both can be analyzed with a unified theory of the determination of the incomes of different families in different generations.

REFERENCES

Becker, Gary S. (1964 - 1st ed.) (1975 - 2nd ed.). *Human Capital: A Theoretical and Empirical Analysis.* New York: Columbia University Press for the National Bureau of Economic Research.

Becker, Gary S. (1967). "Human Capital and the Personal Distribution of Income: An Analytical Approach" (Woytinsky Lecture, No. 1). Ann Arbor: Institute of Public Administration, University of Michigan. Reprinted in Becker, G.S. (1975). *Human Capital*, 2nd edition. New York: Columbia University Press for the National Bureau of Economic Research, 94-144.

Becker, Gary S. (1974). "A Theory of Social Interactions". *Journal of Political Economy* 82, No. 6 (November/December), 1063-93. Reprinted in Becker, G.S. (1976). *The Economic Approach to Human Behavior.* Chicago: University of Chicago Press.

Becker, Gary S. (1980). *A Treatise on the Family.* Chicago: University of Chicago Press.

Becker, Gary S. and Tomes, Nigel (1976). "Child Endowments and the Quantity and Quality of Children". *Journal of Political Economy* 84, No. 4, Part 2 (July/August), S143-62.

Becker, Gary S. and Tomes, Nigel (1979). "An Equilibrium Theory of the Distribution of Income and Intergenerational Mobility". *Journal of Political Economy* 87, No. 6 (December).

Blau, Peter M. and Duncan, Otis Dudley (1967). *The American Occupational Structure.* New York: Wiley.

Blinder, Alan S. (1973). "A Model of Inherited Wealth". *Quarterly Journal of Economics* 87, No. 4 (November), 608-26.

Blinder, Alan S. (1976). "Inequality and Mobility in the Distribution of Wealth". *Kyklos* 29, Fasc. 4, 607-38.

Blinder, Alan S. and Weiss, Yoram (1976). "Human Capital and Labor Supply: A Synthesis". *Journal of Political*

Economy 84, No. 3 (June), 449-472.

Boudon, Raymond (1974). *Education, Opporunity and Social Inequality*. New York: Wiley.

Cavalli-Sforza, Luigi L. and Feldman, Marcus W. (1973). "Models for Cultural Inheritance. 1. Group mean and within group variation". *Theoretical Population Biology* 4, No. 1 (March), 42-55.

Champernowne, David G. (1953). "A Model of Income Distribution". *Economic Journal* 63, No. 250 (June), 318-351.

Chiswick, Barry R. (1974). *Income Inequality: Regional Analysis Within a Human Capital Framework*. New York: Columbia University Press for the National Bureau of Economic Research.

Conlisk, John (1974). "Can Equalization of Opportunity Reduce Social Mobility?". *American Economic Review* 64, No. 1 (March), 80-90.

Ghez, Gilbert R. and Becker, Gary S. (1975). *The Allocation of Time and Goods Over the Life Cycle*. Human Behavior and Social Institutions, No. 6. New York: Columbia University Press for the National Bureau of Economic Research.

Heckman, James J. (1976). "A Life-Cycle Model of Earnings, Learning and Consumption". *Journal of Political Economy* 84, No. 4, Part 2 (August), S11-44.

Houthakker, Hendrick S. (1975). "The Size Distribution of Labor Incomes Derived from the Distribution of Aptitudes" in W. Sellekaerts (ed.) *Econometrics and Economic Theory: Essays in Honor of Jan Tinbergen*. New York: Macmillan.

Loury, Glenn C. (1979). "Intergenerational Transfers and the Distribution of Earnings". *Econometrica*, forthcoming.

Mandelbrot, Benoit (1962). "Paretian Distributions and Income Maximization". *Quarterly Journal of Economics* 76, No. 1 (February), 57-85.

Mincer, Jacob (1958). "Investment in Human Capital and Personal Income Distribution". *Journal of Political Economy* 66, No. 4 (July/August), 281-302.

Okun, Arthur M. (1975). *Equality and Efficiency: The Big Tradeoff*. Washington D.C.: Brookings Institution.

Pareto, Vilfredo (1935). *The Mind and Society*. Vol. 3. New York: Harcourt Brace.

Parsons, Donald O. (1977). "On the Economics of Intergenerational Relations", mimeo, Ohio State University (August).

Rawls, John (1971). *A Theory of Justice*. Cambridge, Mass.: The Belknap Press of Harvard University Press.

Rosen, Sherwin (1978). "Substitution and Division of Labour". *Economica* 45, No. 179 (August), 235-250.

Roy, Andrew D. (1950). "The Distribution of Earnings and of Individual Output". *Economic Journal* 60, No. 239 (September), 489-505.

Sargent, Thomas J. and Wallace, Neil (1975). "'Rational' Expectations, the Optimal Monetary Instrument, and the Optimal Money Supply Rule". *Journal of Political Economy* 83, No. 2 (April), 241-254.

Tomes, Nigel (1978). "A Model of Child Endowments, and the Quality and Quantity of Children". Ph.D. dissertation, University of Chicago.

FOOTNOTES

1. This paper is written jointly with Nigel Tomes. A fuller version appeared in the *Journal of Political Economy* 87 (December 1979).

We are indeed indebted to Gale Mosteller for excellent research assistance. We received valuable comments from Aloisio Araujo, Lawrence Kenny, Sam Peltzman, Sherwin Rosen, Michael Rothschild, Jose Scheinkman, George Stigler, a referee, and from participants in seminars at The University of Chicago,

National Bureau of Economic Research, University of Western Ontario, The University of California (Santa Barbara), Harvard University, Princeton University, The Ohio State University, and the 1978 Summer Meetings of the Econometric Society.

Our work has been supported by grants to NBER and the University of Chicago from the Alfred Sloan Foundation and the Lilly Endowment. This report has not undergone the review accorded official NBER publications.

2. See Mincer (1958) and Becker (1967); also see the "abilities" models of Mandelbrot (1962), Roy (1950), Houthakker (1975), and Rosen (1978).

3. We ignore life-cycle considerations in this essay, even though many discussions of inequality really refer only to different stages of the life-cycle variation in income; the allocation of resources over the life-cycle has been rather fully analyzed elsewhere (Ghez-Becker 1975, Heckman 1976, and Blinder-Weiss 1976).

4. Family income is a special case of "social income" introduced in Becker (1974).

5. The effect of risk aversion on the amount invested in children is ambiguous in the sense that the effect depends on the third derivative of the utility function (see Loury 1979).

6. In an interesting article on social mobility Conlisk (1974) assumes an equation structure with a reduced form similar to equation (14) (see his equation (16), p. 84). However, his structure is not derived from utility maximizing behavior and does not incorporate the relations between the coefficients of I_t^i, e_t^i, v_{t+1}^i and u_{t+1}^i implied by maximizing behavior and found in equation (14), such as the effect of a change in r on β and α. Moreover, the coefficients in his equations are not related to market or household characteristics, such as rates of return on investments or the importance of children in parental preferences.

7. From equation (16),

$$\sigma_I^2 = \alpha^2\sigma_u^2 \sum_{k=0}^{\infty} \beta^{2k} + \alpha^2\sigma_v^2 \sum_{k=0}^{\infty} \left[\frac{\beta^{k+1}-h^{k+1}}{\beta-h}\right]^2$$

$$= \frac{\alpha^2\sigma_u^2}{1-\beta^2} + \alpha^2\sigma_v^2 \sum_{k=0}^{\infty} \frac{\beta^{2(k+1)}+h^{2(k+1)}-2h^{k+1}\beta^{k+1}}{(\beta-h)^2} \text{ if } \beta, h < 1.$$

The summation in the second term can be written as

$$\left[\frac{\beta^2}{1-\beta^2} + \frac{2}{1-h^2} - \frac{2h\beta}{1-h\beta}\right] \frac{1}{[\beta-h]^2} \quad ,$$

or as

$$\frac{\beta^2(1-h^2)(1-h\beta)+h^2(1-\beta^2)(1-h\beta)-2h\beta(1-h^2)(1-\beta^2)}{[\beta-h]^2(1-h^2)(1-\beta^2)(1-h\beta)}$$

which equals

$$\frac{[\beta-h]^2(1+h\beta)}{[\beta-h]^2(1-h\beta)(1-h^2)(1-\beta^2)}$$

A simpler and more transparent derivation of the equilibrium variance follows from taking the variance of both sides of equation (14):

$$\sigma_{I_{t+1}}^2 = \beta^2\sigma_{I_t}^2 + \alpha^2h^2\sigma_{e_t}^2 + 2\alpha\beta h\, Cov_{I_t e_t} + \alpha^2\sigma_v^2 + \alpha^2\sigma_u^2 \quad (*)$$

Moreover, since $e_t^i = a + he_{t-1}^i + v_t$,

$$Cov_{I_t e_t} = \beta h\, Cov_{I_{t-1}e_{t-1}} + \alpha\sigma_e^2 .$$

Since, in equilibrium with stationary variances and covariances.

$$Cov_{I_t e_t} = Cov_{I_{t-1} e_{t-1}} \,, \qquad \sigma^2_{I_{t+1}} = \sigma^2_{I_t} = \sigma^2_I$$

$$\text{and} \quad \sigma^2_{e_{t+1}} = \sigma^2_{e_t} = \frac{\sigma^2_v}{1-h^2}$$

equation (*) can be written as

$$(1-\beta^2)\sigma^2_I = \frac{\alpha^2\sigma^2_v}{1-h^2} + \frac{2\alpha^2\beta h\,\sigma^2_v}{(1-\beta h)(1-h^2)} + \alpha^2\sigma^2_u \,.$$

Hence

$$\sigma^2_I = \frac{\alpha^2}{1-\beta^2}\sigma^2_u + \frac{\sigma^2(1+\beta h)}{(1-h^2)(1-\beta h)(1-\beta^2)}\sigma^2_v \,.$$

8. That is, the result neglects the effect of a change in rates of return on the average level and distribution of investments in human capital (see Becker 1964, or Chiswick 1974). One analysis that does consider the effect on the equilibrium distribution of investments does not find a clear-cut relation between income inequality and rates of return (see Becker 1967).

9. The equilibrium variance of income would equal

$$\sigma^2_I = \sigma^2_y + \sigma^2_e + \sigma^2_u = \sigma^2_y + \frac{\sigma^2_v}{1-h^2} + \sigma^2_u$$

and average income would be

$$\bar{I} = \bar{y} + \bar{e} = \frac{\bar{e}}{1-d} \,,$$

where d is defined in equation (19). Then

$$CV^2_I = (1-d)^2 CV^2_u + (1-d)^2 CV^2_e + d^2 CV^2_y$$

$$= (1-d)^2 CV_u^2 + \frac{(1-d)^2}{1-h^2} + CV_v^2 + d^2 CV_y^2$$

where $CV_y = \sigma_y / \bar{y}$.

10. Since

$$I_{t+1}^i = \beta I_t^i + \alpha e_{t+1}^i + \alpha u_{t+1}^i ,$$

$$R(I_{t+1}, I_t) = \frac{\beta \sigma I_t}{\sigma_{I_{t+1}}} = \beta$$

because e_{t+1} is independent of I_t if $h = 0$, and in equilibrium, $\sigma_{I_t} = \sigma_{I_{t+1}}$.

11. Since

$$I_{t+1}^i = \beta I_t^i + \alpha h e_t^i + \alpha u_{t+1}^i + \alpha v_{t+1}^i + \text{a constant},$$

then by definition of the multiple correlation coefficient,

$$R^2(I_{t+1}\ I_t, e_t) = \frac{\beta^2 \sigma_{I_t}^2 + \alpha^2 h^2 \sigma_{e_t}^2 + 2\alpha h \beta\ Cov_{I_t e_t}}{\sigma_{I_{t+1}}^2}$$

$$= \beta^2 + \frac{\alpha^2 \sigma_{e_t}^2}{\sigma_I^2} \left(h^2 + \frac{2h\beta}{1-h\beta}\right) > \beta^2$$

since in equilibrium

$$Cov_{I_t e_t} = \frac{\alpha \sigma_e^2}{1-h\beta} \quad \text{(see footnote 6).}$$

If $\frac{\sigma_u^2}{\sigma_e^2} \equiv 0$,

$$\sigma_I^2 \equiv \frac{(1+h\beta)^{2}}{(1-h\beta)(1-\beta^2)} \sigma_e^2 \quad \text{(see equation (17))},$$

and then

$$R^2 \equiv \beta^2 + \frac{(1-\beta^2)h(2\beta+h-\beta h^2)}{1+h\beta}, \text{ where } \frac{\partial R^2}{\partial h} > 0.$$

12. $\dot{g}_m = \frac{\partial g_m}{\partial m} = \frac{\beta^m log\, \beta - h^m log\, h}{\beta - h}$.

If $\beta > h$, $\dot{g}_m \gtrless 0$ as $(\frac{\beta}{h})^m \lesssim \frac{log\, h}{log}$ since $\beta < 1$.

Since the right hand side is constant and the left hand side increases indefinitely as m increases, g_m must reach a single peak at a finite m and then decline monotonically. Therefore, since $g_1 = 1$ and $g_2 = \beta + h$, g_m falls for all m when $\beta + h < 1$ and reaches a peak at $m > 1$ when $\beta + h > 1$. The maximizing value of m is found from

$$\dot{g}_m = 0 = \beta^m \, log\, \beta - h^m \, log\, h,$$

or

$$\hat{m} = \frac{log\, \{\frac{log\, h}{log\, \beta}\}}{log\, \beta - log\, h},$$

If $\beta = kh$, $1 < k < \frac{1}{h}$, then

$$\frac{\partial \hat{m}}{\partial h} = \frac{1}{h} \frac{1}{log\, h \, log\, kh} > 0 ,$$

or increases in β and h that keep their ratio constant would increase $\hat{m}$.

2. APPLICATION OF THE THEORY OF SUPERFAIRNESS

William J. Baumol

It is a great honor to have been asked to give the Harry Johnson Lecture. The quality of his contributions sets us all a performance standard which we must admire profoundly. But this is not the only reason I appreciate the opportunity so deeply. For Harry Johnson was a friend with whom I shared many interests, not the least of them woodcarving, with which we frequently distracted our colleagues at professional meetings. I flatter myself that Harry would have approved of this lecture as an attempt at application of theoretical analysis - an objective he pursued so effectively.

Recently, a group of theorists including Foley, Varian, Pazner, Schmeidler and others, have laid out the foundations of a theory of equity in the economy's distribution and production processes upon which we can build an analysis of some of the equity issues in a variety of policy problems. I will review some of this analysis and provide a diagramatic interpretation which will facilitate our discussion. Then I will show how the theory can be applied to some policy issues, using the choice among rationing techniques to illustrate the application process.[1]

1. *Superfair Distributions in the Two-Good Case*

Consider the distribution of two perfectly divisible commodities among n persons. Suppose each individual is initially assigned exactly $1/nth$ of each good. That distribution is obviously fair (nonstrictly superfair) since no individual will prefer anyone else's share. Now, let the individuals trade freely among themselves. If their tastes differ they will generally carry out some exchanges. Moreover, in the absence of cheating or misrepresentation, every participant must gain from such an exchange. The resulting distribution must then be superfair in the sense that each individual ends up with what in that person's estimate is worth at least $1/n^{th}$ of the total, and to all who have done any trading it must be even better than that.

Let us see how in theory we can determine which distributions of a set of commodities are superfair. Figure 1 is a modified Edgeworth box in which, as usual, the dimensions of the box show the *total* amounts of the two commodities available for distribution. Curve I_1 represents one indifference curve of individual 1. However, at this point the diagram departs from the usual representation, for curve I_1' is *not* an indifference curve of the *other* individual, but is simply the indifference curve I_1 redrawn "upside down" so that I_1 and I_1' are perfecty symmetrical in their respective relation to the origins O_1 and O_2. We will refer to I_1' as the *symmetric image* of I_1, and henceforth the prime will be used to denote all such symmetric images.

Definition. a distribution is called (nonstrictly) superfair if each class of participants prefers its own share to the share received by any other group.[2]

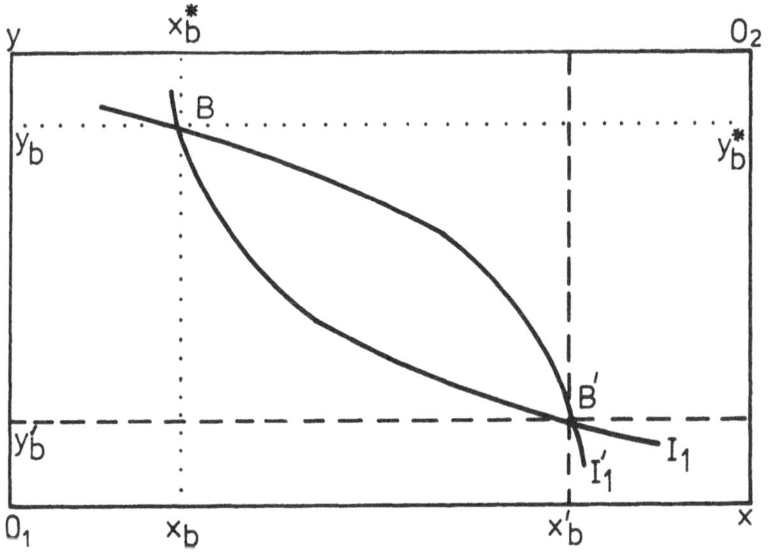

Figure 1

Points B and B' are the two intersections of I_1 and I_1', and it is clear that B' is the symmetric image of B. We will see now that B and B' are both exactly on the boundary of distributions which individual 1 considers fair from his selfish viewpoint. Point B represents the situation in which quantities $(O_2x_b^*, O_2y_b^*) = (O_1x_b', O_1y_b')$, corresponding to point B', go to the other individual, 2. But since B' and B are, by construction, indifferent to individual 1 it follows that the distribution represented by B is exactly fair in the eyes of individual 1. That is, this person is indifferent between what is assigned to him at point B and what is assigned to the other person. Obviously, for the same reason, point B' is also at the border line of fairness to individual 1.

By repeating this construction using other indifference curves of individual 1 we obtain a set points B, B_1, B_2,.. B', B_1', B_2' ... (not shown). The locus of these points is individual 1's fairness boundary. In exactly the same way, using indifference curves of the other person, we obtain individual 2's fairness boundary (Figure 2).

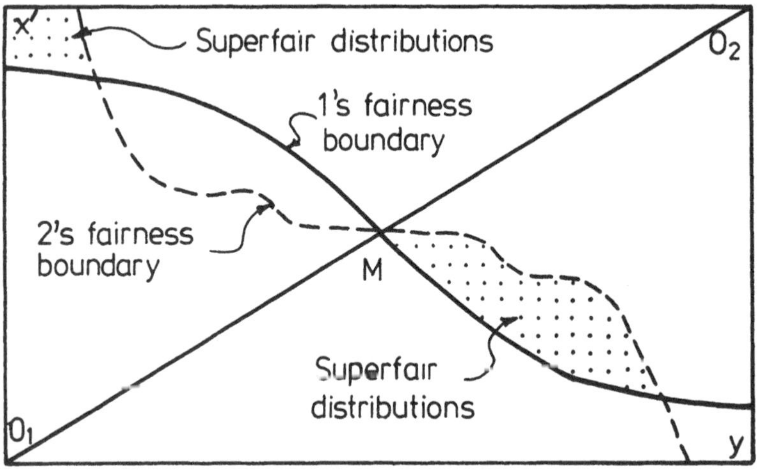

Figure 2

Any point further from O_1 than 1's fairness boundary must obviously be more than fair to 1 in 1's own opinion. The same must be true of points further from O_2 than 2's fairness boundary. It follows that any point that lies above 1's fairness boundary but below 2's fairness boundary must be *strictly superfair*. In Figure 2 there are two regions, the shaded areas, which contain such points. This is the set of points of superfair distributions.

2. *Properties of the Fairness Boundaries*

We know something about the shapes and location of the curves that bound the fairness regions. We will now derive three properties of the fairness boundary: *a*. It must go through the midpoint of the diagram; *b*. it must be symmetrical about the midpoint of the diagram; and *c*. it must have a negative slope. First we will show that it must go through the midpoint, the point in the diagram representing indentical distributions of the available goods to all parties. To find that point, draw the line segment O_1O_2 connecting the two origins of the Edgeworth box. Now draw in the midpoint, *M*, of this line segment. We know that both individuals' fairness boundaries must go through point *M* since at *M* each individual receives exactly the same amount of each good so that at that point each person must be indifferent between the bundles assigned the two persons.

Second, by the symmetry of points *B* and *B'* in Figure 1 we see that either individual's fairness boundary must be symmetric about point *M* in the following sense: its shape to the left of *M*, relative to axes yO_1x must be identical with its shape to the right of *M* relative to axes $y'O_2x'$.

Finally, it can be shown that if an individual's indifferences curves are negatively sloped, continuous and non-intersecting, that person's fairness boundary must have a negative slope.[3]

We may ask also whether the fairness boundary will always exist. We have

Proposition 1. where the individual's utility function and hence the indifference map is continuous, if the individual is not sated in the commodities in question, the fairness boundary must extend to the edges of the Edgeworth box. The fairness boundary will then always exist. In particular, in the two-commodity case it will extend continuously from the upper or left hand boundary of the Edgeworth box, *through the mid point* to the symmetric point on the lower or right-hand boundary.

Proof. As we have seen, the mid point of the Edgeworth box, the point of equal distribution to all parties will always, trivially, lie on the fairness boundary. Hence, by continuity, the boundary must always also exist in a neighborhood of this point. Next note (Figure 2) that, by assumption, for individual 1, his origin O_1 will necessarily be unfair so long as the available quantities of at least some of the goods are positive because at that point individual 1 gets nothing and the goods all go to other parties. By the nonsatiety assumption, then, 1 will envy the parties who do get goods and so O_1 will fail the fairness criterion for 1. Analogously, O_2, the opposite origin, will be more than fair to 1 in his own opinion. Now, as one moves along the boundary of the Edgeworth box from O_1 coming steadily closer to O_2, the degree of envy of individual 1 must decline steadily, since the move involves more and more of the available inventory of the goods going to 1. By continuity there must be some point, *p*, on this path intermediate between O_1 and O_2 at which 1 is indifferent between what is assigned to him and what is assigned to that other individual who in 1's opinion is most favoured. By definition, *p* must lie on 1's fairness boundary.

The remainder of Proposition 1 follows immediately by the continuity assumption, and the symmetry property of the fairness boundary.

3. *Properties of the Regions of Superfairness*

We see that the set of (nonstrictly) superfair distributions must contain *M*, but it is generally not symmetric about *M*. Given one such region to the right of *M*, the symmetric region to the left of *M* will never be superfair since in the former 1's fairness boundary must lie below 2's so that in the latter, 2's fairness boundary must lie above 1's (Figure 2).

We also see that the superfair regions may be disconnected and may contain portions of the axes.

Proposition 2. The superfair region will generally not be located symmetrically within the Edgeworth box and it may not be convex or a single connected set of points.

We notice also that the region of superfair distributions

will tend to lie along the negatively sloping diagonal of the Edgeworth box, *yx*. For it must include *M*, which lies on that diagonal. Moreover, it follows from the negative slopes of the fairness boundaries that the zone of superfair distributions must slope downward to the right. That is, of course, no more than the intuitive statement that if two distributions are to be considered fair, and one of the distributions assigns individual 1 more of one good, then it must compensate *2* by assigning her more of the other good.

The reader may well wonder whether the contract curve, i.e., the locus of Pareto optimal solutions, contains any superfair distributions. The answer, apparently due to Varian, is that, in general, it will. To see this, consider an initially equal distribution of all goods (point *M*). If the contract curve happens to contain *M*, the result follows since *M* is fair by definition. Assume next that the contract curve does not go through *M* and consider the intersection point *K*, of the two individuals' offer curves that begin from *M*, as in the usual international-trade diagram (not shown). Then the standard proof shows that *K* must lie on the contract curve--it must be Pareto optimal. But *K* must also be superfair because at the prices given by the slope of the common price line segment *MK* each individual has the same range of choices available. Letting K_1 and K_2 be the bundles chosen by 1 and *2* at *K* (where, by construction, the two bundles add up to the available quantities of the two goods) 1 thus reveals a preference for K_1 over K_2 and the reverse is true for *2*. Consequently *K* is necessarily superfair as well as Pareto optimal. Thus we have the result now well known in the fairness literature.

Proposition 3. In the exchange of fixed quantities of *n* commodities among *m* individuals there always exists at least one Pareto optimal solution which is superfair.

4. *Rationing: Application of Superfairness Theory*

As an exercise designed to illustrate the applicability of superfairness analysis to concrete issues I will discuss what the theory tells us about the equity of the various rationing methods. Specifically I will deal with two rationing procedures 1. *points rationing* in which individuals are each assigned fixed numbers of ration points (their points incomes) which they can use to "buy" the rationed commodities at a fixed (parametric) point price for each commodity. 2. *rationing with salable points*, the case in which the individual pays for goods with both points and money, and is free to purchase or sell points for money.

On efficiency grounds the literature generally considers points and money rationing to be superior to fixed rations, and considers rationing with salable points to be still better.

I will show that

a) With points rationing any market-clearing equilibriumsolution will be superfair.

b) In general, the equilibrium under rationing with salable points need not be fair, much less superfair.

Thus, there will be cases in which the equilibrium with salable ration points will be inferior in terms of the superfairness criterion to the case where sale of points is prohibited, even if the former arrangement is superior in terms of resource allocation, something which is itself not as clear as usually assumed.

5. *Points Rationing With Money Prices for Goods*

In reality, points rationing has always involved the payment of money as well as points in exchange for goods. Each rationed commodity has its money price, determined by market forces, as well as its points price determined by the authorities. As has long been recognised, this makes the individual consumer's decision problem one involving maximization of utility subject to *two* linear constraints: the money budget inequality and the points budget inequality, with the feasible region being a convex polyhedron.

Since the analysis is most pertinent to a case involving inflationary pressure, it is useful to assume that the two parties represented in our Edgeworth box have, between them, more than enough money to purchase the available quantities of the two outputs. This means that individuals 1 and *2*'s price lines will not coincide. They will have the same slopes since, in the absence of price discrimination, they will face the same relative prices. However, with 1 the individual whose origin is the lower left hand corner of the box, 1's budget line, I, will lie above and to the right of *2*'s (Figure *3*), meaning that the two together can, at current prices, afford to buy more than the available quantities of the two goods (Figure *3*). Notice that the two together cannot afford to end up at a point such as *A* that lies above I. It is true that *2* has the money to pay for the quantities of *X*

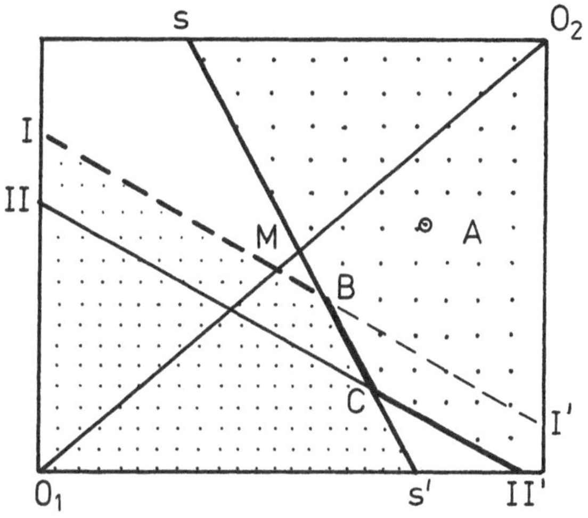

Figure 3

and *Y* assigned to her by that point (because it lies nearer to her origin than her budget line). But since *A* lies above 1's budget line he cannot afford to get to it. For exactly the same reason no point below *2*'s budget line is financially feasible. That is, the two parties can only afford to get to points lying on or between their budget lines *I* and *II*.

We can now see easily what happens if the authorities decide to impose points rationing. As we know, this amounts to the introduction of a new points budget line, *ss*', which cuts through point *M* of equal division. An equilibriumpoint must now satisfy both the monetary and the budget constraints. That is, it must lie on *ss*' and, as we have just seen, on or between the two monetary budget lines *I* and *II*. This leaves us with only the line segment *BC* of *ss'* that lies between *I* and *II*. No other point in the diagram is consistent with the constraints.

This can be seen in a slightly different way. The region that is feasible for I consists of all points which lie below *both* his money and his points budget line, and will therefore be the shaded region whose northeast boundary is *IBs'*. Similarly, *2*'s feasible region must lie above and to the right of the southwest boundary *sCII'*. The only positions common to the two feasible regions and, hence, feasible for both parties are those lying on line segment *BC*, as just noted.

But this is true only at the relative points prices whose ratio is equal to the slope of price line *ss'*. If the authorities select other points prices the points price line will rotate through *M*. The feasible price lines will range from a vertical price line, *vv'*, along which the points price of *Y* divided by the points price of *X* equals zero, to horizontal price line *hh'*, along which the reciprocal of that price ratio is zero (Figure *4*).

As the points budget line rotates counterclockwise from *vv'* to *hh'* in Figure *4*, the feasible line segment *BC* (from Figure *3*) covers the two shaded regions in Figure *4* lying between money budget lines *I* and *II*. That is, only points

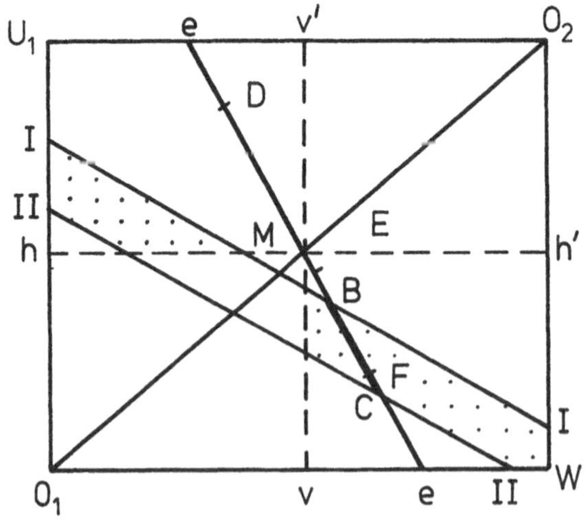

Figure 4

in this shaded region can conceivably be attained under points rationing. But this is not the end of the story. Such a point can be attained only if two conditions are satisfied: (*i*) if the points prices selected are those that clear the market, and (*b*) the equilibrium point on the corresponding points budget line happens to fall in one of the two shaded regions in Figure *4*. That is, suppose *ee* in Figure *4* is the points budget line that clears the market. If a position such as *D* or *E* on that line is the points equilibrium, the arrangement will not work because individual 1 will lack an amount of money sufficient to get to the purchases he would like to make with the ration points in his possession. Only if the equilibrium happens to fall at a location such as *F* on line segment *BC* on *ee* will the points rationing clear the market. It will then work most admirably. As we will now see, it will clear the market, it will eliminate all inflationary pressure, it will be Pareto optimal and it will be superfair. We know it will clear the market because it places both persons at a common position in the Edgeworth box. We know it will stop the inflation, at least in the prices of the two rationed commodities, since neither individual will have any ration points left over to bid for more and so each will be left with a useless amount of money in excess supply. If effect, each person's money constraint becomes ineffective, with the points budget line the only effective constraint. The only (marginal) exception occurs if the equilibrium point happens to fall at either *B* or *C*, the endpoints of the feasible line segment, and here one person will still have an excess stock of money while the other person's money will just suffice for that individual's purchase, so that even in these exceptional cases inflationary pressure will also be eliminated. Finally, we know that the solution will be Pareto optimal and superfair, because with money no longer an effective constraint upon either party the equilibriumis tantamount to a market clearing equilibrium under pure points rationing.

The superfairness follows from our usualargument. The points rationing scheme simply amounts to the establishment of an artificial price line *ee* which goes through the point of equal distribution, *M* (figure 4). This artificial price line is just a substitute for the market price line. The only basic difference between the two is that the market price line would presumably not have contained the equal distribution point, *M*. Now, since points budget line, *ee* goes through *M*, it must offer identical purchase opportunities to both parties - since they have identical points incomes and face identical points prices. But unless they end up at point *M*, because of the negative slope of the points price line, any equilibrium point on *ee* will give *different* bundles of goods to the two parties. Since each has had the option of purchasing without increased points expenditure the combination that goes to the other party but has not chosen to do so, each reveals a preference for his own commodity bundle as against the other person's. Therefore, on the usual premises of revealed preference theory, the distribution must be superfair, indeed, *strictly* superfair. From all this we conclude

Proposition 4 Points rationing with money prices will not always be able to produce a market clearing equilibrium. However, when it does, it will be Pareto optimal and superfair.

6. Rationing with Salability of Points

We come, finally, to the variant of points rationing which has recommended itself to many economists. The idea is to create, along with points rationing, an organized market in which points can be bought and sold at a price that equates their supply and demand. It is argued that the result must be Pareto optimal and that it must constitute a Pareto improvement over the equilibrium when ration coupons are not salable since all trades of ration points for money must be voluntary and so, as usual, there must be mutual gains from the trade.

We will note first that this argument is not necessarily valid; that is, we will see that it is false under rather plausible assumptions. Second, we will show that even where the argument *is* valid the resulting equilibrium may well be inferior to the unsalable points equilibrium on more than one equity criterion. We may observe that the gains-from-trade argument for the Pareto superiority of salability of points is valid only if such sales do not generate a detrimental externality in the form of what may be described as a loss of the feeling of fairness in the system. Suppose that most people consider it unfair for the wealthy to be able to get more than their "fair share" of rationed goods. Given the opportunity, a large majority of the public might choose to vote to prevent everyone (including themselves) from participating in such sales. Yet once such sales become legal so that the wealthy will be able to get additional points on the market, an opponent of the arrangement gains nothing by withholding his own surplus points from the market. Certainly he obtains gains from such trades, if legal trades will take place in any event. But his gains may be greater still if the market for points is eliminated altogether. The problem is that other persons' sales of ration points create detrimental externalities by offending (nearly) everyone's sense of fairness. Here, as usual, the market is unable to cope with such externalities problems, and the resulting free market solution, can be purely illusory.[4]

Before we are able to use our fairness criterion to examine the fairness of the equilibrium under salability of points we must first characterize that equilibrium.

When points can be bought and sold freely the two constraints that characterize normal points rationing are effectively reduced to a single constraint. For then money and ration points simply become two different forms of purchasing power which can be transformed into one another at the current market price of points. One can see this clearly by writing out the relevant constraints.

Since we can easily generalize our argument, let there be n commodities and q individuals and let

x_{ab} = the quantity of commodity A obtained by individual B

x_a = the quantity of commodity A available to the economy

p_a = the market price of A

c_a = the number of ration points required to buy a unit of A

m_b = B's money income

z = the number of ration points issued per person

z_b = the number of points bought (sold) by B, and

p_z = the market price of a ration point.

Then individual *B's* money and points constraints are, respectively

$$\sum_a p_a x_{ab} + p_z z_b = m_b \quad (b=1,\ldots\ldots,q) \qquad (1)$$

$$\sum_a c_a x_{ab} = z + z_b \qquad (2)$$

Multiplying the ration points constraint (2) by p_z and adding the result to money constraint (1) we obtain the one effective constraint for individual *i*,

$$\sum_a (p_a + p_z c_a) x_{ab} = p_z z + m_b \quad (b=1,..,q) \qquad (3)$$

where, following Becker, we may describe $p_z z + m_b$ as individual *B's* full income, *i.e.*, it represents m_b, the money available to him directly as well as the money value of the points issued to him, $p_z z$. This full income can be disbursed among the available goods in any way the individual desires. Each unit of good *A* he buys costs him p_a in money and c_a in ration points, each worth p_z dollars on the market. Thus each unit of *A* effectively costs $p_a + p_z c_a$ (the "full price" of *A*). For any two goods *X* and *Y*, the slope of the individual's money price line (1) is obviously $-p_x/p_y$, that of the points constraintline (2) $-c_x/c_y$, and that of the full income line with salable ration points is

$$-(p_x + p_z c_x)/(p_y + p_z c_y). \qquad (4)$$

Clearly (4) will lie between the slope of the money price line and the points budget line. It will equal the former when the price of points, p_z, is zero, and will approach the latter as p_z approaches infinity. Similarly, for any two individuals *R* and *S*, relative purchasing power will obviously change from m_r/m_s to

$$(m_r + p_z z)/(m_s + p_z z) \qquad (5)$$

We may conclude at once

Proposition 5 Salability of points amounts to a partial equalization of the real incomes of the individuals. The greater the money value of $p_z z$, the points issued per person, relative to the available money incomes, the greater the equalization that will occur.

However, so long as the number of ration points issued and their market price both remain finite, as is normally to be expected, a regime of rationing via salable points will amount only to a partial equalization of incomes, as indicated by (5), along with a modification of relative prices towards the ratios decided upon by the authorities, in accordance with (4).

We have seen from (5) that the greater the total money value of the ration points issued the nearer the solution will be to that under pure points rationing, since the less the share the initial endowments of money income will have in the individual consumers' full income. We may generally expect such a maximal value of the ration points to correspond to the issue of some (intermediate) number of points. For, obviously, the issue of a sufficient number of ration points to make them absolutely redundant will drive their price and, hence, their total market value to zero. Similarly, if no ration points are issued their total value will also necessarily be zero. Hence, there will presumably be some intermediate number of points, z^*, which maximizes the total market value, $p_z z^*$, of the ration points issued.

How, then, do we evaluate the outcome of points rationing with a market in ration coupons? Assuming away the externalities problem raised at the beginning of this section, the result will obviously be Pareto optimal since it involves free exchange at the fixed "full" prices $p_a + p_z c_a$. But will the result be equitable?

Here we deal not just with the distribution of purchasing power, but the way in which it is used, *i.e.*, the equilibrium under the rationing arrangement and every person's attitude toward what he receives under it relative to what is received by each other person.

We have seen that under points rationing equilibrium

will occur somewhere on the contract locus and at a point that lies in a region of superfair distributions. In the complete absence of rationing of any sort, if the market is competitive the solution will also lie somewhere on the contract locus, but it is implausible that this equilibriumwill be superfair. With salability of ration points and in the absence of externality problems, we know from (5) that the distribution of real income will be intermediate between that under pure points rationing and that under the free market solution without rationing. Consequently, if over the relevant range the contract locus is everywhere single valued in every variable expressed as a function of the other variables, the solution under salability of ration points will be intermediate between those under pure points rationing and that yielded by a competitive market without rationing.

Proposition 6. Under rationing with resalability of points the solution may be superfair but need not be so. It can be expected to lie closer to a region of superfair solutions than the free market solution without rationing. If no resalable points solution is superfair, the solution which is likely to be closest to a superfair region is that which results when the authorities issue that number of ration points, z^*, which maximizes $p_z z^*$, the total market value of all the ration points available.

7. *Concluding Remarks*

While this paper has dealt with many issues related to a variety of forms of rationing, its primary purpose has not been to provide another analysis of rationing. Rather, its goal has been to show that the superfairness criterion is operational - that it can be applied to concrete problems and that with its aid one can derive results which are not all obvious in advance. Of course, rationing was selected for that purpose because, of all economic equity issues, it seems to lend itself most readily to this sort of approach.

Something else that emerges is the impression that the views of non-economists on the subject of rationing have a basis more solid than some of the discussions in our literature would seem to imply. For example, salability of ration points does not turn out to be the unmixed blessing we sometimes suggest it to be, and "the common man" is shown to have reason for suspecting its fairness.

All in all, then, superfairness analysis represents a breakthrough which may permit us to begin to deal in rational terms with the fairness issues raised so often by policy makers, which we have so often been forced to evade.

Of course, it cannot be claimed that the superfairness approach is "value free" - but neither is the allocative efficiency sort of advice which has not troubled our consciences much in the past. And, like our allocative-efficiency work, superfairness analysis rests as much on the judgments and preferences of the individuals affected as it does on our own.

REFERENCES

Duncan Foley "Resource Allocation and the Public Sector", *Yale Economic Essays* 7, (Spring, 1967)

E.A. Pazner and David Schmeidler, "A Difficulty in the Concept of Fairness," *Review of Economic Studies*, XLI, July 1974, pp. 441-3

H.R. Varian, "Equity, Envy and Efficiency," *Journal of Economic Theory*, 9, September 1974, pp. 63-91

H.R. Varian, "Distributive Justice, Welfare Economics, and the Theory of Fairness," *Philosophy and Public Affairs*, Volume 4, Spring 1975, pp 223-247

FOOTNOTES

1. Princeton and New York Universities. I should like to thank the National Science Foundation and the Sloan Foundation whose grants greatly facilitated the work reported here.

2. In Varian's terminology, this means that no participant is *envious* of any other. Varian calls such a distribution "equitable" reserving the term "fairness" to refer to a distribution which is both equitable *and Pareto optimal*. I prefer to avoid his terminology for it invites confusion between issues of allocative efficiency and equity which it is one of our purposes to disentangle On these issues see Varian (1974, 1975).

3. I am indebted to Dietrich Fischer for this observation.

4. Alternatively, one can view this case as a prisoner's dilemma problem. If the persons affected can get together and impose abolition of the market in ration points everyone, or nearly everyone, may gain. However, in isolation, each individual has little choice but to act in a manner which is to his immediate advantage, everyone ending up with a net loss as a result of everyone else's actions. The relationship between the externalities problem and the prisoner's dilemma game has long been recognised.

3. CONTRACT THEORY, TEMPORARY LAYOFFS AND UNEMPLOYMENT: A CRITICAL ASSESSMENT

Christopher A. Pissarides

1. *Introduction*

The story of the inability of neoclassical economic theory to provide a rationale for the macro phenomena that preoccupied economists in the post-Keynesian era is by now well known, and does not need repeating. However, two points are worth mentioning, since they bear directly on the topic under discussion. First, if there is non-trivial unemployment in an economy, it is quite likely that firms will be able to influence the supply of labour to themselves by varying their wage offer. This realisation, which was first noted for commodity markets by Arrow (1959), opened up the whole area of optimising wage determination, which previously had relied on Lipsey's (1960) *ad hoc* theorising. Second, and following directly from the first, if wages do not change to accommodate unemployed workers, this must be due to firms' unwillingness to change them. This unwillingness may be due either to ignorance about the effects of wage change, or to some other elements that induce firms to choose wage rigidity despite the existence of queues or vacancies. Wage rigidity can be therefore seen as an optimal policy at the individual level (although perhaps not at the aggregate level), and not as an exogenously imposed "friction" as in the early rationalisations of Keynesian economics.

As is well known, frictionless neoclassical theory contains nothing that suggests that firms may choose not to vary their wages when demand changes. It is therefore clear that if we are to explain wage rigidity and layoffs within a neoclassical framework (something which we accept for the purposes of this discussion, without necessarily arguing that this is the best way to improve macrotheory) some new elements have to be introduced into the traditional model. A large number of authors, following Stigler's (1961) lead, relied on ignorance about the location and wage offers of potential employers to explain the existence of and cyclical changes in unemployment (for a representative sample see Phelps *et al.*, 1970). However, it was soon realised that, despite Alchian's (1970) remarks to the contrary, these models could not explain wage rigidity and demand-related unemployment. At best they offered reasonable explanations of the determinants of the outflows from unemployment when there are many vacancies available, but they could not explain either the existence of layoffs, or large-scale departures from full employment.

The failure of the job-search models to explain wage rigidity and layoffs led to the search for new theories, always working within the traditional utility and profit maximising framework of neoclassical micro-economics. The best-known examples of these new models fall into two groups, the so-called contract theory of Baily (1974), Azariadis (1975) and Gordon (1974) (BAG), and the theory of temporary layoffs of Baily (1977) and Feldstein (1976). In attempting to explain unemployment all models place unique emphasis on the existence of unemployment compensation that is at least partly financed from sources outside the typical firm and workers examined by the models. This paper offers a critical assessment of these models of wage rigidity and unemployment.

2. *The BAG Theory: Wage Rigidity and Involuntary Unemployment*

The BAG Theory was originally put forward as a theory that could explain optimal wage rigidity and "involuntary" unemployment, and had almost immediately been accepted by the profession at large as a theory that succeeded in doing so. (With certain notable exceptions - several of the criticisms mentioned below can be found scattered in journal articles.) The basic idea relates to the attitudes of firms (entrepreneurs) and workers towards fluctuations in their income streams. The argument is that for a given mean value of their respective income streams, firms are better placed to bear fluctuations than workers because the former have better access to capital markets, they hold more diversified portfolios than workers whose main asset (human capital) cannot be diversified, or are simply less risk averse. As a result, firms agree to bear the brunt of stochastic demand fluctuations, offering a better overall job package to their workers, who will agree, as a result, to work for lower mean wages.[1]

It is important to emphasize, before the models are set out, what the models mean by "wage rigidity" and "involuntary unemployment", since a lot of confusing statements about these have been made in the literature. First, by wage rigidity is meant that the firm will offer a wage rate that is independent of its <u>own</u> output price, but fixed in <u>real</u> terms. Thus we have here theories of complete indexation of money wages to an average price level such as the CPI. Second, the firm may not find it optimal to keep employment constant when there are random fluctuations in output-price, so it may resort to a policy of layoffs when demand for its product drops. However, it is quite important that (1) this is <u>not</u> an implication of differential risk attitudes, the main innovation of contract theory, but of the existence of non-trivial unemployment compensation (or leisure from "unemployment holidays"), and (2) if anything, the risk attitudes assumed by the models imply that there should be <u>less</u> layoffs than otherwise.

Thus, if we follow BAG and place differential risk attitudes at the centre of "contract theory", the inescapable conclusion is that contract theory implies that the chances of observing "under-employment equilibrium" (Azariadis' 1975 term) are considerably reduced. On the other hand, the models of Feldstein (1976) and Baily (1977), which have the same structure as BAG, except that they assume risk neutrality all round, imply that layoffs are quite likely to take place.

However, it is still the case that in all these models, unemployment arises because some firms may choose to place their workers temporarily on the unemployment register to benefit from the subsidisation that the government offers through its unemployment compensation programme. If output markets are competitive this view has nothing to say about cyclical unemployment, since in this case fluctuations in aggregate demand are fully reflected in fluctuations in prices, and through the indexation of money wages to prices implied by the theory wage schedules respond to these fluctuations immediately. With competitive output markets the models provide, at best, descriptions of the effects of temporary shifts in demand amongst firms, so they are related more to structural than to cyclical unemployment. But their implications about wages and employment here are not different from those of the traditional neoclassical model with competitive output and labour markets. According to the latter, an economy-wide drop in demand shifts every industry's demand for labour to the left, and so leads to a shift in the aggregate labour-demand schedule, reducing the equilibrium money wage; an industry-specific drop in demand does not move the aggregate schedule and so does not alter the equilibrium money wage, but shifts the industry's own curve leading to reduced employment at the same wage. Thus, money wages are insensitive to industry-specific demand changes, but they respond to economy-wide changes, as the contract theory predicts.

However, the validity of this argument depends crucially on price-taking and full market-clearing in both commodity and labour markets. If commodity markets do not clear, in the sense that firms are sales-constrained over the cycle, then the BAG models may be shown to imply layoffs in response to economy-wide drops in demand. At the extreme where the retail price index is fixed, or follows a predictable course, with the trade-cycle manifested in shifts in the entire demand schedule, the firm will offer a fixed real wage and respond to the cyclical downswing by laying off workers. Clearly, the existence of unemployment here depends on the existence of a sales constraint, which is outside the model. But if the latter can be shown to exist then this is also a sufficient condition for the existence of involuntary unemployment (something <u>not</u> true in traditional theory).[2]

The next section develops a formal model, similar to that of Azariadis (1975) to demonstrate these and other less important propositions. Section 4 discusses temporary layoffs, and section 5 offers some preliminary remarks on an alternative explanation of the phenomenon, placing more emphasis on the monopsony power that firms are likely to have when their workers are endowed with firm-specific capital.

3. *A Formal BAG Model*

Following Azariadis (1975) suppose that the demand for the firm's output is subject to random fluctuations, described by a probability distribution over a finite number of states of nature. Both firm and workers know this probability distribution. We make the critical assumption that workers are attached to firms, because of high mobility costs, so in order to attract workers the firm has to offer a contract (implicit or explicit) whose value depends on both its immediate and longer-run employment strategy. Commodity and labour markets are competitive; the firm is a price-taker in output markets and has to offer a contract to its employees that is at least as good as some exogenously given contract (which employees can get elsewhere). Let

p_i = the price of the firm's output in state i

q_i = the general price index in state i

L = the total number of workers attached to the firm (offered the contract)

L_i = employment in state i

w_i = money wage rate in state i

z = unemployment compensation or units of leisure

ϕ_i = probability of state i occurring

In each state of nature the firm chooses at random L_i of its L workers and offers them w_i. The rest are placed on the unemployment register. If the production function is $f(L_i)$ the firm maximises real expected profits

$$\pi = \sum_i \phi_i \frac{p_i}{q_i} f(L_i) - \sum_i \phi_i \frac{w_i}{q_i} L_i \tag{1}$$

Workers plan to stay with the firm for more than a single period, so they expect to experience the firm's employment strategy in more than one state of nature. We begin by making the extreme assumption that no worker plans to quit to take another job, so workers expect to be employed in state i with probability L_i/L, and be unemployed and waiting for a recall with probability $(1 - L_i/L)$. Since workers do not suffer from money illusion their utility from employment is $u(w_i/q_i)$ and from unemployment $u(z/q_i)$, and so their expected utility from the job offer is

$$U = \sum_i \phi_i \frac{L_i}{L} u\left(\frac{w_i}{q_i}\right) + \sum_i \phi_i \left(1 - \frac{L_i}{L}\right) u\left(\frac{z}{q_i}\right) \qquad (2)$$

Usually it is assumed that $u'' < 0$, so workers are risk averse, whereas firms are not.

The firm is constrained along two dimensions. First, in order to recruit the labour force L, it has to offer a job contract (implicit or explicit) that is worth at least as much as workers can get elsewhere. If the value of the latter is U^*, then the constraint is

$$U \geq U^* \qquad (3)$$

Second, the firm cannot employ in any state more than L workers, so

$$L \geq L_i \text{ for all } i \qquad (4)$$

Profits (1) are maximised subject to (3) and (4). Let λ be a Kuhn-Tucker multiplier associated with (3), and $\phi_i \mu_i$ a multiplier associated with (4). The firm maximises with respect to w_i, L and L_i. Differentiating first the expected profit expression (1) with respect to w_i we obtain

$$-1 + \frac{\lambda}{L} u'\left(\frac{w_i}{q_i}\right) = 0 \qquad (5)$$

This condition clearly implies that $\lambda > 0$, so (3) holds with equality, and, more important, it implies that the real wage w_i/q_i is state-invariant - the "wage rigidity" result. This result depends crucially on the differential risk attitudes assumed, since the second-order maximisation conditions require $u'' \leq 0$. If $u'' > 0$ (5) does not hold at the profit maximisation point, whereas if $u'' = 0$ then (5) is independent of w_i/q_i, and so no unique profit-maximising solution for the latter exists. We return to a discussion of these results later. At present we continue by assuming $u'' \leq 0$ and denoting the optimal state-invariant real wage by w^*. By the non-uniqueness of w_i/q_i when $u'' = 0$ there is no loss of generality if we assume that the real wage is state-invariant even when $u'' = 0$. Since as we show below there are unique solutions for L_i and L irrespective of whether $u'' > 0$ or $u'' = 0$, if $u'' = 0$ the optimal w^* is simply found by substituting the optimal L_i and L into the constraint (3). (On this see Baily, 1977, p. 1054.) For simplicity we also assume that the unemployment compensation z is linked to the retail price index, so we write z^* for a state-invariant real unemployment compensation.

Should now the firm ever find it optimal to refuse to employ part of its work force at the pre-announced wage w^*? To answer this question we differentiate (1) with respect to L and L_i taking into account the constraints (3) and (4). This gives

$$\sum \phi_i \mu_i = \frac{\lambda}{L^2} \sum \phi_i L_i [u(w^*) - u(z^*)] \tag{6}$$

$$\mu_i = p_i^* f'(L_i) - w^* + \frac{\lambda}{L} [u(w^*) - u(z^*)] \tag{7}$$

$$\mu_i \geq 0 \text{ and } \mu_i(L - L_i) = 0, \tag{8}$$

where p_i^* is the firm's relative price in state i. Condition (8) implies that the question whether there are states of nature where the firm is not fully employed reduces to whether it is optimal to choose $\mu_i = 0$ for some i, since if $\mu_i > 0$ then $L_i = L$. Now, condition (6) implies that since in general $w^* > z^*$, at least one μ_i is positive, so there are some states of nature where the firm is fully employed. Layoffs in some state i will be optimal if setting $L_i = L$ violates (7), i.e. if

$$p_i^* f'(L) - w^* + \frac{\lambda}{L} [u(w^*) - u(z^*)] < 0,$$

Using (5) we find that layoffs will take place in state i if

$$p_i^* f'(L) < w^* - \frac{u(w^*) - u(z^*)}{u'(w^*)} \tag{9}$$

It is clear from (9) and the condition $\mu_i > 0$ for some i

that if the firm's relative price p_i^* is state-invariant there will be no layoffs: the existence of layoffs requires that the firm's relative price should vary over states.

Now if such variation occurs the optimality of layoffs requires that the right-hand side of (9) must be positive (since p_i^* can never be negative). Thus a necessary condition for the existence of layoffs is

$$w^* u'(w^*) + u(z^*) - u(w^*) > 0 \tag{10}$$

Our purpose is to show that under these conditions risk aversion on the part of workers reduces the likelihood of layoffs - and so the main assumption of BAG increases the changes of observing full employment at all times.

This is shown simply by considering (10) under risk neutrality, i.e. if $u = a + bw^*$, with $b > 0$. Then the right-hand side of (9) becomes equal to z^*, and so (9) states the obvious proposition that the firm will lay off workers if the value of their marginal product falls short of the unemployment compensation that they can get from the government. Suppose now workers are risk averse. We aim to show that layoffs may not take place even if the value of the worker's marginal product is less than z^*, i.e., the right-hand side of (9) is now equal to some other $\hat{z}$ than is less than z^*.

To demonstrate this we use the fact that since $u(\ )$ is continuous and monotonic it satisfies the First Mean Value Theorem

$$u(w^*) - u(z^*) = u'(x)\ (w^* - z^*)$$

where $w^* \geq x \geq z^*$. Substituting in (9) we get

$$w^* - \frac{1}{u'(w^*)}\ [u(w^*) - u(z^*)] = w^* - \frac{u'(x)}{u'(w^*)}\ (w^* - z^*) \equiv \hat{z}$$

But if $u'' < 0$ then $u'(w^*) < u'(x)$ and so, using the fact $w^* > z^*$

$$\hat{z} < w^* - (w^* - z^*) = z^*.$$

Thus the firm will resort to layoffs if the value of the marginal product of its employees is less than some critical value $\hat{z}$, which is less than the level of unemployment compensation; differential risk attitudes imply that in equilibrium there should be less unemployment than otherwise. If there is unemployment in some states of nature then this must be due to the high unemployment compensation available, or to the high leisure-value attached by workers to unemployment. It is instructive to consider how high this unemployment compensation will have to be before the possibility of layoffs can arise under risk aversion, by considering simple utility functions exhibiting constant relative risk aversion. If the relative risk aversion is unity then

$$u(w^*) = \log w^*,$$

and so the right hand side of (9) is positive if

$$\frac{z}{w} > \frac{1}{e},$$

or z/w (the "replacement ratio") must be at least 37 per cent. If the relative risk aversion coefficient is $r < 1$ then

$$u(w) = w^{1-r},$$

so (9) requires

$$\frac{z}{w} > r^{\frac{1}{1-r}}$$

If, for instance, $r = 0.5$ then the replacement ratio must be at least 25%. On the other hand if $r > 1$

$$u(w) = -w^{1-r},$$

so if, e.g., $r = 2$ the replacement ratio must be at least 50%. These values of the replacement ratio are not insignificant, especially when it is recalled that these are necessary but not sufficient for layoffs; in addition p_i^* must be very small, so layoffs will take place either when a firm does not share in a general boom or when the firm loses demand to other firms.

Before proceeding we offer a simple intuitive explanation for the results obtained so far. It should be apparent by now that the BAG theory relies on two crucial elements for its results, differential risk attitudes and unemployment compensation. Consider a wage and employment policy characterized by random fluctuations, and let $\bar{y}$ be the mean value of total wage payments (i.e., the mean of $w_i^* L_i$ for every state i) and σ_y^2 their variance. The firm is risk neutral, so it is interested only in the mean value of its wage bill $\bar{y}$, being indifferent about σ_y^2. But workers are risk averse, so they evaluate the firm's job offer by taking into account both y and σ_y^2; given $\bar{y}$ a positive σ_y^2 reduces the attractiveness of the firm's offer. Thus, given these differential risk attitudes, it is to everyone's advantage to set $\sigma_y^2 = 0$, since then the firm's offer becomes more attractive without being more costly. This will normally require constancy in both wages <u>and</u> employment.

However, the second element of the theory, unemployment compensation, implies that the firm stands to gain from employment fluctuations, since they enable it to make use of the subsidisation offered by the government to the unemployed to increase the attractiveness of its job offer. Thus, differential risk attitudes lead to constancy of both w^* and L_i, unemployment compensation leads to fluctuations in L_i; the net outcome will obviously be constancy of w^* but either constancy or fluctuations in L_i depending on the relative magnitudes of risk aversion and unemployment compensation involved.

Finally, we demonstrate the conjecture made at the end of the last section, that sales-constrained firms that experience stochastic variations in these constraints will adopt a policy of layoffs even if these variations are economy-wide. Thus, we impose the constraint that the firm's sales in any state i do not exceed D_i.

Quite interestingly, we can demonstrate that if (10) is not satisfied the firm will again not adopt a policy of layoffs. In this case the cost of laying-off a worker is so high, in terms of the worker's expected utility, that the firm prefers to hoard labour in the downswing. To demonstrate this, suppose that $f(L_i) > D_i$, hence the firm bears the cost of L_i workers but sells only D_i. Condition (5) is clearly still valid, indicating the optimality of a fixed wage contract, but now (7) becomes

$$- w^* + \frac{u(w^*) - u(z^*)}{u'(w^*)} = \mu_i \qquad (11)$$

If (10) is not satisfied the LHS of (11) is positive, so $\mu_i > 0$, and $L_i = L$ in all states of nature is still optimal.[3]

However, if (10) is satisfied then labour hoarding is never optimal, since it would make $\mu_i < 0$, which violates (8). Hence the firm produces up to D_i in every state i. Given this, it is trivial to show that if the firm is sales-constrained in any state j then (10) is sufficient for the optimality of layoffs in that state. This follows since by assumption $f(L) > D_j$, and since (10) is satisfied $f(L_j) = D_j$. Hence $L_j < L$.

Thus for the sales-constrained firm (10) is both necessary <u>and</u> sufficient for layoffs. Moreover if the firm is sales-constrained in any state, layoffs in that state are always higher than layoffs without the constraint. More importantly, the sales constraint does not have to be peculiar to the firm for the optimality of layoffs - economy-wide changes in "effective demand" associated with the cycle also produce layoffs. (But it should again be emphasized that the theory does not have anything to say about the origin of sales constraints.)

4. *Temporary Layoffs*

It is clear that the layoffs in the BAG theory are of a "temporary" nature, since workers are attached to the firm and they evaluate the mean utility from a job offer over all states of nature, not just over the current state.

Normally these layoffs will be followed by rehires, and although the laid-off worker is (*ex post*) worse off, his layoff cannot be said to be involuntary. Over a long horizon all workers will share equally in layoffs, so on average the effect will be the same as variations in hours, except that with layoffs, workers get the additional benefits of state-financed unemployment compensation.

The models of Feldstein (1976) and Baily (1977) explore in detail the possibility of temporary layoffs without adopting what appears to be the main BAG assumption - differential risk attitudes. The model explored in detail by the former and used in empirical work elsewhere (e.g. Feldstein 1978) is essentially a BAG model with a linear utility function and a non-stochastic wage rate. (Recall that when $u(\ )$ is linear the first-order conditions cannot be solved uniquely for the optimal wage rate in every state of nature.) His main result is that if there is any subsidization of layoffs by the government, layoffs may be adopted as an optimal policy. This follows simply from condition (10). If the utility function is linear it is very easy to show that the condition for layoffs is simply $z > 0$, which is equivalent to Feldstein's (1976, p. 948) result.

The Feldstein-Baily models also consider variations in hours of work in response to demand fluctuations. Feldstein assumes that hours enter as a separate factor in the production function, whereas Baily uses the more traditional specification of lumping together men and hours. Variations in hours is advantageous from one point of view: in a depression the firm can reduce hours uniformly, increasing the marginal product of labour and offering more leisure to all workers. However, variations in the number of workers enables the firm to benefit from the unemployment subsidy, so although the firm may choose to respond to a depression by lowering hours, the existence of the subsidy makes layoffs more likely than otherwise. Baily (pp. 1051-2) offers an intuitive description of the adjustment process. As output price falls, hours are lowered, as in traditional theory. After a certain point workers will find themselves earning less than unemployment insurance, so the firm places them on the unemployment register to benefit from the subsidy. (This result requires that as hours fall the hourly rate does not go to infinity.) Thus although including variations in hours may qualify the results and make layoffs less likely, it is still true that if there is exogenous unemployment compensation, layoffs are a real possibility as an optimal response to a drop in demand. As in the BAG model with linear utility, unemployment compensation in these models induces layoffs simply by acting as a floor on weekly earnings.[4]

That unemployment compensation acts as a floor on weekly earnings and so may induce unemployment if the value of the marginal product of labour falls below it should not surprise any neoclassical economist. The main interest from these models is their empirical relevance - what proportion of layoffs is actually due to this subsidization, how many workers are recalled to their former jobs and how many quit to take another job. It is also quite interesting that it is not unemployment compensation *per se* that creates unemployment but external financing of compensation: if z of the last section is financed by a tax on either the firm or the workers attached to it, no layoffs can arise in response to z as an optimal policy. Thus, a way to reduce these layoffs (if this is considered desirable) is to tax firms according to their layoff rate, something pursued in the U.S. to some limited extent and in the U.K. with respect to lump-sum redundancy payments.

Feldstein (1975, 1978) argues that a large portion of unemployment in the U.S. can be explained by temporary layoffs. Others (e.g. Clark and Summers (1978), Akerlof and Main (1978)) argue that the picture is not as straightforward as presented by Feldstein. It is not our purpose here to discuss the empirical significance of the theory, although it may be stated that in Britain there is no strong evidence of a significant temporary-layoff rate, despite the full subsidization of unemployment benefit. Instead I offer here three comments on the theoretical structure of the model, which are directly related to the question of layoffs.[5]

First, temporary layoffs take place when the decrease in demand is known to be temporary by both firms and workers. A permanent decrease in demand results in a decrease in the number of people offered the contract (L in the notation of the last section) and not in an increase in the temporary layoff rate, $L - L_i$. By a permanent decrease in demand we mean a leftward shift in the price distribution ϕ, so both firms and workers should be able to distinguish between shifts in ϕ and movements between states within ϕ. The theory has nothing to say about the former, which produces permanent layoffs.

Second, by offering subsidization in the form of unemployment compensation the government increases the attractiveness of job offers, as can easily be seen from equation (2). Thus unemployment compensation in these models plays (partly) the role of an employment subsidy, and so, like other subsidies, it should be expected to increase the firm's permanent labour force. This can indeed be shown to be the case, since if L is endogenous the model predicts $\partial L/\partial z > 0$. However, this subsidy can be enjoyed only if there are layoffs, and so if $L_i < L$ we obtain $\partial L_i/\partial z < 0$. Thus the effect of increasing the subsidy is to increase the firm's labour force when it is fully employed, and decrease it when it has workers on temporary layoff; put differently, the subsidy reduces "permanent" unemployment but increases "temporary" unemployment. The overall effect of the subsidy is ambiguous in general, but if the production function is restricted to Cobb-Douglas mean unemployment can be shown to increase. As expected, this increase is not as much as Feldstein's (1976) model implies, which assumes that L is fixed independently of z.[6]

Finally, even with temporary layoffs, if there are earning opportunities elsewhere, and moving costs are not infinite, workers may search for alternative employment whilst waiting for a recall. Both Feldstein (1976) and Bradshaw and Scholl (1976) found some evidence for such alternative search, and Baily (1977) incorporated it in his formal model. We show below that if this is taken into account the theory of layoffs derived from the model has some strong implications about layoffs during the cycle which require further scrutiny. In general these results are not very favourable to the view of unemployment derived from these models. (That the model may not be able to cope with quitting was also noted and discussed by Akerlof and Miyazaki (1978), but for quite different reasons.)

5. *Job Search During Layoff*

The contract theory of unemployment relies very heavily on the existence of costs associated with job changing (including search costs). In the previous sections, we looked at a special case where these costs were infinite once the individual accepted the contract. In this section we relax this restriction by assuming that individuals do search for alternative employment during layoff.

The possibility may be treated quite generally within the framework of the BAG Theory.[7] Since labour markets are competitive, the value of job-contracts is given exogenously to every firm and worker as U^* (see equation (3)). Thus if a worker on temporary layoff searched and found alternative employment, the value of that employment to him would be U^*. But finding and accepting this alternative employment (either permanently or on a temporary basis until a recall from the old firm involves costs. These costs are higher the higher the moving costs, c, the lower the unemployment compensation, z, and, crucially, the lower the probability of finding alternative jobs, a. Thus, in general, instead of writing $u(z)$ for the utility from layoff, as in (2), we may write $V(c, z, a, U^*)$, with V_1 negative and all other partial derivatives positive. Replacing $u(z)$ by $V(\ )$ in (2) and going through the same analysis we find that layoffs are more likely the higher the value of $V(\ )$.

Thus, once again higher z induces more layoffs. For obvious reasons lower moving costs c also induces more layoffs. But for our purposes the most important new element in this extension is the probability of finding alternative employment, a; the higher this probability, the greater the incidence of layoffs, since in tight markets characterized by high a the cost of the layoff to the worker will be lower. Thus it would appear that if the firm takes into account contract values given by expression (2) in choosing its layoff policy (irrespective of whether $u(.)$ is linear or not) it will be more likely to resort to layoffs when jobs elsewhere are plentiful. If several firms adopt a similar policy forcing the economy to move towards a state of high unemployment, then layoffs will be checked.

This element of the theory is remarkably similar to the well-known feature of job-search theory relating quitting and aggregate unemployment. In the latter, quitting is more likely in conditions of full employment because then workers know that their unemployment durations will be short. If the economy starts moving away from full employment because of too many quits, workers stop quitting because they see their chances of finding alternative employment reduced. Because of this, a theory based on quits cannot explain nontrivial cyclical swings in unemployment. By analogy, a theory of temporary layoffs built on the principles of BAG or Baily-Feldstein (1976) cannot be expected to explain nontrivial departures from full employment: most of the pro-cyclical layoffs that contribute to the cyclical swings in unemployment must be due to some other elements not present in these theories.

It is not surprising that a theory based on voluntary additions to unemployment should have these implications. The state of unemployment is in general less desirable the higher the national rate of unemployment (because durations are in general positively correlated with the rate), so voluntary unemployment should decline as national unemployment rises. Yet it is well known that temporary layoffs are much higher in downswings than in upswings, contributing significantly to the cyclical behaviour of the unemployment stock (see Feldstein 1975, p. 737). The remainder of this section sketches briefly an alternative explanation of temporary layoffs, based partly on Oi's (1962) model of firm-specific training and partly on the theory of search. This alternative is consistent with the results of Feldstein on the role of unemployment compensation but it is also consistent with the cyclical behaviour of temporary layoffs.[8]

Suppose that all (or most) workers are endowed with firm-specific capital, which makes their marginal product in their current employment higher than in other firms. Since firms are monopsonists with respect to workers endowed with firm-specific capital, they will not offer them their full marginal product in wages, but something less; conversely, their own workers are more valuable to them than outside searchers, so they will offer more than what their workers can get elsewhere, in order to induce them to stay. Suppose then a wage rate has been fixed, and the firm experiences a drop in demand, which reduces its desired labour force. The firm can either (a) hoard labour, keeping it idle or using it to build up inventories, or (b) lay off workers. Since workers have firm-specific training, the firm would rather re-employ these workers when demand picks up again than recruit new workers. On the other hand, workers would also like to return to their old firm, because their wages there are higher. But if the cost of the layoff is high, workers may search for alternative employment.

This suggests that firms will hoard labour if employment opportunities elsewhere are plentiful or if unemployment costs are high, but may adopt layoffs when employment opportunities elsewhere are sparse and unemployment costs low. Thus, although unemployment compensation does raise the chances of a layoff, firms are less likely to lay off workers in the upswing than in the downswing, because in the latter case there is a higher chance that the worker will still be unemployed and available for recall when the firm's demand picks up. Moreover, since the costs of remaining unemployed rise with duration, firms may discourage their workers from searching by keeping durations short. Thus, a firm may recall workers before demand picks up and at the same time lay off other workers, ensuring in this way that workers remain attached to it. If the expected duration before a recall is not long, workers may not search for alternative employment at all.

The predictions of this alternative explanation of layoffs concerning unemployment duration, recalls, and search during layoffs are consistent with the evidence presented by Feldstein (1975, 1978). Contrary to Feldstein's (1976) own explanation, or the one that can be derived from BAG and Baily (1977), this alternative explanation views the firm as exploiting its monopsony power with respect to workers with firm-specific training, within imperfectly-competitive constraints imposed by the market. Moreover, this alternative view is also consistent with the observation of layoffs following economy-wide decreases in demand, and not simply firm-specific decreases, as BAG argue.

6. *Conclusions*

In this paper we considered recent neoclassical attempts to provide a rationale for wage rigidity and layoffs.

Consideration of the "implicit contract theory" of Baily (1974), Azariadis (1975) and Gordon (1974) revealed that the critical assumption of differential risk attitudes made by these models (risk-neutral firms and risk-averse workers) leads to index-linking of money wage rates and sub-optimality of layoffs in the absence of exogenous unemployment compensation. If there is unemployment compensation then firms suffering a temporary drop in demand not experienced by other firms may lay off part of their workforce. If output markets do not clear, then layoffs may be more widespread.

Abandoning the assumption of differential risk attitudes introduces an indeterminacy (non-uniqueness) in the optimal wage offer, but whatever the wage it increases the chances of layoffs. The condition required for a layoff now is simply that the marginal product of labour fall below the (exogenous) unemployment compensation or disutility of work. We have argued that the rationalisations of frequent lay-offs and recalls (observed in the U.S.) within an implicit contract model, or the similar models of Feldstein (1976) and Baily (1977), are not as convincing as more traditional explanations that place more emphasis on firm-specific training and the monopsony power that firms and workers enjoy as a consequence.

It would thus appear that with competitive output markets the contract theory has an implication about wage offers that is neither new to neoclassical theory nor empirically valid in the short run; the theory has nothing to say about non-clearing output markets, which might rescue some results; and finally the theory's framework (especially its innovation of differential risk attitudes) is not helpful to the study of temporary layoffs, complicating an otherwise simple model that relies on exogenous unemployment compensation or disutility from work for layoffs.

REFERENCES

Akerlof, G. and Main, B. (1978). Unemployment Spells and Unemployment Experience. *Special Studies Paper* 123, Federal Reserve Board.

Akerlof, G. and Miyazaki, H. (1978). The Implicit Contract

Theory of Unemployment Meets the Wage Bill Argument (October).

Alchian, A.A. (1970). Information Costs, Pricing and Resource Unemployment. In Phelps.

Arrow, K.J. (1959). Towards a Theory of Price Adjustment in M. Abramovitz *et al.*, *The Allocation of Economic Resources*. Stanford.

Azariadis, C. (1975). Implicit Contracts and Underemployment Equilibria. *Journal of Political Economy* 83, 1183-1201.

Baily, M.N. (1974). Wages and Employment under Uncertain Demand. *Review of Economic Studies* 42, 37-50.

Baily, M.N. (1977). On the Theory of Layoffs and Unemployment. *Econometrica* 45, 1043-63.

Bradshaw, T.F. and Scholl, J.L. (1976). The Extent of Job Search During Layoff. *Brookings Papers on Economic Activity* 2, 515-24.

Clark, K.B. and Summers, L.H. (1978). Labor Force Transitions and Unemployment. *NBER Working Paper No. 277* (August).

Feldstein, M.S. (1975). The Importance of Temporary Layoffs: An Empirical Analysis. *Brookings Papers on Economic Activity* 3, 725-44.

Feldstein, M.S. (1976). Temporary Layoffs in the Theory of Unemployment. *Journal of Political Economy* 84, 937-57.

Feldstein, M.S. (1978). The Effect of Unemployment Insurance on Temporary Layoff Unemployment. *American Economic Review* 68, 834-46.

Gordon, D.F. (1974). A Neoclassical Theory of Keynesian Unemployment. *Economic Inquiry* 12, 431-59.

Lipsey, R.G. (1960). The Relation between Unemployment and the Rate of Change of Money Wage Rates in the U.K. 1862-1957: A Further Analysis. *Economica* 27, 1-31.

Oi, W. (1962). Labor as a Quasi-fixed Factor. *Journal of*

Political Economy 70, 538-55.

Phelps, E.S. (1970). *Microeconomic Foundations of Employment and Inflation Theory*. New York.

Stigler, G.J. (1962). Information in the Labor Market. *Journal of Political Economy* 70, 94-105.

FOOTNOTES

This paper arose out of notes that I prepared for discussion at the Centre for Labour Economics' Unemployment Seminar at LSE. I benefitted from preliminary discussions with John Sutton and Marios Clerides, and from the comments of the members of the Unemployment Seminar, especially Stephen Nickell and Nicholas Rau. After the completion of the first draft of this paper I saw a paper by Akerlof and Miyazaki (1978) where some of the criticisms discussed in section 3 below are also made.

1. However, since mean wages are known and workers have long horizons, aversion to wage fluctuations must clearly be due to capital market imperfections. The theories do not model capital market imperfections explicitly but simply talk of risk-averse workers and risk-neutral firms (and they have been criticised for doing so by Feldstein (1976)).

2. Even if we accept the existence of non-market-clearing as a datum there may still be problems with the BAG assumptions that may alter the results summarized in the text. Thus, if there is commodity rationing it is not clear that real incomes are sufficient representations of workers' welfare, whereas the theory requires that workers may be indifferent to fluctuations in the rationing constraint but be averse to fluctuations in real income.

3. Azariadis (1975, p. 1192) calls the LHS of (11) the "reduction in labor cost accomplished by eliminating one job in any state". If this is positive the firm <u>increases</u> its costs by dismissing workers, so no such dismissals take place.

4. It is quite straightforward to introduce hours in the formal model of section 3 and demonstrate these claims.

5. It should perhaps be emphasized that being critical of the particular theory of temporary layoffs put forward in Feldstein (1976), Baily (1977) or BAG, does not necessarily deny the empirical significance of the phenomenon. Indeed, close reading of Feldstein (1978, esp. p. 835) reveals that for empirical research into this question it is necessary to take account of factors not present in the formal models under discussion here.

6. Baily (1977, p. 1059) considers variations in L emphasizing the greater employment variation that results from the increase in L and the decrease in $L_i < L$.

7. The results of the next two paragraphs can also be derived from Baily's (1977) specification of mobility.

8. The ideas below will be formalised in a future paper.

DISCUSSION : JOHN D. HEY

This most interesting paper by Christopher Pissarides represents a further contribution to the now sizeable literature motivated by the desire to provide acceptable microtheoretic explanations for important *disequilibrium* phenomena - particularly those of unemployment and inflation. Since the inception of this new field of theoretical endeavour, two particular potential explanatory factors (for these disequilibrium phenomena) have dominated the literature: first, uncertainty; and second, adjustment costs. While much of the recent literature (job search, contract theory, and the theory of temporary layoffs) has been predominantly concerned with the first of these, perhaps *one of the messages* emerging from Pissarides' paper is that the profession should not go overboard in favour of this uncertainty approach, but should also keep the second factor (the existence of adjustment costs) firmly under consideration; in particular, he draws attention to the friction introduced by the existence of firm-specific human capital. A *second important message* of this paper is that perhaps more is claimed of some of the existing models than can actually be delivered by them; in particular, attention is drawn to the role of contract theory as an explanation of temporary layoffs. (Though I must admit to some confusion here: I had always thought of contract theory as being a way of explaining, *inter alia,* why university teachers in the U.K. were paid so little - they were trading-off salary against security of tenure.) I would like to examine these conclusions, and indeed appraise the whole thrust of the paper, within the structure of the following taxonomic framework.

			time t+1		
			E	U	N
	Employed	E	ee	eu	en
time t	Unemployed	U	ue	uu	un
	Not in labour force	N	ne	nu	nn

Any model of the type under consideration is essentially concerned with three stocks and nine flows - those depicted in the schema above. Single capital letters denote stocks, while pairs of lower case letters denote flows. In the former category are the Employed (E), the Unemployed (U) and those Not in the labour force (N); these stocks are represented by the rows (at time t) and the columns (at t+1) of the above matrix. The flows are the cells in the above matrix (ee, eu, en, etc.); the most important of these for the present paper are those which are classified as LAYOFFS or QUITS (flows eu and possibly en) and HIRING and REHIRING (flows ue and possibly ne). (As an aside it is interesting to note that, whereas superficially it appears straightforward to distinguish between layoffs and quits according as to whether the firm or the worker has initiated the separation, in actuality the dichotomy is not always that clear; for instance, as Pissarides points out, the separation may be mutually agreeable.)

Before discussing the various theoretical explanations of the flows in the above matrix, it would seem useful to distinguish between *equilibrium* and *disequilibrium* within the labour market. Equilibrium, which exists when the stocks (E, U and N) are constant through time (or, possibly, when they are changing in a predetermined fashion - a case I wish to exclude for reasons of expositional simplicity) can be of two types: *static* (when the net flows are all zero) or *stationary* (when the net flows are non-zero, but constant). Disequilibrium occurs when the stocks and the net flows are changing (in a non-predetermined manner) through time. Now it appears to me that all the models that Pissarides discusses (including his own) - and indeed most of the other models in this general so-called 'disequilibrium' area - are models of *stationary equilibrium.* If this is so, then the models have *nothing whatsoever to say about the effect of overall declines in aggregate demand* - such a phenomenon is outwith their framework of reference; Pissarides' attempts to discuss the models' abilities to predict behaviour in such a case is therefore illegal. I will return to this point shortly.

Let us first turn briefly to the flows in the above matrix, and check which theories can (or purport to) explain them. First, job search theory (which, I feel, the author dismisses rather too summarily) is normally used to explain flows ue and uu, but it can also explain flows ee and eu, and indeed possibly en, un, ne, nu and nn. However, it is important to note that such explanations are all *as viewed from the worker's point of view* (the behaviour of the firms is treated as exogenous) - in particular, all quits are voluntary on the part of the worker. Second, contract theory can explain flows ee, eu, ue and uu - but now essentially *as viewed from the firm's point of view* (the behaviour of the workers is treated as exogenous). Temporary layoff theory is almost identical in its intended coverage (though the inclusion of the word 'temporary' emphasises the 'stationary equilibrium' - rather than 'disequilibrium' - nature of the model). Third, there are other uncertainty-type models which can explain various flows; for example, some unpublished work by C.J. McKenna at the University of York examines the role of learning (by firms about the productivity of workers, and by workers about the working conditions in firms), and shows how flows ee, eu, ue and uu can be explained within a market model. Fourth, (though certainly not finally) is Pissarides' own model - sketched out rather tantalisingly in the closing pages of the paper - which appears to explain the same four flows: ee, eu, ue and uu.

As I hope is apparent from the above discussion, the various theories that have been (and are being) developed are not particularly competing theories: indeed in most cases they are complements rather than substitutes. Some look from the firm's point of view, some from the worker's; some posit uncertainty, some the existence of adjustment costs. Taken together, they constitute the pieces of a jig-saw puzzle which is slowly taking shape. What we surely need now is a genius who can actually put the pieces together (in a consistent fashion - which, as I have argued elsewhere, is a difficult problem); surely we do not want to throw any of the pieces away?

I would now like to turn to the examination of an important distinction frequently referred to by Pissarides: the distinction between an *industry wide* drop in demand and an *economy wide* drop in demand. In terms of my taxonomy, this is the distinction between (a fluctuation within) a *stationary equilibrium* state and a *dis-equilibrium* state. As I have already mentioned above, I do not think any of these models have very much to tell us about the latter situation. This is since these models assume a given (and known) probability distribution; in contrast, presumably the crucial feature of a general economy wide drop in demand is that the probability distribution is *changing*, and it is changing in an *unforseeable fashion*.

(Without wishing to get hung up with semantics, this would seem the only sensible way to attach any meaning to the concept of 'an exogenous decrease in aggregate demand'.) In terms of Pissarides' model, an economy wide drop in demand is an unforseen change in the ϕ_i values.

These considerations lead to a very important general point. In most models, the probability distributions are assumed given and known; no learning takes place or is modelled. Thus the true values of the ϕ_i are always known. But, if we wish to model an economy wide drop in demand, we need to model behaviour when the ϕ_i *may change*. Now, and this is very important, how can any economic agent tell whether an observation (on some random variable) is a random observation from the old distribution or whether it is the first random sample from some new distribution? In other words, *how is a shift* (in the probability distribution) *recognised?* (As an aside, one might ask how the worker checks whether the contract, implicitly or explicitly entered into, is actually being enforced? Moreover, how do the workers check whether the equilibrium condition EU = U* is being maintained? Indeed, what meaning can be attached to this *equilibrium* (note the importance of this word) *condition* when the possibility of disequilibrium exists?)

Once it is admitted that a shift (in the probability distribution) may be difficult to recognise, and thus might be ignored or its magnitude mis-estimated, then the existence of dis-equilibrium (as distinct from stationary equilibrium) states must also be admitted. However, the existing theories have very little, if anything, to say about such states. (It is interesting to recall Arrow's 1959 comment to the effect that dis-equilibrium confers monopsony power on price-setters; this point is neatly echoed by Pissarides' modelling of monopsony power in the final pages of his paper.) The essential point here is that general dis-equilibrium type phenomena cannot be modelled in what is an essentially equilibrium framework; thus the *correct* emphasis in the theories under discussion is on *temporary* layoffs rather than on *unemployment*.

Before concluding, there are four minor points.
(1) Most of the models assume a perishable (non-storable) commodity; thus inventories play no role. However, if the product were storable, then inventories could be used to

absorb part of the uncertainty. Indeed, we could perceive such inventories as stores of labour - since labour itself is instantly perishable and non-storable. (2) The sales-constrained model appears somewhat odd in that price-*taking* behaviour seems no longer optimal when sales are constrained by demand. (3) While lump-sum redundancy payments might be useful (in a stationary equilibrium model) as a device for cutting down on temporary layoffs, they might also have the effect (in a disequilibrium model) of cutting down on *em*ployment in the first place. (4) In the sketch of his own model towards the end of the paper, Pissarides seems to be suggesting that workers might be 'fooled' into staying with a firm that lays them off frequently for short periods whereas they would not stay with a firm that laid them off infrequently for long periods (even though the expected duration of layoff were the same in both cases).

Overall, Pissarides has provided a very elegant characterisation of the contract theory and temporary layoffs theory, and has shown how the main conclusions of these theories emerge from this characterisation. He has carefully highlighted the crucial assumptions of these models, and has put their achievements into a useful perspective. Notwithstanding the various reservations noted above (particularly those concerning the 'correct' direction for such research, and the appropriate methodology for 'dis-equilibrium' analysis), Pissarides' paper represents an important appraisal and critique. Moreover, his concluding pages whet our appetite for his forthcoming further contributions in a field in which he is already an acknowledged expert.

4. DOMINANT FIRM MODELS OF RESOURCE DEPLETION

A.M. Ulph and G.M. Folie

INTRODUCTION

The models presented in this paper analyse the equilibrium price and output paths that occur in an industry depleting an exhaustible resource, where some of the firms act as a cartel which sets the path of prices over time, while another group of firms, the fringe, takes the path of prices as given and sets output to maximise the present value of the fringe's profits. The cartel is aware that the prices it sets will determine the fringe's supply, and so selects a price path which maximises the present value of the cartel's profits, taking account of the fringe's response. The resulting *dominant firm* equilibrium will be shown to consist, in general, of two phases - a 'competitive phase', in which price follows the path a perfectly competitive industry would set, and a 'monopoly phase', in which the price follows a price path a monopolist would set. The decision problem confronting the cartel can then be characterised as selecting how much of its resources it should allocate to each phase.

Interest in models of partially cartelised markets arises naturally from the realisation that such a structure characterises many real-world exhaustible resource industries, of which the crude oil industry is probably of greatest interest. The issues one might hope such models would illuminate include what are the likely future paths for output and prices, how far does the existence of the fringe constrain the ability of the cartel to raise prices, what are the likely welfare losses imposed by the cartel and how might public policy affect such losses, and how stable is such a cartel likely to be? It could be argued, however, that one does not need to develop a particular theory of exhaustible resource cartels to answer such questions. There is already a substantial literature on both exhaustible resources and on imperfectly competitive markets, and an appropriate blend of results from both areas of theory could yield the required insights.

No doubt such an approach would be a useful first step, but the purpose of this paper is to show that a proper consideration of partially cartelised exhaustible resource industries generates a number of results which run counter to the intuitions one derives from both the theory of exhaustible resources in its competitive and monopolistic forms, and from the theory of partially cartelised markets applied to inexhaustible commodities. Four particular results will be derived.

First, under plausible cost assumptions, it will be shown that it will pay the cartel to split its production into two distinct phases, with an intervening period in which only the fringe produces. Second, when it is assumed that the cartel and the fringe have identical costs of production, a frequently invoked assumption, then the equilibrium for the dominant firm model is equivalent to the equilibrium for the Nash-Cournot model, in which the cartel assumes that the fringe's output does *not* respond to the price path it sets, Salant (1976), Ulph and Folie (1978a, 1978b). Third, if the cartel has a reasonable cost advantage over the fringe, then the profits of the fringe will be *lower* in the dominant firm equilibrium than they would have been in a perfectly competitive equilibrium. Finally, if the cartel has a substantial cost advantage over the fringe then the monopoly phase of production can take place before the competitive phase. For some of these cases, where the cost advantage is very marked, lowering the cost of the fringe's production will cause the prices charged by the cartel in the monopoly phase to *rise*. Moreover the price path in the monopoly phase is *higher* than it would be if the entire industry was monopolised. This has the interesting consequence that, if we define welfare as the sum of consumer and producer surpluses discounted over time, an attempt to weaken the impact of the cartel by making the fringe act competitively rather than monopolistically, can actually lower welfare.

The first two of these results are entirely new, but the second two have some antecedents. The fact that the fringe's profits may be lower in a partially cartelised market has been demonstrated for a wide range of Nash-Cournot and quasi-dominant firm models (Ulph and Folie, 1978a, 1978b), and this paper extends the results to dominant firm models. The fourth result is related to work by Gilbert and Goldman, (1978) and Hoel (1978), although in both cases the fringe is assumed to supply an inexhaustible substitute resource. Both papers note that lowering the cost of this substitute resource may cause the price initially set by the cartel to rise, and Hoel notes that the price set by the cartel may be higher when the substitute resource is owned by a fringe of competitive firms than when it is controlled by the cartel itself. This paper confirms these results for the case where the substitute resource is also exhaustible and shows that the higher price set by the cartel in the partially cartelised market may lower welfare. Gilbert and Goldman show that welfare may be higher when there is *no* substitute resource, which is a somewhat different result, and seems to hold only when the cartel's resources are very large.

It is important to note the way in which the market is supposed to operate in this paper. The cartel announces prices for all future time periods for the resource and the fringe responds by announcing output plans. To ensure that these plans are realised it is assumed that there is either a set of binding contracts or a set of future markets in which all trades occur now and no recontracting is allowed. In the terminology of differential games, these are *open-loop strategies*. This is of considerable importance for it will be shown that there are cases where these strategies are *dynamically inconsistent* - that is where it would pay the cartel to deviate from its announced strategy at some future date. In a world without binding contracts or perfect future markets the equilibria described here would not be appropriate. Thus while the model deals with allocation of the resource over time, it is a meta-static model, rather than really dynamic. This is also true of all the other treatments of this problem referred to in this paper.

Finally it should be noted that the model employs a number of simplifying assumptions - extraction costs are independent of current and cumulative output levels and there is a linear demand curve which does not change over time. Gilbert (1978) analyses a dominant firm model with rather different assumptions - there are no extraction costs and demand is constant - elasticity (with elasticity less than one) with a backstop technology that will be supplied with infinite elasticity at some finite price. None of the results listed above can occur in Gilbert's model.

THE MODEL

There are two groups of firms, a cartel group, indicated by subscript c, and the fringe group, inidcated by subscript f. Within each group the firms will be assumed to be identical, so each group can be treated as a single firm. X_c and X_f are the reserves of the cartel and fringe respectively. It will be assumed that costs of production of both groups are independent of both current and cumulative output, and K_c, K_f will denote the unit production costs of the cartel and fringe respectively.

Although the two groups have different costs, they produce a homogeneous output, and the demand for this resource in every period is given by the demand curve,

$$p = F - aq$$

where p is market price and q is the quantity demanded. For notational simplicity no time subscripts for variables are used, and this should case no confusion.

Finally, all firms face the same rate of discount, δ .

The market operates by the cartel announcing a path of prices over time for the resource. The fringe takes this price-path as given and selects a path of output which maximises the present value of its profits. The cartel is aware of the influence its price path has on the fringe's supply, so for any price path it can calculate how much will be demanded in each time period, how much the fringe will supply in each time period, and hence how much production will be required from the cartel's resources. The cartel will select a price path which allows supply and demand to be balanced in each time period, which does not require cumulative production by the cartel to exceed its initial reserves, and which maximises the present value of the cartel's profits.

What will the cartel's chosen price path look like? To take account of the fringe's production there will clearly need to be some phase - which will be denoted the 'competitive phase' - during which the fringe firms deplete their resources. As is now well-known, during such a phase the present value of marginal profits to the fringe must be constant, otherwise a rearrangement of the fringe's production would yield higher profits to the fringe. Thus, during the competitive phase, price will follow the path

$$p = K_f + \rho_1 e^{\delta(t-\sigma_1)} \tag{1}$$

where σ_1 is the start of the competitive phase, and ρ_1 is the present value of marginal profits, or 'exhaustion rent', evaluated at σ_1 .

While all the fringe's resources will be depleted during the competitive phase, it is possible that the cartel may also choose to produce during this phase. Let X_{c1} denote the amount of resources devoted by the cartel to the competitive phase, $0 \leqslant X_{c1} \leqslant X_c$. How will the cartel allocate this production within the competitive phase?

At time t , the present value of the cartel's per unit profit from producing during the competitive phase is

$$(K_f + \rho_1 e^{\delta(t-\sigma_1)} - K_c)e^{-\delta t}$$

or

$$(K_f - K_c)e^{-\delta t} + \rho_1 e^{-\delta\sigma_1}$$

If $K_f > K_c$, then the present value of unit profits declines over time, so it will pay the cartel to concentrate its production of X_{c1} at the start of the competitive phase. Letting $\bar{\sigma}$ denote the time it would take to deplete the cartel's resources, X_{c1}, then $\bar{\sigma}$ is defined by

$$\frac{1}{a}\int_{\sigma_1}^{\sigma_1+\bar{\sigma}} \left(F - K_f - \rho_1 e^{\delta(t-\sigma_1)}\right)dt = X_{c1} \tag{2}$$

and the present value of the cartel's profits from depleting X_{c1} , valued at σ_1 , can be shown to be

$$U(X_{c1}) = \frac{1}{a\delta}\left\{\rho_1\delta\bar{\sigma}(F + K_c - 2K_f) - \rho_1^2(e^{\delta\bar{\sigma}}-1) + (F - K_f)(K_f - K_c)(1 - e^{-\delta\bar{\sigma}})\right\} \tag{3}$$

If $K_c = K_f$, then the present value of unit profits to the cartel is constant throughout the competitive phase. Thus, like the fringe, the cartel is indifferent about when it produces, and the present value of the cartel's profits, at time σ_1, are

$$U(X_{c1}) = \rho_1 \cdot X_{c1}$$

Finally, when $K_f < K_c$, production will be concentrated at the end of the competitive phase. Letting τ_1 denote the length of the competitive phase, and $\bar{\sigma}$ the length of time it takes to deplete the cartel's resources, X_{c1}, then $\bar{\sigma}$ is defined by

$$\frac{1}{a}\int_{\tau_1-\bar{\sigma}}^{\tau_1} (F - K_f - \rho_1 e^{\delta t})\, dt = X_{c1}$$

and the present value of the cartel's production is

$$U(X_{c1}) = \frac{1}{a\delta}\left\{\rho_1\delta\bar{\sigma}(F + K_c - 2K_f) - \rho_1^2(1 - e^{-\delta\bar{\sigma}})e^{\delta\tau_1} + (F - K_f)(K_f - K_c)(e^{\delta\bar{\sigma}} - 1)e^{-\delta\tau_1}\right\} \tag{4}$$

This completes the discussion of the competitive phase. Since, in general, it cannot be assumed that $X_{c1} = X_c$, it remains to discuss how the cartel acts outside the competitive phase. This will be denoted the 'monopoly phase', because, since the fringe's production is taken account of by the inclusion of the competitive phase in the price path, the cartel is now free to act as a monopolist. The cartel will allocate its remaining reserves, $X_{c2} = X_c - X_{c1}$, so that the present value of marginal profits is constant in each period. Since marginal revenue is $M = 2p - F$, the monopoly price path is given by

$$p = \tfrac{1}{2}(F + K_c) + \rho_2 e^{\delta(t-\sigma_2)} \quad .... \quad (5)$$

where $2\rho_2$ is the exhaustion rent corresponding to the monopoly phase and σ_2 is the start of the monopoly phase.

While the cartel is able to price like a monopolist during the monopoly phase, there is nevertheless an implicit constraint - the price path set during the monopoly phase cannot yield the fringe a higher implicit profit than it can earn during the competitive phase. This requires that for all t during the monopoly phase

$$\left[\tfrac{1}{2}(F + K_c) + \rho_2 e^{\delta(t-\sigma_2)} - K_f\right] e^{-\delta t} \leqslant \rho_1 e^{-\delta\sigma_1}$$

or

$$\tfrac{1}{2}(F + K_c) + \rho_2 e^{\delta(t-\sigma_2)} \leqslant K_f + \rho_1 e^{\delta(t-\sigma_1)}$$

Letting $P_1 = K_f + \rho_1 e^{\delta(t-\sigma_1)}$

and $P_2 = \tfrac{1}{2}(F + K_c) + \rho_2 e^{\delta(t-\sigma_2)}$

denote the 'competitive' and 'monopoly' price paths respectively, the competitive phase occurs when $P_1 \leqslant P_2$, while the monopoly phase occurs when $P_2 \leqslant P_1$. The equality between the price paths will occur only at the point of transition from one phase to the other, and this reflects the obvious characteristic of an equilibrium path that it be continuous. For any discontinuities would present profitable opportunities for switching resources between the two phases.

The above consideration means that there are three possible arrangements for the two phases, depicted in Figure 1(a), (b) and (c):

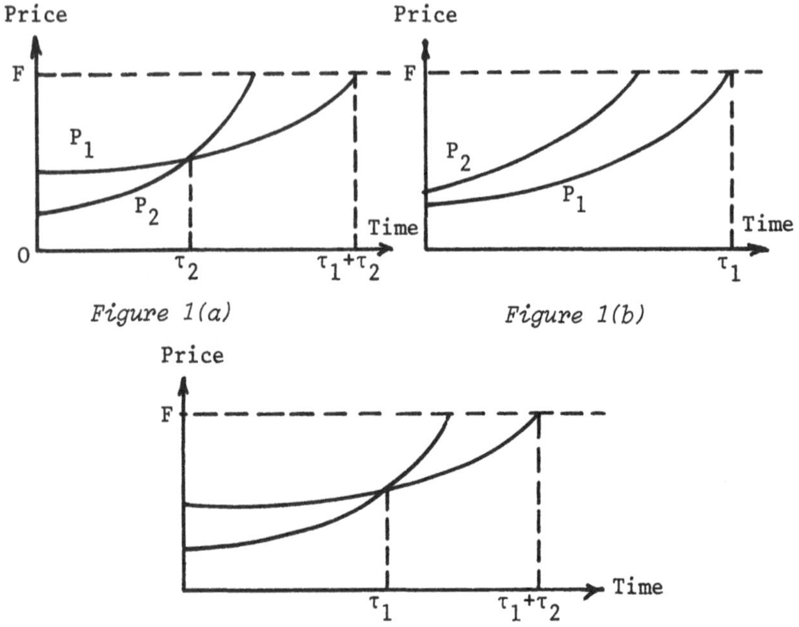

Figure 1(a) *Figure 1(b)*

Figure 1(c)

Figure 1. Determination of Phases

Case I is shown in Figure 1(a), with the monopoly phase, of duration τ_2, coming first, and the competitive phase, of duration τ_1, second. A necessary condition for Case I to occur is $K_c < \frac{1}{2}(F + K_c) < K_f$, for if this was not the case then the fact that P_1 lies initially above P_2 would imply that

$$\rho_2 e^{-\delta\sigma_2} < \rho_1 e^{-\delta\sigma_1}$$

and then P_2 would lie below P_1 for all t, an impossibility.

At the other extreme, Case III illustrated in Figure 1(c), the competitive phase comes first (with $P_1 < P_2$) followed by the monopoly phase, $P_2 < P_1$. By analogy with Case I, a necessary condition for Case III to occur is $K_f < \frac{1}{2}(F + K_c)$.

Finally, in between is Case II, in which there is no monopoly phase at all. A sufficient condition for this case to occur is $K_f = \frac{1}{2}(F + K_c)$, since this is the only solution allowed for this condition.

This describes the order in which the two phases of the dominant firm solution can occur. To complete the solution it is necessary to determine the way the cartel decides how much of its resources to devote to each phase, and the values of four variables ρ_1, ρ_2, τ_1, τ_2, - the exhaustion rents and duration for each phase.

Consider first the case where $\frac{1}{2}(F + K) < K_f$, so that either a case I or Case II might occur. To begin, assume some arbitrary split of the cartel's resources between the two phases, X_{c1}, X_{c2}. Then the exhaustion rent and duration of the competitive phase can be determined by solving the problem of a competitive industry endowed with resources $X_f + X_{c1}$, all of uniform cost of extraction K_f, and with demand $P = F - aq$. The solution for ρ_1 and τ_1 is given by the two equations

$$\frac{1}{a}\int_0^{\tau_1} (F - K_f - \rho_1 e^{\delta t})\, dt = X_f + X_{c1}$$

$$K_f + \rho_1 e^{\delta \tau_1} = F$$

where the latter condition says that price at the end of the competitive phase must be sufficiently high to choke off demand for the resource. The value of the cartel's profits at the start of the phase are $U(X_{c1})$, as derived earlier in Equation (3).

Now the variables ρ_2, τ_2 are determined by considering the problem confronting a monopolist with resources X_{c2}, costs K_c, demand $P = F - aq$ where the terminal price is constrained to be $K_f + \rho_1$, the price at the start of the competitive phase. The equations determining ρ_2 and τ_2 are thus

$$\frac{1}{a}\int_0^{\tau_2} (F - \tfrac{1}{2}(F + K_2) - \rho_2 e^{\delta t})\, dt = X_{c2}$$

$$\tfrac{1}{2}(F + K_c) + \rho_2 e^{\delta\tau_2} = K_f + \rho_1$$

It can be readily shown that the value of the cartel's profits in the monopoly phase is given by

$$V(X_{c2}) = \frac{1}{4a\delta}\left\{(1-e^{-\delta\tau_2})\left[(F-K_c)^2 - e^{-\delta\tau_2}(2K_f+2\rho_1-F-K_c)^2\right]\right\}$$

Thus the total present value of profits to the cartel corresponding to the allocation of its reserves X_{c1}, X_{c2} is given by

$$W(X_{c1}, X_{c2}) = V(X_{c2}) + e^{-\delta\tau_2}U(X_{c1})$$

The cartel determines its optimal allocation of its resources between the two phases by choosing X_{c1}, X_{c2} so as to

$$\mathit{Max}\ W(X_{c1},X_{c2})\ \text{s.t.}\quad X_{c1} + X_{c2} = X_c \quad .$$

If the solution to this is $X_{c2} = 0$, then a Case II solution is achieved.

If $\tfrac{1}{2}(F + K_c) > K_f$, then a similar algorithm is used, only now the monopoly phase is solved first (with terminal price F), and then the competitive phase, with terminal price $\tfrac{1}{2}(F + K_c) + \rho_2$. $W(X_{c1}, X_{c2})$ will of course become

$$W(X_{c1}, X_{c2}) = U(X_{c1}) + e^{-\delta\tau_1}V(X_{c2})$$

where now $V(X_{c2}) = \frac{1}{4a\delta}(F-K_c)^2\left(1-e^{-\delta\tau_2}\right)^2$

Finally, if $\tfrac{1}{2}(F + K_c) = K_f$, then a Case II solution results, and all that is required is to solve the problem of a competitive industry with resources $X_f + X_c$, costs

K_f, and demand $P = F - aq$.

This completes the description of the general solution of the dominant firm model. In general it will consist of two phases - a competitive and a monopoly phase. If the cartel has a substantial cost advantage over the fringe, i.e. $\frac{1}{2}(F + K_c) < K_f$, then the monopoly phase, if it exists, will come first. Otherwise the cartel must wait till the end of the competitive phase before acting as a monopolist.

It may be worth commenting on why it will usually pay the cartel to produce some of its resources during the competitive phase, rather than reserving all its production for the monopoly phase. The obvious advantage of switching resources out of the monopoly phase is that this raises the price to be obtained during the monopoly phase, at the expense of lowering the price during the competitive phase. This latter disadvantage, however, is offset by a second consideration. When the monopoly phase comes first, Figure 1(a), the existence of the fringe puts an upper limit, $K_f + \rho_1$, on the price that can be set during the monopoly phase. Switching resources into the competitive phase allows the cartel to price above $K_f + \rho_1$, although of course ρ_1 falls as more resources are switched into the competitive phase. In Case III, where the monopoly phase comes last, the existence of the fringe firms acts to *delay* the time at which the cartel can act like a monopolist, so that when the cartel switches resources into the competitive phase it obtains the benefit of earlier profits. Thus, while the cartel is sacrificing part of its opportunity to act as a monopolist, it gains the advantage of higher prices during the monopoly phase, plus the opportunity either to price beyond the constraint set by the fringe or to make earlier profits, and these benefits will ensure, in general, that it will be worthwhile setting $X_{c1} > 0$.

DYNAMIC INCONSISTENCY

The previous section outlined the possible dominant firm equilirbia that can arise in the model studied in this paper. In deriving these equilibria it was assumed that the cartel would announce the price it would set for the resoruce at each point of time and the fringe would announce its output level for each point of time. To realise such equilibria would require either binding contracts or a complete set of future markets in which all dealings were completed at the beginning of time and no recontracting is allowed. In the absence of such institutional features, it is conventional to appeal to some notion of rational expectations about the future behaviour of agents. Such a rational expectations equilibrium will coincide with equilibrium computed in the previous section only if the latter is dynamically consistent, i.e. at each point in time it pays the cartel to continue playing their announced strategies. It is easy to demonstrate that in general the equilibria of the previous section are not dynamically consistent.

Consider a Case III equilibrium for $K_f < K_c$. This will consist of three phases. Up to time t_1, say, there will be competitive prices and only the fringe produces. From t_1 to t_2, say, there are competitive prices, and only the cartel produces, while after t_2 the cartel produces at monopoly prices. The intermediate phase is crucial when the cartel is announcing its strategy for it allows a smooth transition from competitive prices to monopoly prices. But once t_1 is reached in real time, the fringe's resources would be exhausted and the cartel is free to set monopoly prices immediately. If the fringe anticipates such behaviour, it will hold back production to make a capital gain, and this destroys the original equilibrium. So the Case III equilibrium is not dynamically consistent.

It should be noted that some equilibria will be dynamically consistent. Thus no problem arises in a Case I equilibrium or in the model of Gilbert (1978). For the remainder of this paper it will be assumed that an appropriate institutional framework is available to ensure that the equilibria derived in the previous section can be realised.

TWO SPECIAL CASES

In this section two particular cases will be examined since they present some interesting features. Both cases concern Case III solutions, in which the competitive phase precedes the monopoly phase, and for which a necessary condition is that $K_f < \frac{1}{2}(F + K_c)$. This section considers two subcases of this condition - subcase A in which $K_c < K_f < \frac{1}{2}(F + K_c)$ and subcase B for which $K_f = K_c$.

Subcase A: $K_c < K_f < \frac{1}{2}(F + K_c)$

In this subcase the competitive phase will consist of two subphases, in the first of which the cartel produces by itself and in the second of which the fringe produces by itself. But this has the immediate implication that the cartel's production takes place in two unconnected periods - the first part of the competitive phase and the monopoly phase, with the fringe's production occuring in between.

To demonstrate that such cases do exist, consider the example where the parameters are $X_c=1000$, $X_f=500$, $K_c=0$, $K_f=10$, $F=100$, $a=2$, $\delta=.1$. Then it can be calculated that the dominant firm solution consists of $X_{c1} = 640$, $X_{c2} = 360$, yielding a maximum profit to the cartel of 5261.4.

The splitting of the cartel's production into two phases is contrary to what one would expect from the theory of exhaustible resources for it does not occur in models of competitive, monopolistic, or Nash-Cournot market structures. It has the important implication that in addition to the welfare losses introduced by monopolistic pricing practices, there are now production inefficiencies due to more expensive resources being extracted while cheaper resources are still available.

Subcase B: $K_c = K_f$

The result to be demonstrated for this particular set of parameters is that the dominant firm equilibrium is equivalent to the Nash-Cournot equilibrium(Salant, 1976). In a Nash-Cournot model, the cartel takes the output path of the fringe as *given*, and selects a price path which maximises present value of profits. Equilibrium occurs when the price path assumed given by the fringe is the one selected by the cartel, while the output path assumed given by the cartel is the one the fringe chooses. Since this is a completely different assumption from the one embodied in the dominant firm model one would expect the equilibria to differ. However, for this particular case, they are equivalent.

To prove the equivalence, one might as well assume that $K_f = K_c = 0$. For ease of notation the competitive price path will be written as:

$$P_1 = \rho_1 e^{\delta t}$$

and the monopoly price path

$$P_2 = \frac{F}{2} + \frac{\rho_2}{2} e^{\delta t}$$

Also, let σ denote the time at which the competitive phase ends, and τ the time at which the monopoly phase ends. Then the five equations determining the five variables ρ_1, ρ_2, σ, τ, X_{c1} which characterise the dominant firm equilibrium can be written as

(6) $0 = \rho_2 e^{\delta\sigma} + F\ log\ F - F - 2a\delta(X_c - X_{c1}) - F\ log\ \rho_2 - F\delta\sigma$

(7) $\delta\tau = log\ F - log\ \rho_2$

(8) $0 = \rho_1 + F\delta\sigma - \frac{F}{2} - \frac{\rho_2}{2} e^{\delta\sigma} - a\delta(X_f + X_{c1})$

(9) $\delta\sigma = log\ F - log(2\ \rho_1 - \rho_2)$

(10) $\frac{\partial W}{\partial X_{c1}} = \frac{\partial W}{\partial X_{c2}}$

It was shown by Salant (1976) and Ulph and Folie (1978a) that the Nash-Cournot solution also consists of a period of simultaneous production, which will be denoted by $(O-S)$, followed by a period when the cartel aloneproduces, denoted $(S-T)$. There are also exhaustion rents, R_1 and R_2 to be determined, and the four equations defining R_1, R_2, S and T where shown in Ulph and Folie (1978a) to consist of

(11) $\delta FS + 2R_1 - R_2 = a\delta X_f + F$

(12) $\delta S = log\ F - log\ (2R_1 - R_2)$

(13) $R_2 = F\ log\ R_2 + 2a\delta X_c + F\delta S - F\ log\ F + 2R_1 - R_2$

(14) $\delta T = log\ F - log\ R_2$

Clearly equations (7) and (9) are identical to equations (14) and (12). Simple linear combinations of (11) and (13) allow them to be re-written as

$$(15) \quad 2R_1 = 2a\delta(X_c + X_f) + F\ log\ R_1 - F\delta S - F\ log\ F + 2F$$

$$(16) \quad R_2 = F\ log\ R_2 + a\delta(2X_c + X_f) + F - F\ log\ F.$$

Equally simple manipulation of (6) and (8) transform them to become:

$$(17) \quad 2\rho_1 = 2a\delta(X_c+X_f) + F\ log\ \rho_1 - F\delta\sigma - F\ log\ F + F$$

$$(18) \quad \frac{\rho_2}{2}e^{\delta\sigma} + \rho_1 + a\delta X_{c1} - \frac{F}{2} = F\ log\ \rho_2 + a\delta(2X_c+X_f) + F$$

$$- F\ log\ F$$

(15) and (17) are clearly identical, so the two sets of equations are equivalent if

$$\rho_2 = \frac{\rho_2}{2}\ e^{\delta\sigma} + \rho_1 + a\delta X_{c1} - \frac{F}{2}$$

or

$$a\delta X_{c1} = \rho_2 - \rho_1 + \frac{F}{2} - \frac{\rho_2}{2}\ e^{\delta\sigma}$$

Tedious algebraic manipulation of equation (10) shows that this is indeed the case.

While a specific functional form for the demand curve has been used to prove the equivalence of Nash-Cournot and dominant firm equilibria when both groups of firms have identical constant marginal costs of production, the fact that Gilbert (1978) was able to obtain a similar result in a model with a different demand structure suggests that the result may be fairly general. Thus what is often taken to be an innocuous simplifying assumption - essentially ignoring production costs - turns out to be quite restrictive.

When costs of production differ between the cartel and the fringe, the equivalence between the solutions of the two models disappears. In the first place, it is demonstrated in Ulph and Folie (1978a) that the Nash-Cournot model will generally contain periods of simultaneous production between the fringe and the cartel, whereas no such period exists in the Dominant Firm model. More importantly, however, it has been proved in Ulph and Folie (1978b) that equilibria for the Nash-Cournot model exist in which the cartel's profits are lower than they would have been in a competitive equilibrium. Clearly, this cannot be a feature of a dominant firm equilibrium, so, as one would expect, the equilibria of the Nash-Cournot and Dominant Firm models will be different.

One final point should be made about this case. Consider equations (11) and (12) of the Nash-Cournot solution. Together they determine S and $(2R_1-R_2)$. But equations (11) and (12)depend only on X_f , not on X_c. Thus, by the equivalence of the Nash-Cournot and dominant firm solutions, the duration of the competitive phase, σ, is independent of X_c.

This has the immediate implication that when $K_f = K_c$, all solutions are of the Case III type. First, it is proved that there could be at most one Case II solution Suppose there are two values of X_c, $\bar{X}_c$ and $\bar{\bar{X}}_c$, say, such that the dominant firm model yields solution with $\bar{X}_{c2} = 0$, $\bar{\bar{X}}_{c2} = 0$. Then the competitive price has to satisfy the terminal requirement that $K_f + \rho_1 e^{\delta\sigma} = F$, so that with σ fixed, so is ρ_1 . But with ρ_1 and σ independent of X_c , aggregate demand is independent of X_c , so that in at least one of the solutions aggregate demand cannot equal initial resources, which is excluded. Thus there can be at most one value of X_1, $\bar{X}_c$ say, for which there is no monopoly phase.

But this too is impossible - for consider any $\bar{\bar{X}}_c < \bar{X}_c$. Now for $\bar{X}_c$,$\bar{\rho}_1$ is found such that $K_f + \bar{\rho}_1 e^{\delta\sigma} = F$, while for

$$\bar{\bar{X}}_c, \bar{\bar{\rho}}_1$$

is found such that $K_f + \bar{\bar{\rho}}_1 e^{\delta\sigma} = G < F$. So $\bar{\bar{\rho}}_1 < \bar{\rho}_1$. Hence aggregate demand along the curve $K_f + \bar{\bar{\rho}}_1 e^{\delta t} (0 \leq t \leq \sigma)$ must be greater than aggregate demand along the curve $K_f + \bar{\rho}_1 e^{\delta t} (0 \leq t \leq \sigma)$. But this is impossible, for in the first case aggregate demand must equal $\bar{\bar{X}}_{c1} + X_f$, while in the second case it equals $\bar{X}_{c2} + X_f$, and by assumption

$$\bar{\bar{X}}_{c1} + X_f < \bar{\bar{X}}_c + X_f < \bar{X}_{c2} + X_f ,$$

a contradiction.

Thus it has been proved that for $K_f = K_c$ no case II solutions are possible. A fortiori, this suggests that when $K_f < K_c$, no case II solutions are possible. Hence, a sufficient condition for case III solutions to occur is $K_f \leq K_c$.

COMPARISON WITH COMPETITIVE EQUILIBRIA

In this section the solutions of the dominant firm model will be compared with those of the perfectly competitive model and it will be demonstrated that wherever a case I or case II solution to the dominant firm model occurs, then the profits of the fringe firms are *lower* in the dominant firm solution than in the competitive solution. This means that in these cases the cartel is gaining at the expense of both consumers and competitors. Since the arguments are identical to those used in the Nash-Cournot case (Ulph and Folie, 1978a) details are omitted.

It was demonstrated in the previous section that a necessary condition for either a case I or case II solution to occur is $K_f > K_c$. With this cost condition a perfectly competitive market will deplete the cartel's resources first and then deplete the fringe's resources. The competitive solution thus consists of finding R_1, R_2, S and T such that

$$\int_0^S (F - K_c - R_2 e^{\delta t})dt = aX_c$$

$$K_c + R_2 e^{\delta S} = K_f + R_1 e^{\delta S}$$

$$\int_S^T (F - K_f - R_1 e^{\delta t})dt = aX_f$$

$$K_f + R_1 e^{\delta T} = F$$

The solution is shown as the dashed line in Fig. 2(a) and Fig. 2(b).

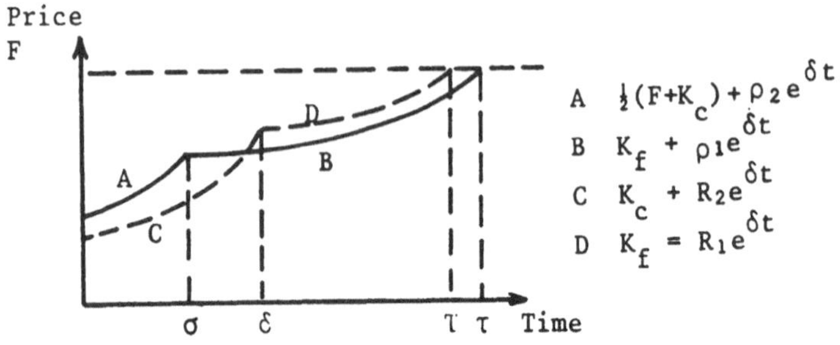

Figure 2(a)

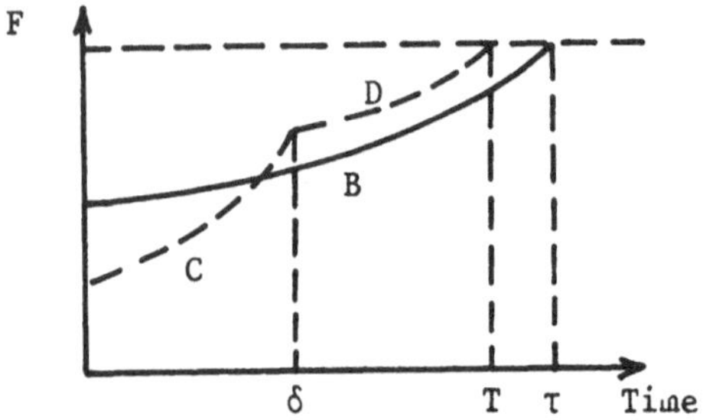

Figure 2(b)

Figure 2: Competitive and Dominant Firm Equilibria

The heavy line in Figs. 2(a) and 2(b) represents the solution of the corresponding dominant firm model. That the price paths for the two models have to be related to each other as shown in Fig. 2(a) and 2(b) is proved in Ulph and Folie (1978a). It is most easily seen in Fig. 2(b) where if $K_f + \rho_1 e^{\delta t}$ lay above $K_f + R_1 e^{\delta t}$, then the price path for the dominant firm solution would lie everywhere above the price path for the competitive solution, which is impossible since the same amount of resources is being depleted in both cases.

However, since in both cases $K_f + R_1 e^{\delta t}$ lies above $K_f + \rho_1 e^{\delta t}$, this means that $R_1 > \rho_1$; that is the present value of the unit exhaustion rent on the fringe's resources is greater in a competitive market than in the dominant firm model. Since exhaustion rents are the only source of profits to the fringe in this model, this demonstrates that the fringe's profits are lower in a partially cartelised market than in a competitive market. As noted in the introduction, this result conflicts with the intuition derived from models of partially cartelised markets handling inexhaustible commodities, where the existence of a cartel is usually to the benefit of the fringe firms.

Since $\frac{1}{2}(F + K_c) < K_f$ is a sufficient condition for a case I or case II solution to occur, it is also a sufficient condition for the fringe to be worse off after the formation of the cartel. However, a necessary condition for a case II solution to occur also includes costs in the range $K_c < K_f < \frac{1}{2}(F + K_c)$, so that even with a fairly small cost advantage the cartel may be able to benefit at the expense of the fringe. This is similar to the situation that occurs with Nash-Cournot models.

Finally, it should be noted that when $K_f \leq K_c$, the fringe must always benefit from the formation of the cartel. This is illustrated in fig. 3, where again the dashed line represents the competitive equilibrium and the solid line the dominant firm equilibrium. Details can be found in Salant (1976), or Ulph and Folie (1978a).

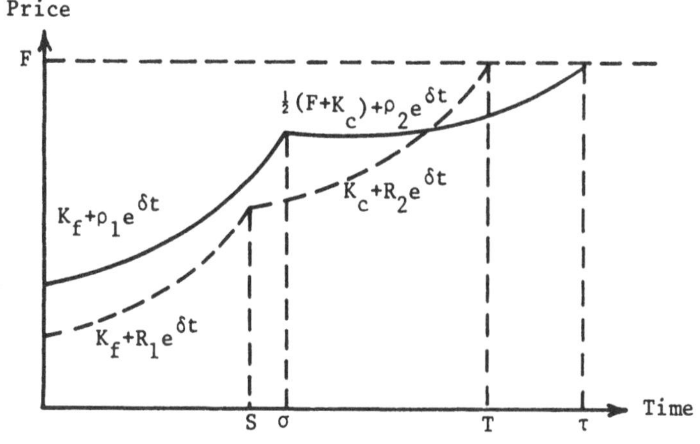

Figure 3: Competitive and Dominant Firm Equilibria

COMPARISON WITH PURE MONOPOLY EQUILIBRIA

In this section only a Case I outcome to the dominant firm model is considered, and this will be compared to the outcome that would result if all the resources were controlled by a monopolist, as might occur if the fringe firms joined the cartel. It will be shown that the effect of the fringe joining the cartel would lead to the price of the exhaustible resource initially *falling*. While the price in the fully monopolised market will eventually move above the price in the partially cartelised market, the initially lower price can lead to the welfare losses from a fully monopolised market being smaller than the welfare losses of the partially cartelised market. This is an example of a second-best result - that a partial attempt to introduce competition into a monopolised market can make matters worse.

Given the complexity of the model, it is easiest to see what is involved by considering some particular examples. In the examples considered, the parameters are $F = 100$, $a = 2$, $X_f = 500$, $X_c = 1000$, $\delta = 0.1$, $K_c = 0$; the parameter K_f, which must exceed 50, takes the values $90, 80, 70, 60$. The results are shown in Table 1. For each value of K_f the solutions to the dominant firm model (D) and the fully monopolised model (M) are presented.

Consider first the effect on the dominant firm solution of lowering the cost of the fringe's resources. The first line shows the impact of this on the initial price, that is $\frac{1}{2}(F + K_c) + \rho_c$. As K_f falls from 90 to 60, the initial price rises from 50.33812 to 50.36172.

Thus lowering the costs of the fringe's resources causes the price charged by the cartel in the monopoly phase to rise. The reason for this rather surprising result is that the lowering of the fringe's costs has two effects on the price set by the cartel. The obvious effect is to lower the terminal price that must be reached at the end of the monopoly phase, namely $K_f + \rho_f$, exerting a downward pressure on the price set in the monopoly phase. However, the lowering of the fringe's costs denies the cartel further opportunities for charging very high prices, and the cartel responds to this by increasing the amount of its resources devoted to the competitive phase. This is shown in row 4 where X_{c1} increases as K_f falls. Since X_{c2} is now falling, this has the effect of increasing the exhaustion rent, ρ_c, earned in the monopoly phase. As Table 1 shows, this second effect dominates the first effect.

The reason the increase in the initial price seems a surprising result is that in competitive or monopolistic markets only the first effect takes place. For in both cases the cheapest resources will be depleted completely along a price path in which the present value of the exhaustion rent remains constant, and then the more expensive resources are depleted along another price path in which, again, the present value of the exhaustion rent is constant. Thus each resource has its own distinct price path, and the effect of lowering the costs of the more expensive resource must lower the price path in the initial phase. This is illustrated by the results presented for the pure monopoly model (M) in Table 1. As the costs of the more expensive resources, (K_f), falls the initial price also falls.

A comparison of the dominant firm and monopoly solutions yields another interesting result. The initial price is *higher* under the dominant firm model than under the fully monopolised model. The reason is the same as that outlined above; monopolising the fringe's resources raises the *initial* price to be charged in the second phase and hence would raise the price charged in the first phase; but in the partially cartelised market the cartel responds to the existence of the fringe by lowering the amount of resources it devotes to the monopoly phase, which drives up the rent earned by the cartel in the monopoly phase. When the fringe's costs are very expensive, the second effect is stronger than the first.

The last row in Table 1 computes a measure of welfare as the discounted sum of producers and consumers surplus in each period, which is the measure used by Gilbert and Goldman (1978). This shows that the effect of the initially higher price charged in the dominant firm model is sufficient to cause welfare to be *lower* in the partially cartelised market than in the fully monopolised market. This is a good example of a second best result - making part of the market a bit more competitive can lower welfare for it ignores the interaction between the fringe's behaviour and the cartel's behaviour; specifically, it ignores the fact that the cartel will respond to the fringe by reducing the amount of its resources it depletes in a monopolistic way.

As noted in the introduction, the results of this section are related to those of Gilbert and Goldman (1978) and Hoel (1978). Both these papers deal with a model in which the exhaustible resource is controlled by a cartel, but there is also a 'backstop' inexhaustible technology which is more expensive than the exhaustible resource. Both models show that lowering the cost of the backstop may cause the initial price set by the monopolist to rise, and this paper demonstrates that this result also applies when the 'backstop' is itself an exhaustible resource. Hoel noted that the price set by the cartel may be higher when the 'backstop' technology is controlled by a group of competitive firms than when the 'backstop' is controlled by the cartel. This paper extends the result to an

Table 1.

K_f	90		80		70		60		100
Model	D	M	D	M	D	M	D	M	D/M
Initial Price	50.33812	50.33737	50.34211	50.33138	50.34284	50.3204	50.36172	50.30359	50.33919
Length of Monopoly Phase	47.73	48.93	44.75	47.93	40.78	46.94	33.61	45.95	49.93
Date of Final Exhaustion	158.73	258.93	107.73	157.73	89.37	123.60	79.01	105.92	49.93
X_{c1}	5	-	30	-	80	-	210	-	-
X_{c2}	995	-	970	-	920	-	790	-	-
Welfare	18160.23	18160.46	18163.26	18170.87	18176.65	18194.85	18192.38	18219.16	18157.28

exhaustible 'backstop' resource, and also shows that this may be sufficient to cause welfare to be lower under a partially cartelised than a fully monopolised market.

Gilbert and Goldman demonstrate that when the cartel has very large resources, then the level of welfare may be higher when there is *no* backstop technology than when such a backstop technology exists. In the model of this paper this is equivalent to setting $K_f = F$, and this is shown in the last column of Table 1. As can be seen, this example does not confirm Gilbert and Goldman's result, welfare here being lower than in any case where the fringe produces. However, Gilbert and Goldman's result is proved with $X_c \to \infty$, and this is probably not of much interest. The second-best result proved in this paper appears to be of more interest.

CONCLUSIONS

This paper has examined the pattern of depletion that will result in a market for an exhaustible resource where part of the resource is owned by a cartel and the rest by a group of competitive firms. It was shown that the cartel's problem can be presented as deciding how much of its resources to allocate to each of two phases - a competitive phase and a monopoly phase, where the order of the phases depends on the costs of production. Despite the simplicity of the model, it is capable of producing a range of possible outcomes (wider than those studied by Gilbert (1978)), and yields a surprising number of results. These concern the splitting of the cartel's production between two phases which could be separated in time by production by the fringe, the equivalence of dominant firm and Nash-Cournot models under certain assumptions, the possibility of dynamic inconsistency, the possibility that formation of the cartel could be at the expense of fringe profits, and the possibility that making a fully monopolised market a bit more competitive may lower welfare.

It is obviously important to consider how robust these results might be, and it is hoped to present such results at a later date, but experience with the Nash-Cournot model suggests that the results will hold up under a wide range of assumptions.

REFERENCES

Gilbert, R.J., (1978), "Dominant Firm Pricing in a Market for an Exhaustible Resource", *Bell Journal of Economics*, Vol. 9, No. 2, pp. 385-395.

Gilbert, R.J., and Goldman, (1978), "Potential Competition and the Monopoly Price of an Exhaustible Resource", *Journal of Economic Theory*, Vol. 19.

Hoel, M., (1978), "Resource Extraction, Substitute Production, and Monopoly", *Journal of Economic Theory*, Vol. 19, pp. 28-37.

Salant, S.W., (1976), "Exhaustible Resources and Industrial Structure: A Nash-Cournot Approach to the World Oil Market", *Journal of Political Economy*, Vol. 84, pp. 1079-1093.

Ulph, A.M., and Folie, G.M., (1978a), "Exhaustible Resources and Cartels: an Inter-Temporal Nash-Cournot Model", *Discussion Paper 31*, School of Economics, University of New South Wales, Sydney.

Ulph, A.M., and Folie, G.M., (1978b), "Gains and Losses to Producers from Cartelisation of an Exhaustible Resource", *C.R.E.S. Working Paper R/WP26*, Australian National University, Canberra.

FOOTNOTE

1. We are very grateful to Paul Geroski, Alan Ingham, David Newbery and David Ulph for helpful comments on earlier versions of this paper. In particular David Newbery pointed out a mistake in the results presented in an earlier version of Table 1. Of course we are responsible for all remaining errors.

DISCUSSION: DAVID M.G. NEWBERY

This is an important paper which makes a number of significant contributions to the theory of exhaustible resources. First, it employs a solution concept - that of von Stackelberg - which appears best suited to the analysis of the international oil market. Other writers have concentrated on the more tractable alternatives of perfect competition, pure monopoly, or Cournot-Nash oligopoly, none of which is satisfactory for the oil market. Those writers who have recognised the importance of the presence of both a cartel and a competitive fringe have either made convenient simplifying assumptions (inelastic demand and a backstop, as in Gilbert, 1978) or resorted to computer simulation for the solution (Cremer and Weitzman, 1976). Second, it develops a method which allows the price path to be largely solved algebraically (though the authors appear to use a computer for the last step of determining the amount sold by the cartel during the competitive phase). The drawback of the computer approach is that it is more difficult to see what influences the solution, and correspondingly harder to gain insight into the problem. An analytical, or, even better, a diagrammatic approach makes the problem more transparent and hence more fruitful. Third, this method allows a wider range of assumptions about cost and demand, which is not only useful for practical applications, but also useful in demonstrating the special nature of earlier results. These are well summarised in the conclusion to the paper. Finally, the paper draws attention to the possibility of dynamic inconsistency, which I have been studying closely in the context of tariffs on oil imports (Newbery and Maskin, 1978). These problems are of topical interest in the debate on macro-economic policy when agents hold rational expectations (Kydland and Prescott, 1977, Buiter, 1980).

There is much to comment on in the paper, but I shall confine my remarks to two issues - the method of solution of the price path, and the resolution of the problem of dynamic inconsistency. Elsewhere (Newbery, 1980) I have argued that in certain cases it is possible to solve the rational expectations von Stackelberg equilibrium path diagrammatically, and I shall illustrate this for the case considered in section 5 of the paper, where the authors compare the Case I outcome when the fringe either joins the cartel or competes with it. The price path with a competitive fringe is shown in Figure 1 below. The price trajectory is BCE, with exhaustion at date T and price F, during BC the cartel is unconstrained by the fringe, during CD the cartel is constrained by the competitive price path CDE, but in the sole supplier. The cartel exhausts at D, and the fringe then supplies along DE. The location of these points is found as follows. The point E is fixed at the choke price, F, and the price at date x years <u>before</u> exhaustion is, using the notation of the paper:

$$p_x^f = K^f + (F - K^f)e^{-\delta x}$$

Demand at each date is thus determined, and the length of the phase DE is such that consumption over this period is equal to total fringe stocks.

At the point D the cartel's marginal rent (marginal revenue less marginal cost) must be equal to the competitive price (since the fringe imposes a limit price path CDE on the cartel), and along AD the marginal rent rises at the rate of interest. Along BC the unconstrained monopoly price implied by the marginal rent is below the competitive price path, but between C and D the cartel must limit price. The length of the phase BCD is again determined by the condition that cumulative consumption is equal to the cartel's stock of oil.

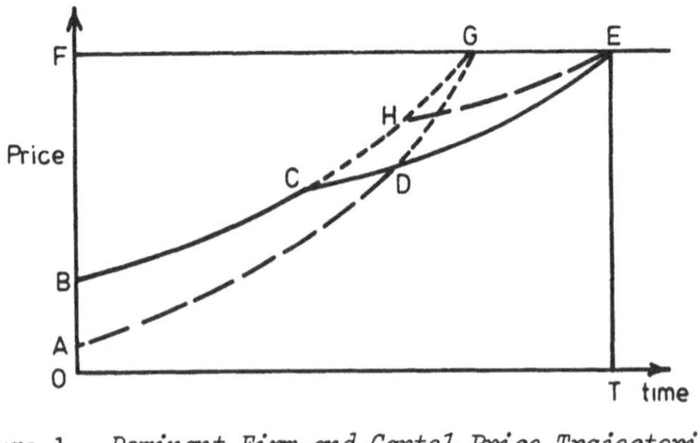

Figure 1 *Dominant Firm and Cartel Price Trajectories*

The advantage of this approach is that we can immediately prove that the initial price must be reduced if the fringe joins the cartel. Fix the terminal price at E, and, since the marginal revenue is equal to the price at the choke price *F* (or E), once the fringe joins the cartel its marginal revenue must now follow the path CDE up to the point E. The price associated with this marginal revenue is the path HE. As shown, at H the fringe's (monopoly) price meets the cartel's price path BCHG, so that BCHE is a possible price trajectory for the unified cartel - except that it lies above the previous trajectory BCDE. There is thus less consumption along the new price path, which means that the date of starting must be earlier, and hence the initial price lower.

The second-best welfare effects of encouraging monopoly are rather similar to those discovered by Gilbert and Newbery (1979, Appendix p.11) and it may be possible to develop a simple diagrammatic analysis along the lines presented there.

Consider the solution proposed by Ulph and Folie for the case where the fringe has lower extraction costs than the cartel. In Figure 2 the direction of time has been reversed to emphasise that the fixed point from which the price path is computed is the price at the date of exhaustion, *F*. The marginal revenue trajectory, FBE, again satisfies the condition that the cartel's marginal rent rises at the rate of interest up to the date of exhaustion, and in turn fixes the monopoly price path FAD. The competitive price path is ABC, steeper than the marginal revenue path if, as we assume, the fringe has lower extractions costs than the cartel.

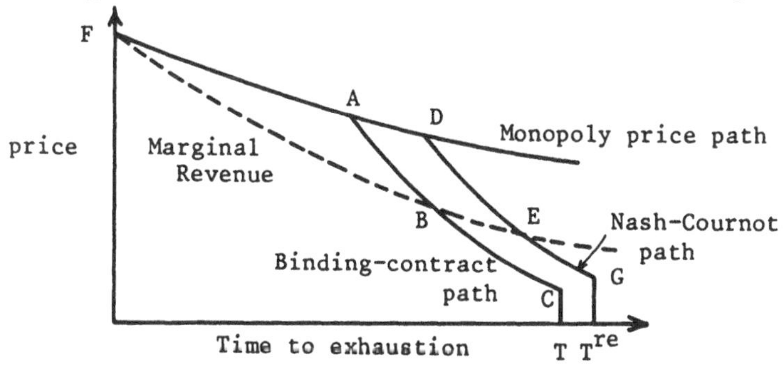

Figure 2 *Price Trajectories for the case of dynamic inconsistency*

The cartel is the sole supplier along BA, where it is assumed to be constrained by the competitive price path, and also along AF, where it is unconstrained. Since the cartel can freely transfer oil between the start of its extraction (point B) and the final date (point F), present discounted marginal rent must be equated at these two points, so they must both lie on the marginal revenue trajectory FBE. This condition, together with the requirement that the cartel's stock be exhausted over FAB, fixes the price path, whilst BC is likewise fixed by the requirement that the fringe exhausts over BC. The time elapsed before exhaustion is therefore T.

Now, the cartel will only be constrained to follow the price path BA if the fringe can freely transfer oil from CB to BA, which it can only do before the plan unfolds. If, at the initial date, the fringe and cartel sign binding contracts, then this option is available to the fringe and the Ulph-Folie solution will indeed prevail. In the absence of binding contract, if the fringe exhausted itself along CB, it would be unable to sell during BA, and the cartel would be free to raise its price to the monopoly path FAD. The fringe would anticipate a price jump at B, and will delay extraction, thus disrupting the proposed solution. The Ulph-Folie solution is therefore not a rational expections equilibrium.

The rational expectations equilibrium in the absence of binding contracts must have the fringe supplying until the price has risen to the monopoly path, at which point there is no incentive for any jump in price after the fringe is exhausted. In general, it is difficult to characterise the rational expectations price path in any simple way, although it can be computed recursively using the technique developed in Maskin and Newbery (1978). However, it converges to the Nash-Cournot equilibrium path GEDAF at D, and the Nash-Cournot path has therefore some appeal as both an approximation to the rational expectations path, and as a dynamically consistent path. More precisely, it describes a supply strategy for the fringe, in which it supplies inelastically along GED, which removes any temptation of deviation by the cartel. Along ED both the fringe and the cartel supply, and the cartel's supply is fixed by the position of the marginal revenue trajectory FBE and the competitive price path DEG. (The full details are given in Newbery, 1980).

Now that the cartel only supplies a fraction of the market along DE, the monopoly phase DF, will be longer than under binding contracts (AF), if the same total stock is to be exhausted over both phases. The average price is higher, and the time taken to exhaustion, T^{re}, is longer than with binding contracts. The fringe benefits from a higher initial price (G instead of C), and the cartel suffers from its inability to bind itself to a credible extraction plan. Maskin and Newbery showed that their monopsonist might be made worse off than in the competitive equilibrium, and the same might happen here, for Ulph and Folie (1978) claim that a Nash-Cournot equilibrium might give lower profits to the cartel than the competitive equilibrium. The absence of binding contracts may have serious costs for the cartel.

Finally, Ulph and Folie argue that dynamic inconsistency is practically unimportant as in fact the OPEC cartel has lower extraction costs than the fringe, hence ruling out this particular problem. However, if OPEC faces lower discount rates than the fringe (as seems to be the case), than the competitive price path may be steeper than the marginal revenue path, and the problem remains. This case is discussed in more detail in Newbery (1980).

REFERENCES

Buiter, W.H. (1980), The Macroeconomics of Dr. Pangloss: A Critical Survey of the New Classical Macroeconomics, *Economic Journal*, 90 (1), 34-50.

Cremer, J. and Weitzman, M. (1976),'OPEC and the Monopoly Price of World Oil', *European Economic Review*, 8, 155-164.

Gilbert, R.J. (1978), 'Dominant Firm Pricing in a Market for a Exhaustible Resource', *Bell Journal of Economics* Vol 9, No 2, 385-395.

Gilbert, R.J. and Newbery, D.M.G. (1979), 'Pre-emptive Patenting and the Persistence of Monopoly', Economic Theory Discussion Paper 15, Cambridge.

Kydland, F.E. and Prescott, E.C. (1977), 'Rules rather than discretion: the inconsistency of optimal plans', *Journal of Political Economy*, 85 (3), 473-91.

Maskin, E, and Newbery, D.M.G., (1978), 'Rational Expectations with Market Power - The Paradox of the Disadvantageous Tariff on Oil', Warwick Economic Research Paper No 129.

Newbery, D.M.G. (1980),'Oil Prices, Cartels and the problem of dynamic inconsistency', Mimeo Cambridge.

Ulph, A.M. and Folie, G.M. (1978), 'Gains and Losses to Producers from Cartelisation of an Exhaustible Resource', C.R.E.S. Working Paper R/WP26, Australian National University, Canberra.

ACKNOWLEDGEMENTS

I am grateful to Alastair Ulph for further clarifying the distinction between the Nash-Cournot and dominant firm equilibrium and hence correcting my initial comments.

5. PROPERTY AND COMMODITY TAXES AND UNDER-PROVISION IN THE PUBLIC SECTOR

N. Topham

1. *INTRODUCTION*[1]

Much attention has been devoted to selecting a vector of tax rates that minimises distortion in the private sector of the economy; relatively little attention, on the other hand, has been devoted to a consideration of the relationship between the tax regime and public-sector efficiency. It is surprising that this is the state of affairs, because Wicksell (1896) saw clearly the reason for the relationship between public-sector supply and the tax structure. Wicksell's adoption of the principle of unanimity[2], rather than majority voting, as the constitutional method of approving expenditures was influenced by the fact that the poor, who were presently disenfranchised, would shortly have the vote and thus political power. For:

> "Once the lower classes are definitely in possession of the power to legislate and tax .... (they) may impose the bulk of all taxes upon the rich and may at the same time be so reckless and extravagant in approving public expenditure to which they themselves contribute but little that the nation's mobile capital may soon be squandered fruitlessly".

Wicksell, who welcomed democracy, despite the attendant dangers of the poor following the example of his own ruling class, was here saying that once the poor were in power they could so organise the tax regime that the tax-price per unit of public expenditure facing them would be negligible and hence they would vote for a large (too large) public sector. The tax regime and the size of the public sector were inextricably linked in Wicksell's analysis through the instrument of tax prices facing the majority of voters.

The Lindahl (1919) voluntary-exchange model unfortunately diverted attention from this point. It emphasised the necessity of preference-revelation. If public goods were to be supplied, some knowledge of marginal valuations was necessary in order to determine optimal quantities and the associated benefit tax. But if tax bills were to be a function of information supplied, 'rational' individuals would understate their preferences. Much subsequent work has concerned itself with these problems, which were given their more recent emphasis by the pioneering work of Samuelson (1955) and Musgrave (1958). In the real world, however, we find ourselves - at least in the medium term - faced with an existing array of taxes[3]. Given knowledge of this tax structure, consumers can work out for themselves their tax share of public-expenditure programmes. In these circumstances, it is rational to reveal one's preferred budget size. The problem of free-riders and the difficulties of preference revelation are not the decisive issues for the applied economist.

Minimising distortion in the private-sector would usher in a vector of tax rates that would tax heavily the necessities of life, and the distributional consequences of such a tax programme are well known. What is also widely recognised is that lump-sum benefit taxation is associated with an efficient level of public goods. And it needs only to be stated to be obvious, if it isn't already, that in a median-voter model the actual level of public-sector provision depends on the tax costs per unit of public-sector output faced by the median voter. The purpose of this paper is to weld these three statements together into a simple theoretical structure. In the next section, the circumstances under which a tax on a commodity is a benefit tax is considered and an operational measure of the distributive effects of various taxes is obtained. And those in society who would gain and those who would lose from an incremental change in public expenditure are identified. Section 3 states the criteria for efficiency in public-goods supply and considers the circumstances under which they are met. The broad conclusion is that they are met, except in isolated instances, only under tax neutrality. If the tax regime is redistributive from rich to poor (that is, willingness to pay minus tax costs is positive (negative) for the rich (poor)), the level of public-sector provision is too low. This occurs if the taxes are levied on commodities whose income elasticity is less than 1.5 to 2, and conversely. Various income distributions are considered. A change financed by lump-sum taxes is investigated. In section 4, the aggregate level of provision for a good supplied under private markets is compared with the aggregate level of provision of the same good supplied in the public sector - under majority voting. This provides perspective for the earlier section. If income elasticity for the social good is less than one, the broad conclusion is that public-sector supply may be larger (depending on tax prices) than the private sector supply: for higher values of this parameter there is only a presumption this holds. Finally, in section 5 we introduce government and the attendant bureaucracy. It may be argued that median-voter models do not work too well in the real world[4]. That may well be so. However, if a government decides to provide more for everyone than the median voter would demand for himself, it is a mixed blessing. Obviously the disparity between efficient and actual levels of output is reduced: but since in the case of under-provision, the rich want more of the good than the poor, the relative position of the poor is worsened by this executive action.

2. *TAX NEUTRALITY & PUBLIC GOODS SUPPLY*

Problems associated with preference revelation and free riders have led many writers in public finance to concentrate on the tax side of the government budget. The search for an analytical link between the provision of social goods and the determination of the tax structure has been largely abandoned. Since leisure cannot be taxed and if lump-sum taxes are ruled out, as they usually are in the real world, the best that can be done is the imposition of a set of distorting taxes which raises the required revenue but at the same time minimizes the deadweight loss. Such a set of taxes is said to be *optimal*.

Uniform tax rates have adverse relative effects on commodities with high price elasticities. When taxation is the focus of attention, what is required is that the dead-weight loss per £ of revenue collected is the same for all commodities, and this implies that the proportionate reduction in demand should be the same for all commodities. Let the tax rate on a commodity h he expressed as $r = t/q$, where t is tax paid per unit of h consumed and q is the after-tax price. The change in price induced by the tax is rq and the optimal tax rule can be written as:

$$\varepsilon = \frac{dh/h}{dq/q} = \frac{s}{r}$$

$$\text{i.e. : } r = s\varepsilon^{-1}$$

where ε is price elasticity of demand. The tax rate on a commodity should be lower the lower its own price elasticity of demand. This is the inverse elasticity rule of the optimal-tax literature in its simplest form.[5]

Once a tax regime is declared before voting takes place, it is irrational not to reveal preferences for public goods. When this is so, some knowledge of tastes for publicly-supplied goods can be derived from empirical work and in this way approximate measures of public-goods evaluation attempted. Since normally tax schedules *are known* in advance, these considerations raise the possibility of forging an analytical link between the tax and expenditure sides of the budget. Once this link is made it is possible to relate the efficiency of public-sector provision to the tax regime chosen. This problem has been virtually ignored in the literature.

The median voter does not equate his marginal rate of substitution between the public good and the numeraire with the former's resource cost but with the full *economic costs of taxation* that he faces at the margin. The optimal tax literature takes the level of public expenditure as given; but the choice of commodity for tax purposes is an important determinant of these tax costs and thus of public-goods supply. And once it is possible to discern how other individuals in society value the level of public goods provision chosen by the median voter, a judgement about its allocative efficiency can be made.

Lump-sum benefit taxation provides an optimal level of public goods. Benefit taxation implies that each taxpayer is taxed in line with his demand for public services, and at those tax prices everyone demands the same level of public-goods supply. An individual is charged the same price for all units and consumers' surplus is not taxed away by charging higher tax prices for inframarginal units. If an individual's *fiscal residual* is defined as willingness to pay less the tax price per unit he is required to pay, in the special case of benefit taxation fiscal residua are everywhere zero. Such a tax is said to be neutral in its distributive effects.

What one generally has in mind when one thinks of a benefit tax is a personalised lump-sum tax. In that circumstance, there are no distortive effects in the private sector to contend with. Commodity taxes, by contrast, do have distortive effects; so it will clarify matters if the question is posed, When is a commodity tax a benefit tax? Obviously, for a commodity tax to be a benefit tax it must be distributionally neutral, and the conditions for tax neutrality are set out in the analysis below. They are important because they have a direct bearing on the efficiency of public-goods supply, as will become clear in the next section. In addition to its distributional effects, a commodity tax also bears directly on individual attitudes to the taxed commodity. First, an increase in public-goods supply implies an increase in the required tax yield and hence a change in the after-tax price of the taxed commodity. An objective of optimal taxation is to minimise the deadweight loss associated with distortion of this nature. Second, an increase in the provision of the public good allows a reduction in the consumption of the taxed commodity if it is a close substitute of the public good (and *vice versa* if it is a complement). For a commodity tax to be a benefit tax, the tax must be distributionally neutral and these two effects must be zero.

The median voter equates his marginal rate of substitution between the public good and the numeraire not simply with the tax price he faces but with the wider concept of the *economic costs of taxation* to him at the margin. His fiscal residual, as it has been defined above, may not be zero - indeed in what follows it will not be so except in the special case when the two effects above are either zero or cancel, and this latter can occur only in the case of complementary goods. However, a commodity tax may still be said to be distributionally neutral if the ratio of willingness to pay (MRS) to actual tax costs at the margin is the same for all individuals. As will become clear, this is the circumstance in which all individuals would vote for the same level of public-goods supply. If the tax is not neutral and favours, for example, the rich, this implies that at the margin the MRS of a rich person is greater than his marginal economic costs of taxation, in which case he will vote for an increase in public goods supply. Tax neutrality rather than distortion is what is crucial for public-sector efficiency.

To shed further light on these matters, consider the case of a proportional tax on commodity h. There is one public service (z) and one taxed commodity. The following assumptions are made at this stage of the analysis:

(i) individuals differ only in income;

(ii) their utility fuctions are additively separable;

(iii) the median voter chooses the level of public service under simple majority voting; and

(iv) the public budget is balanced and taxation is the sole source of revenue.

Assumption (i) is not crucial to the analysis, but it facilitates the exposition. Obviously tastes differ within an income class, but by and large it seems reasonable to assume that a representative from an income class will exhibit tastes similar to one from another income class, and that the two individuals differ only in income. Assumption (ii) is widely used when broad categories of commodities are being analysed, as here, in which case the cross effects are expected to be negligible. This assumption could be relaxed without much difficulty for some of the earlier results, but the later results would be difficult to derive as a general case. Assumption (iii) is widely used and has a secure place in the literature of public choice. However, it is not at all crucial to the analysis of this section, and in section 5, where a bureaucratically-determined level of the public service is considered, it is dropped.

The focus of attention is the provision of public good z, and the amount to be supplied is chosen by the median voter; this amount depends, among other things, on his income and the tax-price he faces. Government revenue is derived wholly from the tax on commodity h whose after-tax price is $q = p + t$, where p is the constant net-of-tax price. The resource cost of z is invariant and defined as ρ, and the government's budget is balanced when $tH = \rho z$ with H the aggregate level of consumption of h.

Let $v(y,q,z)$ be the indirect utility function of a man with income y. By Roy's identity the demand for the taxed commodity for a man with y is:

$$h(y,q,z) = -v_q/v_y \qquad \text{.... (1)}$$

where v_q and v_y are partial derivatives. The solution for the tax rate $t(z)$ is found from the equation:

$$\rho z = t\Sigma h(y,p+t,z) \qquad \text{.... (2)}$$

In voting for a level of provision, consumers can take account of (2) and assume that the population will adjust its consumption of h when its price increases; for as z increases so does t and thus q. But they may assume that H is fixed, or at least ignore any feedback, and in this circumstance:

$$t = \rho z/H \qquad \text{.... (2a)}$$

Suppose voters do allow for the effect of z on h through t. The voter with median income ($\hat{y}$) maximises his indirect utility function $v(\hat{y},p+t(z),z)$ with respect to z:

$$\hat{v}_q\, t'(z) + \hat{v}_z = 0$$

or, by Roy's identity:

$$\hat{h}\, t'(z) = \hat{v}_z/\hat{v}_y \qquad \text{.... (3)}$$

The left-hand side of (3) is the marginal economic cost of taxation confronting the consumer, which he brings into equality with his marginal rate of substitution between z and y.

Consider first whether an incremental change in z would be universally approved. If z changes, so does t, and an individual with income y is better off if the marginal utility of the public goods exceeds his incremental tax costs times the marginal utility of income:

$$v_z > t'(z).hv_y \qquad \ldots (4)$$

By assumption (ii), $v_{yz} = 0$ and so $v_z = \hat{v}_z$. Using (3) and (4), we see that an individual with y gains if:

$$hv_y < \hat{h}\hat{v}_y \qquad \ldots (5)$$

If $y > \hat{y}$, (5) holds if hv_y is a decreasing function of y. Sato (1972) has shown that a separable utility function of the generalised CES type has the property that elasticities are approximately constant. Thus the Engels functions, $h = y^{\theta}$ and $v_y = y^{-\sigma}$, can be fed into (5) to yield:

$$y^{\theta-\sigma} > \hat{y}^{\theta-\sigma} \qquad \ldots (6)$$

If the elasticity of the marginal utility of income is greater than income elasticity of demand (i.e., $\sigma > \theta$), hv_y is a decreasing function of y and greater z benefits the rich and is not approved of by the poor.

It may be that voters consider H fixed, so that t is determined by (2a). In this case, (3) becomes:

$$h\frac{\rho}{H} = \hat{v}_z/\hat{v}_y \qquad \ldots (7)$$

But of course h is a function of its after-tax price, and increased z requires additional tax revenue; so individual adjustments to h and thus H will occur, even though consumers do not recognise this when they vote for the supply of z. Therefore, using (3) and (7), those who gain from an incremental increase in z are the individuals for whom:

$$hv_y < \frac{\rho}{H\ t'(z)}\hat{h}\ \hat{v}_y \qquad \ldots (8)$$

Differentiation of (2) yields:

$$t'(z)\ (\Sigma h + t\Sigma h_q) = \rho - t\Sigma h_z \qquad \dots\ (9)$$

Additive separability implies that inferiority and complementarity are ruled out. Therefore $h_z < 0$, and hence equation (9) implies (as it would if $h_z = o$):

$H\ t'(z) > \rho$

because $h_q < 0$. Here again, then, the rich benefit and the poor lose out as a consequence of there being an incremental increase in z, provided hv_y is a decreasing function of y. Otherwise the obverse is true and the poor gain and the rich don't when z is increased. Estimates for these parameters are readily available. Evidence for σ is that it is in the region of 1.5 to 2 whilst, for example, θ approximates to 1 for a property tax, and in this case hv_y is a decreasing function of y[6].

Thus far, the analysis has considered only marginal changes. We turn now to consider fiscal residua, and we enquire, When is a tax a benefit tax? From (3), we have an expression for the marginal rate of substitution of the median voter:

$\hat{MRS} = \hat{h}\ t'(z)$

Using (9):

$$h\ t'(z) = \rho\frac{h}{H}\ \frac{\{1-w\}}{\{1+s\}}$$

where $w = h_z.z/h$; $s = r\varepsilon$, with $\varepsilon = h_q.q/h$, and $r = t/q$. Here r is the tax rate, and s is related to the optimal-tax rules; for as we saw on p.110 $r = s\varepsilon^{-1}$. Note that the first term on the right-hand side is the tax-price per unit faced by the voter, whilst the bracketed term combines the two effects discussed on p.111 above.

The fiscal residual of the median voter is not necessarily zero because of the bracketed term. It is positive when:

$\hat{h}\ t'\ (z)\ z > t\hat{h}$

$$t'(z) > \frac{\rho}{H}$$

$$\frac{1-w}{1+s} > 1$$

By assumption (ii), $w < o$, whilst s is negative[7]. Although his fiscal residual is positive, the median voter is in equilibrium and thus in *fiscal balance*.
For the median voter:

$$\hat{MRS}.z = \frac{1-w}{1+s} t \hat{h} \qquad .... \quad (10)$$

For an individual with income y:

$$MRS = k \frac{1-w}{1+s} t h \qquad .... \quad (11)$$

If k is greater than 1, the tax is neutral, and an individual with $y > \hat{y}$ enjoys a positive fiscal balance, which is an increasing function of y. Divide (11) by (10)[8]:

$$MRS/\hat{MRS} = k (h/\hat{h}) \qquad .... \quad (12)$$

By the same considerations that led to (6):

$$k = (y/\hat{y})^{\sigma-\theta} \qquad .... \quad (13)$$

If $y > \hat{y}$ and k is less than one. For a commodity tax to be a benefit tax, the second condition to the one mentioned on p.111 above is that we must have $\sigma = \theta$. So far as the example of a property tax is concerned, there is an *a priori* case that it is not a benefit tax because it is not distributionally neutral.

The intuitive explanation of tax neutrality is straightforward. As income rises, its marginal utility falls; so that at the margin £s paid in tax are worth less and less. At the same time, expenditure on h rises for a normal good ($\theta > 0$) and the tax price a consumer faces increases with income. If the two offset each other precisely ($\sigma = \Theta$), the tax is distributionally neutral[9]. All consumers demand the same quantity of the public good. Any voting system would provide the same amount of z. If $\sigma > \theta$, as is the case with a property tax, for the rich willingness to pay exceeds their tax cost, and they want more z to be supplied. The poor will vote for a reduction in public expenditure in these circumstances. Whether the poor benefit from an enhanced 'social wage' depends in part on the way in which it is financed.

The analysis illustrates a remark by Lindahl (1928), referring to the provision of a public garden: "Half the rate payers are fairly well-to-do, the other half are rather poor. The subjective utility of the garden may be taken to be roughly the same for all; but utility in terms of money is much higher for the rich than it is for the poor, for the rich can pay the same sum much more easily than can the poor".

The optimal tax rules at their crudest level require high tax rates on commodities with low price elasticities of demand, and h can be any commodity. For those with $y > \hat{y}$, a fall in θ widens the inequalities at (5) and (6). For those above median income, a fall in θ is tantamount to choosing, for the purposes of public finance, a commodity with a lower income elasticity of demand. But we know both from the general formula of Frisch[10] and from the known properties of the separable utility function assumed that $\sigma \simeq \theta/\varepsilon$. Since σ is constant, a fall in θ implies a reduction in ε. Thus, as the optimal tax literature makes explicit, there are distributional issues to be faced up to if the decision is made to tax heavily goods with low elasticities of demand. What has been demonstrated in this section is that this is also true when both sides of the fiscal budget have been taken into account.

Of course, if $\theta > \sigma$, as it might for a luxury good, the boot is on the other foot; the tax system is then redistributive from rich to poor. Historically, the tax system has operated in this way. In the seventeenth century, indirect taxes were placed on luxuries and regarded as more progressive than poll taxes[11]. A century later, William Pitt ('the younger') actually managed to make a 'poll' tax progressive. According to his contemporary Robert Burns, the intention of Pitt's tax on hair-powder was explicit[12]:

Pray Billy Pitt explain thy rigs,
This new poll tax of thine!
"I mean to mark the Guinea pigs
From other common swine".

All well and good: but as we have indicated there are two sides to the coin, and when tax regimes are known in advance a rational voter will balance public sector provision with the tax costs it imposes on him. The quantity of social goods the median voter will choose will depend on his tax costs at the margin, and these in turn depend on the commodity chosen to bear the tax. In a voting model, the level of the budget and the tax system chosen to finance it are inextricably linked.

3. *Public Sector Efficiency*

Allocative efficiency in the public sector requires that certain criteria are met. For the purposes of this paper, these are:

MRS = marginal tax cost (a) (all individuals)

ΣMRS = marginal economic cost (b)

Condition (a) is satisfied by lump-sum benefit taxes and is the Lindahl condition. In the case of commodity taxes however, the indirect effects of distortionary taxation have to be taken into account in determining the indirect effects of distortionary taxation have to be taken into account in determining the marginal tax cost. Condition (b) is not identical with the Samuelsonian condition, which refers to lump-sum taxes; condition (b) here considers whether condition (a) is met in aggregate. The question now posed is, how does the choice of commodity to tax affect efficiency so defined in the public sector?

Concentrating on (b), we enquire whether there is under-provision in public-goods supply. Efficiency requires ΣMRS.z = mtH. From (11):

ΣMRS.z = mt (kh)

where $m = (1-w)/(1+s)$. Therefore, we require to know whether:

$$mt\Sigma(kh) > mtH$$

$$\Sigma(ka) > n \qquad \text{.... (14)}$$

where $a = h/\bar{h}$

The multiplier $k = (y/\hat{y})^{\sigma-\theta}$ can be re-written:

$$k = (y/\tilde{y})^{\sigma-\theta} \, (\tilde{y}/\hat{y})^{\sigma-\theta} \qquad \text{.... (15)}$$

where $\tilde{y}$ is the income of an individual who consumes $\bar{h}$ of the taxed commodity. Equation (15) can be substituted into (14):

$$(\tilde{y}/\hat{y})^{\sigma-\theta} \, \Sigma a^{\sigma/\theta} > n \qquad \text{.... (16)}$$

For a distribution of income skewed to the left $\tilde{y} > \hat{y}$, and so the first term LHS is greater than one if $\sigma > \theta$. Suppose for now that m equals one. We are left with:

$$f(a) = \Sigma a^{\sigma/\theta} > n \qquad \text{.... (17)}$$

Noting that $\Sigma a = n$, we can maximise (17) subject to this constraint to yield:

$$\frac{\partial f}{\partial a_1} = (\sigma/\theta)a_1^{(\sigma/\theta)-1} = \lambda \qquad \text{.... (18)}$$

where λ is the Lagrangian multiplier. Since $\lambda = (\sigma/\theta)a^{(\sigma/\theta)-1}$ is monotonic, it follows that the n equations of form (18) imply that $a_1 = a_2 \,....\, = a_n$. Moreover, $\partial f/\partial\lambda$ informs us that at its turning point, (18) has $\Sigma a^{\sigma/\theta} = n$, and since $\Sigma a = n$, we know from this condition that $a_1 = a_2 = \,....\, = a_n = 1$. Second-order conditions show that this is a minimum provided $(\sigma/\theta) > 1$.

$$\text{i.e.: } \Sigma a^{\sigma/\theta} > n \qquad \text{.... (19)}$$

provided $(\sigma/\theta) > 1$ and incomes are not everywhere equal[13].

Taken together, (19) and (16) imply that the aggregate efficiency condition is not met unless tax neutrality prevails. If $\sigma > \theta$, the level of public-sector provision is too low. But the converse also holds: public-sector provision is too high if $\sigma < \theta$. A tax on a luxury to finance a project will bring about a level of provision that is too high, given a normal distribution of income and simple majority voting. It is clear from (16) that these results are unaffected in sign if the distribution is skewed to the left, so that $\bar{h} > \hat{h}$; the first term on the left multiplies the LHS by a factor in excess of 1 and the resulting discrepancy between ΣMRS and tax costs widens.

These results apply only to the utility function under consideration. Nevertheless, although not generally true, I suspect they are true more often than not. Bowen (1943) described a situation where majority voting would satisfy condition (b). His tax regime was a poll tax. As Stephen Salter and I have shown elsewhere, a Bowen equilibrium is satisfied in such a circumstance by a system of linear demand curves derived from a quadratic utility function. In this case, individual welfare losses from under- and over-provision cancel out because the rate of change of the marginal rate of substitution is constant; but the demand function has zero income elasticity of demand; and therefore although the family of preference maps coupled with equal tax shares meets condition (b) but not (a), it does lend support to the conjecture that, even when preferences are revealed and tax shares fixed in advance, satisfying the Samuelsonian but not the Lindahl condition will occur only in isolated cases.

Leaving aside these conjectures, we now turn to discuss the link between the tax regime adopted and its effects on the disparity between actual and efficient levels of provision in the public sector. It is clear from inspection of (16) that the disparity between the LHS of (16) and n widens when θ is decreased. What consumers are willing to pay for the output chosen by the median voter is an inverse function of θ. Moreover, the disparity between efficient and actual levels of output widens the more leftward skewed is the distribution of income - that is, the greater is $\bar{y}$ than $\hat{y}$. Lowering θ is tantamount to selecting a commodity with a lower ε for taxation purposes; this affects adversely not only the distribution of income, it has also a deleterious effect on efficiency in the public sector. What people in aggregate are willing to pay for the 'social wage', as chosen by the median voter, exceeds total tax costs when $\sigma > \theta$; the excess demand of the rich outweighs the desire for less z by the poor.

Now in the previous section, it was demonstrated that a marginal change financed by commodity taxes would be undesirable when $\sigma > \theta$. The level of provision has now been shown to be inadequate in total: individuals in aggregate were willing to pay more than was collected from them to finance public programmes. There is therefore some method of public finance that can make everyone marginally better off. Suppose a marginal change in z is financed by lump-sum taxes. This is the Samuelson version of condition (b), albeit the distortionary effects of taxation are allowed for in evaluating individuals' willingness to pay. The change in z costs $\rho.dz = \Sigma dy$, and recalling the individual indirect utility functions:

$$dv = v_y d_y + v_z d_z$$

$$= v_y\{dy + (v_z/v_y)dz\}$$

So everyone can be made better off if

$$\Sigma(v_z/v_y) > \rho \qquad \ldots \quad (20)$$

We again assume that $v_{yz} = o$ and that taxpayers are aware of the effects on h of a change in z:

$$v_z = \hat{v}_z = t'(z)h\,\hat{v}_y$$

So condition (20) can be rewritten:

$$\hat{h}\,\Sigma(\hat{v}_y/v_y) > \rho/t'(z) \qquad \ldots \quad (21)$$

To simplify matters, suppose y is distributed normally and let $\theta = 1$ so that $\hat{h} = \bar{h}$. Then (21) becomes:

$$\bar{h}\Sigma(y/\bar{y})^{\sigma} > H/m$$

$$\text{i.e., } m\Sigma(y/\bar{y})^{\sigma} > n \qquad \ldots. \ (22)$$

Inequality (22) holds provided $\sigma > 1$ and $m > 1$, by analogous argument to that on p. . Relaxing the assumptions just made does not affect the result provided $\theta < 1$ and the distribution is leftward skewed, which in any event are the cases we are interested in. What has been shown is that a system of individual lump-sum taxes could be used to finance an incremental change in z and the lump-sum tax payments could be tailored to make everyone better off. This underlines the inadequate nature of public expenditure when financed by a commodity tax.

Finally, in the case where voters ignore the effects of a change in z on purchases of h, since now:

$$v_z = \hat{v}_z = (\rho/H)\hat{h}\,\hat{v}_y$$

condition (20) becomes:

$$\hat{h}\Sigma(\hat{v}_y/v_y) > H \qquad \ldots. \ (23)$$

If $\hat{h} = \bar{h}$, the equivalent of (22) is in this case:

$$\Sigma(y/\bar{y})^{\sigma} > n \qquad \ldots. \ (24)$$

which again is true if $\sigma > 1$.

4. *PUBLIC AND PRIVATE SECTOR PROVISION*

So far we have considered only public goods. But the state is responsible for supplying many private goods, which in principle could equally well be provided by the private sector. This section considers *aggregate* levels of provision in these alternative locations of activity. The choice of tax base determines the level of public expenditure voters would most prefer. We have seen that this level may be less than aggregate willingness to pay for that quantity. The public sector distributes its services arguably more equitably, but does it in aggregate provide less than the private sector would supply?

The switch from public goods to private goods is readily accommodated. The constant resource costs of public goods is ρ and conversion to private goods requires their price to be denoted as ρ/n.

The state supplies to each individual the quantity the median voter demands for himself. Assuming constant elasticities over the range, we consider individual demands in the public sector. The distortionary tax cost an individual faces depends on his purchase of the taxed commodity and thus on his income: $m(h/H)\rho/n$. The median voter has a demand function for the publicly-supplied good of:

$$\hat{z} = A\hat{y}^{\alpha} [m(\hat{h}/H)(\rho/n)]^{\beta}$$

$$= Ay^{\alpha+\theta\beta}\{m(1/H)(\rho/n)\}^{\beta} \qquad \text{.... (25)}$$

The assumption of identical utility functions with individuals differing only in income is retained. If $\theta = |\alpha/\beta|$, all individuals demand the same quantity of the public service; the expression $A\{.\}^{\beta}$ is independent of any one individual's income. For separable utility functions, $\sigma \simeq \alpha/\beta$ in the public sector, just as equivalent ratios approximate to σ in the private sector.

Thus (19) is simply a different way of denoting commodity-tax neutrality as in equation (13), where $\theta = \sigma$. When $\theta = |\alpha/\beta|$, equation (25) describes the Lindahl solution, which is also Pareto optimal[14].

Since the public provision of the service implies that all individuals are coerced to consume the same amount as the median voter, the level of public-sector provision is simply:

$$n\hat{z} = nA\hat{y}^{\alpha}\{m(h/H)(\rho/n)\}^{\beta} \qquad \ldots \quad (26)$$

There are individual variations in the amount consumed when h is supplied privately, and in this model such variations are simply a function of income. Aggregate provision in private markets would amount to:

$$\Sigma z = A(\rho/n)^{\beta}\Sigma y^{\alpha} \qquad \ldots \quad (27)$$

We wish to consider under what circumstances private-market provision would exceed public provision. This occurs if:

$$\Sigma z \; > \; n\hat{z}$$

$$\text{i.e. } (1/n)\Sigma y^{\alpha} > \; \hat{y}^{\alpha} \; \{m(h/H)\}^{\beta} \qquad \ldots \quad (28)$$

First, ignore the bracketed term on the RHS and consider only whether:

$$(1/n)\Sigma y^{\alpha} > \hat{y}^{\alpha} \qquad \ldots \quad (29)$$

Inequality (29) compares mean consumption in private markets with a median choice in the public sector. Obviously, in a society homogeneous in income, the two levels of provision are the same. But in the real world the variance of the income distribution is invariably positive. Suppose $\hat{y} = \bar{y}$.[15] In this case an inspection of (29) informs us that the inequality does not hold if $\alpha = 0$ or if $\alpha = 1$; in both these cases, the levels of provision in each sector are the same.

Equation (29) can (when $\hat{y} = \overline{y}$) be rewritten ignoring the brackets:

$$(1/n)\Sigma(y/\overline{y})^{\alpha} > 1 \qquad \dots. \ (30)$$

Since $\Sigma(y/\overline{y}) = n$, we know from p.119 that provided the society is not homogeneous in income, inequality (30) holds if $\alpha > 1$. If $\alpha < 1$, the inequality does not hold, and in this case public-sector provision is greater than private (market) provision. Thus although earlier we have shown circumstances where public-sector provision is too low in the sense that aggregate willingness to pay exceeded tax costs, we have now demonstrated that there are situations where a level of provision that is too low in this sense may yet be greater than the amount private markets would supply, and in the public sector the distribution amongst individuals would be more equitable.

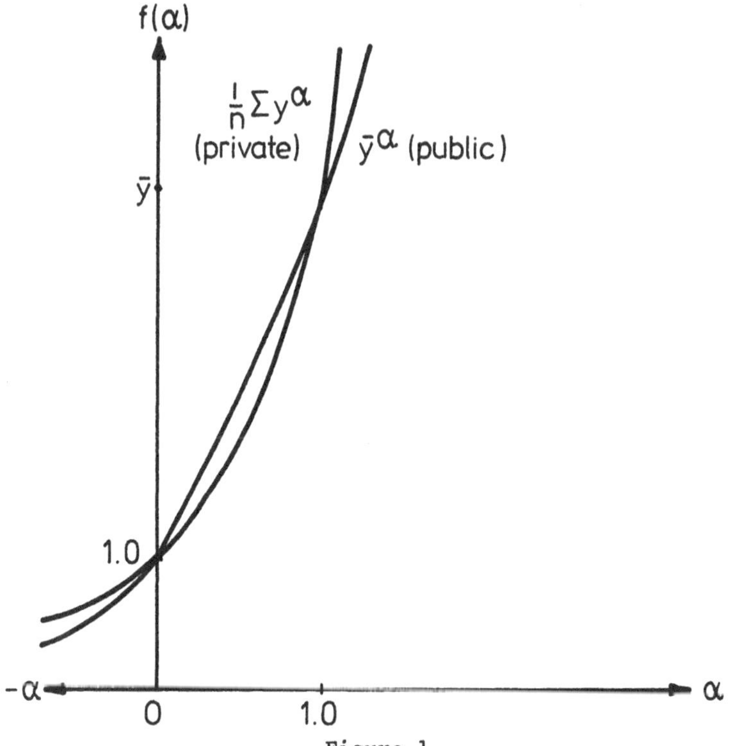

Figure 1

Even for a normal distribution of h, $\hat{y} = \bar{y}$ only if $\theta = 1$. If $\theta < 1$, $\hat{y} < \bar{y}$. In this latter case. the paragraph above is reinforced. If $\theta > 1$, $\hat{y} > y$, and it may not then be true that inequality (29) holds.

Now consider the bracketed term in (28). This can be rewritten.

$$\{(m/n)/(\hat{h}/\bar{h})\}^{\beta}$$

The term $\hat{h}/\bar{h}$ is marginally less than one for a positively skewed distribution of income - $\bar{y} > \hat{y}$. Earlier discussion evaluated m as greater than one, but not excessively so. The population parameter n is of course a large number. Thus the bracketed term represents a small fraction. Price elasticity is negative and generally less than one; so the whole term is greater than one. Thus it is unlikely in these circumstances for private market provision ever to exceed public-sector provision. As α increases, so does β given the relationship $\alpha \simeq \sigma\,\beta$. And as β increases in modulus value so does the expression $\{.\}^{\beta}$. The larger is n the more likely that public sector provision will exceed what private markets would supply. And of course in the public sector the distribution is more egalitarian. These considerations need to be set against the general theme of under-provision in the public sector.

5. *POLITICIANS AND BUREAUCRATS*

A median-voter model casts government as a neutral processer of signals received. It may be that both politicians and bureaucrats to a large measure determine public-sector supply. Presumably it is greater than that which the median voter would choose and thus the disparity between levels of provision is somewhat reduced if under-provision is the problem. All this looks like a scenario where bureaucrats could claim some justification for their activities[16]. Unfortunately, that is not the case. First, if luxuries are taxed, their type of executive impetus would only drive the public sector further away from its optimum. And there is also a further problem. To be sure, the executive can abrogate consumer preferences, but not without attendant distributional complications. Consider a new bureaucratically determined (z_b) level of output. In equation (25), everything is known except $\hat{z}$. Now replace $\hat{z}$ by z_b and solve equation (25) for y_b:

$$y_b = \{z_b A^{-1} [m(1/H)(\rho/n)]^{-\beta}\}^{1/(\alpha+\theta\beta)} \quad \text{.... (32)}$$

Everything in (32) is known except y_b and when this is determined its value allows us to identify the member of the society who would have chosen the level of provision that is bureaucratically determined. This information (which can be derived given knowledge of the parameters of the respective demand functions in the public and the private sectors) can then be fed into the various equations in section 2. Whether the tax expenditure package remains regressive for a particular group of individuals is readily determined by feeding the y_b from (32) into (13). Equation (13) becomes:

$$k = (y/y_b)^{\sigma-\theta} \quad \text{.... (33)}$$

If $\sigma > \theta$ and $y > y_b$, $k_j > 1$, and the fiscal residual remains positive for all $y_j > y_b$.

The lower is the ratio in (33), the less is k for taxes on non-luxuries. However, it is easy to misinterpret what is going on here. Recall that k has reference to marginal evaluations only and ignores consumer's surplus. If $k > 1$, this implies that the individual wants more of the good, and conversely. When a tax is redistributive from rich to poor, as we have defined it, the rich want more, the poor less. Executive action to produce more improves the lot of the rich and worsens that of the poor, who are driven further from their optimum.

The quotation by Wicksell that set off this enquiry has been investigated only partially. Tax regimes were given in advance and there has not been space to investigate the alternative, although precisely how one would formulate voting over tax regimes simultaneously with voting for expenditure levels is not a simple question. In some governmental structures, moreover, tax regimes are *given* constitutionally. Local government employs more than one in ten of the labour force in this country and its tax regime is confined to one tax base, as it has been since time out of memory. However, assuming Wicksell's nightmare ($\sigma < \theta$) came to pass where the majority poor placed inordinate tax burdens on the rich, executive action would then benefit the very poor only - all those who fell in the category $y < y_b$.

Nevertheless, an enlightened and well-intentioned executive could move to close the gap between aggregate willingness to pay and tax revenues, albeit not without facing up to the distributional implications of its actions.

6. CONCLUDING COMMENT

This paper has sought to emphasise that the tax regime and the level and efficiency of the public sector are inextricably linked. Although concerned with only one social good and one taxed commodity, the analysis can be extended to accommodate taxes on a number of commodities.

The main finding of this paper for a separable utility function with approximately constant elasticities - with individuals differing only in income, and with the median voter choosing - were:

(i) If a publicly-supplied good is financed with a proportionate tax on a commodity whose income-elasticity is less than the elasticity of the marginal utility of income schedule:

- (a) the fiscal basket is regressive;
- (b) the level of provision is too low; and
- (c) the rich want more, the poor less.

(ii) Switching the tax to a commodity with a lower income elasticity benefits the rich at the expense of the poor; and if the income distribution is positively skewed, the level of public-service provision falls.

(iii) Bureaucratically-determined increases in the provision of the publicly-supplied good benefit the rich who want more whilst driving the poor further from their optimum; but such an incremental move is possible with lump-sum taxes.

The analysis raises questions for the optimal tax literature, because clearly deadweight losses are limited in the private-sector only at the expense of failing to meet efficiency conditions in the public sector. In this model, only full tax neutrality attains the efficiency condition.

Point (iii) reminds us that increases in public-expenditure programmes on distributional grounds can only be justified under that criterion if the tax regime necessary to finance them is stipulated and analysed in advance. However, the paper made no comment about the distribution of income, nor did it address the issue of income transfers.

In the case of many commodities, the tax rate cannot be personalised and progression in the rate structure is not possible. Housing provides an exception. But whilst distributional issues can be resolved in this way, the level of provision in a median-voter regime depends on the tax-price he faces - if the distribution of income is negatively skewed, progression could have a deleterious effect on public-sector supply. Further research in this direction is needed.

As a whole, the paper has raised more questions than it has answered. It was positive in the sense that it asked whether in aggregate willingness to pay exceeded tax costs. Where this was the case, it was shown that it was possible to make everyone better off with lump-sum taxes financing an incremental change in z. These being ruled out, whether z should move up or down is a question that requires a social welfare function to to deliver a normative response.

The problem of voting over tax instruments was not addressed and the relationship between this problem and the one analysed in the paper has not been spelt out. Likewise a social welfare function was not brought in because such a device and a median voter are mutually exclusive. If the two happen to be compatible, we could learn something about the social welfare function from the choices made by a median voter.

Finally, this paper originated as a problem in local-government economics. Discussions of extending the tax base to allow greater local autonomy have thus far been carried on at quite a banal level in this country. Tax regimes in local government are determined in advance and it is not a small sector of the economy. Obviously, welfare maximisation demands that considerations of both the optimal tax literature and the issues raised here should feature on the agenda of any future discussions.

REFERENCES

Aaron, H.J. (1975). *Who Pays the Property Tax*? Washington Brookings.

Aaron H.J. & McGuire, M. (1970. Public Goods and Income Distribution. *Econometrica* 38, 907-920.

Atkinson, A.B. (1977). Optimal taxation and the direct versus indirect tax controversy. *Canadian Journal of Economics* 10, 590-606.

Barlow, R. (1970). Efficiency Aspects of Local School Finance. *Journal of Political Economy* 78, 1028-40.

Baumol, W.J. & Bradford, D.F. (1970). Optimal Departures from Marginal Cost Pricing. *American Economic Review* 60, 265-283.

Bergstrom, T.C. & Goodman, R.P. (1973). Private Demands for Public Goods. *American Economic Review* 63, 280-296.

Bowen, H.R. (1943). The Interpretation of Voting in the Allocation of Economic Resources. *Quarterly Journal of Economics* 58, 27-48.

Brown, A. & Deaton, A. (1972). Models of Consumer Behaviour. *Economic Journal* 82, 1145-1236.

Buchanan, J.M. (1964). Fiscal Institutions and Efficiency in Collective Outlay. *American Economic Review* 54, 277-235.

Buchanan, J.M. & Brennan, G. (1978). Towards a Constitution for Leviathan. *Journal of Public Economics* 8, 255-273.

Frisch, R. (1959). A Complete Scheme for Computing All Direct and Cross Demand Elasticities in a Model with Many Sectors. *Econometrica* 27, 177-196.

Grigson, G. (1977). *Epigrams and Epitaphs* London: Faber and Faber.

Lindahl, E. (1919). Just Taxation - A Positive Solution. Reprinted in R.A. Musgrave & A.T. Peacock (1958). *Classics in the Theory of Public Finance* London: Macmillan.

Lindahl, E. (1928). Some Controversial Questions in the Theory of Taxation. Reprinted in Musgrave & Peacock, *op. cit.*

Mueller, D. (1979). *Public Choice*, Cambridge: Cambridge.

Musgrave, R.A. (1959). *The Theory of Public Finance.* New York: McGraw Hill.

Pommerehne, W.W. (1978). Institutional Approaches to Public Expenditure: Empirical evidence from Swiss municipalities, *Journal of Public Economics* 9, 255-80.

Salter, S.J. & Topham, N. (1978). Migration and Option Demand for Local Public Goods. *Salford Papers in Economics* 78-2.

Samuelson, P.A. (1954). The Pure Theory of Public Expenditure. *Review of Economics and Statistics* 36, 386-9.

Sandmo, A. (1976). Optimal Taxation - An Introduction to the Literature, *Journal of Public Economics* 6, 37-54.

Sato, K. (1972). Additive Utility Functions with Double-Log Consumer Demand Functions, *Journal of Political Economy* 80, 102-24.

Stern, N. (1976). The Marginal Valuation of Income. In Artis, M.J. & Nobay, A.R. (ed.) (1977). *Studies in Modern Economic Analysis* London: Blackwell.

Stiglitz, J.E. (1974). The Demand for Education in Public and Private School Systems. *Journal of Public Economics* 3, 349-86.

Whitehead, C. (1971). A Model of the U.K. Housing Market. *Oxford Bulletin of Statistics* 33, 245-66.

Wicksell, K. (1896). A New Principle of Just Taxation. Reprinted in Musgrave, R.A. & Peacock, A.T., *op.cit*.

FOOTNOTES

1. I am deeply indebted to J.A. Mirrlees for saving me from an error of omission and for help with

the consequential reformulation of the problem. Previous drafts were given to staff seminars at the Universities of York and Salford. Additional help, which was provided by Richard Barnett, Stephen Salter, Michael Sumner, Leighton Thomas, and Robert Ward, is gratefully acknowledged. None of these is implicated in the views expressed nor responsible for errors that remain.

2. Wicksell did not intend that his principle of unanimity would guarantee that all marginal evaluations would be met. A voter would approve the budget on an all-or-nothing basis; thus unanimity merely guarantees that everyone gains some consumer's surplus from the public budget. This leaves, of course, a good deal of room for the bureaucracy to operate, which we consider in section 6.
3. Brennan and Buchanan (1977) have recently addressed and analysed constitutional issues associated with the choice of tax structure. Local governments are often confined to property as a tax base, but other possibilities are suggested occasionally. These long-term problems are not discussed here.
4. Pommerehne (1978) shows, as might be expected, that median-voter models work better in Switzerland where referenda are not uncommon.
5. See Baumol and Bradford (1970) and Sandmo (1976). Of course other considerations are dealt with in the literature surveyed. But however we write the tax "rule", it does not affect the basic issue: the dichotomy between expenditure and taxes is an artificial one.
6. On the value of σ, Brown and Deaton (1972) and Stern (1976) summarising the evidence suggest a figure of approximately 2. On the value of θ, Whitehead (1971) suggests a figure of approximately 1; studies in the U.S. suggest a similar value - see for example Aaron (1975) and references therein.

7. Suppose assumption (ii) is relaxed. Whether w is positive or negative is now not clear. If the good to be taxed is a complement to z, then its consumption rises when z increases - the textbook example is a tax on televisions to finance television channels, historically we had the road fund, and currently we have the betting tax. But public services might just as easily be financed by taxing 'substitutes' - a tax on locks to finance police patrols. Earmarking is not common in the real world, and although on balance public services substitute for private provision, the tax burden is so widely spread that it is perhaps safer to regard w as near zero. Hence $(1-w)/(1+s) > 1$.
8. The method adopted here is similar to Aaron and McGuire (1970). But whereas they were able to make statements only about relative tax shares, the analysis here is able to evaluate the fiscal residual of each individual in society on an absolute basis. Note that because elasticities are approximately constant, the bracketed terms in (10) and (11) are taken to be population constants.
9. In an early paper, Buchanan (1964) derived the conditions for neutrality on an intuitive level. He concluded that the income elasticity of the public good divided by its price elasticity should equal the elasticity of the tax price schedule. The ratio of income to price elasticity approximates to σ whilst the elasticity of the tax-price schedule is no more than the income elasticity of demand of the taxed commodity. (If the basis of the tax is a proportionate income tax, the elasticity of the tax-price schedule is simply unity). Thus Buchanan's early conjuncture amounts to $\sigma = \theta$.
10. Frisch (1959) showed that if utility functions are additive all income and price elasticities stand in a common relationship to one another:

$$-\sigma = -\theta(1-v\theta)/(-\varepsilon+v\theta)$$

where v is the proportion of the budget spent on the commodity in question whilst θ and ε are respectively income and price elasticity of demand. Frisch called σ the money flexibility of marginal utility of income. Sato showed that a generalised CES type utility function yields approximately constant income and own-price elasticities. He goes on to show that σ measures the overall elasticity of substitution with no cardinal implications; that is, it measures the overall (average) curvature of indifference surfaces (see Sato, p.108).

11. Atkinson (1977), p.600.
12. Quoted in Grigson (1977).
13. Stiglitz (1974) derives a similar result and shows over-provision occurs if $\sigma > 1$. He analyses a tax that is proportional to income and the results here are easily modified to show that this is the case. However, he was concerned with education, which almost invariably is financed by a property tax, and under a proportional property tax, tax payments are proportional to income only if $\rho = 1$. Distortion effects are also ignored by Stiglitz.
14. Barlow (1970) argued that under-provision occurred when $\alpha > \beta$. This statement is not generally true and over-provision occurs if $\theta > |\alpha/\beta|$. Bergstrom and Goodman (1973) point out that a Lindahl equilibrium is attained if $\theta = |\alpha/\beta|$.
15. This occurs if $\theta = 1$.
16. Mueller (1979) provides a useful survey of the literature on bureaucracy.

DISCUSSION : J. MIRRLEES

In his stimulating paper, Neville Topham identifies an important and fascinating set of issues. Much of the discussion I presented at the conference has been superseded by the revised version of the paper. Consequently I shall confine myself to a few general remarks.

It is not easy to decide how best to pose the question, whether a democracy would tend to provide too few public goods. One needs a theory of voting decisions and their effects; and one needs a feasible standard of comparison, a way of organizing the economy that is a genuine alternative to the model representing real-world provision. Neville Topham takes as his model of democratic provision an economy in which tax revenue is obtained by taxing one commodity, such as buildings, and its members vote on the level of public good provision, allowing for the effect on the general tax level of alternative levels of provision. His comparison models are, first, similar economies in which the tax base is different; and, second, an economy in which public-good efficiency conditions apply.

The majority-voting model seems to be a good one to start from. But one needs to know what voters believe are the tax consequences of any particular level of public good provision. For example, they might or might not allow for the effects on demand for commodities in the tax base. The fashionable assumption of rational expectations suggests that they allow for such effects. Casual conversation with voters suggests that the individual cost of new public expenditures is generally greatly underestimated, and plays only a small part in the voter's decision.

It is an interesting observation that the choice of tax base affects the voting-equilibrium level of the public good. An optimal choice of tax base should no doubt reflect that consideration. Indeed the literature on preference revelation is, in a sense, directed to that question, for it contemplates radical redesign of the way the tax system responds to the level of provision (and declared preferences). Is it not odd to contemplate a society in which taxes are set optimally, and public goods chosen by vote? In representative democracy, something like this may happen: some issues affect the outcome of elections, others are determined by members of the government or civil servants. I do not think the division between these two classes of decision splits tax from expenditure decisions. One possible model is that expenditures are chosen by majority vote conditional on a given tax system, and the tax system is chosen by majority vote conditional on the level of public expenditure. But for that model, there is no point in asking what happens if a different tax base is chosen. One has to compare directly with some alternative model where the voters are more or less sophisticated, or where you or I get to choose everything for the general good.

This brings us back to the central question, whether public expenditure is too high. An answer can be given only if there is a method of comparing alternative outcomes. I do not think that Samuelson's efficiency rule for public goods is any help here. It applies only when there are optimal lump sum taxes and subsidies; and these are not possible. Furthermore the voters in these models know they are not possible, or at least are not in operation.

Could optimal tax theory come to the rescue? I think it can. Given the way Topham has set up his model, we could compare a naive government that has set up optimal taxes, given the level of public goods set by voters, with a sophisticated government that has chosen a tax system to maximize welfare, taking into account the effects of the system on voting behaviour. Would public expenditure be greater or less in the second case? The answer must depend on the relative importance of the public good, on the margin, to different income groups, *and* the effect of increased expenditure on tax revenue. Whether a county council should spend more on schools really does depend on whether that attracts higher tax payers to the county.

In that way we are led to think about the agreements that local governments ought to reach with one another, and the extent to which it is desirable for decisions to be taken locally. There is another issue of similar type that is central: how should the issues voters decide about be split up? Splitting them geographically has obviously undesirable properties. Does splitting the issues finely always have predominantly undesirable effects? In particular, are frequent elections, or referenda, bad? There are hints in Topham's work that splitting issues - here taxes and expenditures - is a bad thing. I do not know any general answers, but surely this is an important and manageable general question.

6. LIFE INSURANCE AND ASSET HOLDING IN THE UNITED KINGDOM

A. F. Shorrocks

1. *INTRODUCTION*[1]

One of the more important legacies of the Royal Commission on the Distribution of Income and Wealth is the series of Personal Sector Balance Sheets constructed by the Central Statistical Office. Provisional estimates for 1975 and 1976 first appeared in *Economic Trends* (January 1978). These balance sheets are updated and improved versions of those compiled by Revell (1967), and provide estimates of aggregate holdings of various assets.

Prior to this the only available estimates of asset holdings were those published by the Inland Revenue and derived from estate data using the estate multiplier method. These figures are subject to a number of shortcomings, due primarily to the fact that they relate only to that part of the population and of personal wealth covered on death by probate returns. Most of the limitations are listed in the notes to *Inland Revenue Statistics*. They are also discussed at length in Revell (1967) and Atkinson and Harrison (1977). However the quantitative significance of the imperfections and omissions in the estate multiplier figures was perhaps not easily appreciated until estimates of total personal holdings in a variety of assets were made available via the official personal sector balance sheets.

A comparison of aggregate asset totals derived from the CSO balance sheets and the Inland Revenue estimates of wealth holdings reveals considerable differences between the two sets of figures. The balance sheet, for example, suggested that the net wealth of households totalled £284 billion in 1975 compared to an estate multiplier figure of £190 billion. Similar differences are apparent for individual asset categories. These discrepancies have prompted attempts to reconcile the two sets of figures and the most recent and elaborate example is the paper by Dunn and Hoffman (1978). Their table 2 identifies

11 sources of variation between balance sheet and estate multiplier estimates of asset holdings, covering points such as differences in the date of valuation, differences in coverage and the fact that some wealth holdings are exempt from estate duty and consequently do not appear in the valuation of estates.

Of the individual items in this table, two stand out as being significantly more important than all the other adjustments. Both appear under the column entitled "Differences in method of valuation" and concern consumer durables and life insurance policies. The consumer durables item arises because the estate duty statistics use realisable values which are much lower (estimate £27 billion) than the written down replacement values used in the balance sheet. The life insurance figure is the result of valuing life insurance at maturity value for estate duty purposes (which is appropriate) and then assigning the same maturity valuation to all policies held by the living population (which is certainly not appropriate). This would inflate estate multiplier wealth by £37.5 billion, if it were not for compensating adjustments due to other factors, notably "Differences in coverage".

Whilst the difference between the estate multiplier and balance sheet valuation of consumer durables is due to different choices of alternative, acceptable bases of valuation, corresponding to the usual distinction between the "sell up" and "going concern" value of an asset, the same cannot be said of the life insurance calculations. The estate multiplier figures are simply a gross exaggeration.

The need to provide estimates of wealth holdings when life policies are appropriately revalued has been recognised by both the Inland Revenue and the Royal Commission (1979, paragraph 4.56). As regards the appropriate alternative basis for valuation, surrender values are thought to be unreasonably low and general opinion seems to be in favour of a valuation based on the reserves held by life insurance companies. Provisional estimates have been made of the downward adjustment to the value of life policies in each age group which would need to be applied and these are reported in Dunn and Hoffman (1978, p.109). They range from a 97% reduction for those aged under 25 to a 20% reduction for those over 85.

After making these adjustments Dunn and Hoffman report an increase of 2.1% in the Gini coefficient for wealth inequality from the initial value of 62% in 1975. This is a fairly modest change given that life insurance values are reduced by £21.8 billion in aggregate, or about 10% of total net wealth.[2] However, the impact of the adjustment is more pronounced when other aspects of asset holdings are examined.

This paper investigates how the revaluation of life policies affects the relationship between wealth holdings and age (Section 3) and the importance of specific types of assets to various sex, age and wealth groups (Section 4). Before embarking on these issues, the pattern of life insurance holdings is considered in detail (Section 2).

2. *THE VALUE OF LIFE INSURANCE HOLDINGS*

Data published in *Inland Revenue Statistics* (1977, table 110) indicated 12.65 million life policy holders in the UK in 1975, 60.2% of the population covered by the Inland Revenue data. The total value of life policies is given at £29.18 billion, an average of £2,307 per policy holder. This constitutes 15.3% of the £190.29 billion aggregate net wealth.[3] Life insurance coverage does not vary greatly between the sexes (67.2% of men compared to 50.1% of women), but the *value* of life policies does differ substantially. The value of male life insurance holdings is reported as £25.34 billion, or 21.9% of their aggregate net wealth; that for women is £3.84 billion, or 5.2% of aggregate net wealth.

Using unpublished data kindly made available by the Inland Revenue[4], it has been possible to calculate the percentage of wealth held in the form of life policies for a number of separate age and wealth range categories. Figures for males in Britain in 1975 are reported in Table 1. These show considerable variation in the importance of life insurance as an asset, with the proportion of wealth held in this form declining with both age and wealth level[5]. It is the figures for the youngest age groups which are most noticeable. Males aged 25-34 are estimated to hold 43.9% of their assets as life insurance, and this proportion rises to over a half for those with net estates in the range £10,000-£50,000. For those aged 18-24 the overall proportion is 58.4%, whilst those with net estates of £10,000-

TABLE 1: Life Insurance at Maturity Value as a Percentage of Net Capital[d] Males, GB, 1975

Age Group	18-24	25-34	35-44	45-54	55-64	65-74	75-84	85+	All Groups
Net Estate Range (£000's)									
Under 1	42.9	35.3	48.7	42.5	19.9	178.6[c]	10.8	4.0	39.4
1-3	55.2	39.7	37.1	27.8	11.2	15.1	3.9	6.9	33.5
3-5	56.6	43.2	29.7	20.0	15.8	2.3	1.6	1.7	30.2
5-10	64.5	44.6	27.8	17.9	8.0	2.6	1.5	2.0	25.7
10-15	75.0	50.3	32.1	19.0	8.3	2.0	1.3	2.3	28.2
15-20	54.4[a]	51.8	33.2	16.8	8.1	2.8	1.2	.7	27.8
20-50	59.0	52.1	31.1	18.0	6.9	2.6	1.3	1.7	24.4
50-100	20.2[a]	33.1	14.4	14.8	6.1	2.8	1.7	2.0	12.8
100-200	-[b]	1.6[a]	6.2	7.6	5.1	2.7	1.6	2.4	4.7
Over 200	-[b]	15.3[a]	8.0[a]	1.8	1.3	1.4	2.9	2.7	4.7
All Estate Classes	58.4	43.9	28.1	16.6	7.2	2.9	1.7	2.0	23.1

Notes:

a. Based on estimated sample sizes of less than ten. The average sample size over all 80 cells was 239.

b. No male estates recorded in these cells.

c. The lowest wealth class includes a high proportion of insolvent estates, hence the low net capital for this group and the very high life policy proportion.

d. Estate values are net of funeral expenses and capital gains tax payable at the time of death. Net wealth figures published by the Inland Revenue exclude funeral expenses (approximately 0.8% of net wealth) from the deductions. Net capital also excludes the very small capital gains liability (approximately 0.04% of net wealth).

TABLE 2: Life Insurance as a Percentage of Net Capital. Males, GB, 1975

Age Group	18-24	25-34	35-44	45-54	55-64	65-74	75-84	85+	All Groups
Net Estate Range (£000's)[c]									
Under 1	2.2	6.1	19.2	20.5	10.1	375.4	8.3	3.2	11.3
1-3	3.6	7.3	12.9	11.9	5.4	9.6	2.9	5.6	8.3
3-5	3.8	8.4	9.5	8.1	7.8	1.4	1.2	1.3	7.1
5-10	5.2	8.8	8.8	7.1	3.8	1.6	1.1	1.6	6.2
10-15	8.3	10.8	10.6	7.6	3.9	1.2	1.0	1.9	7.2
15-20	3.5[a]	11.4	11.1	6.6	3.8	1.7	0.9	0.6	7.3
20-50	4.1	11.6	10.1	7.2	3.2	1.6	1.0	1.4	6.6
50-100	0.8[a]	5.6	4.0	5.7	2.8	1.7	1.3	1.6	3.7
100-200	-[b]	0.2[a]	1.6	2.8	2.4	1.7	1.2	1.9	1.8
Over 200	-[b]	2.1[a]	2.1[a]	0.6	0.6	0.9	2.2	2.2	1.1
All Estate Classes	4.0	8.6	8.9	6.5	3.4	1.8	1.3	1.6	5.8

Notes:

a. Based on estimated sample sizes of less than ten.

b. No male estates recorded in these cells.

c. Individuals are classified by their net estate before the life insurance adjustment is applied: see comments in the text.

£15,000 have 75% of their assets in the form of life insurance[6]. Bearing in mind that those in the youngest age groups will typically have paid premiums for only a few years, these proportions are clearly gross exaggerations.

Table 2 presents comparable figures when life policies are reduced to their equity value, using the equity-maturity ratios for each age group reported in Dunn and Hoffman (1978)[7]. To make this adjustment it was assumed that, within each age-net estate cell, life insurance constitutes an identical proportion of each persons assets. Whilst this assumption may be a reasonable first approximation, it is undoubtedly wrong since many men have no life insurance coverage at all. However, in the absence of data on individual estates, any other method of adjustment would also require some fairly arbitrary assumptions and would be considerably more difficult to implement. Notice that the reduction in the valuation of life policies leads to a corresponding fall in net capital and net wealth. The upper and lower limits for each wealth class therefore have to be amended accordingly and may bear little relation to the net estate ranges indicated on the left-hand side of the table. In particular it is not strictly appropriate to aggregate over age groups to give the figures in the last column, although this has been done for purposes of comparison[8].

The overall impact of the adjustment is to reduce the aggregate value of life policies held by males by about 80% and aggregate net capital by approximately 20%, so that life insurance falls from being 23.1% of net capital to 5.8%. Within any age-wealth cell, the proportion of assets held in the form of life insurance now rarely exceeds 12%. There is still a tendency for the importance of life insurance to fall as wealth increases, but the relationship with age has changed. The proportion of assets held as life policies shows considerably less variation over the age groups compared to Table 1; and the proportion now increases initially with age, reaching a maximum in the 35-44 age group.

Similar adjustments to the value of life policies have been performed for females in 1975, and for males and females in 1976 (these relate to the United Kingdom, rather than Great Britain). The effect of the adjustment is similar to that already found for males in 1975, as can be seen from the summary data provided in Table 3.

TABLE 3: Life Insurance as a Percentage of Net Capital, by Estate Range and Age

Net Estate Range (£000's)	Life Insurance at Maturity Value				Adjusted Life Insurance Valuation			
	Males GB 1975	Males UK 1976	Females GB 1975	Females UK 1976	Males GB 1975	Males UK 1976	Females GB 1975	Females UK 1976
Under 1	39.4	97.5	23.2	27.4	11.3	87.1	7.8	6.6
1 - 3	33.5	38.3	13.3	21.6	8.3	9.9	3.1	3.9
3 - 5	30.2	27.0	10.4	9.2	7.1	6.0	2.5	1.9
5 - 10	25.7	27.9	7.5	8.3	6.2	6.7	1.7	2.0
10 - 15	28.2	27.3	6.4	6.6	7.2	6.8	1.6	1.2
15 - 20	27.8	29.8	3.9	5.6	7.3	7.9	1.3	1.5
20 - 50	24.4	26.0	5.5	5.5	6.6	7.0	1.7	1.6
50 - 100	12.8	12.8	2.7	3.9	3.7	4.1	1.2	1.5
100 - 200	4.7	10.4	3.5	4.6	1.8	2.9	1.3	1.6
Over 200	4.7	2.4	2.9	4.7	1.1	0.9	1.2	1.4
Age Group								
18 - 24	58.4	47.9	26.2	36.4	4.0	2.7	1.1	1.7
25 - 34	43.9	45.2	16.9	19.6	8.6	9.0	2.4	2.8
35 - 44	28.1	28.4	9.2	12.2	8.9	9.0	2.5	3.4
45 - 54	16.6	16.7	7.4	5.1	6.5	6.6	2.7	1.8
55 - 64	7.2	6.9	3.3	3.3	3.4	3.2	1.5	1.5
65 - 74	2.9	2.5	1.5	1.6	1.8	1.5	0.9	0.9
75 - 84	1.7	1.8	1.0	1.2	1.3	1.3	0.8	0.9
Over 85	2.0	1.5	1.0	0.8	1.6	1.2	0.8	0.7
All Groups	23.1	23.4	6.2	6.7	5.8	5.9	1.7	1.7

For males in 1976 the value of life insurance is reduced from 23.4% of net capital to 5.9%. The maturity value of life insurance held by women was 6.2% of net capital in 1975 and 6.7% in 1976, and these are adjusted downwards to 1.7%. Both before and after the valuation adjustment there is a general tendency for life insurance to decline in importance as the level of wealth increases, although the relationship does not always appear to be monotonic[9]. As regards the pattern over age groups, the decline in the importance of life insurance holdings as age increases, apparent in the maturity value figures, does not apply to any of the four sets of adjusted data. As a proportion of total assets, life policies always begin by increasing with age and, with one minor exception, achieve a maximum in the 35-44 age range.

3. THE AGE-WEALTH PROFILE

The relationship between wealth holdings and age has received considerable attention in the literature because of the connection with the life cycle savings hypothesis. If life cycle considerations are important in determining accumulation and asset holdings, wealth levels are likely to show considerable variation with age. Furthermore, wealth is expected to increase with age during the earlier stages of the life cycle and then decline, as individuals approach the end of their lives and begin to dissave.

The life cycle savings hypothesis has important implications for the way in which wealth inequality is interpreted, since observed differences in wealth levels may arise simply because individuals are viewed at different points of the life cycle[10]. Variations in wealth by age, to the extent that they reflect the chosen lifetime plans of individuals, contribute "spuriously" to wealth inequality and thus tend to exaggerate its significance. The significance of this factor will depend, *inter alia,* on the shape and steepness of the age-wealth profile. Moreover, the correspondence between the observed shape and the theoretically anticipated hump pattern, provides a basis for judging whether individuals follow an optimal lifetime savings plan, and an indirect test of the life cycle savings hypothesis itself.

In its first report the Royal Commission (1975, p.115) placed particular emphasis on the age-wealth profile. Using estimates for 1954, 1963-67 and 1972, they noted a general tendency for the average level of wealth to rise consistently with age, and not to decline at the end of the lifespan[11]. They also noted a trend over time towards a flatter profile. This is particularly noticeable in the case of men in 1972 whose age-wealth profile is virtually horizontal. However these observations are based on the unadjusted Inland Revenue figures for which life policies are assigned their maturity value. This assignment will distort the shape of the age-wealth profile since the ratio of maturity to equity value is systematically related to age, and also shows a substantial variation over the age groups. Using maturity values will lessen the degree to which average wealth varies with age and therefore reduces the apparent relevance of life cycle factors. This in turn may influence the importance attributed to accumulation for life cycle purposes, relative to that attached to other determinants of wealth holdings. Valuing life insurance at maturity could also account for the observed trend over time towards a flatter age-wealth pattern if life insurance coverage among the young is increasing[12].

The impact on the age-wealth profile of changing life policies from maturity to equity value can be gauged from Table 4. The figures reported are estimates of various top percentiles of the distribution of net wealth within each age category[13]. Percentiles have been chosen in preference to estimates of mean wealth by age, since the latter are particularly sensitive to assumptions made concerning the wealth of those not covered by the Inland Revenue data (approximately half of the population: see Table 4) and to the problem of small samples in the highest wealth ranges.

When life policies are valued at maturity, the estimates for British men in 1975 suggest that wealth more than doubles between age groups 18-24 and 25-34, and rises again into the next age category, at which point wealth appears to peak, except for those at the very top of the distribution. After applying the adjustments to the value of life policies, the wealth of the youngest age group is reduced by a factor of around 2.5 and that of the 25-34 age group by around 1.75, with successively smaller adjustments to the remaining groups. The net effect is

TABLE 4: Unadjusted and Adjusted Percentile Values by Age. GB, 1975

	Age Group	18–24	25–34	35–44	45–54	55–64	65–74	75–84	85+
Males, before adjustment for life insurance valuation									
Minimum net Wealth of top	1%	17594	36749	48435	55889	59589	58830	64700	89592
	5%	8588	18804	22991	22988	21453	20480	23794	34662
	10%	5418	13534	16272	15272	13235	12300	14203	20655
	20%	2451	9282	11355	10255	8278	6383	8550	12000
Males, after adjustment for life insurance valuation									
Minimum net Wealth of top	1%	7185	21825	40012	50204	57525	58189	64449	89210
	5%	2821	10174	17647	20390	20569	20257	23716	34552
	10%	2089	7490	12269	13481	12631	12183	14157	20604
	20%	1055	5370	8697	9009	7850	6322	8519	11955
Male 1975 Mid Year Population (thousands)		2688	3763	3152	3289	2872	2114	726	125
Percentage of Estates recorded in Estate Duty Data		44.6	68.3	70.8	67.7	52.9	42.2	49.1	60.7
Females, after adjustment for life insurance valuation									
Minimum net	1%	7458	16021	29123	39349	52492	52412	58314	66521
	5%	2196	6961	11835	16100	20102	22078	24547	27510
	10%	– a	4447	6864	10157	12639	14082	15763	17057
	20%	– a	1690	2691	5093	5695	7232	9117	9967

Note: a. Percentile estimates below £5000 are probably unreliable and should be treated with caution. Estimates values below £1000 are not reported.

for the profiles to become steeper at the bottom of the age range, and to peak about ten years later, somewhere in the neighbourhood of 50 years of age.

The percentile values before and after adjustment for life insurance valuation are plotted in Figure 1[14] and illustrate the changes described above. The profiles as a whole seem to provide little evidence in support of life cycle savings. The initial increase with age conforms to expectations, but the decline in middle age in the lower cross section profiles is reversed during the retirement period.

It has been argued that this departure of the observed profile from the anticipated hump pattern can be explained by the omission of pension rights from the definition of wealth[15]. If the actuarial value of rights to a future stream of pension income is imputed to individuals this will help to restore the hump characteristic, since the present value of pension rights is substantial in comparison to marketable forms of wealth and varies significantly with age, attaining a maximum somewhere around the date of retirement. However the actuarial value of pension rights for those aged 80 is not likely to be very high, and it is not clear that the decline in the value of these rights above age 80 will be sufficient to offset the increase in the value of marketable wealth, which appears to increase by about 40% between those aged 75-84 and those above 85[16].

Shorrocks (1975) suggests another explanation for this phenomenon at the end of the lifespan. If wealthy people have a lower mortality rate than average, as the data on mortality by social class suggest, then the group of surviving individuals will not be a random sample of their cohort of contemporaries. Even when the negative correlation between mortality and wealth is low, the probability of surviving beyond, say, age 80 can be much higher for the wealthier members of society. This change in the composition of the surviving population will tend to inflate the average wealth of older age groups relative to theoretical predictions based on the behaviour of a representative individual. The figures provided in Table 4 for the male population in each age group show that the rapid decline in population, and hence the importance of the composition effect, takes place about the age of 70. This is exactly the point at which the cross-section wealth profiles begin their unexpected rise[17].

Figure 1 Wealth Profiles by Age: Males, 1975

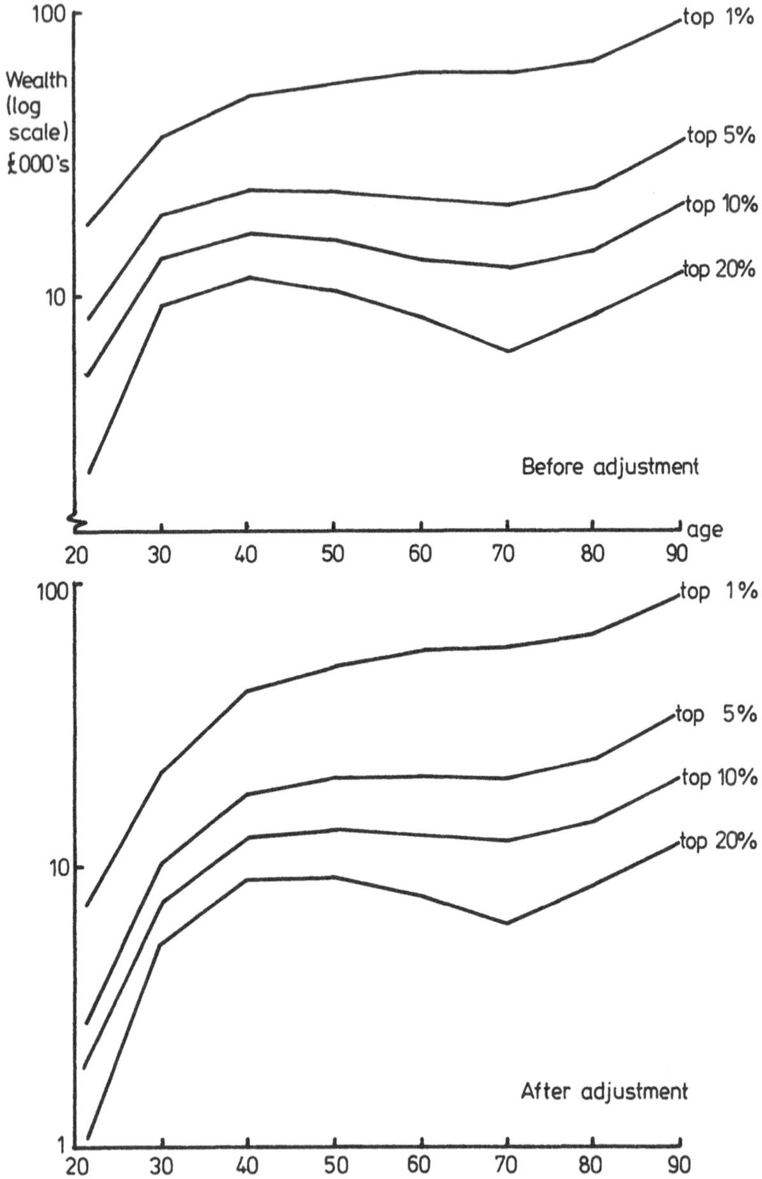

Table 4 also provides percentile values for women, after life insurance has been revalued on an equity basis. These data show a consistent trend towards increasing wealth with age, with no indication of a hump pattern. However the propensity for widows to inherit from their husband's estate makes it difficult to draw conclusions regarding the life cycle savings hypothesis.[18]

4. THE COMPOSITION OF ASSET HOLDINGS

Revaluation of life insurance policies results in changes in the proportion of total wealth held in specific types of assets. If the portfolio composition was similar for different sex, age and wealth groups, the impact of this revaluation would be relatively easy to assess. The percentage of wealth held in assets other than life insurance would simply be scaled up in the same proportion. However, if there is a systematic variation in the portfolio composition by sex, age or wealth level, then the fact that the life insurance adjustment also varies with these factors makes the overall impact difficult to estimate unless disaggregated data are available.

Published data on the asset composition of wealth holdings suggest that the type of assets held does depend on all three factors. This can be seen from the break--down of assets by sex published by the Inland Revenue (1977, Table 110) and their breakdown by wealth range (1977, Table 113). Evidence for variation in holdings of company securities by age is provided by the Royal Commission (1979, Table 6.10). Unfortunately none of this published information is conclusive, since in presenting the relationship with each single determinant, aggregation has taken place over the other two. Thus it is not clear, for example, whether the apparent variation over age groups is simply due to underlying differences in asset holdings with wealth combined with different wealth distributions for the age groups. However the disaggregated data used in this study has enabled the impact of these three factors to be examined separately. The results suggest that each is associated with significant differences in portfolio composition, and that the level of wealth is the single most important determinant.

TABLE 5: Asset Holdings as a Percentage of Net Capital, Before and After Adjustment for Life Insurance Valuation

Asset Category	Males 1975 Before Adjustment UK[a]	Males 1975 Before Adjustment GB	Males 1975 After Adjustment GB	Females 1975 Before Adjustment UK[a]	Females 1975 Before Adjustment GB	Females 1975 After Adjustment GB	All 1975 Before Adjustment UK[a]	All 1975 Before Adjustment GB	All 1975 After Adjustment GB
Unlisted UK Government Securities	1.1	1.1	1.3	2.5	2.5	2.6	1.7	1.6	1.8
Government and Municipal Securities	0.9	0.8	1.0	2.3	2.3	2.4	1.5	1.4	1.5
Unlisted Shares	3.0	3.3	4.0	1.4	1.5	1.6	2.4	2.6	3.1
Listed Shares	4.7	4.8	5.8	11.1	9.6	10.0	7.2	6.7	7.4
Money on Mortgage	2.1	1.9	2.3	2.4	2.3	2.5	2.2	2.0	2.4
Building Society Deposits	5.5	5.4	6.6	10.7	10.4	10.9	7.5	7.4	8.3
Insurance Policies	21.8	23.1	5.8	5.2	6.2	1.7	15.3	16.7	4.2
Cash and Bank Deposits	7.6	7.2	8.8	11.5	11.3	11.8	9.1	8.8	10.0
Household Goods	4.0	3.9	4.8	3.5	3.4	3.6	3.8	3.7	4.3
Trade Assets	3.6	3.6	4.4	1.2	1.3	1.4	2.7	2.7	3.2
Other Personal Wealth	9.9	10.1	12.2	8.3	8.6	9.0	9.3	9.5	11.0
Land	5.0	4.5	5.5	2.5	1.9	2.0	4.0	3.5	4.1
Freehold Residential Buildings	39.8	40.5	49.5	38.2	40.5	42.4	39.2	40.5	46.7
Leasehold Residential Buildings	3.6	3.3	4.1	4.1	4.1	4.3	3.8	3.6	4.2
Other Landed Property	0.9	0.7	1.0	0.6	0.6	0.6	0.7	0.7	0.8
Personal Debts	-5.3	-5.6	-6.8	-2.4	-2.7	-2.8	-4.2	-4.5	-5.2
Property Debts	-8.1	-8.5	-10.4	-3.3	-3.8	-4.0	-6.2	-6.7	-7.9
All Financial Assets	46.7	47.5	35.7	47.2	46.1	43.5	47.0	47.0	38.7
Gross Personal Wealth	64.3	65.0	57.1	60.2	59.4	57.4	62.7	62.8	57.2
Gross Landed Property	49.2	49.1	60.1	45.5	47.1	49.3	47.8	48.3	55.9
Net Personal Wealth	58.9	59.4	50.3	57.8	56.7	54.7	58.5	58.3	52.0
Net Landed Property	41.1	40.6	49.7	42.2	43.3	45.3	41.5	41.7	48.0

Note: a. Derived from *Inland Revenue Statistics* (1977), Table 110.

Table 5 shows how the adjustment made to the valuation of life insurance affects the asset composition pattern between the sexes. There are 17 broad types of assets and debts, which together define net capital, and five composite asset categories. The types of assets have been chosen for comparability with published data, and the correspondence with the categories used by the Inland Revenue is indicated in the Appendix.

Two sets of figures are based on life policies valued at maturity. Those for the UK are derived from published Inland Revenue information. They differ a little from the GB estimates obtained with the disaggregated data because of the slightly different populations to which they relate, and because the published data have been subject to smoothing by the Inland Revenue. The unadjusted figures show differences between the sexes in holdings of particular types of assets, but the general pattern is similar. Men and women hold roughly the same proportion of their wealth in the form of financial assets and in residential buildings. Men incur higher levels of debt, but after debts are subtracted, the division of net capital into net personal wealth and net property is very close to that for women. The most noticeable feature is perhaps the tendency for women to hold more liquid financial assets - savings and local authority bonds, gilt edge stocks, listed shares, cash and deposits in banks and building societies.

When life policies are revalued, the asset percentages for men generally rise by a factor in the range 20-25%. The total for all financial assets falls by 12%, due to the reduction in the value of life insurance, and this is offset by an increase of 11% in gross property, and an increase of 9% in net property. The revaluation of life policies has a smaller impact on the asset holdings of women, but the asset shares of all categories other than life insurance increase by a factor in the region of 5%, and there is an overall shift of 2% of wealth from personal assets to property. Taken together, the adjustments made to the asset composition of male and female wealth holdings now show that women hold 8% more of their wealth in the form of financial assets and 11% less of their wealth as landed property, which, even taking into account the more pronounced difference in liabilities between the sexes, still leaves men with a substantially higher net property percentage. The aggregate adjusted figures for males and females combined indicates that almost exactly half of

TABLE 6: Asset Holdings as a Percentage of Net Capital, Life Assurance at Maturity Value. Males, GB, 1975

Estate Range (£000's)

Asset Category	<1	1-3	3-5	5-10	10-15	15-20	20-50	50-100	100-200	200+	All Estate Classes
Unlisted UK Government Securities	6.4	1.6	1.7	1.4	0.9	1.3	0.8	0.7	0.6	0.8	1.1
Government and Municipal Securities	0.0	0.0	0.4	0.3	0.2	0.5	0.9	1.8	2.2	3.0	0.8
Unlisted Shares	0.8	0.7	0.2	0.2	0.0	-0.1[a]	2.4	8.1	10.4	21.9	3.3
Listed Shares	4.9	1.7	1.3	0.7	0.8	1.8	4.5	8.7	11.7	28.2	4.8
Money on Mortgage	5.5	2.8	1.7	1.2	0.9	1.7	2.3	3.0	3.3	2.3	1.9
Building Society Deposits	5.7	7.9	6.7	5.4	4.3	6.9	6.8	5.3	3.2	1.1	5.4
Insurance Policies	39.4	33.5	30.2	25.7	28.2	27.8	24.4	12.8	4.7	4.7	23.1
Cash and Bank Deposits	31.6	18.2	13.6	7.1	5.1	5.8	5.8	6.0	5.3	9.3	7.2
Household Goods	14.6	6.7	5.4	4.9	3.8	3.8	3.0	2.4	2.4	3.7	3.9
Trade Assets	3.9	0.3	0.8	1.3	0.8	2.5	6.1	9.4	8.3	3.8	3.6
Other Personal Wealth	35.9	26.8	17.7	11.7	7.7	8.2	7.0	8.0	11.1	6.4	10.1
Land	1.1	0.0	0.2	0.3	0.2	1.1	4.1	14.2	18.8	16.7	4.5
Freehold Residential Buildings	17.8	9.2	29.1	49.6	57.4	46.6	41.9	29.4	22.6	9.5	40.5
Leasehold Residential Buildings	0.1	1.6	4.2	5.8	4.1	4.3	2.2	1.3	2.0	0.8	3.3
Other Landed Property	0.6	0.7	0.1	0.0	0.1	0.2	1.0	1.8	2.3	2.6	0.7
Personal Debts	-58.4	-7.7	-3.5	-3.2	-2.5	-3.4	-5.7	-8.3	-7.2	-14.4	-5.6
Property Debts	-10.0	-4.0	-10.0	-12.4	-12.2	-9.0	-7.7	-4.5	-1.7	-0.4	-8.5
All Financial Assets	94.2	66.4	55.8	41.9	40.5	45.9	48.1	46.2	41.5	71.2	47.5
Gross Personal Wealth	148.7	100.2	79.8	59.8	52.9	60.2	64.2	66.0	63.3	85.1	65.0
Gross Landed Property	19.6	11.5	33.7	55.8	61.8	52.1	49.3	46.8	45.6	29.6	49.1
Net Personal Wealth	90.4	92.5	76.3	56.6	50.4	56.9	58.5	57.7	56.1	70.7	59.4
Net Landed Property	9.6	7.5	23.7	43.4	49.6	43.1	41.5	42.3	43.9	29.3	40.6

Note: a. Negative values can result from Inland Revenue practice regarding the revision of provisional estate valuations See, for example, Inland Revenue Statistics (1977), Table 106 (especially footnote 3).

TABLE 7: Asset Holdings as a Percentage of Net Capital, Adjusted Life Insurance Valuation. Males, GB, 1975

Estate Range (£000's)

Asset Category	<1	1-3	3-5	5-10	10-15	15-20	20-50	50-100	100-200	200+	All Estate Classes
Unlisted UK Government Securities	9.3	2.2	2.2	1.7	1.2	1.7	1.0	0.7	0.6	0.8	1.3
Government and Municipal Securities	0.1	0.0	0.5	0.3	0.2	0.7	1.1	2.0	2.3	3.1	1.0
Unlisted Shares	1.1	1.0	0.3	0.3	0.1	-0.1	3.0	8.9	10.8	22.7	4.0
Listed Shares	7.2	2.3	1.7	0.9	1.1	2.3	5.6	9.6	12.1	29.2	5.8
Money on Mortgage	7.9	3.9	2.1	1.5	1.2	2.3	2.9	3.3	3.4	2.4	2.3
Building Society Deposits	8.4	10.9	9.0	6.8	5.5	8.9	8.5	5.8	3.3	1.1	6.6
Insurance Policies	11.3	8.3	7.1	6.2	7.2	7.3	6.6	3.7	1.8	1.1	5.8
Cash and Bank Deposits	46.2	25.1	18.1	8.9	6.7	7.5	7.3	6.7	5.4	9.6	8.8
Household Goods	21.4	9.2	7.2	6.2	5.0	4.8	3.7	2.6	2.4	3.8	4.8
Trade Assets	5.7	0.4	1.1	1.6	1.1	3.2	7.5	10.4	8.6	3.9	4.4
Other Personal Wealth	52.7	37.0	23.6	14.7	10.1	10.4	8.6	8.8	11.4	6.6	12.2
Land	1.6	0.0	0.3	0.4	0.3	1.4	5.1	15.7	19.3	17.3	5.5
Freehold Residential Buildings	26.1	12.7	38.6	62.6	74.2	59.8	51.8	32.5	23.3	9.9	49.5
Leasehold Residential Buildings	0.2	2.1	5.6	7.3	5.3	5.5	2.7	1.4	2.1	0.8	4.1
Other Landed Property	0.8	0.9	0.1	0.1	0.1	0.2	1.3	2.1	2.4	2.7	1.0
Personal Debts	-85.4	-10.6	-4.6	-4.0	-3.3	-4.3	-7.0	-9.2	-7.4	-14.9	-6.8
Property Debts	-14.6	-5.5	-13.3	-15.6	-15.7	-11.6	-9.6	-4.9	-1.8	-0.4	-10.4
All Financial Assets	91.5	53.7	41.2	26.7	23.1	30.5	35.9	40.6	39.7	70.1	35.7
Gross Personal Wealth	171.3	100.3	73.1	49.2	39.1	49.0	55.7	62.5	62.2	84.6	57.1
Gross Landed Property	28.7	15.8	44.8	70.4	79.9	66.9	60.9	51.7	47.0	30.8	60.1
Net Personal Wealth	85.9	89.7	68.5	45.2	35.9	44.6	48.7	53.3	54.8	69.6	50.3
Net Landed Property	14.1	10.3	31.5	54.8	64.1	55.4	51.3	46.7	45.2	30.4	49.7

total wealth is held in the form of landed property, a somewhat different picture than suggested by the unadjusted data.

The impact of life policy revaluation on the relation--ship between asset holdings and wealth level can be seen by comparing the data for males in Tables 6 and 7. Here it would certainly not be appropriate to apply the same adjustment factor to all assets (other than life insurance) at all wealth levels, although within each wealth range it does appear that all asset proportions are adjusted upwards by roughly the same multiple.

As far as the individual asset types are concerned, it is difficult to see any obvious changes in the relationship of holdings to wealth level induced by the adjustment. However the impact is noticeable on all financial assets, where the variation with wealth is more pronounced in Table 7. In addition, property becomes significantly more important in the portfolio for levels of wealth between £5,000 and £50,000. Within this range more capital is held in the form of property (net of debts) than in the form of personal assets (also net of debts), reversing the pattern obtained from Table 6. Also noticeable is the importance of property for men in the £10,000 - £15,000 wealth class, even when large property debts are taken into account.

Finally, the age group variation in the proportion of wealth held in financial assets is provided in Table 8. When life insurance is valued at maturity there seems to be little variation in these percentages either with age or sex. If anything, the figures suggest a decrease in the importance of financial assets over the younger age groups, followed by an increase in importance after retirement. After revaluation of life insurance, the tendency for women to hold a higher proportion of their portfolio in the form of financial assets is apparent for all age groups except the youngest. In addition there is greater variation in the percentages with age, and little evidence to suggest that financial assets initially decline in importance as people become older.

5. *SUMMARY AND CONCLUSIONS*

Information on personal wealth in the UK is obtained primarily from estate duty data, from which estimates of the asset holdings of living persons can be made using

TABLE 8: Holdings of Financial Assets as a Percentage of Net Capital, By Age Group

	Age Group								
	18-24	25-34	35-44	45-54	55-64	65-74	75-84	85+	All Ages
Life Insurance Valued at Maturity									
Males, GB, 1975	71.4	58.1	44.7	40.4	41.0	45.7	48.8	54.7	4.75
Males, UK, 1976	72.1	60.5	46.3	41.6	43.0	47.4	51.7	59.3	49.5
Females, GB, 1975	57.9	44.1	37.3	41.4	46.3	48.2	54.5	61.4	46.1
Females, UK, 1976	54.3	47.4	44.2	41.6	49.0	50.9	55.1	63.1	48.7
Adjusted Life Insurance Valuation									
Males, GB, 1975	34.1	31.7	29.9	33.2	38.5	45.0	48.5	54.5	35.7
Males, UK, 1976	47.9	34.4	31.8	34.5	40.8	46.9	51.5	59.2	38.0
Females, GB, 1975	43.5	34.3	32.7	38.5	45.3	47.9	54.4	61.3	43.5
Females, UK, 1976	29.4	36.4	38.5	39.6	48.1	50.6	55.0	63.1	45.9

the estate multiplier method. One of the consequences of the direct application of this method is an overvaluation of life insurance policies. This occurs because the maturity value appearing in the estate figures is also assigned to all life policies held by the living population. A comparison with the total value of life policies given in the personal sector balance sheets suggest that this inappropriate assignment of maturity values tend to inflate estate multiplier wealth by £37.5 billion were it not for other compensating factors relating to the valuation of life policies for estate duty purposes.

Despite the quantitative significance of the life insurance overvaluation, very little is known about the distortions it causes in the published information on personal wealth holdings. This paper has concentrated on two important issues; the relationship between wealth holdings and age; and the composition of the asset portfolio of individuals. The impact of life insurance valuation on each of these has been examined by comparing the patterns obtained when life insurance is valued at maturity with those resulting from a reduction in life policy values to an equity basis.

For the cross section age wealth profiles the adjustments have a noticeable effect. The profiles become steeper over the younger age groups, indicating a faster rate of wealth accumulation, and the peak in the cross section pattern shifts upwards towards the age of retirement. However both the unadjusted and adjusted sets of profiles subsequently rise again after the age of 70.

The asset composition of wealth holdings was investigated using 17 broad types of assets and debts. The revaluation of life insurance tends to raise the shares of other assets by a factor of 20-25% in the case of men and by around 5% for women. Landed property becomes a larger proportion of total wealth and is subsequently higher in the wealth holdings of men, a feature not apparent in the unadjusted data. Furthermore the substitution of equity values for life policies reveals significant variation in the importance of financial assets for the different sex, age and wealth groups, which again was less pronounced with the unadjusted data.

APPENDIX: Asset Category Definitions

Asset Types	*Rows*	*Inland Revenue Asset Categories*[a]
Basic Categories		
Unlisted UK Government Securities	(1)	1,2
Government & Municipal Securities	(2)	3-10
Unlisted Shares	(3)	11,12
Listed Shares	(4)	13-15, 17-19
Money on Mortgage	(5)	20,22,23
Building Society Deposits	(6)	21
Insurance Policies	(7)	26
Cash & Bank Deposits	(8)	27-30
Household Goods	(9)	25
Trade Assets	(10)	31-37
Other Personal Wealth	(11)	24,30A,39-41
Land	(12)	49,50
Freehold Residential Buildings	(13)	51
Leasehold Residential Buildings	(14)	53
Other Landed Property	(15)	52,54-57
Deductions against Personal Wealth	(16)	43,46
Deductions against Landed Property	(17)	59,60
Composite Categories		
All Financial Assets	(1)-(8)	1-23,26-30
Gross Personal Wealth	(1)-(11)	1-41
Gross Landed Property	(12)-(15)	49-57
Net Personal Wealth	(1)-(11),(16)	1-41,43,46
Net Landed Property	(12)-(15),(17)	49-57,59,60

Notes: [a] See *Inland Revenue Statistics*(1977), Table 103.

REFERENCES

Astin, J.A. (1975). The Distribution of Wealth and the Relevance of Age. *Statistical News*, February, 1-28.

Atkinson, A.B. (1971). The Distribution of Wealth and the Individual Life Cycle. *Oxford Economic Papers* 23, 239-254.

Atkinson, A.B. and A.J. Harrison. (1978). *Distribution of Personal Wealth in Britain*. Cambridge: Cambridge University Press.

Central Statistical Office. (1978). Personal Sector Balance Sheets. *Economic Trends 291.*

Davies, J.B. and A.F. Shorrocks. (1978). Assessing the Quantitative Importance of Inheritance in the Distribution of Wealth. *Oxford Economic Papers* 30, 138-149.

Dunn, A.T. and P.D.R.B. Hoffman. (1978). The Distribution of Personal Wealth. *Economic Trends* 301, 101-118.

Flemming, J.S. (1979). The Effects of Earnings Inequality, Imperfect Capital Markets and Dynastic Altruism on the Distribution of Wealth in Life Cycle Models. *Economica* 46, 363-380.

Inland Revenue Statistics. (1977). London: HMSO.

Oulton, N. (1976). Inheritance and the Distribution of Wealth. *Oxford Economic Papers* 28, 86-101.

Revell, J.R.S. (1967). *The Wealth of the Nation*. Cambridge: Cambridge University Press.

Royal Commission on the Distribution of Income and Wealth. (1975). *Report No.1. Initial Report on the Standing Reference*. London: HMSO.

Royal Commission on the Distribution of Income and Wealth. (1979). *Report No.7. Fourth Report on the Standing Reference*. London: HMSO.

Shorrocks, A.F. (1975). The Age-Wealth Relationship: A Cross Section and Cohort Analysis. *Review of Economics and Statistics* 57, 155-163.

FOOTNOTES

1. This study was undertaken as part of the SSRC financed Programme in Quantitative Economics at the LSE. I should like to thank the Inland Revenue for supplying the disaggregated data on asset holdings. Mr Bugden, Mr Dunn and Mr Hoffman were very helpful

in answering my queries relating to the data and provided valuable comments on an earlier draft of the paper. Richard Glendinning provided extremely valuable research and computing assistance.

2. Dunn and Hoffman (1978), Table A, p.117. That the overall Gini value should show little change is not surprising. To the extent that life insurance adjustment reduces wealth holdings at all levels in the same proportion, the Gini will remain unaffected. The change that does take place arises because those at the top of the distribution tend to hold a smaller proportion of their assets in the form of life insurance, a pattern that is reinforced by the fact that they are predominantly women and in the older age groups. Thus the adjustment reduces their wealth by a lower factor than average. This leads to a downward shift in the Lorenz curve, and an increase in the Gini value. This is partially offset in the Dunn and Hoffman calculations by adjustments made for insurance equity missing from the estate data (relating, for example, to group life cover) which have an equalising impact.
3. The first report of the Royal Commission (1975, Table 48) provides a time series of aggregate asset holdings. The value of life policies as a percentage of net wealth varies between 11.9% and 16.9% over the period 1960-1973, and shows a slight upward trend over time.
4. The data consists of estimates of the number of individual owners and the total value of holdings of specific types of assets, disaggregated by sex, age (10 categories) and wealth range (10 classes). Some 65 different basic types of asset and debts are identified, as well as 38 composite asset categories. The data relate to persons above age 18 in Great Britain during the calendar year 1975 (approximately) and to those in the United Kingdom during 1976. The coverage of these populations is not complete since a large number of small estates do not require probate. This leads to an underrepresentation of lower wealth holders (the data correspond to the "Series A" wealth estimates - see for example *Inland Revenue Statistics*, 1977, Table 114) and may introduce a slight bias into the figures that result from aggregating over age groups and wealth classes, as the implicit weighting of groups may not be correct. Furthermore, there are reasons to suspect that probated estates with low net

estate values (say, less than £5000) are not a random sample of wealthholdings in this range, and this may distort the pattern of asset holdings amongst low wealth holders. (for example, the importance of debts is likely to be exaggerated).

5. The overall figure of 23.1% of Net Capital differs slightly from the 21.9% computed from published sources. The variation may be due to the different geographical regions (Britain versus the UK); to the exclusion of data on those aged below 18 and the "age not known" category from Table 1; and to the "smoothing" adjustments applied to the estate multiplier estimates by the Inland Revenue.
6. Table 1 does not fully reflect the variation in the significance of life policies in asset holdings, since the figure reported in any cell is an average for those estates falling in that age group and estate range, irrespective of whether they included life insurance. Thus, for example, for males aged 18-24, insurance policies account for 59% of the value of estates in the range £20,000-£50,000, but this rises to 83% if estates without life insurance are excluded.
7. These ratios are likely to differ significantly between males and females in a given age group due to the different types of policies chosen. Unfortunately, separate ratios for each of the sexes are not available, so the overall ratios have been applied throughout. This may bias the results, although the direction and quantitative significance of the distortion is difficult to assess. A similar bias may arise if the type of policy chosen is related in some systematic way with the amount of wealth held in forms other than life insurance.
8. This qualification does not apply to the figures for "All Estate Classes".
9. The impression may be misleading because of the inappropriateness of aggregating over age groups when the data has been adjusted: see the earlier comments in the text.
10. The basic reference is Atkinson (1971), but see also Oulton (1976), Davies and Shorrocks (1978) and Flemming (1979).
11. It should be borne in mind that data on cross section age-wealth profiles in a single year are not directly applicable to a theory of asset holdings over the lifetime of individuals. Because the profiles are

expected to be shifting upwards over time due to real growth effects, a hump pattern in the cross section age wealth profile is necessary but not sufficient to ensure a similar pattern for the average experience of a cohort through time: see Shorrocks (1975).

12. There are other explanations of the time trend. The period under consideration was one in which house prices rose rapidly, so the changing relative prices of assets will tend to raise the (relative) average wealth of the young in-so-far as they hold a larger proportion of their wealth in the form of property. Astin (1975, p.28.3) suggests that the trend towards a flatter age pattern was due to this rise in house prices coupled with an increase in home ownership in the younger age groups.
13. An exact Pareto distribution was assumed for inter--polation within each wealth range. This is equivalent to assuming a piecewise linear curve for log F(x) against log x, where x indicates the wealth level and F(x) is the proportion of individuals with wealth greater than x.
14. Percentile values are plotted at the midpoint of the age groups and at 90 years for those over 85.
15. This argument presupposes that individuals regard an entitlement to a pension as a substitute for certain other assets and that their savings behaviour differs from whatever it would have been in the absence of those rights. Imputing the full actuarial value of pension rights essentially assumes that individuals regard them as perfect substitutes for marketable forms of wealth.
16. The average value of state pension rights for various age groups is given in the first report of the Royal Commission (1975, p. 92). These indicate a value to males aged 75-84 of £4,116 compared to £1,860 for those aged 85 and above.
17. One curiosum of wealth distribution data is the number of high wealth holders over 85 years of age when life cycle and tax avoidance arguments would suggest considerably lower amounts would be optimal. Here, for instance, the figures indicate the existence of about 1250 males above 85 with wealth exceeding £90,000.
18. Of course the reverse operates for widowers and although it will be quantitatively less significant, it may contribute to the rise in wealth holdings over

the retirement period. Both retired men and women may also still be inheriting from parents and other relatives.

DISCUSSION: D.M.W.N. HITCHENS

According to the life cycle theory of wealth accumulation, average wealth is expected to rise steadily with age and fall away after retirement as persons draw on savings to finance old age. Some inequality in the wealth distribution as a whole is expected from this, and inequality within age groups is expected because of differences in the pattern of earnings and savings.

Looking at the young age groups in particular - the accumulation of wealth from earnings is not likely to have been carried far and the dominant influence is therefore likely to be inheritance, and gifts intervivos. At the other end of the age spectrum inheritance is also likely to be important - apart from the fact that the wealthy probably live longer they also have more time to collect inheritances (and dissipate them if received early).

Tony Shorrocks has re-examined the wealth-age profile by his downward valuation of life assurance policies from the Inland Revenue use of maturity values to the admittedly more realistic equity values. This has greatest effect on the younger age groups for whom life insurance at death is a large proportion of their wealth - and hence the revised data shows a stronger life-cycle effect.

Since I believe that inheritance rather than life-cycle effects dominate the inequality in the distribution it is worth spending a moment discussing the strength of that relationship.

The work that Colin Harbury and I (1979) undertook can be summarised very quickly and easily:

> Two thirds of male top wealth leavers were preceded by wealthy fathers. This proportion has not changed much this century. Lower down the wealth scale the association is still strong and nearly all such persons were preceded minimally by fathers who were in the top half of the wealth distribution, and when the wealth of other relatives such as fathers-in-law, grandfathers and so forth are brought into the picture the relationship becomes stronger. In the case of wealthy women 95% were preceded by wealthy fathers or husbands or both.

And intermarriage between the rich took place in three fifths of the cases we looked at[1].

Moving to the conjectural. Shorrocks'adjustment is only one of a number suggested by Dunn and Hoffman (1978) to improve wealth data in order to match wealth estimated by mortality multipliers with those of the balance sheet of total wealth.

These include the allocation of wealth between the population included in the estimates derived from mortality multipliers - and the rest (the excluded population); and the limitations of the estate duty multiplier method itself.

Within the included population a number of problems arise. Tony examined the overvaluation of life policies and drew attention to the undervaluation of consumer durables though the quantitative effect of the latter on the age-wealth profile has not been commented on.

I limit myself to a comment on the mortality multipliers themselves. These blow up the wealth of those dying in any year to that of the living in that year by assuming that those dying in a particular age, social class, sex category are a random sample of the living population.

Dunn and Hoffmann point to a category of mortality that might not reasonably reflect those with living wealth. These are persons dying of chronic illnesses who might be expected to dissave as death approaches, and whose wealth would therefore certainly under-represent that of the living.

There is another aspect of this strand of thinking. Social class, on which mortality multipliers are based reflect similarities in the living conditions of different groups of people - their life styles and environment. Mortality is also associated with individuals' occupations - and if occupational mortality overrides the social class categories in particular age groups - the wealth of the dead no longer fully reflects the wealth of the living.

There is some evidence in the recent Registrar General's report on Occupational Mortality (1978) which indicates that death standardised by social class is more prevalent in certain occupational orders - for example those employed in agriculture, engineering and construction.

In the group of persons most affected by Tony Shorrocks' adjustment - those aged below 35 - the most likely cause of death is from accidents (including poisonings and violence). Though a large proportion of these are caused by traffic accidents a significant proportion are related to accidents at work. Those occupational orders more prone to death from all causes among the young include for example - agriculture, construction, transport, the armed forces etc. - and in as much as they leave wealth and are expected to have different wealth and income profiles from the less prone - professional and technical, administrators and managers, paper printing, etc. - they cannot be expected to be randomly representative of the living population.

A related point is that death from accidents may attract insurance benefits over and above that of the individual's own life policy and would tend to exaggerate the expected wealth of the living. Today's North Sea oil rig disaster is indeed a sad case in point, and considerable compensation is expected to be paid.

Our own research tends to suggest that inheritance among the rich is related to certain occupational orders e.g. agriculture, food, drink and tobacco, metal manufacture etc., while self-made wealth is related to others, e.g. chemicals, metal goods nes, clothing[2].

One wonders whether the necessarily small number of observations among the young age groups provides a satisfactory sample from which to estimate the wealth of the young. The Royal Commission's (1975) evidence of a shifting of the age wealth profile from one which is steep to one which is flat - over the period of the mid fifties to the early seventies - may reflect such data problems.

In summary I believe inequality in wealth is largely due to inheritance and only to a small extent to life-cycle effects. And second, much more detailed attention should be drawn to the uncertainties which surround the underlying data used to estimate the living wealth especially of the young.

REFERENCES

Dunn, A.T. and Hoffman, P.D.R.B. (1978), The Distribution of Personal Wealth, *Economic Trends, 301, 101-118.*

Harbury, C.D. and Hitchens, D.M.W.N., (1979), *Inheritance and Wealth Inequality in Britain,* Allen and Unwin.

Registrar General for England and Wales (1978), *Decennial Supplement: Occupational Mortality,* London: HMSO.

Royal Commission on the Distribution of Income and Wealth (1975), *Initial report on the standing reference,* London: HMSO.

FOOTNOTES

1. The proportions given here depend on the definition of having a wealthy father. See Harbury and Hitchens (1979) chapter 3 for different proportions arising from different criteria.

2. The strength of the relationship is greater in some occupations than others. See Harbury and Hitchens (1979) chapter 6.

7. UNEMPLOYMENT EQUILIBRIUM WHEN PRODUCTION IS A FUNCTION OF AVERAGE HOURS AND NUMBER OF WORKERS

P. Madden

Introduction[1]

The literature on fixprice equilibrium with rationing has provided a number of insights into the foundations of employment theory [5,8]. Specifically it shows how price rigidities and quantity constraints may lead to an equilibrium with persistent excess supply of labour. Probably the worst assumption used in these models is that the price rigidities are exogenously given. However, we are not at all concerned with the most important issue of relaxing this assumption in this paper. It is another issue which occupies us.

This is the fact that the rationing literature fails to provide any convincing reasons for unemployment in the everyday sense of the word (i.e. some workers work, some do not). The approach of Malinvaud [8] for instance is to assume that an excess supply of labour is rationed amongst workers by a queuing rationing mechanism. No justification for this mechanism is given, however. Moreover it is not at all essential for any existence argument. One may replace it with a uniform rationing assumption and generate equilibria as Malinvaud does but the only unemployment (in our sense) equilibria will then involve zero employment. We therefore define non-trivial unemployment equilibrium (NUE) as an equilibrium in which some workers work and some workers do not work. The objective of this paper is to explain NUE.

We will be concerned throughout with a very simple economy. Since the phenomenon we are interested in is a labour market phenomenon we shall consider a self-contained economy which consists essentially of a labour market. Specifically there is a capitalist and a number of workers. The capitalist can produce a single output from inputs of workers' labour services and retains profits in the form of output; workers can supply their labour and consume the output. As threatened above, we shall use the assumption of an exogenously given price system. The paper can then be viewed in two parts.

First we look in detail at a standard convex model using the typical fixprice equilibrium concept, Dreze equilibrium [2,4]. The search is for convincing reasons for NUE. Some positive results are obtained, along with rather more negative results. While the positive results are of interest, in the light of the negative results they hardly constitute a convincing explanation of why the economy should suffer from NUE.

We therefore turn to some casual (and some not so casual) empiricism regarding labour markets to suggest a non-convex technology (via a production function where production is a function of average hours and number of workers) and alternative equilibrium concepts to Dreze equilibrium. The outcome seems much more promising as a basis for a theory of unemployment.

The convex economy

There is one capitalist who produces a single output from the labour services of the n workers in the economy according to a given technology. The capitalist is indicated by a superscript 0 and the workers are indicated by superscripts $i = 1,\ldots n$. Output is denoted by a subscript 0 and the labour services of the ith worker are denoted by a subscript i. z^i_j then denotes the net trade by agent i in good j;

$$z^i = (z^i_0,\ldots z^i_n) \text{ and } z = (z^0,\ldots z^n).$$

The set of feasible trades for the capitalist is denoted T^0. We assume:

$$T^0 = \{z^0 \mid z^0_i \geq 0,\quad i = 1,\ldots n;\ z^0_0 \geq -f(z^0_1,\ldots z^0_n)\} \qquad (1)$$

The first part of this definition of T^0 says that the capitalist cannot supply labour services of any type. The production function, $f(z^0_1,\ldots z^0_n)$ indicates the maximum output the capitalist can produce given the vector of inputs $(z_1^0,\ldots z_n^0)$; the second part of the definition of T^0 says that the capitalist cannot supply more output than he can produce. The production function in this convex economy satisfies the following restrictions:

$$f(z_1^0,\ldots z_n^0) \text{ is a continuous, concave, increasing function and } f(0) = 0. \tag{2}$$

Given a net trade z^0, the capitalist can achieve a net output consumption of $f(z_1^0,\ldots z_n^0) + z_0^0$. The utility derived by the capitalist from the net trade z^0 is a continuous, increasing function of his net output consumption:

$$u^0(z^0) = u^0\left[f(z_1^0,\ldots z_n^0) + z_0^0\right] \text{ and is continuous and increasing in } f(z_1^0,\ldots z_n^0) + z_0^0 \tag{3}$$

The set of feasible net trades for the *i*th worker is denoted T^i. We assume that worker *i* can supply up to *a* (> *0*) units of the *i*th labour service but can supply no other good. Hence we assume throughout that T^i is a closed, convex unbounded subset of $\hat{T}^i = \left\{z^i \mid 0 \geq z_i^i \geq -a \text{ and } z_j^i \geq 0\ j \neq i\right\}$. We also assume $0 \in T^i$.

The utility derived by the *i*th worker from the net trade z^i is a continuous, strictly quasi-concave and increasing function of z_0^i and z_i^i only:

$$u^i(z^i) = u^i(z_0^i, z_i^i) \text{ and is continuous, strictly quasi-concave and increasing in } z_0^i \text{ and } z_i^i. \tag{4}$$

Now *0* must be in the boundary of T^i and so discontinuities in workers' Walrasian excess demand functions are not ruled out by the assumptions made so far about T^i. To avoid this problem the assumption we actually make about T^i is:

$$T^i = \left\{ z^i \mid z^i \in \hat{T}^i \text{ and } u^i(z_0^i, z_i^i) \geq u^i(0) \right\} \tag{5}$$

Figure 1 illustrates the typical values of z^i which can satisfy this assumption:

Figure 1

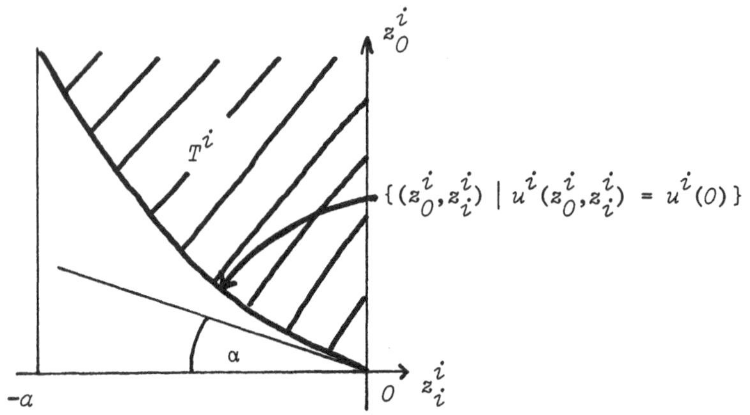

$u^i(0)$ is referred to as the ith workers' minimum utility level. R^i (= tan α in Figure 1) is the maximum real wage at which the ith workers' Walrasian demand is zero; this is referred to as the ith workers' subsistence or reservation wage. Under the assumptions made, R^i is uniquely defined and non-negative; it may be zero.

We complete the description of the convex economy with some definitions and an assumption.

The net trade z is feasible if $\sum_{i=0}^{n} z^i = 0$ and if $z^i \in T^i$, $i = 0,1,\ldots n$.

The net trade z is Pareto efficient if it is feasible and if there exists no other feasible net trade $\hat{z}$ such that $u^i(\hat{z}^i) > u^i(z^i)\ \forall i$.

We say that the ith worker is employed in the net trade

z if $z_i^0 > 0$. The level of employment in the net trade z is the number of employed workers in z.

We say the net trade z involves non-trivial unemployment if the level of employment in z exceeds zero but is less than n.

A non-trivial unemployment equilibrium is an equilibrium net trade z (in some sense) which involves non-trivial unemployment.

We make the following assumption:

The net trade $z = 0$ is Pareto inefficient. (6)

In the next section we assume (1) - (6) without further mention. Economies satisfying (1) - (6) are referred to as convex economies.

Non-trivial unemployment equilibrium in the convex economy

For completeness, let us start by looking at the special case of Dreze equilibrium where no quantity constraints are binding. In other words let us look for NUE in Walrasian equilibrium.

A Walrasian equilibrium exists for the convex economy and the Walrasian equilibrium net trade is Pareto efficient. Since 0 is a Pareto efficient net trade for the set of workers, it then follows from (6) that the Walrasian equilibrium net trade involves some employment ($z_i^i \neq 0$ some $i = 1,\ldots n$). It need not be the case however that all workers are employed in the Walrasian equilibrium. Suppose we have the following situation.

Let $\theta_i(z)$, $i = 1,\ldots n$ be defined as follows for any feasible net trade z where $z_i^0 > 0$:

$$\theta_i(z) = \frac{f(z_1^0,\ldots z_{i-1}^0, z_i^0, z_{i+1}^0 \ldots z_n^0) - f(z_1^0,\ldots z_{i-1}^0, 0, z_{i+1}^0 \ldots z_n^0)}{z_i^0}$$

$\theta_i(z)$ is a measure of the "marginal product" of the ith worker in the net trade z. Consider the assumption:

For some i, $\theta_i(z) \leq R^i$ for all feasible net trades z. (7)

If (7) is satisfied by worker i, it is obvious that this worker will be unemployed in the Walrasian equilibria of the convex economy. We therefore have:

Proposition 1 If (7) is satisfied all Walrasian equilibria are NUE.

All we have here is that workers with a very low productivity or a very high reservation wage will be unemployed in Walrasian equilibrium. This is of course well known. Moreover the reaction of most economists seems to be that this type of unemployment is not something to worry about, that it is inevitable in some sense. The reason for mentioning Proposition 1 here is that it is not clear why such a view should be taken. Tautologically, if society's sole objective is Walrasian equilibrium then, of course, we should not concern ourselves with this type of unemployment; the economists' recommendation is non-interference in Walrasian equilibrium. However, if the objective is maximum employment amongst Pareto efficient allocations (for instance) even in our simple capitalist-worker economy, examples of economies whose Walrasian equilibria do not meet this objective are easily found; the economists' recommendation would then be that the government should interfere with the Walrasian equilibrium. The point is simply that we cannot dismiss the unemployment of Proposition 1 without specifying the grounds for such dismissal; and once we specify objectives relatively non-controversial objectives (such as the one above) may make this unemployment in Walrasian equilibrium a matter for concern and intervention. However, I have nothing further to add to this discussion at this stage and I avoid these issues in the rest of the paper. In particular, I move on to an economy where there can be no Walrasian equilibrium which is a NUE and look for reasons for NUE via exogenous price rigidities. This is the identical worker economy defined as follows:

Let $m(z_1^0, \ldots z_n^0)$ be any n vector formed by permuting the elements of $(z_1^0, \ldots z_n^0)$.

(a) $f(z_1^0, \ldots z_n^0) = f\left[m(z_1^0, \ldots z_n^0)\right]$ for all permutations

$m(z_1^0, \ldots z_n^0)$. (8)

(b) $u^1(.) = u^2(.) = \ldots = u^n(.)$

This assumption requires that all workers be identical from the viewpoint of production ((a)) and in terms of their characteristics ((b)). Now from (6) some worker (say i) works in a Walrasian equilibrium net trade z. If some worker is not employed in this Walrasian equilibrium (worker j, say) then in order that $z^0 \in z^0(p)^2$ (where p is the Walrasian price vector) we must have $p_j \geq p_i$. On the other hand since i and j have the same preferences, $z_j^j \neq 0$ since $z_i^i \neq 0$. Thus:

Proposition 2 If (8) is satisfied no Walrasian equilibrium is NUE.

So we turn to Dreze equilibrium proper. The exogenously given price vector is $\bar{p} : \bar{p}_0 = 1, \bar{p}_i \geq 0, \forall i$.

Quantity constraints may operate on demand or supply of each labour service. Since there is only one potential supplier and only one potential demander of each labour service we denote the vector of quantity constraints on labour supply simply as $\underline{G} = (\underline{G}_1, \ldots \underline{G}_n)$ and the vector of quantity constraints on labour demand simply as $\bar{G} = (\bar{G}_1, \ldots \bar{G}_n)$.

Let $z^0(\bar{p}, \bar{G}, \underline{G})$ denote the set of solutions to the problem:

$$max\ u^0(z^0) \text{ subject to } z^0 \in T^0, \sum_{j=0}^{n} p_j z_j^0 \leq 0 \quad \text{and}$$

$$z_j^0 \leq \bar{G}_j, \; j = 1, \ldots n.$$

For $i = 1, \ldots n$ let $z^i(\bar{p}, \bar{G}, \underline{G})$ denote the set of solutions to the problem:

$$\max u^i(z^i) \text{ subject to } z^i \in T^i,\ \sum_{j=0}^{n} \bar{p}_j z^i_j \leq 0 \text{ and } z^i_i \geq \underline{G}_i.$$

Then:

A Dreze equilibrium relative to the rigidities $\bar{p} = (\bar{p}_1, \ldots \bar{p}_n)$ is $\bar{G}$, $\underline{G}$ and z such that:

(i) $z^i \in z^i(\bar{p}, \underline{G}, \bar{G}),\ \forall_i$

(ii) $\sum_{i=0}^{n} z^i = 0$

(iii) if $\bar{G}_i = z^0_i$ then $\underline{G}_i < z^i_i$, $i = 1 \ldots n$

(iv) if $\underline{G}_i = z^i_i$ then $\bar{G}_i > z^0_i$.

Here (iii) and (iv) are conditions which ensure that at most one side of any market is "rationed".

It is in fact very easy to generate Dreze equilibria which are NUE if we allow differing wage rates among the workers. Setting the wage for some workers sufficiently high and for others sufficiently low will lead to NUE provided there is a Pareto improvement on no trade for the capitalist and some proper subset of the workers. However, an explanation of NUE which relies on differing exogenously given wage rigidities for identical workers seems unconvincing. From now on we therefore assume:

$$\bar{p}_1 = \bar{p}_2 = \ldots = \bar{p}_n. \tag{9}$$

So we now turn to the identical worker economy (8) with identical wage rigidities (9). We first show that there is a large subset of such economies for which there are no Dreze equilibria which are NUE.

Let us make the following additional (to (2)) assumptions about the production function

$$f(z^0_1, \ldots z^0_n) \text{ is homothetic} \tag{10}$$

$f(z_1^0, \ldots z_n^0)$ is not quasi-convex. (11)

The homotheticity assumption is not essential but simplifies the argument. Since $f(.)$ is concave it is quasi-concave: assumptions (10) and (11) then merely ensure that the isoquants of $f(.)$ are not linear. Given (8) and (9) it is then easy to see that we cannot have Dreze equilibria which are NUE as follows

(8), (9), (10) and (11) imply:

either (a) $z^0 \varepsilon\ z^0(\bar{p}) \Rightarrow z_i^0 = 0,\ i = 1, \ldots n$

or (b) there is no $z^0\ \varepsilon\ z^0(\bar{p})$ with $z_i^0 = 0$, some $i = 1, \ldots n$.

If we are to have a Dreze equilibrium relative to $\bar{p}$ which is NUE we must have (b). But we must also then have $z_i^i(\bar{p}) =$ 0 some $i = 1, \ldots n$. From (8), $z_i^i(\bar{p}) = 0\ \forall_i = 1, \ldots n$ and we cannot have NUE. So:

Proposition 3 If (8), (9), (10) and (11) are satisfied then there are no Dreze equilibria which are NUE.

Hence the only way Dreze equilibria which are NUE can be generated for the identical worker economy (8) with identical wage rigidities (9), given our simplifying assumption (10), is if (11) is negated:

$f(z_1^0, \ldots z_n^0)$ is quasi-convex (12)

Given the concavity of $f(.)$ ((2)), (12) now implies linear isoquants. Or:

Assumptions (8), (10) and (12) (plus (2)) imply $f(z_1^0, \ldots z_n^0) = g(\sum_{i=1}^{n} z_i^0)$ where $g(.)$ is a continuous concave, increasing function and $g(0) = 0$. (13)

A production function of the form $g(.)$ here is assumed by Malinvaud [8]. He makes use of the fact that there are Dreze equilibria in which the rationing mechanism is of the queuing variety. This implies:

<u>Proposition 4</u> If (8), (9), (10) and (12) are satisfied then there exists $\bar{p}$ and a Dreze equilibrium relative to $\bar{p}$ which is a NUE.

On the other hand there are Dreze equilibria in which the rationing is uniform. This implies:

<u>Proposition 5</u> Assume (8), (9), (10) and (12) and suppose $\bar{p}$ is such that there is a Dreze equilibrium relative to $\bar{p}$ which is a NUE. Then there is also a Dreze equilibrium relative to $\bar{p}$ which is not a NUE.

So to generate Dreze equilibria which are NUE for the economy now being considered the imposition of the apparently totally *ad hoc* assumption of a queuing rationing mechanism is necessary. We finally demonstrate a result which shows why, in a certain sense, queuing (and NUE) is indeed the likely outcome. We do this by considering a stability concept for net trades and observing that for "large" economies the only stable Dreze equilibria in which workers are constrained are NUE. The stability concept is inspired by Grandmont, Laroque and Younes [6] and is as follows.

A coalition S can <u>block</u> the net trade z at p if

(a) $\exists$ a (possibly empty) set of agents T disjoint from S and a net trade $\hat{z}$ such that

(i) $\sum_{j=0}^{n} \bar{p}_j \hat{z}_j^i = 0$, $\hat{z}^i \in T^i$, $\forall_i \in S \cup T$

(ii) $\sum_{i \in S \cup T} \hat{z}^i = 0$

(iii) $u^i(\hat{z}^i) > u^i(z^i)$, $\forall\, i \in S$

(iv) $u^i(\hat{z}^i) = u^i(z^i)$, $\forall\, i \in T$

and

(b) if $\overline{S \cup T}$ is non-empty then for every $V = u \cup T'$ where

T' is some non-empty subset of T and u is a subset of $\overline{S \cup T}$, $\nexists$ a net trade $\hat{\hat{z}}$ such that

(i) $\sum_{j\,0}^{n} \bar{p}_j \hat{\hat{z}}^i_j = 0,\ \hat{\hat{z}}^i \in T^i,\ \forall\, i \in u \cup T'$

(ii) $\sum_{i \in u \cup T'} \hat{\hat{z}}^i = 0$

(iii) $u^i(\hat{\hat{z}}^i) \geq u^i(z^i),\ \forall\, i \in u \cup T'$.

z is said to be a stable net trade at $\bar{p}$ if $\Sigma \bar{p}_j z^i_j = 0,\ \forall_i$ and if there is no blocking coalition to z at $\bar{p}$.

For S to block z therefore requires S to find another set of agents T and a trade feasible for $S \cup T$ which makes all members of S better off and leaves all members of T at the same utility level. Furthermore it must be the case that no subset of those agents left out ($\overline{S \cup T}$) can suggest a counter-proposal to any subset of T which is feasible and at least as good as z for all parties to this counter-proposal. It is not at all clear that this procedure mimics real labour market mechanisms; it does give the desired result however.

Let us make the following assumption for convenience:

$g(.)$ is strictly concave and bounded (14)

The capitalist total demand for labour, $D(\bar{p})$ is then a well behaved function. If $D(\bar{p}) + \sum_{i=1}^{n} z^i_i(\bar{p}) < 0$ we have excess Walrasian supply of labour and these prices are those at which the Dreze equilibria involve worker rationing. We further consider only those $\bar{p}$ at which $D(\bar{p}) > 0$ and $z^i_i(\bar{p}) < 0$ (otherwise all Dreze equilibria are trivial). The question is: do stability considerations favour any particular type of rationing mechanism at such prices? We consider replications of the original economy to answer this.

The t-fold replica of the original economy is comprised

of $t(n+1)$ agents indicated by (i,q) where $i = 0,\ldots n$ and $q = 1,\ldots t$. Two agents with the same index i have the same u^i and T^i. Now clearly if z is a Dreze equilibrium at $\bar{p}$ for the original economy then the t-fold replica of z is a Dreze equilibrium at $\bar{p}$ for the t-fold replica economy. The question now becomes: do all or any of the Dreze equilibria of the original economy give rise to t-fold replications which are stable in the t-fold replica economy for all t?

Any Dreze equilibrium at $\bar{p}$ for the original economy is such that each worker belongs to one of three types:

$$A_1 = \left\{ i \mid z^i = z^i(\bar{p}) \right\}$$

$$A_2 = \left\{ i \mid z^i = 0 \right\}$$

$$A_3 = \left\{ i \mid 0 < | z^i | < | z^i(\bar{p}) | \right\}$$

Given our restrictions on $\bar{p}$ the only possible types of Dreze equilibrium at $\bar{p}$ are those in which the non-empty A_i's are:

(i) A_1, A_2 ; (ii) A_3 ; (iii) A_1, A_3 ; (iv) A_2, A_3 ;

(v) A_1, A_2, A_3.

With one further assumption we show that the only type of Dreze equilibrium at $\bar{p}$ with the required stability is (i). The assumption is that $\bar{p}$ is such that the capitalist must employ at least two workers to meet his demand; or $D(\bar{p}) > -a$.

We consider each type of Dreze equilibria ((i) - (v)) in turn.

(i) Let z be a Dreze equilibrium trade of type (i). A blocking coalition S can include only workers of type A_2 since the capitalist and all other workers are making their best trade at $\bar{p}$ in z. But since z is feasible for $\bar{S}$ requirement (b) for blocking by S is always violated. So no coalition can block and z is always stable.

(ii) Let z be a Dreze equilibrium trade of type (ii) and consider its t-fold replications in the t-fold replica economy. Let S be the coalition of all workers in the t-fold replica economy except the first worker of type 1; let z_{11}^{1} (z_{01}^{1}) denote the labour supply (output demand) of this worker in z. If each worker in S supplies an additional amount of labour equal to $\frac{z_{11}^{1}}{nt - 1}$ and demands additional output equal to $\frac{z_{01}^{1}}{nt - 1}$ then the net trades implied are feasible for $S \cup T$ if T is the set of capitalists. Moreover for n large enough the net trade then satisfies (a) of the blocking definition. The one worker left out of S cannot make a counter-proposal to any subset of T since $D(\bar{p}) > -a$. So (b) is also satisfied and S blocks.

The arguments for (iii), (iv) and (v) are similar to that for (ii). The blocking coalition required in each case is:

(iii) $S = \{\text{all workers of type } A_3\}$

$T = \{\text{all capitalists plus all workers of type } A_1 \text{ except one}\}$

(iv) $S = \{\text{all workers except one of type } A_3\}$

$T = \{\text{all capitalists}\}$

(v) $S = \{\text{all workers of types } A_2 \text{ and } A_3\}$

$T = \{\text{all capitalists plus all workers of type } A_1 \text{ except one}\}$.

We have:

<u>Proposition 6</u> Assume (8), (9), (10), (12) and (14) are

> satisfied and $\bar{p}$ is such that $D(\bar{p}) + \sum_{i=1}^{n} z_i^i(\bar{p}) < 0$, $D(\bar{p}) > 0$, $z_i^i(\bar{p}) < 0$ and $D(\underline{\bar{p}}) > -a$. Then the only Dreze equilibria at $\bar{p}$ whose t-fold replications are stable in the t-fold replica economy for all t are NUE.

We have already remarked that it is not clear that the coalitional blocking of our definition mimics in any way real labour market transaction mechanisms. We should further point out that if we require T to be empty the set of stable allocations at $\bar{p}$ becomes the set of core allocations at $\bar{p}$. But then Proposition 6 ceases to hold: all Dreze equilibria (of every type) are stable in all replications. The rather tortuous definition of stability originally given is the most attractive the author has found which favours NUE in any way for this economy.

To sum up for the identical worker economy. Here Walrasian equilibria cannot be NUE. One can generate Dreze equilibria which are NUE with the unsatisfactory assumption that different exogenous wage rigidities are given for the identical workers. But if all wage rigidities are the same, NUE can be generated in Dreze equilibrium only if the production function has linear isoquants. And in this case any rigidity which allows a Dreze equilibrium which is a NUE will also allow a Dreze equilibrium where all workers are employed. However, there is a stability definition (albeit somewhat contrived) which favours the former type of Dreze equilibrium.

By and large the conclusion from this section is that no satisfactory theory of NUE will evolve from consideration of Dreze equilibria in convex economies. The rest of this paper is devoted to an alternative tack. Here we piece together various pieces of casual (some more so than others) empiricism about real labour markets and generate more plausible rationalisations for NUE. We start by looking at the nature of the production function.

Production as a function of average hours and number of workers

The production function in the identical worker economy of the previous section implied (for instance) that the output from employing 800 men for one hour a day is at least as large as the output from employing 100 men for 8 hours a day. Casual empiricism suggests that this is not the typical case in reality; indeed one expects the reverse inequality. More formally, one expects quasi-convex rather than quasi-concave production functions. There is some less casual evidence for this, as follows.

In the empirical literature on production functions, it has been found that treating the labour input as a function of average hours and number of workers rather than simply as total man-hours gives rise to different estimates of the coefficients on these two variables. Treating the labour input as a Cobb-Douglas function of average hours and number of workers, Feldstein [3] and Craine [1] have found an exponent for average hours in the region of 2 while that for number of workers is less than one.[3] This Cobb-Douglas specification may be written as follows.

Let $N(z_1^0,\ldots z_n^0)$ denote any n-vector which is a non-decreasing permutation of the elements of $(z_1^0,\ldots z_n^0)$; i.e. $N_i(z_1^0,\ldots z_n^0) \geq N_{i+1}\ (z_1^0,\ldots z_n^0)\ i = 1,\ldots n-1$. Notice that if $N^1(z_1^0,\ldots z_n^0)$ and $N^2(z_1^0,\ldots z_n^0)$ are two such permutations then $N_i^1(z_1^0,\ldots z_n^0) = N_i^2(z_1^0,\ldots z_n^0)$, $i = 1,\ldots n$. Suppose $(z_1^0,\ldots z_n^0)$ is such that $N_r(z_1^0,\ldots z_n^0) > 0$ and $N_{r+1}(z_1^0,\ldots z_n^0) = 0$. Then the number of workers is r and the average hours worked by them is $\frac{1}{r}\sum_{i=1}^{n} N_i(z_1^0,\ldots z_n^0)$. The production function of interest is then:

$$f(z_1^0,\ldots z_n^0) = \left[\frac{1}{r}\sum_{i=1}^{r} N_i(z_1^0,\ldots z_n^0)\right]^{\alpha} \cdot r^{\beta} \text{ where } \alpha\ ,\ \beta > 0 \quad (15)$$

When $n = 2$ and $\alpha > \beta$ (which is implied by the Feldstein-

Craine estimates) the unit isoquant implied by (15) is shown in Figure 2.

Figure 2

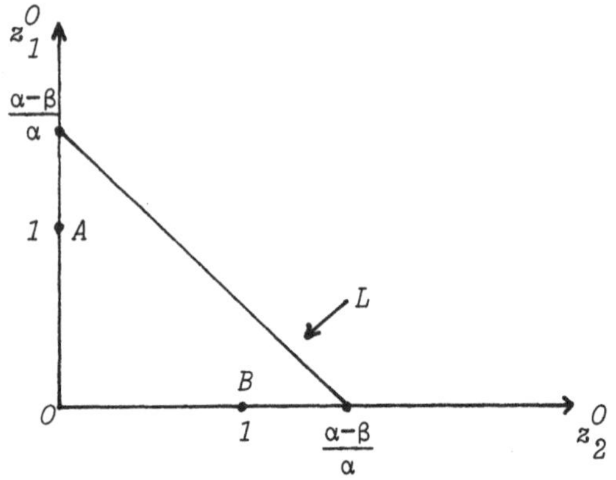

L is the line indicated minus its endpoints and the unit isoquant is $L \cup A \cup B$. The production function is most unusual. In particular, it is quasi-convex in the Feldstein-Craine case, which supports our casual intuition. In addition (15) is not continuous, not increasing and exhibits increasing returns in the Feldstein-Craine case. The only "oddity" in (15) in which we are interested is its quasi-convexity. We therefore consider the following analytically more attractive function:

$$f(z_1^0,\ldots z_n^0) = \sum_{i=1}^{n} (i^\beta - (i-1)^\beta) N_i(z_1^0,\ldots z_n^0)$$

$$\text{where } 0 < \beta < 1 \qquad (16)$$

Both (15) and (16) satisfy the identical worker assumption, (8(a)).

When $n = 2$ the unit isoquant is as shown in Figure 3:

Figure 3

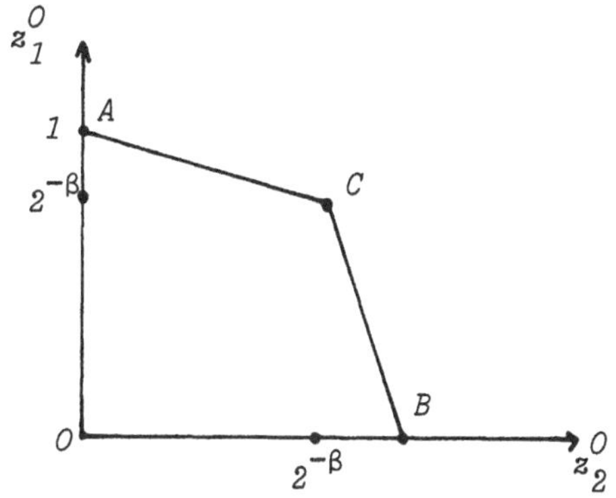

$A\ C\ B$ is the unit isoquant. (16) is continuous, increasing, quasi-convex and exhibits constant returns. If $N_1(z_1^0,\ldots z_n^0) = N_2(z_1^0,\ldots z_n^0) = \ldots = N_r(z_1^0,\ldots z_n^0) = h > 0$ and $N_{r+1}(z_1^0,\ldots z_n^0) = 0$ then (16) collapses to $f(.) = r^\beta.h$, the constant returns version of (15). In effect (16) is a continuous, constant returns modification of (15). It has, in particular, the following most useful property with respect to "marginal products". Suppose initially that $r - 1$ workers are employed. Now add on rth employee who works no more hours than any of the others. The marginal product of this worker ($\theta_r(z)$ in previous notation) is positive, does not depend on z and declines with r. To see this consider $(z_1^0,\ldots z_n^0)$ and $(\hat{z}_1^0,\ldots \hat{z}_n^0)$ where

(i) $N_i(z_1^0,\ldots z_n^0) > 0,\ i = 1,\ldots r$ and $N_{r+1}(z_1^0,\ldots z_n^0) = 0$

(ii) $N_i(\hat{z}_i^0,\ldots \hat{z}_n^0) = N_i(z_1^0,\ldots z_n^0),\ i = 1,\ldots r - 1$ and

$N_r(\hat{z}_1^0,\ldots \hat{z}_n^0) = 0.$

Then from (16) we have:

$f(z_1^0,\ldots z_n^0) - f(\hat{z}_1^0,\ldots \hat{z}_n^0) = \left[r^\beta - (r-1)^\beta\right].\ N_r(z_1^0,\ldots z_n^0)$ and so

$$\frac{f(z_1^0,\ldots z_n^0)-f(\hat{z}_1^0,\ldots \hat{z}_n^0)}{N_r(z_1^0,\ldots z_n^0)} = r^\beta - (r-1)^\beta$$

as required. We denote $\theta_r(z)$ simply by θ_r and we have shown therefore that:

θ_r does not depend on z and $\theta_r > \theta_{r+1} > 0$, $r = 1,\ldots n-1$ (17)

One suspects intuitively that quasi-convex production functions will allow explanations of unemployment which are not possible in the standard case. We now show that this is the case when the quasi-convexity is of the form (16).

Non-trivial unemployment equilibrium in the non-convex economy

The non-convex economy we look at is defined by:

(1), (3), (4), (6), (8), (9) and (16).

So we have an identical worker economy with identical wage rigidities and a technology which is not convex. For convenience let w denote real wage (i.e. $w = \bar{p}_1 = \ldots = \bar{p}_n$). There are in fact Dreze equilibria relative to any $\bar{p}$ for this economy. Moreover if the real wage w exceeds θ_n and is less than θ_1 these Dreze equilibria are NUE. In these equilibria all employed workers are of type A_1 (i.e. $z^i = z^i(\bar{p})$). However, casual empiricism suggests that employed workers do not have a free choice regarding the hours they work. Yet it also seems to be the case that employed workers do not generally face Dreze type constraints on their labour supply. It is not clear, for instance, that the typical 8 hour a day worker is freely choosing to work 8 hours, nor is it clear that he prefers 8 hours to anything less than 8 hours. For these reasons we therefore take the opportunity to introduce two new equilibrium concepts. The first of these involves relatively more competition between workers for employment than the second. We call these equilibria, an equilibrium with free competition and an equilibrium with unions, respectively, although we do not claim much correlation between the behaviour of the "union" in the second of these and the behaviour of trade unions in real labour markets. We now define these equilibria.

The first requirement for both equilibria is the obvious feasibility requirement:

$$z^i \varepsilon T^i \text{ and } z_0^i + w \sum_{j=1}^{n} z_j^i = 0 \tag{18}$$

The second requirement for both equilibria is also the same. For the net trade z to be an equilibrium (in either sense) we require that no agent wishes to cancel his trade on the ith labour market (given the corresponding, budget balancing change in the output trade), for any set of i's $= 1,\ldots n$. Clearly any worker who is demanding the labour services of another worker in z will wish to cancel this trade: in equilibrium worker i will be trading only in output and the ith labour service. The "no cancellation" requirement for workers is then:

$$u^i(z_0^i, z_i^i) \geq u^i(0,0) \tag{19}$$

This simply says that the ith worker does not wish to <u>quit</u>.

For the capitalist the corresponding requirement is as follows. Let:

$$J(z^0) = \left\{ \hat{z}^0 \mid \hat{z}_i^0 = z_i^0 \text{ or } 0,\ i = 1,\ldots n;\ \hat{z}^0 \varepsilon T^0 \text{ and } \hat{z}_0^0 + w \sum_{j=1}^{n} \hat{z}_j^0 = 0 \right\}$$

Then we need:

$$u^0(z^0) > u^0(\hat{z}^0),\ \forall\ \hat{z}^0 \varepsilon J(z^0). \tag{20}$$

This says that the capitalist does not wish to <u>fire</u> any worker.

Finally, we allow some co-operation between agents and

here the equilibria differ. For equilibrium with free competition we allow agents to meet pairwise and to consider whether there is a mutual improvement for them at p involving only goods i and 0 given that they may cancel transactions on labour markets other than i. The procedure is repeated for all pairs and for all $i = 1,\ldots n$. If no improvement can be found in this way, we have an equilibrium with free competition. It is clear that the only such improvements involving goods i and 0 will involve the capitalist and the ith worker. Let:

$$J_i(z^0) = \left\{\hat{z}^0 \mid \hat{z}^0_j = z^0_j \text{ or } 0,\ j = 1,\ldots n,\ j \neq i;\right.$$

$$\left.\hat{z}^0 \in T^0 \text{ and } \hat{z}^0_0 + w \sum_{j=1}^{n} \hat{z}^0_j = 0\right\}$$

Then the requirement is:

$$\forall\, i = 1,\ldots n, \nexists\, \hat{z}^0 \text{ such that} \tag{21}$$

(i) $\hat{z}^0 \in J_i(z^0)$

(ii) $u^0(\hat{z}^0) > u^0(z^0)$

(iii) $u^i(w\,\hat{z}^0_i\ ,\ -\hat{z}^0_i) > u^i(z^i_0\ ,\ z^i_i)$

AN EQUILIBRIUM WITH FREE COMPETITION is a net trade z which satisfies (18), (19), (20) and (21).

The "free competition" evolves from the fact that in (21) worker i may approach the capitalist and persuade him to fire worker j and hire i instead. For equilibrium with unions we remove this possibility. All workers form a union and an alternative to z is accepted if, and only if, it makes some worker better off without making any worker worse off. Se we replace (21) with:

$$\nexists\ z \text{ satisfying (18) such that} \tag{22}$$

(i) $u^0(\hat{z}^0) > u^0(z^0)$

(ii) $u^i(\hat{z}^i) \geq u^i(z^i)$ $\forall$ $i = 1,...n$ with strict inequality for some $i = 1,...n$.

<u>AN EQUILIBRIUM WITH UNIONS</u> is a net trade z which satisfies (18), (19), (20) and (22).

Before proceeding we should remark that there is a close similarity between equilibrium with free competition and Malinvaud-Younes equilibrium [9] and a similar relation between equilibrium with unions and Younes equilibrium [10]. The essential difference is that Malinvaud-Younes and Younes allow agents to cancel (recontract) to <u>any</u> smaller trade rather than just to the zero trade. We have already remarked that freedom to recontract to any smaller trade does not seem to be a characteristic of real labour markets. Hence our equilibria evolve from those of Malinvaud-Younes and Younes by changing the recontracting power endowed on agents in a plausible manner. We now look at the properties of these equilibria in the non-convex economy. We make one additional assumption:

$$u^i(z_0^i\ ,\ z_i^i) = u^i(0,0) \Rightarrow z_i^i > -a \tag{23}$$

This implies that a worker always prefers quitting to working the biological maximum number of hours. For the time being we also take it that $R^i = 0$. We use the following notation. Let b denote the maximum number of hours a worker would work at w before quitting. Let c denote the worker's best choice regarding hours at w. Figure 4 illustrates.

<u>Figure 4</u>

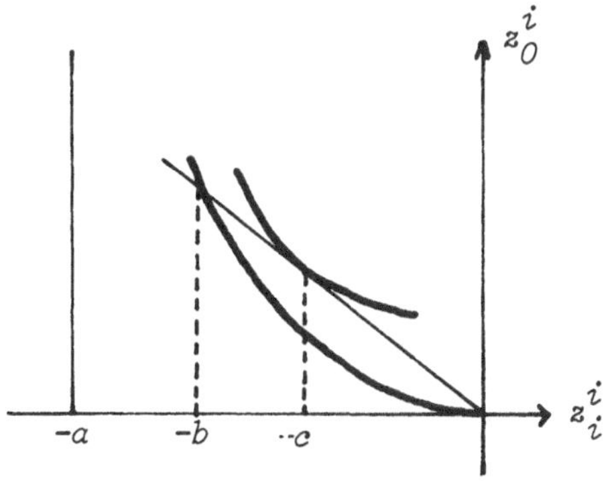

We know from (23) that $a > b > c$. Property (17) allows easy evaluation of the equilibria for this economy. In particular we can find w at which the only equilibria (of either type) are NUE, as follows.

From (17), $\theta_1 > \theta_n$. We consider w such that $\theta_1 > w > \theta_n$. Then either:

(i) $\theta_r > w > \theta_{r+1}$ some $r = 1,\ldots n-1$,

or (ii) $\theta_r = w$ some $r = 2,\ldots n-1$.

We look at (i) first. Let z be defined as follows:

(a) $N_i(z_1^0,\ldots z_n^0) = b$, $i = 1,\ldots r$ and $N_{r+1}(z_1^0,\ldots z_n^0) = 0$.

(b) $z_i^i = -z_i^0$, $i = 1,\ldots n$

(c) $z_j^i = 0$, $j \neq i$, $i = 1,\ldots n$

(d) $z_0^i = -w \sum_{j=1}^{n} z_j^i$, $i = 0,\ldots n$

We show z is an equilibrium with free competition. Generally, $f(z_1^0,\ldots z_n^0) - w \sum_{i=1}^{n} z_i^0 = \sum_{i=1}^{n} (\theta_i - w).\ N_i(z_1^0,\ldots z_n^0)$

At the proposed equilibrium, $f(z_1^0,\ldots z_n^0) - w \sum_{i=1}^{n} z_i^0 = \sum_{i=1}^{r}$ $(\theta_i - w).b$. Since $\theta_r > w > \theta_{r+1}$, $f(z_1^0,\ldots z_n^0) - w\sum z_i^0$ is maximised at the equilibrium under the constraint $z_i^0 \leq b$, $i = 1,\ldots n$. Given this it now follows straight forwardly from the definitions of z and b that z is an equilibrium with free competition.

We now show that the only equilibria are z as defined by (a) - (d). First there can be no equilibrium with more than r men employed since $w > \theta_{r+1}$ and (20) would be violated at such an equilibrium. Also there can be no equilibrium with less than r employed since $\theta_r > w$ and the capitalist and an unemployed worker would violate (21). So the only possible equilibria involve employment of r workers; moreover from (19) each employed worker works at most b hours. For the equilibria to differ from these described by z some employed worker works less than b hours; suppose some worker works d hours, $b > d > 0$. By firing this worker and hiring one of the unemployed for $d+\varepsilon$ hours the capitalist and this unemployed worker violate (21) for some $\varepsilon > 0$ from (23). Hence the only equilibria with free competition are z as described by (a) - (d).

In case (ii) the reasoning is similar. The only difference is that the equilibria are now z defined by

(b), (c), (d) and (e):

(e) $N_i(z_1^0, \ldots z_n^0) = b$, $i = 1, \ldots r-1$, $0 \le N_r(z_1^0, \ldots z_n^0) \le b$

and $N_{r+1}(z_1^0, \ldots z_n^0) = 0$.

So the only difference is that one of the r employed workers may now work anything between 0 and b hours; all others still work b hours however.

We therefore have:

<u>Proposition 7</u> Assume a non-convex economy in which $R^i = 0$ and (23) is satisfied. If $\theta_1 > w > \theta_n$ then there are equilibria with free competition and all such equilibria are NUE. In these equilibria all employed workers except at most one work b hours.

The type of reasoning used here is easily adapted to give, in addition:

<u>Proposition 8</u> Assume a non-convex economy in which $R^i = 0$ and (23) is satisfied. If $\theta_1 > w > \theta_n$ then there are equilibria with unions and all such

equilibria are NUE. In these equilibria all employed workers except at most one work between b and c hours.

For the convex economy nothing like Propositions 7 or 8 is available: the non-convexity we have chosen allows an explanation for unemployment which just cannot be found in the convex environment. It is of further interest that "free competition" between workers in the non-convex economy leads to employed workers working more hours at the going wage than they would optimally choose; one suspects that at least some early "pre-union" labour markets exhibited this phenomenon. Finally we should remark that the assumption that $R^i = 0$ is the least favourable assumption for our argument. If, for instance, $R^i > \theta_n$ then equilibria of either type at all w involve unemployment; in these economies profitable employment opportunities exist but unemployment is inevitable.

Conclusions

The general conclusions from all this are that standard convexity assumptions seem unlikely to allow a satisfactory explanation of unemployment but technological non-convexities may provide the basis for a convincing theory of unemployment. On the usual theorist's criterion of generality I cannot claim too much for the positive results given here in support of the second conclusion. However, if, as the first conclusion indicates, unemployment is fundamentally a non-convex phenomenon there seems to be no alternative, at least at this stage, to the pursuit of various special models.

REFERENCES

1. Craine, R. (1973). On the service flow from labour. *R.E.S.*

2. Dreze, J. (1975). On the existence of exchange equilibrium under price rigidities. *I.E.R.*

3. Feldstein, M. (1967). Specification of the labour

input in the aggregate production function. *R.E.S.*

4. Grandmont, J.M. (1977). Temporary general equilibrium theory. *Econometrica.*

5. Grandmont, J.M. and Laroque, G. (1976). On Keynesian temporary equilibria. *R.E.S.*

6. Grandmont, J.M., Laroque, G. and Younes, Y. (1978). Equilibrium with quantity rationing and re-contracting. *J.E.T.*

7. Leslie, D. and Wise, J. (1980). The productivity of hours in U.K. manufacturing and production industries. *E.J.*

8. Malinvaud, E. (1977). *Theory of Unemployment Reconsidered.* Basil Blackwell.

9. Malinvaud, E. and Younes, Y. (1977). Some new concepts for the microeconomic foundations of macroeconomics. In *Microeconomic Foundations of Macroeconomics* (ed.) G.C. Harcourt. Macmillan.

10. Younes, Y. (1975). On the role of money in the process of exchange and the existence of a non-Walrasian equilibrium. *R.E.S.*

FOOTNOTES

1. I am grateful to participants in seminars at Manchester, Birmingham and the Durham AUTE Conference for helpful comments; particular thanks to Chris Birchenhall, Paul Grout, Mervyn King, Derek Leslie and David Ulph. Errors are the author's fault.

2. $z^i(p)$ denotes the set of Walrasian excess demands for agent i at prices p.

3. Recently Leslie and Wise [7] have reported much lower estimates of the exponent on average hours; indeed in some of their results the exponents on both variables are the same (and less than one) which implies a standard convex technology.

DISCUSSION : DAVID ULPH

I thought this was a very fine paper which dealt with an important and neglected issue. For given the popularity of quantity-constrained equilibrium models of unemployment, it is surprising that so little attention has been devoted to the fact that almost none of these models actually explain unemployment, as distinct from short-time working. In most cases it is simply assumed that excess supply shows up as unemployment.

It comes as no surprise that unemployment can be generated by invoking a form of increasing returns, which makes it cheaper for the firm to produce extra output by having its existing labour force work longer hours than by hiring additional workers. The power of the paper comes in showing that if we want to retain a great deal of the equilibrium structure of these models, *only* some element of increasing returns will do the trick, and in carefully exploring how to handle these increasing returns, which always pose difficulties for equilibrium theory.

My only reservations about the paper are the following.

I think the discussion of the meaning of full employment in the Walrasian economy is a red herring. What Madden shows in his example is that by altering the structure of lump-sum taxes and subsidies one can vary the number of people who would be employed in a Walrasian economy. (Incidentally he employs a rather curious example in which leisure is inferior and an individual is actually subsidised to persuade him to go out to work, but that is clearly an inessential feature of the example.) This is all well known, and indeed is a feature of the literature on optimal income taxation, where one way in which disincentive effects appear is in having some people choose not to go out to work. However in this literature it is always understood that in choosing amongst the allocations generated by different tax structures one is choosing amongst *full employment allocations* in the sense that given the structure of prices and taxes everyone is doing the amount of work they would like to do. I take it that this is the standard definition of full employment. Now while one might quite legitimately be concerned with questions concerning the maximum or optimum levels of employment, the definitions and analysis of these concepts should be kept distinct from those of full employment.

My second reservation concerns the assumption in the final models that workers cannot freely vary their hours of work. While I accept that there are limits to the extent of choice, it seems to me to be important both empirically and theoretically to allow for the possibility of overtime, where people may have some choice as to how much of this they do. Overtime is important theoretically because the non-linear pricing schedule which this introduces is precisely the phenomenon one would expect to arise with increasing returns. One now has to consider how the "fixed price" assumption translates to such a model. Does one assume that all aspects of the labour contract (basic wage rate, standard working week, overtime premium) are given or only some? If the latter assumption is made is variability in some components of the contract sufficient to guarantee full employment? Only by considering what happens when the space of contracts is enriched in response to increasing returns can we have a full understanding of how this phenomenon serves to explain unemployment.

8. GOODWILL - INVESTMENT IN THE INTANGIBLE

John D. Hey

goodwill, n. Kindly feeling to person, favour; cheerful acquiescence, heartiness, zeal; established custom or popularity of business, etc.; privilege granted by seller of business, of trading as recognised successor. (The Concise Oxford Dictionary).

goodwill, n ... (4) The privilege, granted by the seller of a business to the purchaser, of trading as his recognised successor; the possession of a ready-formed 'connexion' of customers considered as an element in the saleable value of a business, additional to the value of the plant, stock-in-trade, book-debts, etc...... (The Oxford English Dictionary).

The subject of goodwill appears to be a highly neglected area as far as present-day economic theory is concerned. A search through the indexes of many of the major theory texts reveals virtually no entries under 'goodwill'; the few references that do exist are brief to the point of perfunctoriness. A visitor from Mars, after reading the economics literature, could be excused for thinking that goodwill was sufficiently unimportant in modern economies for its existence to be ignored.

Such a conclusion would appear to be erroneous - certainly as judged by one's own casual empiricism concerning the frequency and importance of goodwill in everyday life; indeed in many areas of business, trade and commerce, goodwill is the very lubricant of economic life - without it, the ebb and flow of day-to-day transactions would grind to a standstill.

While present-day economic theory would appear to deny the importance of goodwill, this neglect is not reflected in the writings of earlier economists, nor indeed in the present practice of other related disciplines. In particular, lawyers and accountants, long since recognising the import ance of goodwill, have devoted considerable attention to its study. While economists may be mildly amused by the strained endeavours of lawyers and accountants to pin down the precise meaning and implications of goodwill (without the professional expertise of the trained economist to help them), it seems that the time for economists to roll up their sleeves, and join in this difficult task, is long overdue.

It seems generally accepted by legal authorities that the earliest reported legal decision on goodwill was that of *Crutwell* v *Lye* (1810, 17 Ves., 335), during which Lord Eldon made the following remark, which has since formed the basis for legal decisions on the matter: "The Goodwill which has been the subject of sale is nothing more than the probability that the old customers will resort to the old place". (In elucidating the background to this remark, Leake (1930, p.2) notes that: "The class of business under discussion was that of a country wagoner. It was not the name or the personality of the driver, but the place whence he starts and the probability that those who take their goods there will find a carriage for them which form the value of such a business." While we may dispute the implication of Leake's words that the *physical place* conveys goodwill potential, the direction of his remarks is clearly correct).

What is particularly significant in Lord Eldon's statement is the word "probability", and the general implication that goodwill is intangible and ephemeral rather than tangible and permanent.

The *intangibility* of goodwill has long been recognised by accountants (though clearly they are not happy at having to deal with such insubstantial items - one can almost sense the distaste felt by the authors). Equally, the *importance* of goodwill has long been recognised by them; for example, Jones (1970, p.144) remarks that "although of an intangible nature, it is frequently the most valuable asset possessed and its existence goes to the very core of the business." As far as evaluating goodwill in company accounts is concerned, there are two cases to consider, the first, when the company is being sold and a purchase price has been agreed; the second, during the normal life of the company. In the first case, accountants essentially use a tautological approach based on the assumption that the purchase price is the value of (all the assets of) the company; thus, the value of goodwill (that is, the intangible assets of the company) is simply the purchase price less the value of the net tangible assets of the company. The value of goodwill is just a balancing item.

Once a company has been sold, and the 'normal life' of the company recommences, accountants become less sure about the appropriate method of including goodwill in the balance sheets. Indeed, they seem to become rather schizophrenic at this stage: on the one hand, they recognise that there is a fundamental truth underlying their valuation procedure on sale (that is, the case discussed above); on the other hand, their aversion to including such an insubstantial item in the accounts appears to be so great that they want to get rid of it (that is, reduce its valuation to zero) as soon as possible!

The 'fundamental truth' alluded to in the paragraph above is important (and it will form the foundation for our subsequent analysis); it may therefore be useful to spell it out. The practice of ascribing to goodwill the balance between the purchase price and the net value of the tangible assets of the company is an important reminder that a company is more than simply a collection of tangible assets: a (healthy) company is a "going concern"; it has connections, customers, and a reputation. All these have been "built up" in the past, and as such form definite assets to the company. If the market for buying and selling companies is a perfect one, then the purchase price should accurately reflect the value to the company of *all* its assets, both tangible and intangible.

Such considerations lie behind one of the recommended treatments of goodwill in accounting practice. As Jones (1970, p.144) comments, one such way is to value goodwill as the "capitalised value of an annuity in future superprofits". The idea behind this statement is sensible: a firm which has built up a stock of goodwill will generally do better, in the sense of making greater profits, than a firm which has not built up such a stock. To evaluate this stock of goodwill, one simply needs to find the discounted value of profits in excess of some normal return on capital employed. This method is described by Powelson (1955, p.90).

"The method of computation that will appeal most to economists (since it appears to be based on economic principles) is that of capitalising the earning power. For example, if the marginal efficiency of capital can somehow be estimated at ten per cent (perhaps because this is the going rate of return for similar businesses) and if a particular business with net assets of $100,000 is in fact earning $15,000 a year, or a fifteen per cent return, then its goodwill is $50,000. If the net worth of the company is increased to $150,000, through the addition of $50,000 goodwill, its rate of earnings, now reduced to ten per cent, equals the marginal efficiency of capital."

Although there are several items that require elaboration and clarification in the above procedure, particularly with respect to the crucial difference *past* "superprofits" and *expected future* "superprofits" (a point to which we shall return in due course), the basic principle does indeed "appeal to economists". However, it appears that *in practice* accountants do *not* follow the above procedure when deciding on the amount to allocate to goodwill in the balance sheet of a company in its normal existence (that is, when it is not being bought and sold). Indeed, a reading of Jones (1970) suggests that accounting practice consists of trying to write down the value of goodwill (towards zero) as fast as possible. (An examination of some major companies' balance sheets confirms this suggestion). Of course, since goodwill is an asset, its value can be written down only by an *appropriation* of profits. Thus, in practice, the entry under "goodwill" in company accounts tends to be reduced particularly in good years - when profits are high. (In poor years - when profits are low - the practice appears to be to leave the entry for goodwill unchanged, though there are occasions when the figure is increased, in order to 'cushion' the effects of the low profits on other aspects of the balance sheet.[1])

The implication of this accounting practice is that a large figure for goodwill in the balance sheet tends to imply that the company has not made sufficient profits for the value to be written down, while, conversely, a series of healthy profit figures enables goodwill to be written down to an insignificant (or zero) amount.[2] But, of course, this is precisely the opposite of what should happen if the true value of goodwill is the "capitalised value of an annuity in ... superprofits"; indeed, as Jones (1970, p.149) remarks "... {sometimes} goodwill should be read in the negative, i.e. the greater the prominence in the balance sheet, the lower its real value, and vice versa". Or again, according to Jones

(1970, p.148), the most important principle of all is that:

"Any figure shown for goodwill in the balance sheet is at no time a criterion of its actual value to the company."
There is clearly a difficult problem here: if the true value of goodwill ("the capitalised value of future superprofits") is positively related to present profits (as might be expected), then the correct evaluation of goodwill in the balance sheet would lead to considerable fluctuations and instability in the 'healthiness' of the balance sheet; the periodic fluctuations in the company's apparent fortunes would be thereby magnified. In profitable years,goodwill would be written up, and the company would be relatively awash with funds; in unprofitable years, goodwill would be written down, and the company would be relatively starved of funds.

One of the more important implications of the above remarks is that, for empirical purposes, the entry for goodwill in company accounts is likely to prove of precious little value. However, it is of interest to note that an empirical study using such data was carried out in the mid-1930's by Bloomberg (1938). He clearly encountered many of the problems discussed above in deciding upon the 'true' value of goodwill; in many cases he was forced to rely upon judgement. Moreover, the crude nature of the raw data forced him into a rather crude test: he simply divided his (randomly selected sample of) companies into two groups, the first termed the "goodwill" group, the second the "physical asset" group. Although initially he attempted to allocate companies into these two groups solely on the basis of the ratio of intangible assets to total assets, he found this plan impracticable. Eventually, he was forced to resort to "selection by means of a knowledge of the nature of each business". In particular, "Goodwill stocks were considered to be those of companies which were believed to possess a substantial quantity of buyers' attachment. {...} The other group, the physical asset stocks, comprised the shares of companies which possessed natural resources or producing mechanisms and physical plants which were of themselves valuable. They sold undifferentiated products and often manufactured according to specifications. In general, classification was not extremely difficult". (Bloomberg (1938, pp.14-15)). Having divided the companies up into these two groups, Bloomberg's empirical work consisted of analysing the yield on two portfolios - one from each of the two groups consisting of $1,000 worth of stocks in each company. His initial test covered the period from 1912 (the fictitious purchase date) to 1937; this showed quite clearly a considerably greater yield on the Goodwill portfolio. (By 1937 the yield on the Physical Assets portfolio was 7.3%; on the Goodwill portfolio 103.1% (including General Motors) or 26.4% (excluding General Motors)). The trend in the *capital value* of the Goodwill portfolio (excluding General Motors) showed an annual average growth rate of 8.66% p.a., while that for the Physical Assets portfolio was just 0.6% p.a. Several other tests were performed by Bloomberg, but the overall impression was a general tendency for portfolios of goodwill stocks to do better than portfolios of physical asset stocks. This general tendency is rather odd - its persistence through time indicates some reluctance on the part of the market to arbitrage away the difference by bidding up the price of goodwill shares and bidding down the price of physical asset shares. This oddity is noted by Bloomberg (1938, p.60):

"The superiority of the goodwill over the physical asset stocks when both were held over a long period of time makes apparent an under-valuation of the goodwill shares."

Interestingly, Bloomberg advances the explanation that "... the investing public have, in general, regarded goodwill stocks as being charged with a higher degree of risk" (an explanation which he further elaborates later in his study). This explanation is of interest since it highlights once again the intangibility and impermanence of goodwill.[3]

This impermanence is repeatedly emphasised by John R. Commons, one of the few economists to write extensively on the question of goodwill, in both his famous *Legal Foundations of Capitalism*, and his earlier *Industrial Goodwill* (Commons (1924 and 1919 respectively)). For example, in the former he comments (1924, p.273):

"Thus goodwill is an asset, but an extraordinarily evanescent asset. It is held only on good behaviour. Of all kinds of property it most of all demands watchfulness. Good reputation slips away with a few little mistakes left uncorrected ..."

Common's writings provide a rich source for inspiration on the subject of goodwill, and they amply repay detailed study. They clearly stimulated considerable interest at the time of publication, and several writers followed his lead. Foremost amongst these was Foreman who published two articles on the topic in the *American Economic Review* in the early 1920's (Foreman 1923 and 1925 respectively). Similarly, Taussig in the third edition of his *Principles of Economics* (1921) wrote the following (p.175):

"Certainly it pays, and sometimes pays enormously, to create and maintain good will. He who has induced many people to get into the way of buying a particular brand may sell at a price higher than that of his competitors, or sell in greater volume and with more steadiness. No doubt this sort of advantage does not come by accident. It is slowly created by shrewdness, patience, persistence."

It is clear, therefore, that during the post First World War period, economists showed considerable interest in all facets of goodwill and recognised its importance both in everyday economic life and in the valuation of economic enterprises. It is also clear that the prevailing vision of goodwill was that it was a product of a perfectly rational optimising mode of behaviour on the part of both sides of any economic transaction; in general, most economic agents stood to benefit from the existence of a stock of goodwill.[4]

However, as we remarked earlier, present-day economists tend to ignore the existence of goodwill; at best it is relegated to footnotes, at worst it simply fails to appear. Even where it does appear, its nature appears to have subtly changed - no longer is it the product of the rational functioning of economic man, rather it is the product of inertia or ignorance amongst non-optimising humans. Consider the following quote from Joan Robinson's *Economics of Imperfect Competition* (1933, p. 75):

"In so far as the imperfection of the market is due to goodwill there is a certain presumption .... that the elimination of firms will cause the market to become more perfect. The faithful customers of the condemned firms, once dislodged from their adherence to them, may be presumed to choose with greater nicety between the remaining firms, so that each of the remaining firms will have added to their market a fringe of customers whose demand for their particular product is more elastic than the demand of their old customers. If this is the case, prices will be reduced by the concentration of demand, unless marginal costs are rising sufficiently rapidly."

Although Robinson and Taussig are in apparent agreement that the existence of goodwill implies the possibility of higher prices, they clearly disagree about the basis of this implication: to Taussig firms may charge more because they are providing more (namely, the goodwill); to Robinson firms may charge more because of the inertia and ignorance of their customers.

It is high time that we make our own position clear, and provide a definition of goodwill that could form the basis for discussion. We first note that goodwill may exist in a variety of forms; naturally we restrict attention here to those forms of goodwill that are essentially economic in nature - namely those that are part and parcel of economic life. (Though as with any dividing line, its precise position is rather vague: while we wish to include from consideration the goodwill expressed between neighbours, say, the inclusion would not be valid if the neighbours happened to be shopkeeper and customer!). A useful starting point is to classify goodwill by the nature of the market in which it (potentially) exists: thus, we may distinguish *commercial goodwill*, *industrial goodwill* and *financial goodwill* (while the first two of these terms appears to be accepted usage, the third appears to be somewhat less so). We examine these in turn briefly, before returning to more general considerations.

Commercial goodwill is the goodwill which may exist in product markets, or markets for goods and services. Generally, it is conceived of as something which primarily exists at the ultimate end of the chain of production - that is, between retailer and customer. However, this is not to deny that it also may exist between wholesaler and retailer, and between manufacturer and wholesaler, and indeed amongst manufacturers. Thus commercial goodwill is something that may exist coincidentally with the purchase and sale of goods and services.

Industrial goodwill is the goodwill that may exist in labour markets; it is the goodwill that may exist between employee and employer. Finally, *Financial goodwill* is the goodwill that may exist in financial markets; in particular, it is frequently cited as an important element in the relationship between debtor and creditor (though clearly much goodwill exists in such financial trading institutions as the stock exchange and the foreign currency exchanges).

While the actual practice of goodwill differs from case to

case, and from market to market, the basic underlying principle appears to be the same. By enunciating this principle, we may begin to approach a definition. Consider any purchase and sale transaction between a buyer and a seller. The transaction consists of the exchange of some item (a good or a service or an amount of labour or a loan) for some other item. Usually, as Clower has pointed out, in modern day economies one of the items being exchanged is a sum of money. Thus, the buyer gives the seller a sum of money in return for the item being traded. Naturally, the transaction is viewed as being mutually beneficial - in that the seller prefers to have the sum of money rather than the item, while the buyer prefers the item to the sum of money. (This "reciprocity", a term used frequently by Commons, is a crucial aspect of the whole process - a *sine qua non*, no less, unless one of the transactors is being coerced). Once the transaction has been agreed, there are a number of implications - depending upon the terms of the transaction and upon the state of legislation in the country in question. (A typical minimal legal requirement is that the full exchange does in fact take place: if the 'seller' pocketed the money and then refused to hand over the item, or just disappeared as is unfortunately sometimes the case, the 'buyer' would be entitled to some form of legal redress - assuming he could find the 'seller' !).

For the purposes of defining goodwill, it is crucial to distinguish between those implications which are legally binding[5] on the transactors and those which are not. In the former category are certain requirements under common law, under consumer and labour legislation and so on; also in this category are requirements based on the appropriate implementation of any guarantees or indemnities agreed at the point of sale. We wish to exclude all these, legally binding, implications from our present consideration. Instead, we concentrate on those aspects of the transaction which are not legally binding. That is, we focus attention on those aspects which are voluntarily and freely given and taken. Thus, we focus attention on the things that the buyer receives from the seller but which he cannot demand as part of the transaction; and on those things that the seller receives from the buyer but which he cannot demand as part of the transaction. It is crucial to our approach that such items do not become[6] implied parts of the contract; they may be tacit, that maybe tacitly implied; but neither party should feel a necessary grievance if the other party fails to "deliver" the items in question. (Certainly, he may feel "let down", but that is not the same as a legitimate grievance).

The basic principle underlying our view of goodwill is that the provision of such non-legally-necessary items by one party to the other party builds up in the mind of the receiving party some goodwill felt towards the other party. The greater the provision, the greater the increase in the stock. Moreover, such a building-up process, if it exists at all, is likely to be mutual; we suspect that it is unlikely that one party would hoard a large stock of goodwill without reciprocating it in some way; equally unlikely is that the other party would have allowed such a stock to be built up in the absence of reciprocation. As Commons (1919, p. 19) remarks ".... good-will is reciprocity".

Obviously the process may work both ways: the stock of goodwill, which may have been laboriously built-up over many years, could be reduced sharply overnight - if one of the parties fail to provide the expected "little extras". Indeed, we suspect that goodwill is a particularly fragile and tender flower: while it may require constant care and attention for it to flourish, the slightest draught may deal it a death blow.

Examples of such phenomena are numerous; most of us experience such examples every day. As far as commercial goodwill is concerned, they range from the trivial cheery smile of the newsagent to the(unfortunately rare?)garage who will replace free of charge an obviously "Friday-afternoon" car even though the guarantee has expired. As far as industrial goodwill is concerned, examples are provided by employers who keep their staff employed during hard times (when the firm is losing money by keeping them employed), and (reciprocally) by employees who do not quit the firm although prospects elsewhere are apparently much brighter. Loyalty may be an appropriate synonym to use in such circumstances.

Two important pre-conditions must be satisfied before an element of some transaction can be said to be a potential contributor to the goodwill stock; the first is that discussed above, the second flows from it:

(1) The service performed must be *voluntarily* performed; it must *not* be a legally binding part of the transaction;

(2) There must inevitably always be some *doubt* as to whether it will be performed.

The reason why (2) flows from (1) is that, otherwise, it is never performed, or it is always performed. In the former no problem to investigate exists; in the latter, it might as well become part of the legally binding aspects of the transaction. (For example, if a seller of some good would *always* replace it free of charge if ever it (or its replacement etc.) proved faulty, then the seller would presumably benefit by making this total-replacement-policy a *guaranteed* feature of the sale. In other words, there would be no advantage whatsoever in leaving it an implied or tacit part of the initial transaction).

The economic agent who is considering whether to build up a stock of goodwill by the provision of some "extra" in the negotiated transaction has essentially three choices:

(a) to never provide it;

(b) to provide it sometimes; or

(c) to provide it always.

As we have argued above, if the agent opts for (c), then the "extra" in question should simply become part of the offered (and legally binding) contract; as such it would no longer constitute goodwill. Similarly, if the agent opts for (a) no consideration of goodwill exists. Only in case (b) will goodwill be generated.

Absolutely crucial to the choice of (b) - the decision to try and build up goodwill - are the twin ideas that the provision of the "extra" will be profitable (in that some goodwill is better than none), and that, *if the need arises, the agent can stop providing the "extra"*. If times become hard, he can simply stop the provision. *The agent is therefore equipped with a safety valve.* Thus, Marks and Spencers operate a tacit "money back if not satisfied" arrangement because their custom is increased by so doing; however, they retain the right, if things get tough, or if they think that some customer is working a fiddle, to refuse to refund money. Their practice builds up goodwill, yet a safety valve is retained because their practice is not legally binding. Similarly, many firms build up 'good reputations' because they often (though not always) will replace apparently faulty items without charge or quibble if they think the customer has a good case. However, they retain the safety valve of being able to refuse to replace a faulty item: this safety valve provides an important cushion to possible insolvency or bankruptcy. Likewise, for example, universities do not (generally) sack academic staff even though staff student ratios are too high in a particular department; they would be legally entitled to, since the contract merely specifies a period of notice; they tend not to (and presumably can attract staff at lower rates of pay as a consequence), though they retain the right to do so if, for instance, a particular government were to squeeze them severely.

Voluntariness is crucial on both sides of the transaction. Returning to the accountancy definition of the value of goodwill as the "capitalised value of ... superprofits", it should not be inferred from this that monopoly power, or similar restrictive practices, *per se* conveys goodwill value. As has been argued frequently in the courts (see Commons (1924, pp 191 and ff)), the fact that monopolies apparently earn superprofits does *not* imply that these superprofits arrive through goodwill. The fact that the customers of the monopoly are, by definition, not free to go elsewhere for that product means that the customers do not voluntarily choose to purchase from that monopoly. Similar arguments apply to franchises and to protection by patents; Commons (1924, p. 194) puts the case most eloquently:

"Goodwill and franchise are alike in that the owner thereby is raised above the exposure of competition and obtains ordinarily a residual income in excess of what could be obtained if he were fully exposed. But they differ economically and legally; economically in that the customers, in the case of a special franchise, are not free to go elsewhere and choose an alternative except at an onerous expense which gives to the franchise a value somewhat equal to the cost of alternative nuisance; but, in the case of goodwill they are free to go elsewhere without additional cost, and consequently the value given to the goodwill by their willing patronage is a value based on what they voluntarily believe to be a superior service. The value of the franchise is a nuisance value, that of the goodwill is a goodwill value. Both of them reflect the prices of products which possess use-value to the customers, but in one case the price is the value of avoiding a nuisance, in the other the value of avoiding an inferior enjoyment."

However, it should not be thought that monopolies can not generate goodwill. Indeed they can, but not *solely* through the exercise of their monopoly power. We will give an example in due course.

We have now reached the point where we may begin to model formally the processes involved in generating, sustaining and destroying goodwill. Clearly, in an exploratory paper of this kind we cannot hope to give an exhaustive treatment; instead, we adopt the rather more modest aim of providing some simple, but we hope instructive, illustrative examples. Most of these examples are concerned with commercial goodwill, though we will have some things to say towards the end of the paper on industrial goodwill (a topic on which some vaguely related material has already appeared in the form of the 'implicit contracts' literature - of which, more anon).

Of the multitude of possible sources of goodwill that may be modelled (including a "moneyback if not satisfied" *tacit* policy, a "customer is always right" policy, a "cheery smile" policy, etc., etc.), we consider the problem of the replacement of faulty goods. In keeping with our previous discussion, we restrict attention to cases where the replacement is *not* obligatory under law *nor* under the terms of any guarantee. We are therefore considering the replacement of faulty goods outside the terms of any guarantee, or after the expiry of any guarantee period. We assume that the effects of the existence of the guarantee have already been taken into account by the participants in our model, and are thus included in the parameters of the model. From now on, when we refer to faulty goods and their replacement we confine attention to such phenomena *outside* the terms of any guarantee or other legal requirement.

We begin with a very simple model, designed not for its realism but rather for the light it sheds on the importance and functioning of goodwill. Consider a single retailer of some product; we assume for the moment that the retailer has no competitors or alternatively that our retailer's actions have no effect on the actions of its rivals. To make our problem interesting we assume that the good in question may develop a fault; to make our problem simple we assume that the development of a fault renders the good valueless in the eyes of the customers. Clearly the good must be purchased in integral amounts; for ease of analysis (and without loss of generality) we assume that each (potential) demander wishes to buy at most one unit of the good in any one period. (If, on the contrary, a particular individual is a potential demander of, say, three units, we consider him as three (potential) demanders). Potential demanders differ in that the maximum amount that they would be willing to pay for one *fault-free* unit differs; call this maximum amount x, and index potential demanders by this x. (If a particular individual, as instanced above, is a potential demander of three units, then he will appear as three potential demanders with x-values $x_i (i = 1,2,3)$ for the ith unit; if the usual law of demand holds, then $x_1 > x_2 > x_3$).

For the moment we assume that, although individuals differ with respect to this x-value, they are all alike in that they are all risk-neutral.

Clearly the x-value relates to (the maximum amount for) *fault-free* items; since we have assumed that a faulty item is valueless to all customers, then the *actual* demand for a (possibly faulty) item will depend crucially on the attitude of the retailer towards the replacement of, or refund of money paid on, faulty items. There are various strategies open to the retailer, for example, he could:

(1) replace a proportion g of all faulty goods (including faulty replacements, faulty replacements of faulty replacements, and so on);

(2) replace a proportion g of faulty initially-sold goods (but not replace faulty replacements, etc);

(3) refund the purchase price in respect of a proportion g of faulty goods;

(4) replace up to a maximum number n all faulty goods (including faulty replacements, etc., etc.);

(5) replace up to a maximum number n all faulty initially-sold goods;

(6) refund the purchase price in respect of a maximum number n of faulty goods;

(7) and so on.

These are possible alternative strategies; given the choice of one of them, it is necessary to choose the optimal value of g or n as appropriate. Of course, in keeping with our earlier remarks, if it is found that the optimal value of

g or n is zero, then no goodwill will ever exist; likewise if it is found that the optimal value of g is 1 (or of n is the number of items sold), then the retailer's optimal procedure is to declare this strategy formally as part of the transaction ("money *always* refunded", "exchange guaranteed") - again goodwill would not exist.

The full solution to the retailer's problem includes the optimal choice of strategy (amongst (1) to (7) above); we begin, however, with the rather simpler problem of determining the optimal choice of g or n for some of (1) to (7). We concentrate attention on strategies (1) and (3). (We note that (4) to (6) may be more relevant if the upper limit on the exercise of goodwill is presumed to exist for the purpose of avoiding possible bankruptcy; however, (1), (2) and (3) will be very close approximations to (4), (5) and (6), respectively, if $g = n/m$, where m is total goods handed over to customers, if g is *below* the expected failure rate).

Let us begin with strategy (3); that is, the retailer tries to build up goodwill by refunding the purchase price in respect of a proportion g of faulty goods. We consider first the 'general equilibrium' solution - namely that when all potential demanders are relaibly informed of the true value of g. Later, we investigate the considerably more interesting (and complicated) case when the retailer must educate the potential demanders, and the potential demanders must learn, about the true value of g.

Let P denote the price of the good, and p the probability that a particular unit is found to be faulty. Consider a potential demander x, and examine the circumstances under which this potential demander will become an actual purchaser. He will buy if his expected surplus[7] conditional on purchase is greater than or equal to zero (his surplus from not buying). If he buys, his surplus is given by:

$$\text{surplus} = \begin{cases} (x - P) & \text{if item fault-free} \\ 0 & \text{if faulty but money refunded} \\ -P & \text{if faulty but no refund} \end{cases}$$

Thus he will buy if and only if

$$(x - P)(1 - p) + (0)gp + (-P)\, p\, (1 - g) \geq 0,$$

that is, if and only if

$$x \geq P(1 - gp)/(1 - p). \qquad (1)$$

In other words those individuals whose x-values are sufficiently large (greater than the right-hand-side of (1)) will be induced to buy. Note several things about the critical x-value; (i) it equals P if p is zero or g is one; (ii) it is a decreasing function of g and an increasing function of P and p; (iii) it approaches infinity if g is zero and p approaches one.

Suppose now that the number of potential demanders is N and that the distribution of their x-values is represented by the probability density function $f(.)$ (with corresponding distribution function $F(.)$). It follows that the demand, D, that the retailer faces is given by:

$$D = N\{1 - F[P(1 - gp)/(1 - p)]\}\,. \qquad (2)$$

It is clear from this that D is an increasing function of N and g, and a decreasing function of P and p.

We assume that the retailer also is risk-neutral, and that the retailer can purchase any quantity of the good from the wholesaler at a constant cost C per unit. (Alternatively, C can be thought of as the constant marginal cost of producing the good). The retailer's objective is to maximise expected net revenue (that is, net of any expected refunds) less costs; the objective function is thus:

$$V \equiv D[P\,(1 - gp) - C\,] \qquad (3)$$

where D is given by (2).

If the retailer is not allowed to vary P (that is, if the wholesaler or the manufacturer dictates the retail price), then the only decision remaining to the retailer is the "goodwill" decision - that is, the choice of g. The first order condition for maximisation of V with respect to g is:

$$(1 - p)\{1 - F[P(1 - gp)/(1 - p)]\} = [P(1 - gp) - C] \times f[P(1 - gp)/(1 - p)]\,. \qquad (4)$$

The properties of the solution to this depend crucially on the form of the probability distribution. To proceed, we use as the vehicle for our analysis the distribution which would give rise to a *constant-elasticity demand function* in a fault-free $(p = 0)$ or a total-goodwill $(g = 1)$ world; that is, we use the Pareto distribution:

$$\left.\begin{array}{l} F(x) = 1 - a^{b}x^{-b} \\ \\ f(x) = ba^{b}x^{-b-1} \end{array}\right]. \qquad \begin{array}{l} x \geq a \\ \text{(both zero elsewhere)} \end{array} \qquad (5)$$

Clearly, using (2) and (5), if $p = 0$ or $g = 1$, then demand would be given by

$$D = \begin{cases} N\,a^{b}P^{-b} & a \leq P \\ N & 0 < P < a \end{cases}$$

- demand elasticity (above price a) being constant at b. We assume, to make our story sensible, that b is greater than 1 (thus the retailer is operating under elastic demand conditions).

If we substitute (5) into (4) and simplify the resulting expression, we get the following condition for the optimal choice of g:

$$(b - 1)P(1 - gp) = bC$$

or alternatively (6)

$$gp = 1 - bC/(b - 1)P.$$

Of course, gp must lie between zero and one; this restriction implies (in addition to the obvious $C \geq 0$), that (6) holds only if P is greater than $bC/(b - 1)$. If, on the other hand, the price is not sufficiently greater than cost (that is, if P is less than $bC/(b - 1)$), then optimality requires that gp be put equal to zero.

Thus, as P increases from C, the optimal choice of gp remains constant at zero until P reaches $bC/(b - 1)$, thereafter gp increases with P. Other aspects of the optimality condition (6) are of interest: in particular, when P is greater than $bC/(b - 1)$, then the optimal choice of gp is a decreasing function of C and an increasing function of b; in the limit, as the demand becomes totally elastic (b approaches infinity), gp approaches $(P - C)/P$ - namely, the profit as a proportion of the selling price. Finally, it is of interest to note that g and p enter into the optimality condition solely and simply in the form gp; thus changes in the reliability parameter p are exactly offset by changes in the goodwill response g - so that the "expected refund proportion" gp stays unchanged. Moreover, inspection of (3) shows that the expected profit per unit purchased remains constant at $C/(b - 1)$ despite variations in p, though (as (2) shows) the number of customers is influenced by the value of p.

Let us now turn to examine how goodwill affects the participants in the market. Throughout this discussion, we assume[8] that P is greater than $bC/(b - 1)$, so that (6) is the relevant optimality condition. First, as far as the retailer is concerned, it is clear from the nature of the optimisation that he is better off with goodwill than without it - expected profits clearly increase. To be specific the expected gain (using optimal goodwill rather than zero goodwill) is

$$N[a(1 - p)/bP]^{b} C^{-b+1} \{P^{b}(b - 1)^{b-1} - b^{b} C^{b-1} (P - C)\} \quad (7)$$

which can be shown to be unambiguously positive if P is greater than $bC/(b - 1)$.

Second, as far as the customers are concerned, there are two classes to consider: (a) those who would have purchased the good even if goodwill had been zero; (b) those who have been induced to buy the good because of the existence of goodwill. In category (a), as can be seen from (1), are those individuals with x-values greater than $P/(1 - p)$: each of these will have an increased surplus as a result of the goodwill. To be precise, individual x (where x is larger than $P/(1 - p)$ will have his surplus increased by

$$Pgp = [x(1 - p) - P(1 - gp)] - [x(1 - p) - P]. \quad (8)$$

In category (b), as can be seen from (1), are those individuals with x-values between $P(1 - gp)/(1 - p)$ and $P/(1 - p)$: each of these will also have an increased surplus as a result of the goodwill. To be precise, individual x (where x lies between $P(1 - gp)/(1 - p)$ and $P/(1 - p)$ will have his surplus increased by

$$x(1 - p) - P(1 - gp) \quad (9)$$

since surplus before the goodwill was zero. From (8) and (9) an aggregate expression for the total increase in consumer surplus can be derived.

One point is clear - both the retailer and consumers gain from the presence of goodwill. The introduction of goodwill constitutes a Pareto improvement. Another way of expressing this result is as follows: *legislation which attempts to extend the range of the legally binding aspects of transactions may well be counter-productive;* consumers may well not benefit from so-called consumer protection law. The simplest way to put these points into perspective is to consider a legal proposal which forced the retailer to adopt a "sure" policy rather than a "random" policy; that is, a proposal which forced the retailer to choose between putting g equal to zero ("no refund ever"), and putting g equal to one ("refund guaranteed"). From *all* the consumers points of view $g = 1$ is preferred to $g = 0$; in addition, it *may* be the case that the retailer also prefers $g = 1$ to $g = 0$. In our specific example, he would so prefer if

$$P(1 - p)[1 - (1 - p)^{b-1}] > C[1 - (1 - p)^{b}]. \qquad (10)$$

However, it may well be the case that the retailer would prefer $g = 0$ (if forced to choose between that and $g = 1$); in our specific example, he would so prefer if the inequality in (10) was the other way round. In such a case, the proposed legislation would have the effect of making everyone worse off. Indeed in such a case, randomness is a virtue, and goodwill plays a crucial role.

Before we proceed further with this particular formulation, let us consider a slightly different formulation. To be specific, we consider an alternative "goodwill generating mechanism": instead of assuming that the retailer refunds the purchase price in respect of a proportion g of faulty goods (mechanism (3) above), we assume now that the retailer replaces free of charge a proportion g of all faulty goods (including faulty replacements, faulty replacements of faulty replacements, and so on) (mechanism (1) above). In all other respects our model remains unchanged.

As far as the individual consumer is concerned, there are now just two possibilities; either he ends up with a fault-free good or he does not; in both cases he ends up minus the purchase price. He will purchase the good if his expected surplus conditional on purchase is positive, that is if and

and only if

$$x(1 - p)(1 + gp + g^2p^2 + g^3p^3 + \ldots.) - P \geq 0,$$

that is, if and only if

$$x(1 - p)/(1 - gp) - p \geq 0.$$

Thus, he will buy if and only if

$$x \geq P(1 - gp)/(1 - p). \quad (11)$$

Now this is exactly the same condition as under the earlier formulation,despite the fact that for any given g the expected surplus is greater under the second formulation than under the first (to be precise, by a factor $1/(1 - gp)$). Thus, demand is still given by (2), though the profit function (3) needs to be modified. Under the new formulation, this becomes:

$$V = D[P - C/(1 - gp)] \quad (12)$$

where D is given by (2). (Thus profits per unit are greater by a factor of $1/(1 - gp)$. For given P, the first-order condition for optimal choice of g is given by

$$(1 - p)C\{1 - F[P(1 - gp)/(1 - p)]\} = (1 - gp)^2 \times$$

$$P[P - C/(1 - gp)]f[P(1 - gp)/(1 - p)]. \quad (13)$$

Using the Pareto distribution (5) as before), (13) reduces to

$$bP(1 - gp) = (b + 1)C$$

or alternatively (14)

$$gp = 1 - (b + 1)C/bP.$$

These conditions are remarkably similar to, though not identical with, the optimality conditions (6) under the first formulation. To be specific, we now require P to be greater than $(b + 1)C/b$ - which is a smaller number than $bC/(b - 1)$ - (otherwise g should be put equal to zero). Given that P is sufficiently large, goodwill (g) is an increasing function of b and a decreasing function of C/P; the limiting value of

gp as demand becomes infinitely elastic is $(P - C)/P$ again; moreover , g and p appear once again solely and simply in the form gp - our previous remarks therefore apply.

In this alternative formulation, both the retailer and consumers benefit from the existence of goodwill; again, consumer legislation (which forced g to equal either 0 or 1) could be counter-productive.

Which of the two alternatives (in its optimal version) is preferred by the retailer and consumers? Beginning with the former, we see from (2), (3) and (6) that its maximised expected profit under the first formulation is:

$$\begin{array}{ll} N[a(1 - p)(b - 1)/bC]^b \; C/(b - 1) & \text{if } P/C \geq b/(b - 1) \\ N[a(1 - p)/P]^b (P - C) & \text{if } P/C < b/(b - 1), \end{array} \qquad (15)$$

while, from (2) (12) and (14), we see that its maximised expected profit under the second formulation is:

$$\begin{array}{ll} N[a(1 - p)b/(b + 1)C]^b \; P/(b + 1) & \text{if } P/C \geq (b + 1)/b \\ N[a(1 - p)/P]^b (P - C) & \text{if } P/C < (b + 1)/b \;. \end{array} \qquad (16)$$

It is a fairly straightforward, though tedious, exercise to show[9] that for all values of P/C greater than one, the value of (16) is always higher than, or the same as, the value of (15). (Equality occurs only when P/C is less than $(b + 1)/b$). Thus the retailer prefers the second formulation to the first - a result not surprising in view of the common demand function (2) and the different profit per unit functions (3) and (12).

Which do (potential) consumers prefer? Well, under the first formulation, the expected surplus for individual x is given by:

$$\left.\begin{array}{ll} x(1 - p) - bC/(b - 1) & \text{if } x \geq bC/[(b - 1)(1 - p)] \\ 0 & \text{otherwise} \\ & \\ \text{if } P/C \geq b/(b - 1) & \end{array}\right] \qquad (17a)$$

and

$$\left.\begin{array}{ll} x(1 - p) - P & \text{if } x \geq P/(1 - p) \\ 0 & \text{otherwise} \\ \text{if } P/C < b/(b - 1)\ . & \end{array}\right] \quad (17b)$$

Under the second formulation, the expected surplus is given by:

$$\left.\begin{array}{ll} x(1 - p)bP/[(b + 1)C] - P & \text{if } x \geq (b + 1)C/[b(1 - p)] \\ 0 & \text{otherwise} \\ \text{if } P/C \geq (b + 1)/b & \end{array}\right] \quad (18a)$$

and

$$\left.\begin{array}{ll} x(1 - p) - P & \text{if } x \geq P/(1 - p) \\ 0 & \text{otherwise} \\ \text{if } P/C < (b + 1)/b\ . & \end{array}\right] \quad (18b)$$

It is clear from (17) and (18) that for a given individual surplus is never less, but may well be more, under the second formulation than under the first. We note also that more individuals are likely to experience a positive expected surplus under the second than under the first.

Thus both retailer and consumers prefer the second formulation to the first (when both optimally implemented). In a sense this is hardly surprising in view of the basic presumption that consumers would prefer to have a (fault-free) good while the retailer would prefer to have money; the second formulation increases the likelihood that this mutually beneficial exchange takes place.

The whole of the above analysis has proceeded on the basis of a given selling price P. If, in contrast, the retailer is allowed to vary P, then some interesting degeneracies set in. For instance, if V is maximised with respect to *both* P *and* g, the resultant first-order conditions, when solved simultaneously, imply that

$$P(1 - gp) = C = 0 \quad (19)$$

for *both* formulations, and for *all* demand functions (whether constant-elasticity or not) - an equation that in general can not be satisfied. For example, in our second formulation using the x distribution (5), we find that the first-order condition for g requires that:

$$P(1 - gp) = (b + 1)C/b, \tag{20}$$

while the first-order condition for P requires that:

$$P(1 - gp) = bC/(b - 1)\ . \tag{21}$$

Closer inspection reveals that these interior first-order conditions do not have a consistent solution because the actual optimal point is a corner solution. To be precise, since $(b + 1)/b$ is less than $b/(b - 1)$, the optimal strategy is to put $g = 1$ (one of its "corner values"), and to let P be determined by (21); thus, for optimality we require

$$g = 1 \quad \text{and} \quad P = bC/[(b - 1)(1 - p)]. \tag{22}$$

In other words, if the retailer is free to determine the price P in addition to g, he will incorporate "free replacement of faulty items" as a guaranteed part of the transaction, and, adjust his selling price accordingly (so that, in effect, the consumers are paying for the guarantee in a form of mutual insurance policy); goodwill in our sense would not exist. As might be expected, however, demand is restricted by the price-setting behaviour: when price is fixed (and is sufficiently high for g to be nonzero), the set of individuals buying the good are those with x-values larger than

$(b + 1)C/[b(1 - p)]$ (see 18);

when price is determined by the retailer according to (22), the set of individuals buying the good are those with x-values larger than

$$bC/[(b - 1)(1 - p)] \qquad \text{(see (11) and (22))}, \tag{23}$$

a number larger than that above. (As an aside, it may be interesting to note that if the retailer is free to fix price, but is restricted to goodwill values $g = 0$ and $g = 1$, the set of individuals purchasing the good will be the same - namely those with x-values above the expression in (23) - irrespective of which of these two values he chooses).

An alternative way of interpreting the comparative results of the price-fixed and the price-variable cases is to view the latter as showing how goodwill operates as a surrogate price in the former; changing g and changing P are both ways of changing the price paid per fault-free item.[10] This interpretation adds strength to our comments on the possible adverse effects of consumer legislation.

Before terminating our consideration of the price-variable case, we note that whereas the degeneracy (19) holds for all demand configurations, it need not necessarily be resolved in the manner discussed above - this was merely an illustration based on our second goodwill formulation. Other resolutions are possible. For example, the first of our formulations leads to identical equations (namely (6)) for the first-order condition for both P and g, (which is not surprising given that they always enter into V in the form $P(1 - gp)$). Thus, one of the two can be set arbitrarily (within reason), and the other adjusted optimally. In particular, they could be chosen (without any harm to the retailer) so as to maximise total expected consumer surplus (subject to (6)).

We also note that the degeneracy (19) is a consequence of the particular set of assumptions chosen. There are a variety of alternative sets of assumptions which yield interior (and thus non-degenerate) solutions. To go into details would take us beyond the scope of this paper, but some general remarks may be of use; these remarks will also indicate the various ways in which the analysis of this paper may be generalised and extended. An obvious first extension is to incorporate other attitudes towards risk (other than neutrality) into the behaviour of the various participants. As far as the demand side was concerned, non-neutral risk attitudes would imply that P and g would enter into the expression for the critical x-value in ways other than the simple multiplicative form $P(1 - gp)$. As our discussion above implies, this would, in general, lead to a resolution of the degeneracy obtained in the simple model.

Risk aversion could also be introduced on the retailer's side. The obvious way to proceed would be to assume normality of the profit-per-unit-purchased function (in light of the underlying binomial or negative binomial generating mechanism). If the retailer was then assumed to have a constant absolute risk aversion utility function, the trade-off between expected return and variance of return could easily be analysed. We have in fact made significant progress in analysing such a case; the results are interesting though lack of space forbids consideration here.

A third (though clearly not the final) possibility is to introduce some notion of *moral hazard*. To be specific, we might envisage some positive relationship between p and g - reflecting the increased carelessness of individuals when faced with an increased possibility of free replacement. We have also made progress in investigating this case; once again the results prove to be of interest. (For example, as might be expected, the existence of a moral hazard effect implies a reduction in the supply of goodwill).[11]

We now turn to more general considerations. In particular, we note that all the above analysis has been based on a 'general equilibrium' approach; that is, we have assumed throughout that all potential demanders were correctly informed about the true value of the goodwill parameter g. In practice, this is not the case, particularly for a firm newly setting up in business. What we need, therefore, is some description of the process by which consumers become informed about the value of g, and some consideration of how this learning process may affect the behaviour of the firm. We envisage two strands to this learning process - one resulting from the experience of individuals, and one resulting from the transmission of information *between* individuals. Consider first the former.

The best way to consider this process is to imagine an individual freshly becoming aware of the retailer. At this stage he may or may not have some preconceived idea of the possible value of the firm's g (such a preconceived idea could be based on the individual's general past experience of retailers, tempered by particular impressionistic evidence of the retailer in question). Two possibilities arise: first, that the individual's preconceived ideas are sufficiently adverse (relative to the firm's selling price, and the individual's x-value), and are sufficiently strongly held, for the individual to decide right from the outset that his expected surplus is likely to be negative (even taking into account possibly improved evaluations). In such a case, the individual will never buy, and he will thus never have any (direct) evidence on which to change his original preconception of g. Second, the individual's preconceived ideas may be sufficiently favourable, or held sufficiently weakly, for the individual to consider it worth his while having a trial purchase. In this case, he will gain experience as to the firm's goodwill policy, and can use this to 'update' or amend his originally held ideas. Of course, crucial to all these decisions is the number of repeat purchases he expects to make; as a generalisation, the smaller the number of such repeat purchases, the less likely he is to make a trial purchase (other things being equal) - he has potentially less to gain by learning. The reader familiar with the literature will notice the similarity with the "two-armed bandit problem" examined by Rothschild (1974).

An obvious way[12] to model this process is to assume that the individual's subjective evaluation of g during this learning process is representable by a Beta probability density function; the Beta distribution is a conjugate family for samples from the Bernouilli distribution (which is what the individual is observing). If A and B (both positive) are the parameters at some stage, and if they are such that the individual considers purchase potentially worthwhile, then two possibilities arise:

(1) *The item is fault-free:* in this case the individual gets no information about the firm's goodwill strategy (since the need for goodwill to be exercised has not arisen);the individual's beta parameters remain at A and B;

(2) *The item is faulty:* in this case information is generated; the actual information depends upon the goodwill formulation in operation. In particular:

(a) *With our first formulation* (refund a proportion g), then the individual's parameters after the purchase will be:

$$\begin{cases} A + 1 \text{ and } B & \text{if money } \textit{is} \text{ refunded:} \\ A \text{ and } B + 1 & \text{if money is } \textit{not} \text{ refunded.} \end{cases}$$

(b) *With our second formulation* (replace a proportion g), then the individual's parameters after the purchase will be:

$$\begin{cases} A + k \text{ and } B & \text{if } k \text{ faulty and } k \text{ replaced} \\ A + k - 1 \text{ and } B + 1 & \text{if } k \text{ faulty and } k - 1 \text{ replaced.} \end{cases}$$

At any stage, the individual's "best-guess" of the true value of g is given by the expected value(of the beta distribution), namely[13] $A/(A + B)$. This value will fall if the individual experiences a succession of faulty items which are not replaced(or refunded); it will rise if the individual experiences replacements (or refunds). The actual experience will, of course, depend upon the actual value of g, if the individual continued repeat purchasing for long enough, the expected value $A/(A + B)$ would approach g - in the long run he would be perfectly informed. However, he may have become discouraged by a succession of bad experiences - if these led him to stop buying he would never become perfectly informed.

The solution to the individual's optimal learning strategy would constitute a paper in itself; here we merely confine ourselves to some illustrative comments with respect to the first formulation. Here the expected surplus *conditional on knowing the true value of g* is given by

$$ES = x(1 - p) - P(1 - gp) = x(1 - p) - P + Ppg$$

for individual x. If the individual operates on a *myopic* basis, then he will replace g by its expected value $A/(A + B)$, and purchase if $x(1 - p) - P + PpA/(A + B) \geq 0$. Thereafter, he would update A and B according to the rules given above. However, it is important to recognise that this *is* myopic - in that it ignores the possibly beneficial effect of purchase *this* period on expected surpluses in *future* periods through the learning process. A non-myopic strategy would proceed as follows: suppose the individual has an infinite horizon and discounts future surpluses at the rate r. Define by $S(A, B)$ the total expected discounted surplus from following an optimal strategy starting from a period in which the parameters of the beta distribution (modelling the subjective $p.d.f.$ of g) are A and B. It can be shown that S is given by

$$S(A,B) = max\ \{0, \int_0^1 s(g)f(g)dg\}$$

where

$$s(g) = (1 - p)[(x - P) + rS(A, B)] + pg[0 + rS(A + 1,B)]$$
$$+ p(1 - g)[-P + rS(A, B + 1)],$$

and

$$f(g) = [\Gamma(A + B)/\Gamma(A)\Gamma(B)]g^{A-1} (1 - g)^{B-1}$$

This implicity defines the function $S(A, B)$ which determines the optimal strategy: if at some stage, the individual's A and B are such that $S(A, B)$ is positive, then a further purchase should take place; if however, $S(A, B)$ is zero purchasing should cease forever - the retailer has lost the customer for good.

A complete model of goodwill would incorporate such a learning process, it would also incorporate the optimal reaction of the retailer faced with such a process. A realistic model would also include a description of the flow of information *between* potential consumers; in practice, individuals do not learn purely from their own experience, but also from the experience of others. Thus, a general model might describe a shifting market in which there is a continual inflow of new potential consumers, a continual outflow of old customers (who have died or whose tastes have changed, etc.), and a continuing sharing of information and experience. In such a market, the accuracy of general conceptions about the true value of g would be higher the greater the length of time participants stay in the market, and the greater the sharing of information. It is clearly easy to envisage markets in which grave misconceptions of the true value of g may persist for a long time - indeed, one can easily imagine cases wherein, once a general feeling that the true value of g is very low has been established, it takes a long time for a real increase to be perceived.

For a new firm establishing itself in a market, the rate at which the perceived value of g approaches the true value of g depends upon the initial preconceptions of potential demanders to the new firm (an initial dislike may be hard to shake off), upon the rate of information spread between individuals, and upon the rates of inflow and outflow of the market. During this learning period, the firm may be operating at a higher level of goodwill than that "appreciated" by the market; that is, the demand generated is not the profit-maximising demand associated with the actual level of goodwill. But this, of course, is the process of investing in goodwill - of building up a good reputation. However, there is an obvious corollary: if the spread of reputation is at all slow, it may be optimal for the firm to aim at a lower level of goodwill than would be optimal with a faster spread. Alternatively, the firm may encourage the faster spread of information by initially operating at a higher level of goodwill than it intends to do in its long-term steady state. For a firm established in a market, a poor reputation may be something that is very hard to shake off - particularly if the turnover in the market is at all low; after all, most of the non-demanders in the market will have decided that the firm is not worth purchasing from, and they will need a lot of convincing to make them change their minds. For such reasons, loss of reputation (through a run of bad luck, say) can be particularly harmful to an established firm.

We are currently investigating such processes, and hope to report some results in due course. We are also involved in modelling goodwill in other forms and other markets; a brief word about these may be of interest.

One obvious extension is to more explicitly competitive markets - wherein competition is through goodwill rather than price. Here we may envisage a process similar to that discussed above, with consumers moving from firm to firm in the light of their experience. Consider the simplest of such models - with price fixed at P and just two firms. Let p remain the failure rate, and g_i $(i = 1, 2)$ the respective goodwill rates. Suppose consumers buy one unit of the good each period, initially choosing a firm at random, and then staying with that firm until he experiences a non-replaced faulty item; he then switches to the other firm until he experiences a non-replaced faulty item; and so on.[14] Denote by q_i the probability that a consumer, who purchases from firm i in some period will buy from the other firm in the next period. By the "rules of the game", q_i equals $p(1 - g_i) + p^2 g_i(1 - g_i) + p^3 g_i^2(1 - g_i) + \ldots$, that is

$$q_i = p(1 - g_i)/(1 - g_i p)\,. \tag{24}$$

Now let Q_t denote the probability that a customer entering the market at time 1 finds himself a customer of firm 1 in time period t. We have

$$Q_t = (1 - q_1)\, Q_{t-1} + q_2\, (1 - Q_{t-1}),\ (t = 2, 3, \ldots)$$

that is

$$Q_t = Q_{t-1}\, (1 - q_1 - q_2) + q_2,$$

a recursive relation which solves to give (assuming $Q_1 = \frac{1}{2}$):

$$Q_t = [\, 2q_2 + (q_1 - q_2)(1 - q_1 - q_2)^{t-1}]/[2(q_1 + q_2)]\,.$$

If we now assume that a proportion $(1 - k)$ of the market participants leave the market each period, and a similar number of new entrants arrive each period, it is a straight forward matter to show that the proportions of the total market buying from firms 1 and 2 each period (in a steady state) are, respectively,

$[1 + k(q_2 - q_1)/(1 - k + kq_1 + kq_2)]/2$ and

$[1 + k(q_1 - q_2)/(1 - k + kq_1 + kq_2)]/2.$

The first is greater than, equal to, or less than the second, according as q_1 is less than, equal to, or greater than q_2. To cut a long story short, we simply report the results of the mutually consistent optimising decisions of the two firms (assuming price P and cost C); these are as follows:

(1) $P/C \leq 1/[k(1 - p)]$

$g_i = 0 \qquad q_i = p/(1 - p)$ *for both* $i = 1, 2$

(2) $1/[k(1 - p)] < P/C \leq (1 - p + kp)/[k(1 - p)^2]$

either $g_i = 1 \qquad q_i = 0 \qquad$ *for both* $i = 1, 2$

or $g_i = 0 \qquad q_i = p\ (1 - p)$ *for both* $i = 1, 2$

(3) $(1 - p + kp)/[k(1 - p)^2] < P/C$

$g_i = 1 \qquad q_i = 0 \qquad$ *for both* $i = 1, 2$.

The second of these is particularly interesting: if the price/cost ratio is in a certain range, then *either* both firms operate full replacement *or* both firms operate no replacement, which it is is arbitrary, but both firms must do the same. (Thus two saddle points exist). We note crucially that the critical price ratios depend upon k: the larger this is (that is, the smaller the rate of turnover of the market), the smaller the critical price-ratios, and hence the more likely that (total) goodwill exists.[15] A similar result holds if the number of firms in the market increases.

Finally, we note the importance of goodwill in labour markets. Some related work in this direction has already appeared in the "implicit contracts" literature; see, for example, Azariadis (1975). The kind of model we have in mind is one in which firms do not necessarily fire workers in hard times (even though the formal contract legally entitles them so to do); by behaving in this apparently altruistic fashion they are able to attract better workers, or to pay lower wages, or to keep workers in "good times" (that is, in times when it would appear that workers have an incentive to quit and seek better opportunities elsewhere). To make sense in terms of our interpretation of goodwill, this "altruism" must necessarily be random - if, on the contrary, a firm *always* laid off workers or *always* retained workers, no goodwill would ever exist (since in the latter case the job-security would optimally appear as part of the legally binding contract). As with our simple models of commercial goodwill discussed above, a crucial element of descriptions of industrial goodwill is the relationship between the actual values of the firm's goodwill parameters and the (potential) workers' perceptions of the firm's "reliability". In addition, there are symmetrical considerations as far as individual worker's "reliability" is concerned. (By worker's reliability, we mean the reciprocal phenomenon of a worker staying with a firm even when it is apparently in his interests to quit). Some consideration of this latter effect is contained in Grossman (1977).

In conclusion, we must admit that our formal analysis has barely scratched the surface, in the real world, goodwill exists in a multitude of different forms and in many different guises. Moreover, we must admit that our simple illustrative models are crude abstractions of the complex forms that exist in practice. However, we hope that these models are a step in the right direction, and that they capture the essential features of goodwill. We also hope that we have provided a solid theoretical basis for the study of goodwill - particularly crucial to this, we feel, are the twin concepts of *voluntariness* and *reciprocity*. We hope to build further on these foundations in subsequent work. It seems appropriate to leave the final words to Commons (1924, p.273).

"That goodwill should not have found its place in the economic theories of value while it is the crux of legal theories of value and the principal asset of business must probably be explained by the individualistic materialism and hedonism of those theories which sought to eliminate the will as something capricious. Yet goodwill can be seen and felt - seen not in commodities, but in the transactions of business; and felt, not in consumption and production, but in the confidence of patrons, investors and employees."

REFERENCES

Azariadis, C. (1975). Implicit Contracts and Underemployment Equilibria. *Journal of Political Economy* 83, 1183-1202.

Bloomberg, L.D. (1938). *The Investment Value of Goodwill.* The John Hopkins University Studies in Historical and Political Science, Series LV1, No.3.

Commons, J.R. (1919). *Industrial Goodwill.* New York.

Commons, J.R. (1924). *Legal Foundations of Capitalism.* Wisconsin: University of Wisconsin Press.

Degroot, M.M. (1970). *Optimal Statistical Decisions.* New York: McGraw-Hill.

Foreman, C.J. (1927). Economies and Profits of Good-will. *American Economic Review* 13, 209-24.

Foreman, C.J. (1925). Computation of Good-will Profits. *American Economic Review* 15, 652-64.

Grossman, H.I. (1977). Risk Shifting and Reliability in Labor Markets. *Scandinavian Journal of Economics* 79, 187-209.

Heal, G.M. (1977). Guarantees and Risk-Sharing. *Review of Economic Studies* 44, 549-60.

Jones, F.H. (1970). *Guide to Company Balance Sheets and Profit and Loss Accounts* 3rd Edition. Cambridge: Heffer.

Leake, P.D. (1930). *Commercial Goodwill.* London: Pitman.

Powelson, J.P. (1955). *Economic Accounting.* New York: McGraw-Hill.

Robinson, J. (1933). *Economics of Imperfect Competition.* London: Macmillan.

Rothschild, M. (1974). A Two-armed Bandit Theory of Market Pricing. *Journal of Economic Theory* 9, 185-202.

Spence, M. (1977). Consumer Misperceptions, Product Failure and Producer Liability. *Review of Economic Studies* 44, 561-72.

Taussig, F.W. (1921). *Principles of Economics* Vol.1, 3rd Edition Revised. New York: Macmillan.

Zeckhauser, R. (1970). Medical Insurance: A Case Study of the Trade-Off between Risk Spreading and Appropriate Incentives. *Journal of Economic Theory* 2. 10-26.

FOOTNOTES

1. A particularly interesting case, that of *Stapley* v *Read Bros. Ltd.* (1924), is quoted by Jones (1970, p.150). The gist of this case is that the goodwill originally stood at £140,000, and was subsequently written down out of profits over a period of years to £51,000; simultaneously a reserve of £61,000 was created out of profits. The balance of goodwill was then written off against this reserve, reducing the latter to £10,000. In due course, the reserve was built up to £40,000 which was then distributed in the form of fully paid shares by way of a capital bonus. Unfortunately, the company then hit hard times and accumulated losses totalling over £20,000. The next year proved better with profits of some £13,000. At this stage, the directors proposed to pay three years' arrears of preference dividend out of this £13,000, whilst simultaneously writing off the accumulated loss (of over £20,000) *by restoring goodwill in the books at £40,000 and crediting reserve account with this amount.* As might be expected, this proposal caused a few sparks, resulting in an injunction being sought to restrain the directors from this proposed action (for obvious reasons). The final upshot, however, was interesting: Mr. Justice Russell *refused* the injunction on the grounds that the profits used earlier to write off goodwill had not been permanently capitalised.
2. There may, of course, be tax reasons why such a procedure is followed.
3. The implication being that the rate of return on tangible assets is less uncertain than the rate of return on intangible assets; a proposition which few

would want to dispute unless the intangible assets were protected by law (or custom) in such a way that they assumed the characteristics of tangible assets.

4. It may be interesting to note in passing the similarity of the 'goodwill problem' with the Prisoners' Dilemma. Both sides stand to gain from the building-up of goodwill, yet both may be forever tempted to take steps which may result in the destruction of the goodwill stock.
5. As our interest is primarily with the non-legal implications, we ignore problems such as the cost of enforcing legal requirements. We assume that the legal process is such that the law is always enforced at zero cost to the innocent party and at a sufficiently penal cost to the offending party, so that there is never any incentive for the latter to exist.
6. In many areas of law, it appears that repeated usage of a particular custom over a number of years may make that custom into a legally binding contract. For example, public rights of way, or use of unused land. Also we note that the law recognises that legally binding contracts need not be written: verbal statements may well be equally binding.
7. Risk-neutrality has been assumed.
8. If the assumption is invalid, then g should be put equal to zero - goodwill does not exist, and no further discussion is necessary.
9. This follows since $(b + 1)/b \leq (b - 1)^{b-1} (b+1)^{b+1}/b^{2b} \leq b/(b - 1)$ for all $b \geq 1$.
10. Or, as an anonymous referee has pointed out, choosing g is somewhat analogous to choosing product quality. In this respect, the literature on product quality is relevant; see, for example, Heal (1977) and Spence (1977).
11. A useful analogy here is the choice of a deductible in an insurance contract in the presence of moral hazard; see, for example, Zeckhauser (1970).
12. For details, see Degroot (1970) especially pp.160-1.
13. See Degroot (1970, p.40).
14. This is not necessarily an optimal strategy; the latter may be very complex, as Rothschild (1974) indicates.
15. The degeneracy results from the simplifying assumptions. As with the single retailer, more realistic assumptions lead to less degeneracies and more possibilities of interior solutions.

DISCUSSION: IVY PAPPS

A glance at the bibliography reveals that there has been no directly relevant economic literature for the last forty-five years. So I should like to start by thanking John Hey for rescuing the subject from the obscurity into which it has fallen among economists and providing us with an interesting preliminary analysis.

My remarks fall into two main areas.

The first starts out as a comment on semantics but develops, I hope, into a somewhat more substantive point. Mr. Hey pays some attention to the accountants treatment of goodwill and places most emphasis on the impermanence and uncertainty of goodwill. This leads him to a consideration of the generation of goodwill by means of the *uncertain* and *voluntary* provision of extra services on the part of a supplier. Although this generates some interesting results, which I shall discuss later, I think that it has also led to a neglect of some aspects of goodwill which may be more important in the real world.

When accountants (usually at the time when a company is sold) include the value of goodwill in the balance sheet, they are,of course, simply capitalising all returns which are greater than the normal returns on the physical assets. Such supernormal returns have several sources. They may, of course, be simply monopoly profits or rent on specialised factors of production and I agree with John, that there is no useful purpose to be served by considering such returns in an analysis of goodwill since they are already analysed by another branch of economic theory. Second, they may be returns from the kind of behaviour which John analyses in his paper. Third, they may be returns from the *uncertain or certain* services by which the supplier attempts to differentiate his product - and I think that, on the whole, this is the meaning of goodwill which corresponds most closely to popular usage. That is, a firm in monopolistic competition can make its own demand curve less elastic by slightly differentiating its own product from that of its competitors. Lipsey's first year textbook argues that retailing provides a reasonably good example of monopolist competition and it is of some interest that when one thinks of goodwill, the example of retailing again springs to mind. I am not convinced that, in this case, the provision of the service must be uncertain. It seems to me that under certain conditions, some firms will have an incentive to differentiate their products by providing various probabilities of replacement or refund - and the optimal probability for some firms may be unity. Mr. Hey will argue that, in this case, there is no goodwill because replacement or refund will become an enforceable part of the contract and the retailer can charge a price which reflects this. But if the product is differentiated and the retailers can adjust price as well as the level of refunds, then this will presumably be true for all retailers whether they operate a policy of guaranteed refund or not. Moreover, it seems to me to be a little strange to omit from consideration a case which one would consider in common parlance as generating goodwill.

All of this semantic discussion is intended to provide an introduction to the main point I wanted to make which is that I was uncomfortable about the paper's omission of any rigorous discussion of market structure. This worried me because the more I thought about it, the more convinced I was that any discussion of goodwill depended crucially on the market structure being assumed. For example, Mr. Hey obtains most of his results from what is essentially a monopoly model. (Although as he shows later, he has to set the price exogenously to obtain a result.) I wondered what would happen under perfect competition. It is clear that in the long-run, g and P must be set so that

$$P(1 - pg) = C \qquad (1)$$

i.e. $AR = AC$

and quantity demand (and supplied) will be

$$D = Na^{b}C^{-b}\ (1-p)^{b} \qquad (2)$$

That is, LR competitive equilibrium depends only on costs, the parameters of the demand function and the probability of a faulty item. g and P may be set at any values so long as they satisfy equation (1). Notice that no firm has a positive value for goodwill, not because of the parameters of the problem, but because competition will bid away super-normal returns from goodwill as it does from any other factor.

As Mr. Hey shows, with monopoly power the firm can earn supernormal returns by generating goodwill. The profits earned by the monopolist when $g = 0$ are:

$$N\, a^{b} P^{-b} (1-p)^{b} [P-C] \qquad (3)$$

and the *extra* profits due to goodwill are given by equation (7) in the paper.

When I came to consider monopolistic competition - the case which I think is potentially most interesting - I discovered why it had not been analysed in the paper. It is in fact extremely difficult to analyse within this simple framework and, I suspect, impossible if one holds to the assumption that all consumers are risk-neutral. My own feeling is that some progress could be made by allowing individuals to differ in their attitudes to risk and thus provide an incentive for firms to differ in the amount of refund/replacement they offer. In the long-run, of course, one would expect the value of goodwill to be reduced to zero as free entry allows supernormal profits to be bid away but one cannot really analyse this case unless both P and g are allowed to vary. John argues that a determinate solution cannot be found in the case of risk-neutrality and I hope that he will be tempted to consider the case of various degrees of risk-aversion and perhaps consider the implications for product differentiation.

I am forced to the conclusion that, at the moment, this paper has provided us with a theory of goodwill which is directly applicable only to the case of monopoly. However, even here, I think that Mr. Hey has not got as much mileage as he might out of his simple model. For example, although he discusses the important welfare implications, he does not consider the positive implications of equation (7). As I understand it, equation (7) shows the value to the monopolistic firm of its "goodwill behaviour" and it seems interesting to ask how this value varies with conditions facing the firm. It turns out that, under this formulation, the value of goodwill varies negatively with respect to p. That is, firms selling a product with a high probability of a fault will *ceteris paribus* have a low value of goodwill. There may be a possibility of some empirical work here and I would like to see whether the positive implications could be extended.

9. THE VALUE OF NON-MARGINAL CHANGES IN PHYSICAL RISK

M. Jones-Lee

To date, virtually all of the theoretical and empirical work on the "value of life" has concentrated on essentially *marginal* variations in physical risk.[1] The standard argument goes something like this. Suppose that the ith individual's marginal rate of substitution[2] of wealth (a) for (subjective) probability of his own death during some forthcoming period is m_{ii} and (b) for (subjective) probability of the jth individual's death is m_{ij}. The aggregate compensating variation, V, for a safety-improvement scheme yielding small changes in subject probabilities $\delta p_{ij} (i,j = 1...n)$ in a society of n individuals (where p_{ij} is the ith individual's subjective probability of death for the jth individual etc.) is then given by,[3]

$$V = -(\sum_i m_{ii}\delta p_{ii} + \sum_{\substack{ij \\ (j \neq i)}}\sum m_{ij}\delta p_{ij}), \tag{1}$$

the first component of V being the aggregate compensating variation for changes in probabilities of "own" death and the second being that for changes in probabilities of "other people's" death.

Now suppose that the safety improvement is such as to produce a "uniform" variation in physical risk, i.e.

$$(\forall ij)\ \delta p_{ij} = -\frac{x}{n} \tag{2}$$

where n is the number of individuals in society and x is sufficiently small in relation to n to ensure that (1) remains a good approximation.

Substituting from (2) into (1) we get,

$$V = \frac{x}{n}\sum_{i} m_{ii} + \frac{x}{n}\sum_{\substack{ij\\(j\neq i)}}\sum m_{ij}\ , \qquad (3)$$

That is, V is then x *times* the sum of the population average of m_{ii} and the population average of $\sum_{\substack{j\\(j\neq i)}} m_{ij}$.

Furthermore, the expected number of lives to be saved by the scheme is simply x, so that it is natural to regard $\frac{1}{n}\sum_{i} m_{ii} + \frac{1}{n}\sum_{\substack{ij\\(j\neq i)}}\sum m_{ij}$ as the "value of one statistical life".

The problem of placing a value on human life for the purposes of a conventional cost-benefit analysis in allocative decisions that affect safety is therefore reduced to one of obtaining information concerning typical orders of magnitude of m_{ii} and m_{ij}.

A number of criticisms have been levelled against this argument. For example,

(i) For small changes in risk, subjective probabilities are unlikely to show any close correspondence to "objective" probabilities (i.e. an expert's assessment) so that it is not at all clear that these subjective probabilities ought to form the basis for so crucial an exercise as the valuation of safety.

(ii) This approach to the valuation of life and safety makes no distinction between the various modes of death and this may be a significant over-simplification (people may, for example, have a marked preference for death during sleep rather than in, say, a nuclear disaster).

(iii) Equation (1) involves a raw *unweighted* sum of individual compensating variations and as such takes no account of the distribution of income or wealth. Assuming that m_{ii} and m_{ij} are (*cet. par.*) increasing functions of wealth this means that the safety of the rich (and those they care for) will tend to be given relatively greater weight in the allocative decision process than the safety of the poor.[4]

(iv) This approach to taking decisions that affect life and

death is misconceived because cost-benefit analysis *ought* to ask questions about the possibility of actual compensation *ex post* and death is an event for which no sum, however large, could possibly compensate *ex post*. In short, life and death are incommensurable with other commodities and consequently inherently incapable of valuation in monetary terms.[5]

It must be admitted that these criticisms are important and deserve serious consideration in assessing the legitimacy of the proposed procedure for valuing life. Indeed I shall offer some comments on criticisms (i)-(iii) in the final section of this paper - I have dealt at length with criticism (iv) elsewhere[6] and shall therefore not consider it further at this stage. However, the primary purpose of the present paper is to examine, and hopefully rectify, what I believe to be a rather more serious limitation of the approach to valuation of safetyoutlined above, namely that *by its very nature it is capable of dealing only with very small (i.e. marginal) changes in risk*. This limitation is especially serious in view of the fact that one of the most pressing current allocative issues concerns the generation of nuclear power and the disposal of nuclear waste, both of which involve essentially non-marginal changes in physical risk. More specifically, the *International Commission on Radiological Protection (I.C.R.P.)* has recommended:

(i) that no practice shall be adopted unless its introduction produces a positive net benefit;

(ii) all radiation exposures shall be kept as low as reasonably achievable, economic and social factors being taken into account (this is known as the ALARA principle) and

(iii) the radiation dose to individuals shall not exceed the limits recommended for the appropriate circumstances by the I.C.R.P.[7]

Furthermore, the I.C.R.P. has indicated that in assessing "net benefits" and in taking account of "economic and social factors", a conventional cost-benefit analysis is to be employed.

These recommendations have been adopted in a number of countries including the U.K. and indeed the *National Radio-*

logical Protection Board (N.R.P.B.) is currently in the process of evolving specific procedures for putting the I.C.R.P. recommendations into practice in this country. As a result of physiological research, it is now possible to associate with each level of radiation exposure an expected number of "health effects" (e.g. fatal cancers) that will arise in a given population. It is therefore clearly of crucial importance for the N.R.P.B. in implementing the I.C.R.P. recommendations to be able to assign values (or costs) to these health effects. This means that in the case of, for example, fatal cancers, the N.R.P.B. requires values (or costs) for the saving (loss) of *statistical* life. *Furthermore, for decisions involving radiation doses at or near to the I.R.C.P. dose limits it seems unlikely that it will be legitimate to regard x as sufficiently small in relation to n for equation (3) to remain a good approximation.* Clearly, then, what is required is information concerning compensating variations in wealth for essentially *non-marginal* changes in physical risk.

1. *An Analytical Framework*

Let us denote by v_{ij} the ith individual's compensating variation for a change in current period probability of death for the jth individual from $\bar{p}_{ij}$ to p_{ij}. In Jones-Lee (1976) I have shown that under fairly general conditions on preferences and attitudes to risk, v_{ij} will be related to p_{ij} by a function whose graph is of the general form shown in Figure 1.

Now notice that

(i) The marginal rate of substitution, m_{ij}, is simply the modulus of the gradient of this graph at A i.e. $m_{ij} = -\left(\frac{\partial v_{ij}}{\partial p_{ij}}\right)_{\bar{p}_{ij}}$

(ii) Unless there exists a finite sum that will compensate the ith individual for the certainty of the jth individual's death, then v_{ij} becomes unbounded below for some increment

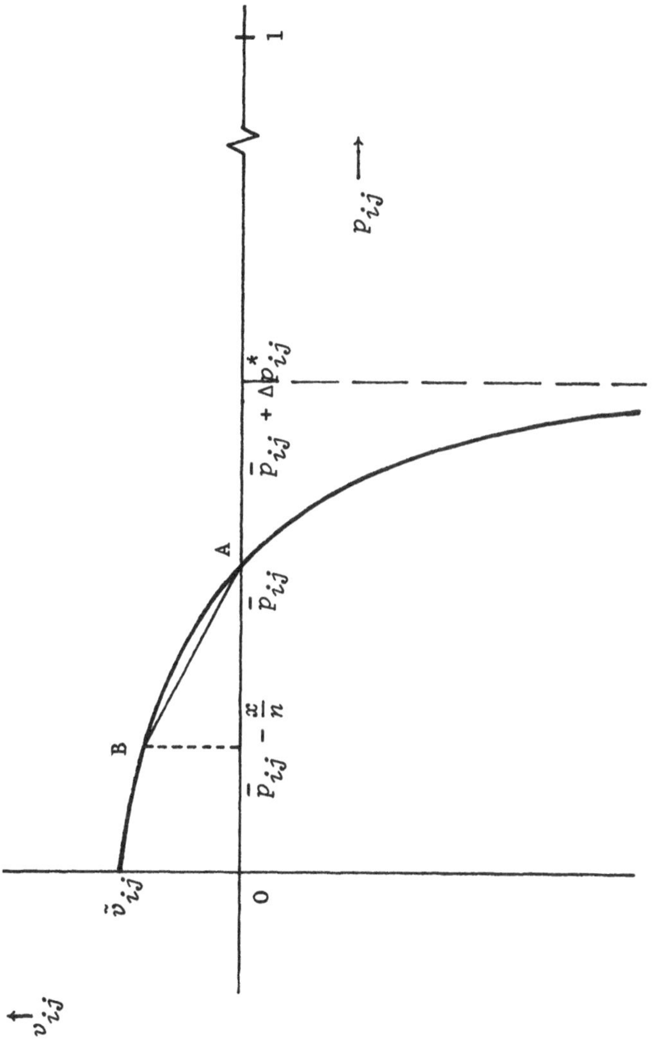
v_{ij}
$\tilde{v}_{ij}$
0
B
A
$\bar{p}_{ij} - \frac{x}{n}$
$\bar{p}_{ij}$
$\bar{p}_{ij} + \Delta p^*_{ij}$
p_{ij}
1

Figure 1

in risk $\Delta p_{ij}{}^{*} \leq 1 - \bar{p}_{ij}$.

It seems natural to refer to such an increment in risk, if it exists, as the ith individual's "maximum acceptable increase in risk for the jth individual". Since it is unlikely that many individuals could be compensated with any finite sum for the certainty of their *own* death during the current period, it will be assumed in what follows that there does indeed exist a "maximum acceptable increase in risk of own death", $\Delta p_{ii}{}^{*}$.

(iii) While it is almost certainly impossible to make life "completely safe" for anyone during a forthcoming period, it is nonetheless convenient to consider the hypothetical safety improvement that does indeed completely eliminate risk during the current period. The ith individual's compensating variation for the complete elimination of physical risk to the jth individual during the current period is denoted by $\tilde{v}_{ij}$.

(iv) The counterpart to equation (3) for a uniform *non-marginal* decrease in risk, $(\forall_{ij})\Delta p_{ij} = -\frac{x}{n}$, is

$$V = \sum_{i} v_{ii} + \sum_{\substack{ij \\ (j \neq i)}}\sum v_{ij} \tag{4}$$

Or, denoting the modulus of the gradient of the chord AB in Figure 1 by μ_{ij},

$$V = \sum_{i} \mu_{ij}\frac{x}{n} + \sum_{\substack{ij \\ (j \neq i)}}\sum \mu_{ij}\frac{x}{n} \tag{5}$$

$$= \frac{x}{n}\sum_{i} \mu_{ii} + \frac{x}{n}\sum_{\substack{ij \\ (j \neq i)}}\sum \mu_{ij} \tag{5'}$$

Clearly, then, for variations in physical risk that involve non-marginal changes in p_{ij}, the value of one statistical life is given by the population averages of μ_{ii} and $\sum_{\substack{j \\ (j \neq i)}} \mu_{ij}$. (Notice that the limits of these averages as $\frac{x}{n} \to 0$ are the averages of m_{ii} and $\sum_{\substack{j \\ (j \neq i)}} m_{ij}$ respectively which identifies (3) as a special case of (5').

Ultimately the size of these population averages (and their relationship with the magnitude of the risk change $-\frac{x}{n}$) is an empirical matter. In the remainder of this paper, however, I shall attempt to establish results concerning the broad order of magnitude of $\frac{1}{n}\sum_i \mu_{ii} + \frac{1}{n}\sum\sum \mu_{ij}$ in relation to $-\frac{x}{n}$ by assuming

(i) that these population averages can be considered by reference to an "average" ("typical", "representative") individual and

(ii) by considering the implications of fairly weak restrictionson this typical individual's preferences and attitudes to risk.

In addition the analysis that follows will concentrate upon μ_{ii} and m_{ii} since much of what is said concerning these also applies, *mutatis mutandis*, to μ_{ij} and m_{ij}.[8] From this point on, therefore, subscripts will be suppressed, m, μ and p denoting respectively m_{ii}, μ_{ii} and p_{ii} for the typical individual.

2. *Some Properties of $v(p)$*

In this section it will be shown that there exists a surprisingly simple relationship between m and Δp^*. It will also be argued that, while $v(p)$ is strictly concave, it may be legitimate in a significant number of cases to treat $v(p)$ as *approximately linear* for $p < \bar{p}$. These results are potentially very important because they provide *a priori* restrictions on the function relating μ and p at key points in its domain of definition. While this in no sense permits us to give a full specification of $\mu(p)$, nonetheless, given the concavity of $v(p)$ it does significantly narrow down the range of possibilities.

In order to derive these results, I shall employ a model developed in an earlier A.U.T.E. paper.[9] The basic assumption of this model is that the individual's preference ordering over joint subjective probability distributions of (a) the present value of his wealth, w, (defined to include discounted future labour income) and (b) the time of his death τ (measured from the present) is representable by the mathematical expectation of a Von-Neumann/Morgenstern type of utility function, U. In addition it will be assumed that U can be satisfactorily approximated by the additive-separable form

$$U(w,\tau) = u(w) + \ell(\tau) \tag{6}$$

with

(i) $(\forall w)\ u'(w) > 0,\ u''(w) < 0,$

(ii) u bounded,

(iii) $(\forall \tau)\ \ell'(\tau) > 0.$

While I have established results for more general forms of U elsewhere,[10] it is convenient both from an analytical and expository point of view to work with the separable form of U particularly because separability implies that if the individual has access to actuarially fair life insurance and annuity markets then he will plan insurance and annuity purchases so as precisely to cover his human capital (i.e. given that he is optimally insured, w will be *independent* of τ). This may at first seem to be an inordinately extensive degree of cover, but it is worth noting that any middle-income individual with a "mortgage protection" policy and an occupational pension scheme having widow's and orphans' benefits, is probably already in a situation in which his human capital is close to being fully covered.

Now suppose that the latest date at which the individual conceives it possible that he will still be alive is T. Let us divide the interval $[0,T]$ into T (short) periods and denote by p_τ the probability of death during period τ *conditional* upon survival of the preceding $\tau - 1$ periods. The individual's compensating variation, v, for a perturbation in the vector of conditional probabilities of death from $\bar{p} = (\bar{p}_1, \bar{p}_2 \ldots \bar{p}_T)$ to $p = (p_1, p_2 \ldots p_T)$ will then satisfy[11]

$$u(w-v) + \mathrm{E}\ell = u(w) + \bar{\mathrm{E}}\ell \tag{7}$$

where

$$\left.\begin{aligned} E\ell &= \ell(1)p_1 + \ell(2)p_2(1-p_1) + \ell(3)p_3(1-p_2)(1-p_1) + \text{etc} \\ &\text{and in particular} \\ \bar{E}\ell &= \ell(1)\bar{p}_1 + \ell(2)\bar{p}_2(1-\bar{p}_1) + \ell(3)\bar{p}_3(1-\bar{p}_2)(1-\bar{p}_1) + \text{etc} \end{aligned}\right] \tag{8}$$

While (7) and (8) could in principle be used to investigate the relationship between v and any configuration of perturbations in $\bar{p}_1\ \bar{p}_2 \ldots \bar{p}_n$, it is of particular interest to consider a *ceteris paribus* variation in $\bar{p}_1$. Setting $p_2 = \bar{p}_2$, $p_3 = \bar{p}_3$ etc., and differentiating through (7) with respect to p_1 we get,

$$-\left(\frac{\partial v}{\partial p_1}\right)_{\bar{p}_1} \;(=m) \;=\; \frac{\bar{E}\ell - \ell(1)}{(1-\bar{p}_1)\; u'(w)} \tag{9}$$

Also, by setting $p_1 = \bar{p}_1 + \Delta p_1$ in (7) we get

$$\Delta p_1 = (1-\bar{p}_1)\frac{[u(w-v) - u(w)]}{\bar{E}\ell - \ell(1)} \tag{10}$$

But, as $\Delta p_1 \to \Delta p_1^*$ so $v \to -\infty$ so that

$$\Delta p_1^* = (1-\bar{p}_1)\frac{[u^* - u(w)]}{\bar{E}\ell - \ell(1)} \tag{11}$$

where u^* denotes sup. $u(w)$.

Combining (9) and (11) then gives

$$m\Delta p_1^* \frac{u'(w)}{u^* - u(w)} = 1 \;. \tag{12}$$

Thus it has proved possible to obtain a very simple expression relating m and Δp_1^*. However, the content and significance of this expression would be substantially illuminated if an operational interpretation could be found for the ratio $\frac{u'(w)}{u^* - u(w)}$. Fortunately it turns out that there is an extremely straightforward and concrete interpretation for this conflation of characteristics of the "utility of wealth" component of U. In Jones-Lee (1980) I have shown that $\frac{u'(w)}{u^* - u(w)}$ provides a natural measure of risk-aversion for small-stake, *large*-prize gambles (the Pratt-Arrow measure of "absolute risk-aversion" RA, it will be recalled is relevant only for small-stake, *small*-prize gambles[12]). In fact $\frac{u'(w)}{u^* - u(w)}$ gives directly the critical win/loss probability ratio that will just induce an individual to participate in small-stake, large-prize gambles[13] (that is, if π is the win-probability that will just induce an individual to undertake a gamble with stake x and net-of-stake prize y, then with x small and y large, $\frac{\pi}{1-\pi}$ is approximated by $\frac{x\, u'(w)}{u^* - u(w)}$, the quality of the approximation improving the smaller is x and the larger is y). This measure is referred to as "asymptotic risk aversion" and is denoted by RL. Its properties and relationship with RA are fully discussed in the paper cited.

Given this, we can rewrite (12) as

$$m\Delta p_1^* \, RL = 1, \tag{12'}$$

which is an expression of extraordinary simplicity and provides a basis, for example, for assessing the compatibility of public sector proposals concerning the value of statistical life on the one hand and legally (or conventionally) imposed hazard limits on the other.[14]

Now let us examine the behaviour of $v(p)$ at the other extreme of its domain of definition, i.e. for $p_1 < \bar{p}_1$ and in particular for $p_1 = 0$. Provided that v is at least three-times differentiable with respect to p_1 then, recalling that $v(\bar{p}_1) = 0$, we can use Taylor's Theorem to write,

$$v(p_1) = (p_1-\bar{p}_1)\, v'(\bar{p}_1) + \frac{(p_1-\bar{p}_1)^2}{2}\, v''(\bar{p}_1) + \frac{(p_1-\bar{p}_1)^3}{6}\, v'''(\hat{p}_1) \tag{13}$$

where $v'(\bar{p}_1)$ denotes $\left.\frac{\partial v}{\partial p_1}\right|_{\bar{p}_1}$ etc. and $\hat{p}_1$ is interior to the interval joining $\bar{p}_1$ and p_1.

But from (7) and (8) it follows that for general values of p_1 (i.e. not just $p_1 = \bar{p}_1$),

$$\frac{\partial v}{\partial p_1} = -\left[\frac{\bar{E}\ell - \ell(1)}{(1-\bar{p}_1)u'(w-v)}\right] , \tag{14}$$

and

$$\frac{\partial^2 v}{\partial p_1^2} = \left[\frac{\bar{E}\ell - \ell(1)}{(1-\bar{p}_1)u'(w-v)}\right]^2 \frac{u''(w-v)}{u'(w-v)} \tag{15}$$

$$= -\left(\frac{\partial v}{\partial p_1}\right)^2 RA \tag{15'}$$

where *RA* is the Pratt-Arrow measure of "absolute risk-aversion evaluated at $w-v$.

Thus, from (15')

$$\frac{\partial^3 v}{\partial p_1^3} = -2\,\frac{\partial v}{\partial p_1}\,\frac{\partial^2 v}{\partial p_1^2}\,RA + \left(\frac{\partial v}{\partial p_1}\right)^3 \frac{dRA}{dw} \tag{16}$$

$$= \left(\frac{\partial v}{\partial p_1}\right)^3 \left(2RA^2 + \frac{dRA}{dw}\right) \tag{16'}$$

Now given $(\forall w)$ $u'(w) > 0$ and $u''(w) < 0$, it is clear from (14) and (15) that $\frac{\partial v}{\partial p_1}$ and $\frac{\partial^2 v}{\partial p_1^2}$ are both *negative* for all values of p_1 for which $v(p_1)$ is defined. However, the sign of $\frac{\partial^3 v}{\partial p_1^3}$ is strictly indeterminate if, as is usually assumed,

RA decreases with wealth. Nonetheless, there are strong grounds for supposing that $\frac{dRA}{dw}$ will normally be small enough for us to ignore its effect and treat $\frac{\partial^3 v}{\partial p_1^3}$ as negative. Thus, for example, consider the exponential and homogeneous forms of $u(w)$, $u(w) = -\alpha e^{-\beta w}$ and $u(w) = -\gamma w^{-\eta}$ $(\alpha, \beta, \gamma, \eta > 0)$. These forms of $u(w)$ in a sense represent limiting cases in the class of utility functions having the desirable "decreasing absolute/increasing relative risk aversion" properties (the exponential utility function has constant absolute and increasing relative risk aversion, while the homogeneous form exhibits decreasing absolute and constant relative risk aversion). In the exponential case $\frac{dRA}{dw}$ is exactly zero. In the homogeneous case we have $RA = \frac{\eta+1}{w}$ and $\frac{dRA}{dw} = \frac{-(\eta+1)}{w^2}$ so that the term $2RA^2 + \frac{dRA}{dw}$ in (16') becomes $\frac{(\eta+1)}{w^2}(2\eta+1)$ which is unambiguously positive. It would therefore seem appropriate to treat $\frac{\partial^3 v}{\partial p_1^3} < 0$ as the "normal" case so that from (13)

$$p_1 < \bar{p}_1 \Rightarrow v(p_1) > (p_1-\bar{p}_1)v'(\bar{p}_1) + \frac{(p_1-\bar{p}_1)^2}{2} v''(\bar{p}_1). \tag{17}$$

But, given the concavity of $v(p)$, it must also be the case that

$$p_1 < \bar{p}_1 \Rightarrow v(p_1) < (p_1-\bar{p}_1)v'(\bar{p}_1). \tag{18}$$

Thus from (12'), (15'), (17) and (18)

$$p_1 < \bar{p}_1 \Rightarrow (p_1-\bar{p}_1)v'(\bar{p}_1) > v(p_1) > (p_1-\bar{p}_1)v'(\bar{p}_1)\left[1-\frac{(p_1-\bar{p}_1)}{2\Delta p_1^*}\frac{RA}{RL}\right]. \tag{19}$$

Clearly, then, the error in treating $v(p_1)$ as linear for

$p_1 < \bar{p}_1$ with, in particular, $\tilde{v} \approx m\bar{p}_1$, depends on the size of the term $\frac{(p_1-\bar{p}_1)}{\Delta p_1^*} \frac{RA}{RL}$. While it is generally true that, with u well-behaved, $RA \geq RL$ (see Jones-Lee (1980)), it is again instructive to consider the exponential and homogeneous forms of $u(w)$. In the exponential case we have $RA = RL$, while in the homogeneous case $\frac{RA}{RL} = \frac{\eta+1}{\eta}$. However, an empirical study by Friend and Blume (1975) suggests that RR ($= \eta + 1$ in this case) is typically between 3 and 5 so that there is probably little error in treating $RA \approx RL$ as the "typical" case. Thus if, for example, $\Delta p_1^* \geq 2\bar{p}_1$ (and with the objective counterpart to $\bar{p}_1$ being about 10^{-3} for the coming year for an individual aged 30-40, this does not seem unduly restrictive) then the error in treating $v(p_1)$ as linear over the entire interval $[0,\bar{p}_1]$ would be at most about 25% and substantially less than this if we restricted attention to, say, the interval $\left[\frac{\bar{p}_1}{2}, \bar{p}_1\right]$. While this argument admittedly lacks the robustness and generality of the earlier result concerning the relationship between m and Δp_1^*, it would nonetheless seem legitimate to treat approximate linearity of $v(p_1)$ for $p_1 < \bar{p}_1$ as the norm rather than the exception.

Combining the results obtained so far we can now give a very much more complete specification of the overall form of $v(p)$ than was possible in Figure 1 (see Figure 2).

This in turn means that the graph of $\mu(p)$ will take the general form as shown in Figure 3.

It has, therefore, proved possible to say quite a lot about the value of non-marginal changes in physical risk on the basis of relatively weak assumptions concerning the preferences of the typical individual. However, we can go just a little bit further. Putting $p_2 = \bar{p}_2$, $p_3 = \bar{p}_3$ etc. in equation (7), it follows that

$$u(w-v) - u(w) = \frac{(p_1-\bar{p}_1)}{1-\bar{p}_1} [\bar{E}\ell - \ell(1)]. \tag{20}$$

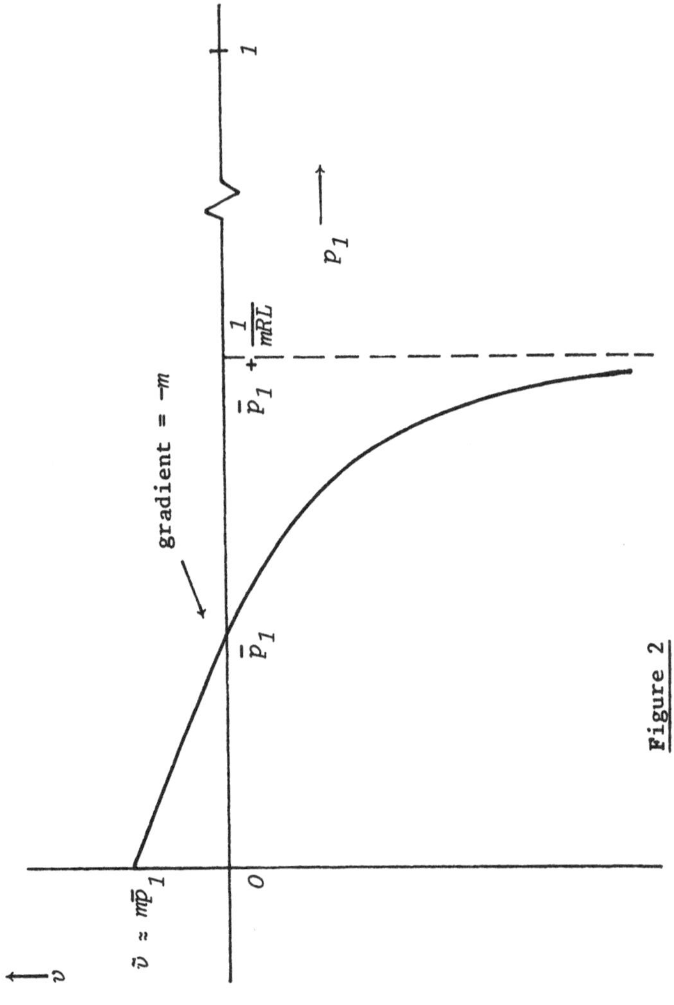

Figure 2

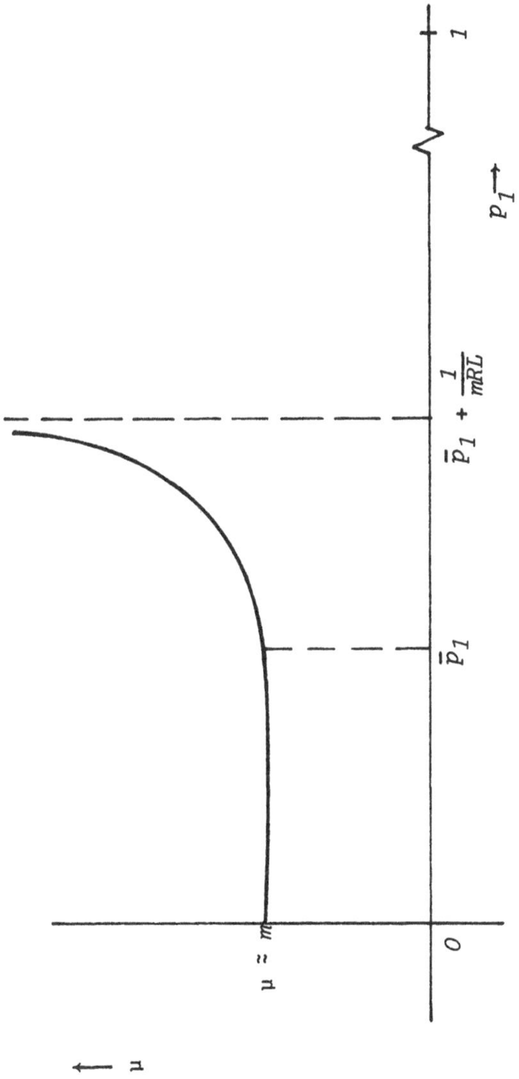

1
$p_1 \rightarrow$
$\bar{p}_1 + \frac{1}{mRL}$
$\bar{p}_1$
0
$\mu \approx m$
$\mu \rightarrow$

Figure 3

Substituting from (11) to (20) we therefore get

$$u(w-v) - u(w) = \frac{(p_1-\bar{p}_1)}{\Delta p_1^*} [u^*-u(w)] \tag{21}$$

or, putting $u^* = 0$ (as we may do given the two degrees of freedom associated with U) and re-arranging,

$$\frac{u(w-v)}{u(w)} = 1 - \frac{(p_1-\bar{p}_1)}{\Delta p_1^*} \; . \tag{22}$$

Clearly then, all that is required to generate a *complete specification* of the relationship between v and p_1 is a set of values for $\bar{p}_1$, Δp_1^* and the parameters of $u(w)$ (notice that we do *not* need any information concerning $\ell(\tau)$[15]). In the next section equation (22) will therefore be used to generate the $v - p_1$ relationship (and hence the $\mu - p_1$ relationship) for various configurations of $\bar{p}_1$ and Δp_1^* for the exponential and homogeneous forms of $u(w)$. Since the parameters of these two classes of utility function are themselves readily interpretable in terms of the Pratt-Arrow risk-aversion measures, full specification of the $v - p_1$ relationship (and hence the $\mu - p_1$ relationship) will require only values for $\bar{p}_1$, Δp_1^* and RA (or RR). Thus, provided that the typical individual's utility of wealth function can be adequately approximated by the exponential or homogeneous forms (and these are, indeed, broadly well-behaved classes of utility function) then we shall have succeeded in acquiring a fairly substantial "feel" for what would appear to be the range of probable orders of magnitude of the typical individual's valuation of non-marginal changes in physical risk.

3. *The Relationship Between v and p_1 for Exponential and Homogeneous $u(w)$*

If the utility of wealth function takes the exponential form, $u(w) = -\alpha\, e^{-\beta w}$ $(\alpha,\beta > 0)$, then equation (22) gives

$$e^{\beta v} = 1 - \frac{(p_1 - \bar{p}_1)}{\Delta p_1^*} \qquad (23)$$

Furthermore, for this class of utility functions $\beta = RA = \frac{RR}{w}$ so that we can write

$$e^{RR\frac{v}{w}} = 1 - \frac{(p_1 - \bar{p}_1)}{\Delta p_1^*} \qquad (23')$$

For the homogeneous utility of wealth function, $u(w) = -\gamma\, w^{-\eta} (\gamma, \eta > 0)$, equation (22) gives

$$\left(1 - \frac{v}{w}\right)^{-\eta} = 1 - \frac{(p_1 - \bar{p}_1)}{\Delta p_1^*} \qquad (24)$$

In this case $\eta = RR - 1$ so that

$$\left(1 - \frac{v}{w}\right)^{1-RR} = 1 - \frac{(p_1 - \bar{p}_1)}{\Delta p_1^*} \qquad (24')$$

Since we are considering a "typical" individual, $\bar{p}_1$ will be set at 10^{-3} and w at £5×10^4 since these are, respectively the (approximate) "objective" probability of death during the coming year for an individual aged between 30 and 40 and the (approximate) present value of average earnings over thirty years discounted at 10%. Given the range of values for RR suggested by Friend and Blume (1975), it would seem appropriate to consider as alternatives $RR = 2$, 5 and 10. Finally for an individual with $\bar{p}_1 = 10^{-3}$, it would be surprising if Δp_1^* exceeded 10^{-1} or were less than 10^{-4} so that Δp_1^* will be given the alternative values 10^{-4}, 10^{-3}, 10^{-2}, and 10^{-1}.

The graphs of v as a function of p for a selection of the consequent combinations of RR and Δp_1^* are shown in Figure 4 for the exponential utility of wealth function and in Figure 5 for the homogeneous form. The corresponding graphs of the implied $\mu - p_1$ relationship are shown in Figures 6 and 7.

Figure 4

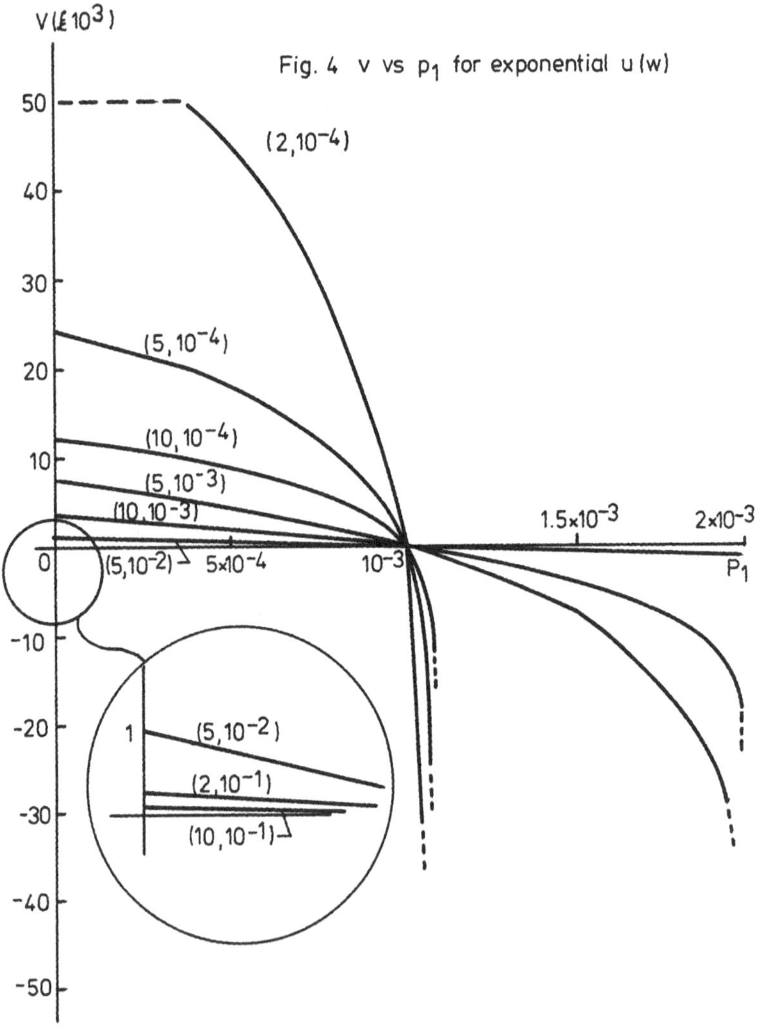
V(£10³)
Fig. 4 v vs p1 for exponential u(w)
50
40
30
20
10
0
-10
-20
-30
-40
-50
(2,10⁻⁴)
(5,10⁻⁴)
(10,10⁻⁴)
(5,10⁻³)
(10,10⁻³)
(5,10⁻²)
5×10⁻⁴
10⁻³
1.5×10⁻³
2×10⁻³
P1
1
(5,10⁻²)
(2,10⁻¹)
(10,10⁻¹)

Figure 5

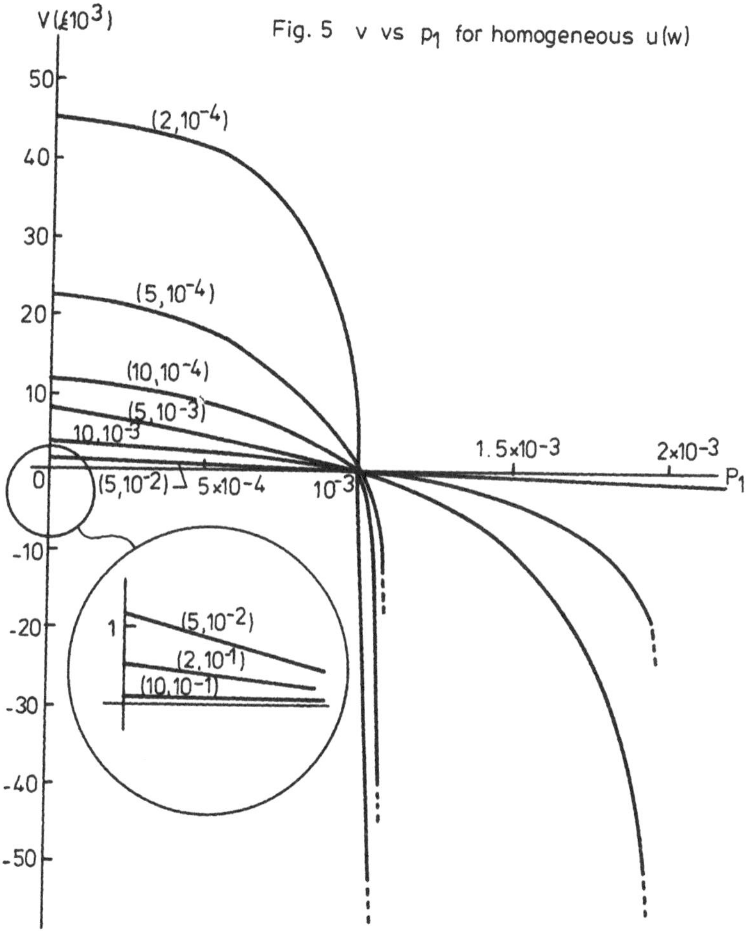
V(£10³)
Fig. 5 v vs p₁ for homogeneous u(w)
50
40
30
20
10
0
-10
-20
-30
-40
-50
(2,10⁻⁴)
(5,10⁻⁴)
(10,10⁻⁴)
(5,10⁻³)
10,10⁻³
(5,10⁻²)
5×10⁻⁴
10⁻³
1.5×10⁻³
2×10⁻³
P₁
1
(5,10⁻²)
(2,10⁻¹)
(10,10⁻¹)

Figures 6 & 7

Fig. 6 μ vs p_1 for exponential u(w)

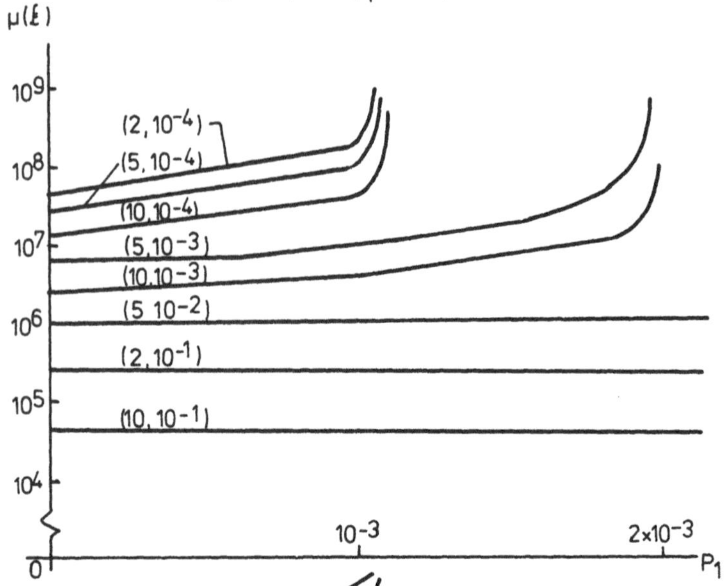

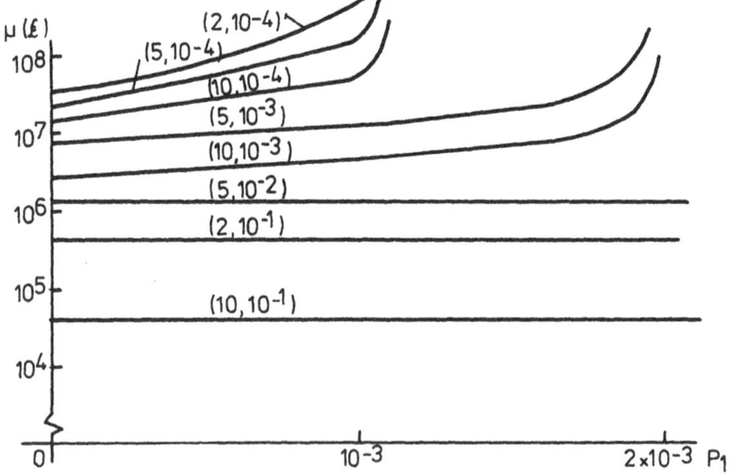

Fig. 7 μ vs p_1 for homogeneous u(w)

These graphs exhibit a number of interesting features. In the first place the $v - p_1$ relationships clearly have the general properties for which I have argued here and elsewhere. In addition, for those cases in which $\Delta p_1^* \geq \bar{p}_1$, the approximate linearity of $v(p_1)$ for $p_1 \leq \bar{p}_1$ suggested in Section 2 is clearly substantiated. Notice that this means that in such cases the distinction between μ and m can be ignored for risk *reductions* and indeed it is clear from Figures 6 and 7 that the distinction becomes significant only for risk increases that carry us close to the maximum acceptable level. Of course, these comments do not apply when $\Delta p_1^* < \bar{p}_1$: with $\Delta p_1^* = 10^{-4}$ it is clear from Figures 6 and 7 that it would be inappropriate to approximate μ by m for other than genuinely marginal variations in risk. Finally it is evident that with the exception of cases in which RR is very small and (more particularly) Δp_1^* rather larger than is suggested by intuition and casual questioning, the value of μ in the region of $\bar{p}_1$, and hence m, is very large indeed. For example, with $RR = 5$ and $\Delta p_1^* = 10^{-2}$ we have $m \approx £1m.$ for both the exponential and homogeneous forms of $u(w)$. This offers some support for the theoretical results derived in Jones-Lee (1978) and for other empirical work which suggests that the appropriate value of statistical life for marginal changes in risk should be somewhat larger than that currently employed in U.K. public sector decisions.

4. *Concluding Comments*

In this paper I have established various results concerning a "typical" individual's valuation (in the form of compensating variations in wealth) of non-marginal changes in physical risk. Given fairly weak restrictions on preferences and attitudes to risk it has proved possible to derive a simple and potentially rather important general restriction on the relationship between m and Δp_1^*. With two further relatively weak conditions on the magnitudes of RL/RA and $\Delta p_1^*/\bar{p}_1$ it was also possible to derive a simple and interesting restriction on the relationship between $\tilde{v}$ and $\bar{p}_1$. Finally, in Section 4 the full $v - p_1$ (and hence

$\mu - p_1$) relationships have been generated for various apparently plausible configurations of utility function parameters etc., for each of the exponential and homogeneous classes of utility function and these results tend to confirm various claims made in this and earlier papers concerning the qualitative and quantitative properties of the "value of statistical life".

The analysis presented here is, however, open to a number of criticisms. Some of these concern the overall approach to the valuation of life and safety and were outlined at the beginning of the paper. Others apply to the specific assumptions, model and methodology employed in this paper. Let me begin by considering the more general criticisms.

Apart from Broome's objections which I have discussed at length elsewhere, the most serious general criticism, in my view, concerns the relationship between subjective and objective probabilities. In a nutshell the problem is this. All of the probabilities that have featured in the analysis are essentially subjective: the $v - p_1$ relationships in Figures 1, 2, 4 and 5 are all, for example, compensating variation - *subjective* probability relationships. On the other hand, the probabilities that will be input data in a cost-benefit analysis will typically be the result of (more or less) expert assessment and will, for want of a better term, be referred to as "objective". Now there is no reason to suppose that subjective probabilities will be equal to, or for that matter bear any simple relationship to objective probabilities.[16] If we consider a particular individual's subjective probability, p_s, as a function of objective probability, p_o, for some event, then the range of possibilities is literally all possible functions $f:[0,1] \rightarrow [0,1]$. In the case of complex and momentous unwanted events like death, one suspects that the functions will either be stepped or else will display a sort of 'hysteresis effect' as shown in Figure 8.

What are we to do about this given that little is known about the "typical" relationship between p_s and p_o (other than that it is unlikely to take the form $p_s = p_o$)? My own views on this matter are fairly radical. I think it is fair to say that conventional cost-benefit analysis is

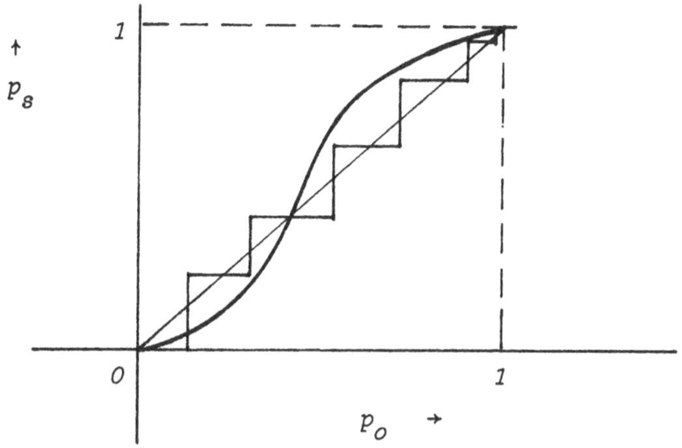

Figure 8

intended, *inter alia*, to take account of individual preferences and that if individual *i* prefers A to B then as far as individual *i* is concerned, cost-benefit analysis will rank A above B. But what if *i*'s preference for A over B is based on faulty information or information that is incomplete in relation to that available to the cost-benefit analyst or expert? I believe that there is then a strong case to be made for simply *ignoring* *i*'s stated ranking over A and B and using instead the ranking that he *would* have if he had access to all available information. (An alternative approach would of course be to *provide* the individual with the information, but in many cases this will be too costly or indeed virtually impossible, especially if the information is highly technical and requires processing skills which the individual does not possess.) Thus, for example, suppose that individual *i* mistakenly believes that sulphur-dioxide is beneficial to health but that for some reason it is impossible to inform him that this belief is mistaken. Should we then accord sulphur-dioxide emissions a *positive* value as far as *i* is concerned, or should we instead take it that if *i* could be apprised of the erroneous nature of his beliefs then he would in fact become averse to such emissions so that, his stated preference notwithstanding, we treat sulphur-dioxide as a cost rather than a benefit from

i's point of view? I find it hard to imagine that many people would seriously wish to defend the former position. If I am right, then it would seem that the appropriate way to establish the aggregate compensating variation for a safety improvement is to set the changes in p_{ij} equal to the expert's assessment of what they should be and then discover the magnitude of the corresponding v_{ij}. That is, we should try to determine the sums that people *would* pay for the safety improvement if their subjective assessments of the consequent risk reductions corresponded with the expert's assessment. It must be stressed that this is not to advocate that we should use the expert's *valuation* of the risk change. The expert's function in this exercise is to estimate the *technical consequences* of the safety improvement. The valuation of these consequences is then, as it were, left to individuals themselves to decide.

Notice that this way of handling the subjective/objective probability problem neatly sidesteps a rather serious pathological possibility that, were it to occur, would render this whole approach to the valuation of safety virtually worthless. It has been suggested that most people may in fact ignore very small risk changes, that is the graph in Figure 8 may indeed be stepped, at least near the origin. If this is the case and we derive values for cost-benefit analysis from individual compensating variations for actual subjective assessments of risk change, then safety improvements implying very small risk changes will be accorded a value at or close to zero. Put another way, whether the saving of one statistical life will be accorded other than a negligible value in cost-benefit analysis will then depend crucially on the size of the population, n, in which this life is to be saved. With n large enough, most people will have $\delta p_s = 0$ and hence $v = 0$ in spite of the fact that $\delta p_o \neq 0$. A methodology which implies that the value of statistical life can be driven close to zero provided only that the population is large enough is, to say the least, suspect. However, no such problems arise if, as I have advocated, δp_s is set equal to δp_o. By the very definition of subjective probability, individuals will prefer smaller to larger subjective probabilities of unwanted events[17] so that v_{ij} will be an unambiguously decreasing function of p_{ij} throughout its domain. We therefore have $\delta p_o \neq 0 \Rightarrow \delta p_s \neq 0 \Rightarrow v \neq 0$ for every individual in society and the consequent impossibility of statistical life being accorded a value of zero.

Now let us consider the objection that no distinction is made in this kind of analysis concerning the various different modes of death. Since it is almost certainly the case that most people would prefer to die one way rather than another, an analysis of the value of changes in the probability of death ought ideally to distinguish between the different ways of dying. However, this is an essentially empirical matter - I know of no way in which anything of significance could be said on the subject in the context of the kind of *a priori* analysis developed in this paper. Until we do have information concerning individual attitudes to death we must therefore rely upon introspection and casual questioning and on the basis of these it is my suspicion that, with the exception of very extreme and unpleasant ways of dying (e.g. under torture or being eaten alive by extra-terrestrial monsters), the impact of people's preferences for modes of death on this kind of analysis would not be very great. I doubt that the aggregate compensating variation for one life saved from death by heart attack would be very much different from one life saved from death in a car accident.

The last of the general criticisms concerns the question of the distribution of income and wealth. This, I think, need not detain us for long. Consider a standard Bergson-Samuelson social welfare function $u_s = f(u_1, u_2 \ldots u_u)$ for a society of n individuals where u_s is a social welfare index and $u_1 - u_u$ are individual utility indices. For the safety improvement yielding small changes in subjective probabilities of death, δp_{ij}, we can then write

$$\delta u_s \simeq \frac{\partial f}{\partial u_1}\frac{\partial u_1}{\partial w_1}\left[\frac{\partial w_1}{\partial p_{11}}\,\delta p_{11} + \frac{\partial w_1}{\partial p_{12}}\,\delta p_{12} + \cdots\right]$$

$$+ \frac{\partial f}{\partial u_2}\frac{\partial u_2}{\partial w_2}\left[\frac{\partial w_2}{\partial p_{22}}\,\delta p_{22} + \frac{\partial w_2}{\partial p_{21}}\,\delta p_{21} + \cdots\right]$$

$$+ \cdots \frac{\partial f}{\partial u_n} \frac{\partial u_n}{\partial w_n} \left\{ \frac{\partial w_n}{\partial p_{nn}} \delta p_{nn} + \frac{\partial w_n}{\partial p_{n1}} \delta p_{n1} + \cdots \right\} \qquad (25)$$

or

$$\delta u_s \simeq - \left\{ \sum_i \frac{\partial f}{\partial w_i} m_{ii} \, \delta p_{ii} + \sum_{i j}\sum_{j \neq i} \frac{\partial f}{\partial w_i} m_{ij} \, \delta p_{ij} \right\} \qquad (25')$$

Equation (1) is clearly the special case of (25') in which the "distributional weights" $\frac{\partial f}{\partial w_i}$ have been set equal and u_s measured in the units of w so that $\frac{\partial f}{\partial w_1} = \frac{\partial f}{\partial w_2} = \cdots \frac{\partial f}{\partial w_n} = 1$ and $\delta u_s = v$. It would clearly be a straightforward matter to build alternative distributional weightings into the analysis, but whatever these were, (21') makes it quite clear that the primary determinants of δu_s (apart from the distributional weights and the δp_{ij}) will still be m_{ii} and m_{ij} or, for non-marginal changes in risk, μ_{ii} and μ_{ij}. I therefore make no apology for effectively ignoring the distributional question in an analysis whose primary concern is with the typical properties of m_{ii} and m_{ij} and their non-marginal counterparts μ_{ii} and μ_{ij}.

Finally let me deal with what I consider to be the most serious specific criticism of the kind of approach employed in this paper, namely that I have not (as claimed) considered the attitudes of a "typical" individual but have, rather, derived results concerning the valuation of physical risk of a sort of economic robot constructed from a set of *a priori* restrictions on preferences and attitudes to physical and financial risk which individually seem not particularly implausible but taken as a whole add up to a gross misinterpretation of what is in fact "typical".

One possible line of defence against this criticism is to take an essentially pragmatic position on the valuation of life and safety. As things stand at present, we have very little hard empirical information concerning individual attitudes to (and more particularly, valuations of) physical risk and indeed it is in the nature of the problem that this empirical information will be rather difficult to acquire and will even then be far from free of ambiguity. These difficulties are in part a result of the subjective/objective probability problem discussed earlier: while it is possible in principle to observe the sum that an individual is willing to pay for a particular safety improvement (or indeed to ask him more or less directly how much he would be willing to pay for any *hypothetical* safety improvement) there remains the very difficult question of what subjective probability change the individual in fact associated with the particular risk reduction. Thus, while it is possible to elicit rates of substitution of wealth for *objective* probability of death (or, more accurately, an expert's assessment thereof) it is altogether another matter to determine the corresponding rate of substitution for subjective probability and it should by now be clear that it is unambiguously the latter that is required. Nonetheless, certain kinds of public sector allocative decisions are such that some sort of valuation of life and safety is literally unavoidable so that given the difficulties associated with empirical estimation of m_{ii} etc., we would appear to have precisely four alternatives. These are:-

(i) Not to attempt an explicit valuation of life and safety but rather to let the valuation emerge *implicitly* by relying on the "hunch/feel/intuition/good sense" etc., of those who are ultimately responsible for taking the decisions.

(ii) To require public sector decision-making agencies to place explicit values on life and safety but again to permit them to so do on the basis of the "hunch/feel/intuition/good sense" of those ultimately responsible.

(iii) To derive values of life and safety by procedures that bear no relation to the principles of conventional cost-benefit analysis (e.g. the loss of net or gross output approaches advocated by Dawson and others).

(iv) To use such information as is available concerning preferences and attitudes to risk to form an educated guess (one hesitates to use the term "estimate") about the nature of "compensating variation/subjective probability of death" relationships that *would* be appropriate for a conventional cost-benefit analysis and *would* emerge if it were possible to resolve the problems of direct empirical estimation.

The objections to approaches (i) - (iii) are well known and need no rehearsal here. This leaves only approach (iv) whose implementation requires that we resolve the difficult question of how precisely to use scant and doubtfully reliable information concerning preferences etc., to educate a guess concerning the population average of m_{ii} and m_{ij} or μ_{ii} and μ_{ij}.

Since the standard procedures of statistical estimation are unlikely to be of much help in a problem such as this, it is necessary to formulate criteria by which such a guess or estimate is to be formed. My own view is that there is much to be said for doing so in accordance with two basic principles:-

(i) The approach employed should be simple and direct if only because the basis of the guess/estimate is then fairly easily intelligible and the whole exercise is less likely to be accorded the spurious reliability that it might otherwise acquire. In addition, one then has something in the nature of a clearly identified "bench-mark" or reference point from which to assess the impact of more complex assumptions and estimation procedures.

(ii) The guess/estimate should lie within the limits defined by the requirement of consistency with such information (e.g. hard empirical or stylised fact) as is available.

The assumption that the "typical" individual is an expected utility maximiser and that the relevant utility function takes the simple separable form specified in (6) can then be defended on the basis of the first of these principles. To be sure, most of us almost certainly violate the Von-Neumann/Morgenstern or Savage axioms from time to time but if one is to make a single summary statement concerning choice under uncertainty, these axioms have the powerful two-fold advantages of simplicity and normative appeal (that is, most of us do not deliberately *choose* to violate the axioms but rather make mistakes in information processing which, when they are pointed out to us, we would prefer to rectify).

The various specific assumptions concerning the properties and parameter values of $U(w,\tau)$ have also been made with reference to the two basic principles. Exponential and homogeneous utility of wealth functions were considered partly because of their simplicity but also partly because they are both bounded above (this eliminates St. Petersburg problems) and because they bracket the "decreasing absolute and increasing relative risk aversion" properties commonly held to be typical. Finally, particular parameter values such as *RR* were set within intervals suggested by existing empirical evidence. Thus, while it may be true that the individual who has been our object of analysis does not deserve to be considered as "typical", I believe that he/she nonetheless displays sufficient consistency with what *is* commonly held to be typical to justify treating the results of the paper as a useful benchmark.

5. *Postscript*

Since this paper was written, the N.R.P.B. has published a consultative document, *The Application of Cost-Benefit Analysis to the Radiological Protection of the Public.*[18]

The primary purpose of this document is to make proposals for the cost to be associated with a unit "collective dose equivalent" of ionising radiation, the "man-sievert". (The sievert is a measure of radiation dose, a *man*-sievert being the exposure of one person to one sievert, *100* people to 10^{-2} sieverts each or 10^{6} people to 10^{-6} sieverts each etc.) While it has been established that the expected number of adverse health effects (e.g. fatal cancers) from one man-sievert is effectively *independent* of the size of the irradiated population, the N.R.P.B. has nonetheless argued for an increasing (and indeed convex) relationship between the cost of a man-sievert and the dose *per capita* (the latter being, of course, inversely proportional to the size of the irradiated population). The basis for this argument is essentially the one presented in Section 1 of this paper, namely that the cost (value) of the loss (saving) of one statistical life depends on the size of the population within which the life is lost or saved because population size determines the magnitude of the risk to which each person is exposed and individual compensating variations are non-linearly related to risk. From a purely qualitative point of view, then, the N.R.P.B. position is gratifyingly consistent with that for which I have argued in this paper. However, when one considers the precise *quantitative* nature of the N.R.P.B. proposals things are, to put it mildly, less satisfactory. The I.C.R.P. dose limit referred to earlier effectively prescribes a maximum acceptable increase of about 6.25×10^{-5} in risk of death during any one year due to radiation exposure. This, then, is the increase in risk at which the N.R.P.B. counterpart to the $\mu - p_1$ relationship becomes vertical, i.e. $\mu \to \infty$. (Notice that while the N.R. P.B. discussion relates to a cost-*dose per capita* function, this can be directly converted into a $\mu - p_1$ function by a straightforward scale adjustment.) But now consider the following passage from the N.R.P.B. document setting out the position on the cost per man-sievert at *very low per capita* radiation doses (which is of course the counterpart to the value of statistical life for *marginal* risk changes).

> "There are therefore three possible evaluations of the value to be assigned to increments of collective dose equivalent made up entirely of dose equivalents below an insignificant level.
>
> (a) A value of zero, based on pragmatic arguments that any finite value will direct resources to reducing doses that are already insignificant.
>
> (b) A value of about £1,000 per man-sievert using only the direct costs of objectively predicted statistical health effects.
>
> (c) A value of about £5,000 to £10,000 per man-sievert using in addition subjective valuations of very low levels of risk.
>
> The Board feels that on balance option (b) represents the most reasonable choice and suggests a value of £1,000 per man-sievert for practical use."
>
> (N.R.P.B., p. 10)

Now notice first that since one man-sievert is taken by the N.R.P.B. to produce detrimental health effects equivalent to about 1.25×10^{-2} deaths, the value of statistical life for marginal risk changes implied by alternative (b) is about £80,000 while under alternative

(c) it is between £½m. and £1m. It is also worth noting that the "direct costs of objectively predicted statistical health effects" referred to in alternative (b) comprise gross output losses and medical costs so that this valuation method is broadly similar to that advocated in Dawson (1971) and currently used by the Department of Transport (though it should be noted that the D.Tp. also includes a more or less arbitrary component for "pain, grief and suffering").

In short, then, the N.R.P.B. has succumbed to the temptation discussed in Footnote 14. Letme therefore conclude by spelling out my objection to the N.R.P.B.'s proposal. I can see a certain cynical logic in proposal (a) if by an "insignificant" dose is meant a dose so small that most people will fail to perceive the increment in risk involved. (I would, however, reject such a proposal on the grounds outlined in Section 4.) On the other hand the accummulated results of both *a priori* and empirical work on the "value of changes in risk" approach to the value of life (including the results presented in this paper), while by no means conclusive, point to values of life of the order of magnitude suggested in proposal (c) rather than those in (b). It therefore seems to me that, if the N.R.P.B. really is in the business of evolving costing and valuation procedures for a conventional cost-benefit analysis, then it must simply make up its mind whether to adopt proposal (a) or proposal (c). There is neither empirical support nor a satisfactory logical basis for adopting proposal (b). Of course, it might be argued that the decision to adopt (b) is essentially a *compromise* between (a) and (c). But then the N.R.P.B.'s position is rather akin to that of the unhappy tourist who, unable to make up his mind whether to visit London or Paris, instructs his travel agent to locate him precisely half-way between the two cities. Those with a passing knowledge of European geography will appreciate that this is a somewhat less than satisfactory (and indeed rather uncomfortable) resolution to the tourist's dilemma.

REFERENCES

Acton, J. (1973). Evaluating Public Programs to Save Lives: The Case of Heart Attacks. RAND Corporation R-950-RC.

Arrow, K.J. (1971). *Essays in the Theory of Risk Bearing*. North Holland.

Broome, J. (1978). Trying to Value a Life. *Journal of Public Economics*, February.

Conley, B.C. (1976). The Value of Human Life in the Demand for Safety. *American Economic Review*, March.

Cook, P.J. and Graham, D.A. (1977). The Demand for Insurance and Protection: The Case of Irreplaceable Commodities. *Quarterly Journal of Economics*, February.

Dawson, R.F.F. (1971). *Current Costs of Road Accidents in Great Britain*. Road Research Laboratory.

Friend, I. and Blume, M.E. (1975). The Demand for Risky Assets. *American Economic Review*, December.

Hammerton, M. (1973). A Case of Radical Probability Estimation. *Journal of Experimental Psychology*, December.

I.C.R.P. Publication 26 (1977). *Recommendations of the International Commission on Radiological Protection*. Pergamon.

Jones-Lee, M.W. (1976). *The Value of Life: An Economic Analysis*. Martin Robertson and Chicago.

Jones-Lee, M.W. (1977). Some Empirical Rigor-Mortis - or an Empirical Procedure for Estimating the Value of Life from Tyre Replacement Data. Paper presented to the Health Economics Study Group Conference, Newcastle.

Jones-Lee, M.W. (1978). Human Capital Risk Aversion and the Value of Life. In Currie, D.A. and Peters, W. (eds.) *Contemporary Economic Analysis, Volume 2* (1980), Croom Helm.

Jones-Lee, M.W. (1978b). The Value of Life in the Demand for Safety: Comment. *American Economic Review*, August.

Jones-Lee, M.W. (1979). Trying to Value a Life: Why Broome Does Not Sweep Clean. *Journal of Public Economics*, October.

Jones-Lee, M.W. (1980). Maximum Acceptable *Physical* Risk and a New Measure of *Financial* Risk Aversion. *Economic Journal*, September.

Kahneman, D. and Tversky, A. (1973). On the Psychology of Prediction. *Psychological Review*, July.

Melinek, S.J. (1974). A Method of Evaluating Human Life for Economic Purposes. *Accident Analysis and Prevention*, October.

Needleman, L. (1976). Valuing Other People's Lives. *Manchester School*, December.

N.R.P.B. (1980). *The Application of Cost Benefit Analysis to the Radiological Protection of the Public: A Consultative Document.* H.M.S.O.

Savage, L.J. (1954, 1972). *The Foundations of Statistics.* Wiley and Dover.

Smith, R. (1973). Compensating Wage Differentials and Hazardous Work. Technical Analysis Paper No. 5, Office of Policy Evaluation and Research, Department of Labor, August.

Thaler, R. and Rosen, S. (1973). The Value of Saving a Life: Evidence from the Labor Market. Paper presented at the *N.B.E.R. Conference on Income and Wealth, Household Production and Consumption*, November.

Usher, D. (1973). An Imputation to the Measure of Economic Growth for Changes in Life Expectancy. *Conference on Research in Income and Wealth, New York: National Bureau of Economic Research, 1971.*

Veljanovski, C.G. (1978). The Economics of Job Safety Regulation: Theory and Evidence: Part 1 - The Market and Common Law. Paper presented to the S.S.R.C. Research Seminar in Law and Economics, Corpus Christi College, Oxford, September.

* This paper arose out of advisory work for the *National Radiological Protection Board*. While I am particularly grateful to M.J. Clark, A.B. Fleishman and G.A.M. Webb of the N.R.P.B. for stimulating discussion etc., neither they nor the N.R.P.B. can be held responsible for any errors or eccentricities contained in this paper. I am also grateful to a referee who pointed out a serious limitation in my original discussion of the approximate linearity of $v(p_1)$ for $p_1 < \bar{p}_1$. The argument presented in this version of the paper owes much to a procedure of proof suggested by the referee.

FOOTNOTES

1. See for example Thaler and Rosen (1973), Conley (1976), Jones-Lee (1976) or Cook and Graham (1977).

2. Marginal rates of substitution are here treated as the *moduli* of relevant derivatives.

3. Strictly speaking, it would also be appropriate to include in V the real resource costs (e.g. medical and police costs) and losses of net output (roughly the excess of a victim's lifetime output over his lifetime consumption) that are avoided as a result of the safety improvement scheme since society benefits by not having to bear these costs. However, these components of V present no serious conceptual problems and are in any case almost certainly of negligible order of magnitude in relation to the terms containing m_{ii} and m_{ij} so that they will be ignored in what follows. Alternatively, it would be possible to regard these avoided costs as part and parcel of m_{ij} but I believe that there are conceptual advantages in treating m_{ii} and m_{ij} as reflecting aversion to death *per se*, rather than to the real resource and output-loss implications of death.

4. This problem is not, of course, specific to the cost-benefit analysis of safety.

5. This particular criticism is due to Broome (1978).

6. See Jones-Lee (1979).

7. See I.C.R.P. (1977).

8. See, for example, Needleman (1976) or Jones-Lee (1976) pp. 114, 139-142.

9. See Jones-Lee (1978).

10. See Jones-Lee (1980).

11. Strictly speaking, (7) requires (a) that life insurance companies do not adjust premia in response to the perturbation in $\bar{p}$ and (b) that the individual does not adjust his degree of cover. For a defence of these assumptions and an analysis of the implications of relaxing them, see Jones-Lee (1978).

12. See, for example, Arrow (1971) p. 95.

13. Thus, quite apart from anything else, this measure of risk aversion is arguably more directly relevant than *RA* for the kind of gambles with which the majority of individuals are indeed confronted: football pools and lotteries abound whereas small-stake, small-prize gambles are relatively rare. This means that empirical estimation of typical orders of magnitude of the risk aversion measure should be a fairly straightforward matter.

14. For example, the I.C.R.P. recommended dose limit for ionising radiation places a limit of about 6.25×10^{-5} on the permissible increase in the risk of death during any one year due to radiation exposure. Furthermore, as was pointed out earlier, the N.R.P.B. is currently in the process of devising specific procedures for implementing the I.C.R.P. recommendations. Suppose that the N.R.P.B. is tempted (as it may well be) to employ a value of statistical life (for small changes in risk) of the order of magnitude currently used by, say, the D.Tp. (e.g. about £100,000) and suppose in addition that the I.C.R.P. dose limit is intended to be reflective of "typical" orders of magnitude of Δp_1^*. (13') then gives a value of about 0.16 for *RL* which implies that the critical win probability for a £1-stake, large-prize gamble is about 0.14. That is, if the I.C.R.P. dose limit and the D.Tp. value of life are

to be compatible, then the typical individual would reject the £1-stake large-prize gamble if the chances of winning were less than about 1 in 7. As a description of typical attitudes to physical and financial risk, this seems improbable to say the least. The only way out of the apparent inconsistency would be either to substantially slacken the dose limit and/or substantially increase the value of statistical life. Indeed, even if the N.R.P.B. dose limit were slackened by a *factor of ten* (to 6.25×10^{-4}) we would still require a value of statistical life equal to many multiples of that used by the D.Tp. to generate "reasonable" values of *RL*.

15. Other than that it is an increasing and generally well-behaved function.

16. There is in fact a large experimental psychology literature on this subject. See, for example, Kahneman and Tversky (1973) or Hammerton (1973).

17. On the standard definition (e.g. Savage's - Savage (1972) p. 31) an individual judges event A subjectively more probable than event B *if and only if* he prefers an act generating a desirable consequence (e.g. survival) under A and a less desirable consequence (e.g. death) under B to an act in which the consequences are reversed, *ceteris paribus*.

18. See N.R.P.B. (1980).

19. In Jones-Lee (1978b) I have suggested that a value of statistical life as high as £1m. (in 1978 prices) is quite consistent with the results of existing empirical work in this area (Acton (1973), Usher (1973), Thaler and Rosen (1973), Smith (1973), Melinek (1974), Jones-Lee (1976, 1977) and Veljanovski (1978)). Furthermore, *a priori* analysis in this field tends to confirm this large order of magnitude for the value of statistical life (see, for example, Conley (1976), Jones-Lee (1976, 1980) and the argument presented in this paper).

DISCUSSION: CLIVE D. FRASER*

This paper represents the latest and, in many respects, the most satisfactory of a series of attempts by Professor Jones-Lee and others to put the Valuation of Life and Limb (VOL) (more precisely, the valuation of changes in risk to life and limb) on more secure foundations within the mainstream of single period and multiperiod consumer theory. I have very little to say about the technical results presented.

Instead, as Professor Jones-Lee deals principally with the positive aspects of compensation and various risk measures, it seems appropriate to treat some neglected normative issues. This is best done by imbedding the issue of the valuation of risk changes within the larger framework of government optimization as the former is unlikely to be insensitive to the latter.

I therefore focus upon what seems to me to be a fundamental and largely unexplored asymmetry in the valuation of physical risk changes: that between what an individual would be prepared to pay for risk reductions, and what he would need to be paid in order to accept a perturbation in (neighbourhood) risks. To illustrate this asymmetry, it is most convenient to return to the single period framework, using familiar notation (see, e.g., [5]), and to interpret the individual's necessary compensation for bearing increased risk as part of a full *ex ante* liability contract received from the government or the appropriate compensatory agency. $U^1(m^o)$ is the individual's certainty equivalent *status quo* utility of wealth m^o in the absence of risk, ρ the incremental project-specific risk to life or/and limb, and $U^d(m^o)$ the individual's death-or-disabled-contingent utility of wealth m^o (where $U^1(m) > U^d(m), \forall m \epsilon (\underline{m}, \infty), \underline{m} \geqq 0$). Compensation which leaves the individual as well off, in a conditional expected utility (CEU; [6]) sense, with the prospect of (implicitly subjective) risk ρ, as with the *status quo* in its absence must satisfy

$$U^1(m^o) = \rho U^d(m^o+c^d) + (1-\rho)U^1(m^o+c^1) \qquad (1)$$

As is usual, we are assuming, *inter alia*, that in the

event of surviving the project, the individual evaluates the utility of wealth with the same function as in the *status quo*. (Thus, e.g., in a multiperiod context, anxiety effects associated with continued survival in a more risky environment would be neglected.) The specification is neutral with respect to (w.r.t.) the *mode* of death/ disability. It assumes nothing about the marginality, or otherwise, of the risk change - except that, if a risk increase exceeds the maximum acceptable, then it will be impossible to find (c^1, c^d) satisfying (1). (However, as we are really within the realm of competing risks, one wonders whether a non-marginal change in any specific risk confronting the individual is likely to have a more than marginal impact upon the overall risk level which he confronts.)

We can call the c^i, $i=1,d$, the *state-contingent compensating variations* in wealth/income and note that they need not be equal and, indeed, are unlikely to be. In other words, a government concerned to fully compensate an individual for the increased risk associated with a project need, *ex ante*, only do so to the extent of *promising* the vector of state-contingent compensation (c^1, c^d) and then having actual payment dependent upon the realized state. Governments do seem to behave in this manner: empirically, most payments for damage, whether to life or limb, to property or amenities, are made *ex post* and not unconditionally. Of course, the sum which an individual would actually *pay* to effect a *reduction* in risk is necessarily state-invariant and corresponds to Jones-Lee's $V(p)$ or $V'(p)$. However, concentration upon what the individual would be prepared to receive for accepting increased risk is justified by noting that the situations which we have in mind are typically ones in which physical risks *are* to be increased.

What are some possible implications of state-contingent versus state-invariant compensation? Very briefly, imagine a government which is concerned to, say, minimize the expected cost of exactly compensating an otherwise adversely affected individual for the prospect of a risky project,[1] and let π by the government's assessment of the relevant "objective" risk to the individual. (π need not equal ρ and is unlikely to.) Furthermore, suppose the government can trade-off between compensation and protective or informational expenditures in that incremental expenditure upon either of the latter can affect its own or/and the individual's assessments of the relevant risks. If e (respectively c) is the expenditure upon protection (respectively information) *s.t.* $\pi(e)$ (respectively $\rho(c)$) exhibits diminishing marginal productivity with regard to such expenditure, and if we resort here to the convenient fiction of government optimization w.r.t. the representative individual, the government's problem in its simplest form can be stated as either

$$\underset{\underline{c}=\{c^d,c^1,c\}}{\text{Min.}} \quad \pi c^d + (1-\pi)c^1 + c \qquad \text{P.1,}$$

$$\text{s.t.} \quad \rho(c)U^d(m^o+c^d)+(1-\rho(c))U^1(m^o+c^1)-U^1(m^o) \geq 0$$

or

$$\underset{\underline{e}=\{c^d,c^1,e\}}{\text{Min.}} \quad \pi(e)c^d + (1-\pi(e))c^1 + e \qquad \text{P.2,}$$

$$\text{s.t.} \quad \rho U^d(m^o+c^d)+(1-\rho)U^1(m^o+c^1)-U^1(m^o) \geq 0$$

or

$$\underset{\underline{e}=\{c^d,c^1,e\}}{\text{Min.}} \quad \pi(e)c^d + (1-\pi(e))c^1 + e$$

$$\text{s.t.} \quad \rho(e)U^d(m^o+c^d)+(1-\rho(e))U^1(m^o+c^1)-U^1(m^o) \geq 0$$

and, perhaps, a "moral hazard" constraint to the effect that

$$U^1(m^o+c^1)-U^d(m^o+c^d) \geq 0 \qquad (2)$$

The individual's equilibria associated with P.1) - P.3) would correspond to his insurance market equilibria at a maximum CEU level of $U^1(m^o)$ provided that actuarial intermediaries possessed the same risk assessment, $\pi(e)$, as the government. In this sense, then, under state-contingent compensation the government is merely compensating the individual by offering him an insurance policy which promises greater than *status quo* wealth in at least one state. It is also worth pointing out that maximum acceptable physical risk, to the extent that it is important, will certainly be no less under such optimal compensating insurance than under its state-invariant counterpart. These features are to be expected because individual valuation of risk changes is no more insensitive to government activities than it is to the availability, or otherwise, of private opportunities for risk-sharing.

Notice, also, that in P.1) - P.3), merely by inspection, if the government is constrained to offer state-invariant compensation (V), its own risk assessment is eliminated from consideration (and its criterion becomes simply minimization of $V + c$, or $V + e$, subject to (1)). Empirically, this is implausible.

Let us therefore consider the state-contingent case and take P.1, just for example. It can be shown[2] that provided $\pi \leqq \rho$ - i.e., provided the individual's risk-assessment is bounded below by the government's[3] - then

$$\text{(i)} \quad \frac{\partial\hat{\rho}}{\partial\pi} < 0 \; ; \qquad \text{(ii)} \quad \frac{\partial\hat{c}^{d}}{\partial\pi} < 0 \; , \; \frac{\partial\hat{c}^{1}}{\partial\pi} > 0$$

most plausibly at an interior solution for $\hat{\underset{\sim}{c}}$, with similar results holding for P.2) and P.3). Thus, there will most likely be an inverse relationship between the two perceived risk assessments. Also, the government's response to an increase in the risk which it perceives is to shift the structure of compensation towards the state whose probability of occurrence has been reduced. Such behaviour is perfectly explicable in terms of self-insurance and self-protection in the sense of Ehrlich-Becker ([2]). (Furthermore, most of these results can be extended to the case where the government is itself a CEU-maximizer concerned to maximize the CEU of the residual from a compensation fund after making protective/informational expenditures and state-contingent compensation payments. This latter situation might arise when individual risks are interdependent and non-marginal so that the usual Law of Large Numbers justification for the government acting like a risk-neutral intermediary breaks down.)

As these seemingly perverse results are associated with state-contingent rather than state-invariant compensation, it might be wondered why one should suggest consideration of the former device. The suggestion arises because, at the purely theoretical level, it can also be shown that state-invariant compensation is likely to lead to the government engaging in less protective expenditure and more informational expenditure than with its state-contingent counterpart, as well as necessarily resulting in a Pareto-inferior outcome. Other perversities associated with state-invariant compensation include the fact that such a restriction leads an optimizing government to be invariant in the trade-off between compensation and information w.r.t. its attitude towards risk. Again, this is implausible empirically.

Now why is all this likely to be particularly important *empirically*? There are several reasons, many of which I have discussed extensively elsewhere ([3]). I therefore reiterate only two here: firstly, and most trivially, if the government is not considered a benevolent-neutral agent and *can* affect, purely cosmetically, the level of risk perceived by the individual, we cannot be sure that it will not do so and thus we might wish to ensure that it minimizes its expenditure on such informational activities.[4] Paradoxically, as such informational expenditures would, *per se*, be unobservables, this is more easily done by allowing the government discretion with respect to the state-contingent structure of compensation than by confining it to state-invariant compensation. In this context, once we relax the implicit assumption that the government is necessarily a benevolent, disinterested agent, we might also be sceptical about Jones-Lee's suggestion that we accept the government "expert's" assessment of the "true" risk. Secondly, although applied welfare theorists normally focus upon *hypothetical* compensation (in the sense of whether potential gainers could or could not compensate potential losers from a project) as the basis for project evaluation, presumably because they are chary of the ethical judgements associated with prescribing actual compensation, it should be apparent, nevertheless, that when compensation is to be *actual* rather than merely *notional*, the precise mode of compensation is likely to have real resource allocation implications. Indeed, this is part of the gist of a recent paper by Cordes and Weisbrod ([1]) on Governmental Behaviour in Response to Compensation Requirements (which constructed and tested a simple deterministic model of project selection by a utility maximizing bureau subject to a compensation-

and-construction-cost budget constraint), the results of which seem to support my contentions.

As important and interesting as is the task of devising measures of the valuation of various changes in risk, therefore, the most important need seems to be that of choosing the structure of compensation which motivates the government to do what is *objectively* best for the individual. Jones-Lee's discussion emphasizes this need in another respect because he provides strong grounds for the belief that, as it is, governments consistently understate the VOL. And, if the government consistently understates the VOL, it follows almost surely that it will consistently under-invest in risk-mitigating activities.

In sum, I would like to say that the assumed state-invariance of compensation used to derive Jones-Lee's elegant results has great pragmatic merits insofar as it admits of the possibility of using market-revealed data as a first approximation to the VOL. Such compensation might well be best in a second-best world. However, as identification of Jones-Lee's $V(p)$ function presupposes precisely the same information on the individual's subjective risk assessments (and, implicitly, ways in which it can be manipulated) as would be required for the determination of optimal state-contingent compensation, and state-invariant compensation can, furthermore, be shown to suffer from a variety of theoretical defects *vis-à-vis* the latter, its usefulness as a *theoretical* vehicle is inevitably circumscribed.

REFERENCES

Cordes, J.J. and Weisbrod, B.A. (1979). Government Behaviour in Response to Compensation Requirements. *Journal of Public Economics* 11, 47-58.

Ehrlich, I. and Becker, G.S. (1972). Market Insurance, Self-Insurance, and Self-Protection. *Journal of Political Economy* 80, 623-648.

Fraser, C.D. (1980). Optimal Compensating Insurance, Informational Asymmetries and Government Discretionary Behaviour, *mimeo*, January, University of York (U.K.). Revised July 1980.

Jones-Lee, M.W. (1980). Maximum Acceptable *Physical* Risk and a New Measure of *Financial* Risk-Aversion, forthcoming, *Economic Journal*.

Jones-Lee, M.W. (1976). *The Value of Life*. London: Martin Robertson.

Luce, R.D. and Krantz, D.H. (1971). Conditional Expected Utility. *Econometrica* 39, 2, 253-271.

FOOTNOTES

* As Professor Jones-Lee informed me beforehand that his presentation would be based more upon the contents of his Economic Journal (1980) article ([4]) than of that submitted for inclusion in the conference proceedings, I have felt it desirable to concentrate my discussion upon an issue relevant to both papers, and, indeed, to the entire Valuation of Life literature.

1. Such a criterion is dual to government maximization of a Bergson-Samuelson Social Welfare Function subject to compensation constraints after appropriate modifications have been made for the possible "publicness" of informational or protective expenditures. The government effectively acts as its own risk-neutral insurer. More generally, in (P.1) - (P.3) below it can also be considered as an active agent manoeuvring strategically against a passive principal.

2. See ([3]).

3. The assumption that $\pi \leqq \rho$ is not at all implausible. For example, it can be shown ([3]) that in the case where the individual's risk assessment is exogenous (insusceptible to protective expenditures), but the government's own is endogenous, the government will either reduce the "true" level of risk as perceived by itself to strictly below that perceived by the individual, should this be possible and necessary, or will not engage in any protective expenditures at all.

4. Alternatively, in (P.2) - (P.3), we might wish to ensure that it maximizes its protective expenditures consistent with (1) and expected cost minimization.

10. PRICE-COST MARGINS, MARKET STRUCTURE AND INTERNATIONAL TRADE

Bruce Lyons

I. Introduction[1]

A large volume of empirical work has related industry price-cost margins to industrial structure both for the U.K. and for the U.S.A.. In the more recent literature, some attempts have also been made to take account of the influence of international trade factors. Following the piecemeal tradition of much of the empirical work in this area, the specification of such estimating equations has been largely *ad hoc*, adding such variables as the import/sales ratio, the export/sales ratio, and/or the rate of tariff protection into a multiple regression analysis.

This paper attempts to provide a more rigorous theoretical foundation to the specification and functional form of such equations by integrating international trade into a model of industrial structure and profitability. The model, presented in section II, is an extension of that derived for non-collusive oligopolists by Cowling and Waterson (1976). This model facilitates discussion of the roles of both homogeneous and differentiated imports and exports, as well as the degree of industrial concentration, in the determination of industry price-cost margins.

In section III, after a brief survey of the existing evidence, the model is tested against cross-section data for 118 U.K. manufacturing industries. Compared with previous *ad hoc* specifications it is found that the significance of the relationship is very much enhanced when the theoretically superior functional form is estimated. The degree of industrial concentration measured by the Herfindahl index, the share of domestic firms in total domestic sales (including imports), and the share of exports in domestic output each have a significant and positive impact on industry price-cost margins.

II. The Model

Following Cowling and Waterson (*ibid.*) we consider an industry with N firms producing a homogeneous product. However, we also allow for competition from imports and for export opportunities. It is assumed that there is no capacity constraint so firms can make independent decisions as to how much to produce for domestic and export sales.

The ith firm wishes to maximise its profits (π_i).

$$\pi_i = pD_i + p_w X_i - c_i(D_i + X_i) - t_i(X_i) \qquad (1)$$

where D_i = domestic production for the domestic market by firm i

X_i = domestic production for the export market by firm i

$c_i(D_i + X_i)$ = firm i's total production costs

$t_i(X_i)$ = firm i's additional (e.g. transport and tariff) costs associated with exporting

p = domestic price

p_w = world price

Domestic price depends on total domestic sales, including imports (M),

$$p = f(D + M), \text{ where } D = \sum_{i=1}^{N} D_i \qquad (2)$$

Symmetric with the domestic equation, the world's inverse demand function,

$$p_w = g(X + W), \text{ where } X = \sum_{i=1}^{N} X_i \text{ and } W = \text{total rest of the world output less } M \qquad (3)$$

Maximising with respect to domestic output,

$$\frac{\partial \pi_i}{\partial D_i} = p + D_i\, f'(D + M)\, \frac{\partial D + M}{\partial D_i} - c_i'\,(D_i + X_i) = 0 \qquad (4)$$

Writing, $\dfrac{\partial (D + M)}{\partial D_i} = 1 + \dfrac{\partial \sum_{j \neq i} D_j}{\partial D_i} + \dfrac{\partial M}{\partial D_i} = 1 + \lambda_i + \theta_i$,

multiplying equation (4) by D_i and aggregating over N firms,

$$pD - \sum c_i'\,(D_i + X_i)\, D_i + \sum D_i^2\, f'\,(D + M)\,(1 + \lambda + \theta) = 0 \qquad (5)$$

where $\lambda = \dfrac{\sum \lambda_i D_i^2}{\sum D_i^2}$ and $\theta = \dfrac{\sum \theta_i D_i^2}{\sum D_i^2}$ (i.e. weighted conjectural variation terms).

Rearranging (5),

$$\frac{pD - \sum c_i'\,(D_i + X_i)\, D_i}{pD} = \frac{H(1 + \lambda + \theta)}{z} \cdot \frac{D}{(D + M)} \qquad (6)$$

where $H = \dfrac{\sum D_i^2}{D^2}$ = the Herfindahl index of concentration

$$z = - \frac{\left(\frac{p}{D + M}\right)}{f'(D+M)} = \text{industry elasticity of demand.}$$

Like Cowling and Waterson, we find the price-cost margin for domestic sales to be an increasing function of H, and inversely related to z; but we also find the share of domestic firms' output in total sales to be a determining factor.

Turning to the export market, equation (1) may be maximised with respect to X_i and aggregated in a similar manner to that employed for the domestic market. Thus,

$$\frac{p_w X - \sum c_i'(D_i + X_i)X_i - \sum t_i'(X_i)X_i}{p_w X}$$

$$= \frac{H_x(1 + \beta + \phi)}{z_w} \cdot \frac{X}{X + W} \qquad (7)$$

where $H_x = \frac{\sum X_i^2}{X^2}$ = an index of export concentration

$z_w = - \frac{\left(\frac{p_w}{X+W}\right)}{g'(X+W)}$ = world elasticity of demand

$$\frac{\partial(X+W)}{\partial X_i} = 1 + \partial \frac{\sum_{j \neq i} X_j}{\partial X_i} + \frac{\partial W}{\partial X_i} = 1 + \beta_i + \phi_i$$

$$\beta = \frac{\sum \beta_i X_i^{\,2}}{\sum X_i^2}$$

$$\phi = \frac{\sum \phi_i X_i^{\,2}}{\sum X_i^2}$$

The left hand sides of equations (6) and (7) show the extent to which the industry is able to raise price above marginal costs, while the right hand sides represent the elements of market structure that permit the exercise of monopoly power. If we assume constant marginal costs equal to average costs, the left hand sides of (6) and (7) become the rates of return on domestic and foreign sales respectively. Industry profit (π), expressed as a proportion of total sales is therefore,

$$\frac{\pi}{pD + p_w X} = \left[\frac{H(1 + \lambda + \theta)}{z} \quad \frac{D}{D+M}\right] \frac{pD}{pD + p_w X}$$

$$+ \left[\frac{H_x(1 + \beta + \phi)}{z_w} \quad \frac{X}{X+W}\right] \frac{p_w X}{pD + p_w X} \qquad (8)$$

The expressions in square brackets represent the rates of return in each market, and the remaining terms are weighting factors.

While, as we have already discussed, a *ceteris paribus* increase in import penetration leads to an unambiguous decrease in potential profitability, the effect of exports is not so clear cut. The share of exports in industry sales affects the industry profit rate primarily via the weighting of domestic and export profit rates. The export share may also have a secondary impact inasmuch as it is related to $(X/X+W)$ and thus market power abroad. The overall effect of exports on profitability therefore depends on the conditions under which goods are traded in the world market relative to the domestic situation.

The respective sizes of the domestic and export rates of return (equations (6) and (7)) depend, *ceteris paribus*, on the relative sizes of:-

(i) z and z_w: it is usually assumed that the world elasticity of demand will exceed the domestic elasticity. However, anticipating the discussion of differentiated products that follows, it may be that exports tend to satisfy the fringe demands of foreign countries. Such demands may be much less price elastic than those in the mainstream domestic market.

(ii) H and H_x: here, there is a basic asymmetry which will probably lead to exports being more concentrated than are domestic sales. Whilst it is quite possible for firms selling domestically not to enter the world market, it is much less likely that a firm will produce only for export. Thus, fewer firms will operate in the export market. Given the greater size and uncertainty of the world market, they will also have a greater probability of having less equal shares than they do in the home market.

(iii) $\lambda + \theta$ and $\beta + \phi$: traditional ties may lead to greater co-operation (more positive or less negative conjectural variations) in the home market, though these terms cannot be seen as totally independent of the degrees of concentration and domestic domination in each market.

(iv) $D/D+M$ and $X/X+W$: it appears to be more clear cut that domestic firms will dominate their own markets to a greater degree than they can abroad. However, remembering that "the world" is in fact a large number of individual national markets, a system of discriminating tariffs, such as Imperial Preference, can result in domestic firms facing protected markets in remote and less industrialised countries. At the same time, there might be substantial import competition at home, from geographically proximous and industrially advanced nations.

Three qualifications must be added to the already equivocal rôle of exports. Firstly, it may not be possible to charge different prices at home and abroad. This may be due either to anti-dumping legislation, or to low transport and tariff costs permitting arbitrage. The problem is now of maximising equation (1) subject to the constraint that $p = p_w$. Price will be related to cost by a weighted average of the structural determinants of profitability in each market. The absence of price discrimination means that overall profitability must be lower than for the unconstrained case, and it is possible that firms will decide not to export at all. Again though, the relationship between overall profitability and the export share is ambiguous.

Secondly, a devaluation will shift the world demand curve, in terms of the domestic currency, upwards in proportion to the exchange rate change. Raw material prices and, therefore, costs will also rise but less than proportionately. The net result, however, is not clear cut. If, for instance, world demand becomes relatively less elastic (as would happen with a linear demand curve), the world will become a more profitable market. On the other hand, it is not at all clear, *a priori*, why demand shifts should be of this nature. For example, a constant elasticity demand curve would shift iso-elastically, raising exports and export profit levels, but without altering marginal (or relative) profitability.[2]

Finally, any empirical relationship between profitability and exports may be subject to an omitted variables problem. Khalilzadeh-Shirazi (1974) argues that "exporting is a risky undertaking which must be rewarded by a risk premium if the firm is to engage in it" (*ibid.*, p. 70). The risk results from high information costs, exchange-rate variation and possible adverse action by foreign governments. If the rate of return on exports includes this risk premium, then industries with higher rates of export may appear to have higher overall rates of return on sales. Alternatively, Caves (1974, footnote 14, p. 8) suggests that there may be a spurious positive association between profitability and exports if comparative advantage is correlated with "market structure traits" which tend to support excess profits. For instance, economies of scale may lead to both high entry barriers and more exports. In this case, the barriers to entry may push up the overall profit rate even though export opportunities are, in fact, acting as a partial restraining factor. Another possibility is that export capacity may frighten off potential entrants. If entry threatens, existing firms need only switch some output from the possibly not very profitable foreign market in order to pursue an effective policy of predatory pricing. In this case, exports are seen as a profitable way of employing the excess capacity whose origin lies in its use as a weapon to ward off entry (*cf.* Spence, 1977). A positive relationship between profitability and exports may therefore be the result of a third factor, rather than any direct causal connection.

So far we have considered only homogeneous imports, exports and domestic production. While product heterogeneity is not easily handled at the firm level, the case of differentiated imports is of some interest. Linder (1961) asserts that different countries have predominantly different tastes for goods within broad product groups. Each country will tend to have a comparative advantage in producing for the home market, and exports result from fringe foreign demand which is not catered for by that country's own producers. Similarly, imports result from domestic demand for less mainstream goods not produced at home. Such a system may be characterised by a domestic industry where all firms produce a homogeneous product, but where price also depends on differentiated imports and rest of the world production. Thus, the price domestic firms obtain in the home market

$$p = f(D,M) \tag{9}$$

and the price they receive abroad

$$p_x = g(X,W) \tag{10}$$

The firm now maximises profits (equation 1) with respect to D_i and X_i, subject to (9) and (10). Following similar manipulations to those employed for the homogeneous case

$$\frac{\pi}{pD + p_x X} = \left[\frac{H(1 + \lambda)}{z_D} - e_{pM}\, e_{MD}\right] \frac{pD}{pD + p_x X}$$

$$+ \left[\frac{H_x(1 + \beta)}{z_x} - e_{p_x W}\, e_{WX}\right] \frac{p_x X}{pD \quad p_x X} \qquad (11)$$

where,[3] $z_D = \dfrac{-(\frac{p}{D})}{f_D(D,M)}$ = domestic elasticity of demand for the domestically produced goods,

$z_X = \dfrac{-(\frac{p_x}{X})}{g_X(X,W)}$ = elasticity of demand for exports,

$e_{pM} = \dfrac{f_M(D,M)}{(\frac{p}{M})}$ = elasticity of price of domestically produced goods with respect to imports,

$e_{MD} = \sum_{i=1}^{N} \frac{D_i}{D} \left(\frac{\partial M}{\partial D_i}\right)\left(\frac{D_i}{M}\right)$ = weighted average conjectural elasticity of imports with respect to the output of the domestically produced good,

$e_{p_x W} = \dfrac{g_W(X,W)}{(\frac{p_x}{W})}$ = elasticity of price of exports with respect to world output, and

$e_{WX} = \sum_{i=1}^{N} \frac{X_i}{X} \left(\frac{\partial W}{\partial X_i}\right)\left(\frac{X_i}{W}\right)$ = weighted average conjectural elasticity of world output with respect to exports.

Other symbols are as defined before.

Each of the above $e_{..}$ elasticities is expected to be negative. For instance, an increase in imports will reduce the demand price of the domestically produced good ($e_{pM} < 0$). Also, the expected change in imports consequent on a change in domestic output (e_{MD}) will be non-positive in all "normal" cases (see Hicks, 1935, pp. 12-16). Similar arguments apply to the elasticities in the export market.

Equation (11) suggests that, in the differentiated case, the industry price-cost margin will be what it would be were there no foreign competition, less an adjustment to take account of (i) the degree of substitutability between the domestically and foreign produced goods (e_{pM}, e_{p_xW}), and (ii) the conjectural elasticity of foreign output (e_{MD}, e_{WX}). We return to the factors underlying and reflecting substitutability in the empirical section of this paper. However, it is useful to note here, how the elasticities under discussion may be related to the actual degree of import penetration in the market.

Caves has argued that "some well-defined products (hereafter *subproducts*) classified to an industry have no close importable substitutes, while others are subject to high cross-elasticities with respect to the prices of imports and face varying amounts of actual import competition. The import share, as a weighted average of these situations, probably reflects the prevelance of subproducts with close importable substitutes." (Caves, 1974, p. 6). Thus, at an empirical level, equation (11) may refer to subproducts in the observable market. Large values of e_{pM} will be reflected in actual import penetration in some subproducts, while low values in others will result in few imports. Ignoring the aggregation problem, Caves' deduction follows. (Note, that although Caves is talking about conventional cross-price elasticities, e_{pM} is analytically identical.) Furthermore, it might be argued that the conjectural elasticity of foreign supply, e_{MD}, will be related to actual supply because firms will become more aware of potential foreign competition, the more such competition is apparent.

In this section, we have developed a model of price-cost margins, market structures and international trade for both homogeneous and differentiated products. Both, it is argued, lead to qualitatively similar conclusions, although the degree of substitutability is an additional feature of the latter case. Before turning to the empirical applicability of such models, we note the possibility of introducing pricing into a dynamic setting.

No mention has yet been made of what determines each industry's imports. In fact, the domestic economy's imports will be someone else's exports and will thus be subject to a similar exercise in maximising behaviour to that in equation (7). It can be seen that the more successful are foreign firms in restricting W and pushing up p_w, the more profitable it is for domestic firms to export. Similarly, the more successful are domestic firms in exercising their market power, the more imports they are likely to attract. Domestic firms may take this directly into account when setting their output levels. They would then maximise the net value of the firm subject to the dynamic constraint that short-run profit maximisation may lead to the loss of long-run profits as imports penetrate the market (*cf.* Gaskins, 1971). In the context of oligopoly, this problem becomes a differential game which suggests that firms interested in long-run profitability may restrict output less than is implied by the above short-run models.

III. The Evidence

The step from a theoretical relationship such as equation (8), to an empirical test is always hazardous. However, the theory developed in section I does provide a number of insights into the empirical specification of equations relating industrial profitability to the degree of international competition. It has long been appreciated that the exercise of market power depends on the industry elasticity of demand. Cowling and Waterson (1976) show formally how industrial concentration, measured by the Herfindahl index, modifies the ability to reach the monopoly solution and we demonstrate that domestic firms can only influence their price-cost margins to the extent that they control total supply to the market ($D/D+M$).

A second implication of our theory is that these elements of market structure interact in their influence on domestic market power. A highly concentrated industry can have little effect on industry price, if imports represent a large proportion of domestic sales. Thus either a competitively structured domestic industry or a substantial degree of foreign competition are substitutes in terms of the control of monopoly power.

Finally, the rôle of exports remains ambiguous. If dumping is not possible and if the demand for exports is more elastic than domestic demand, they will probably provide a competitive influence. Failure to meet either of these conditions could lead to exports raising the industry's rate of profit.

Before looking at some recent U.K. data, we provide a brief review of some of the existing evidence which relates profit rates to measures of import penetration and export propensities.[4] For the U.K., Khalilzadeh-Shirazi (1974) (revised by Caves *et al.* (1975)), shows that the 5-firm concentration ratio and the share of exports in industry sales both positively raised price-cost margins in 1963. The share of imports in industry output was not significant in restraining profitability, which may have been due to the empirical misspecification of the import variable (which in our terms amounted to $M/D+X$). Hart and Morgan (1977) repeat similar regressions on 1968 data, but exclude the export propensity. Neither the concentration ratio nor the import variable are significant in multiple regression. Esposito and Esposito (1971), and Pagoulatos and Sorensen (1976a) provide evidence that similar variables are both significant determinants of industrial profitability in the U.S.; but the latter study shows no influence of exports. Pagoulatos and Sorensen (1976b) confirm the negative effect of imports for most of the E.E.C. countries and also find a generally negative influence of the export propensity. Concentration is only important in the larger economies of France and Germany. Jenny and Weber (1976) and Neumann *et al.* (1979) support these results for France and Germany respectively. Canadian studies (e.g. Jones *et al.* (1973), (1977)), have shown a perverse, positive influence of the import propensity. This might be partially explained by the importance of imported components to the most efficient sectors of the domestic industry and to the misclassification of these components to the assembly industry. House (1973) and Caves and Uekusa (1976) show the concentration ratio (adjusted by House for import competition) to be a significant determinant of profitability in Kenya and Japan, but the export propensity has no effect in either country.

In general, the degree of industrial concentration and the degree of import competition do tend to exert significant influences on industrial profitability.[5] This conclusion remains despite the poor empirical proxies that have been employed. None of the above studies used the Herfindahl index of concentration; each of them used domestic output ($D+X$) as the denominator of the import variable, instead of the more appropriate measure of total sales to the domestic market ($D+M$); and only Hart and Morgan have employed an interactive functional form. As is to be expected, the export propensity has provided ambiguous results. Exports are pro-competititive in the E.E.C. countries where zero tariffs and geographical proximity lead to a highly competitive environment which allows little chance for price discrimination. In the U.K., at least prior to entry into the E.E.C., exports appear to have been more profitable than domestic sales.

In order to illustrate the advantages of a more appropriate specification of the estimating equation, we now turn to a study of U.K. manufacturing in 1968. The data are for a cross-section of 118 MLH (3-digit) industries which is based on a full sample of the manufacturing sector excluding those industries with "miscellaneous" in their titles and those which are nationalised or dominated by public corporations. The numerator of the price-cost margin (π) is measured as value added less wages and salaries, as given by the Census of Production (B.S.O., 1974). H is measured in employment terms (donated by Dr. S.W. Davies), but since export and domestic production are not distinguished by size class, measured H is a combination of actual H and H_x.

Import and export data (in value terms), were obtained from the C.S.O.. Unfortunately, a problem arises in that not all imports are competitive with the domestic supply. The identity of importers is not known and in many cases domestic firms are themselves large importers (e.g. Ford importing Ford Granada cars). This problem is exacerbated by the occasional misclassification of components into the assembly industry and we must rely on total imports being at least an indicator of foreign competition.[6]

Finally, there are no reliable data on demand elasticities, world production nor conjectural variations at this level of aggregation. In the face of these problems, it has been suggested (Cowling and Waterson, 1976), that an empirical study of *changes* in price-cost margins may be less heroic than one of levels. In other words, it may be more reasonable to assume that, for instance, the elasticity of demand is constant over time rather than across industries. We have chosen to reject this approach for three main reasons. Firstly, a study of changes introduces new problems such as the income elasticity of demand in the context of a growing economy. Secondly, slight changes in the industrial classification over the years make the comparibility of industries very difficult. Thirdly, our main aim is to compare the specification of an estimating equation which is suggested by the theory of oligopoly facing international trade, with the *ad hoc* regressions used in those studies outlined above, all of which were estimated in levels.

Given our data limitations, the nearest functional form to equation (8) is estimated as regression 1 (t-ratios are given in parenthesis),

$$\text{(R1)}\quad \pi/S = \underset{(22.51)}{.177} + \underset{(2.26)}{.328}\; H * DDM * DS + \underset{(0.95)}{.195}\; H * XS$$

$$\bar{R}^2 = .037$$

where, π = profits (as defined above)

$S = pD + P_w X$ = total industry output

H = Herfindahl index of concentration (as defined above); it is assumed that the concentration of domestic sales and of exports are the same

$DDM = D/(D+M)$ = the domestic industry's share of the domestic market

$DS = pD/S$ = proportion of industry output sold at home

$XS = p_w X/S$ = proportion of industry output exported

The poor fit of (R1) suggests that too much has been asked of the theoretical restrictions on the functional form, which has implicitly assumed all the elasticity terms, conjectural variations and the share of exports in world supply to be constant across industries.

Furthermore, as have already been discussed, there are problems associated with the exact measurement of *H* and particularly imports. Taken together, these points suggest that a less restrictive estimating procedure may provide better results. (R2) is therefore estimated in linear form,[7]

$$\text{(R2)} \quad \pi/S = \underset{(-0.11)}{0.005} + \underset{(1.41)}{.144H} + \underset{(4.21)}{.191\ DDM} + \underset{(3.71)}{.149\ XS}$$

$$\bar{R}^2 = .161$$

H is significant only at the 8% level on a 1-tail test. However, imports are an effective restraint on market power, and exports exert a positive influence on profitability. (R2) may be compared with the typical regression equation estimated by those papers surveyed above.

$$\text{(R3)} \quad \pi/S = \underset{(15.49)}{.189} + \underset{(0.33)}{.007\ CR5} - \underset{(-3.62)}{.111\ MS} + \underset{(2.88)}{.097\ XS}$$

$$\bar{R}^2 = .113$$

where $CR5$ = 5-firm concentration ratio

$MS = pM/S$ = imports/domestic output ratio

Clearly (R3) is inferior to (R2) both in overall explanatory power, and in the individual significance of the concentration and import penetration variables. A log-linear functional form of (R2) was also tried in order to pick up any interactions between *H* and *DDM*. Unfortunately, three zero values of *XS* required either (i) setting *XS* equal to some arbitrarily small number in order to take logs, or (ii) omitting these observations from the sample, or (iii) making use of the fact that $DS = 1-XS$ and substituting the log of *DS* into the regression. Each of these possibilities was explored, but since the results are not very different from (R2), they are not reported here.

Next, we turn to the question of product differentiation and heterogeneous products. In our discussion of equation (11), it was suggested that *DDM* remains a useful measure of foreign competition even if imports are differentiated from domestic production. However, this one variable is unlikely to pick up all the influence of differentiated products, so two further proxy variables are explored.

The advertising sales ratio (*ADS*) has often been employed in profitability studies, including many of those cited earlier. Comanor and Wilson (1967) argue that firms will advertise more heavily either if the product is *inherently* given to differentiation or if they wish to make their product, *appear* different to that produced elsewhere. Either way, advertising will reflect the degree to which one product within an industry is a substitute for another. A second, statistical reason for including *ADS* in a regression analysis is that due to data limitations, advertising has not been subtracted from the numerator of π/S.

The second proxy for product heterogeneity is less conventional. If domestic and foreign output were completely homogeneous, each country would tend to become either an importer of a good, or an exporter, but not both at once.[8] The more heterogeneous the product, however, the more cross-trading there will be in similar products. The following measure of the heterogeneity of domestic output with respect to world production is therefore suggested,

$HET = \dfrac{X + M - |X - M|}{X + M}$, where $|....|$ represents the absolute value of ....[9] If an industry's products are completely homogeneous, and there is no intra-industry trade, either X or M equals zero, so $HET = 0$. If exports are exactly balanced by imports, the cross-trading of implicitly differentiated goods is at a maximum and $HET = 1$. It is expected that *HET* will raise price-cost margins in that it will reflect the degree of non-substitutability of domestic for foreign products (*cf.* equation (11)). Repeating the previous three regressions with these additional variables,

$$\text{(R4)} \quad \pi/S = \underset{(8.90)}{.124} + \underset{(2.35)}{.306}\, H * DDM * DS + \underset{(1.88)}{.347}\, H * XS$$

$$+ \underset{(4.71)}{1.13}\ ADS + \underset{(3.39)}{.061}\ HET$$

$$\bar{R}^2 = .2258$$

$$\text{(R5)} \quad \pi/S = \underset{(-0.43)}{-.017} + \underset{(1.93)}{.180}\ H + \underset{(3.69)}{.154}\ DDM + \underset{(3.68)}{.136}\ XS$$

$$+ \underset{(4.60)}{1.06}\ ADS + \underset{(2.96)}{.050}\ HET$$

$$\bar{R}^2 = .3123$$

$$\text{(R6)} \quad \pi/S = \underset{(7.99)}{.139} + \underset{(0.68)}{.014}\ CR5 - \underset{(-3.06)}{.087}\ MS + \underset{(3.12)}{.097}\ XS$$

$$+ \underset{(4.55)}{1.08}\ ADS + \underset{(2.68)}{.048}\ HET$$

$$\bar{R}^2 = .2642$$

ADS and *HET* are significant at the 1% level at all times and they considerably improve the statistical fit of each equation, with (R5) now explaining over a third of the variance of price-cost margins. (R5) remains much the best specification with *H* becoming significant at the 3% level on a 1-tail test. The coefficient on *ADS* is not significantly different from unity, so care should be taken before interpreting advertising as an anti-competitive device.

IV. Conclusion

Section II of this paper represents an attempt to integrate international trade into a testable theory of oligopolistic behaviour. Models are developed for both homogeneous goods and for a differentiated case where imports are viewed as imperfect substitutes for domestic production.

A number of existing studies of industrial profitability and international trade are reviewed in Section III, followed by a more detailed investigation of the U.K. experience in 1968. It is found that the Herfindahl index of concentration, the degree of domestic domination of the home market, the export/sales ratio, advertising and a measure of the heterogeneity of traded goods each act to raise price-cost margins. Each of these work in the expected direction, except perhaps, exports. Theoretical considerations lead to an ambiguous prediction as to the overall effect of the export propensity, but the positive sign suggests that either the unusual circumstances of Commonwealth trade, the aftermath of devaluation, or the special characteristics of British products led to export industries being more profitable than those producing primarily for the home market. To the extent that the first of these reasons is true, and going by the experience of the E.E.C. countries, membership of the Common Market may have considerably weakened this export relationship in recent years. By the same token, however, the competitive effect of imports is likely to have been even further strengthened.

REFERENCES

Business Statistics Office (1974). *Report on the Census of Production 1968*. London: H.M.S.O., Vols. 156, 158.

Caves, R.E. (1974). International Trade, International Investment and Imperfect Markets. *Special Papers in International Economics*, No. 10, Princeton University.

Caves, R., Khalilzadeh-Shirazi, J. and Porter, M. (1975). Scale Economies in Statistical Analyses of Market Power. *Review of Economics and Statistics*, Vol. 57, 133-140.

Caves, R. and Uekusa, M. (1976). *Industrial Organisation in Japan*. Brookings Institution, Washington D.C.

Comanor, W. and Wilson T. (1967). Advertising, Market Structure and Performance. *Review of Economics and Statistics*, Vol. 49, 423-440.

Cowling K. and Waterson, M. (1976). Price-Cost Margins and Market Structure. *Economica*, Vol. 42, 267-274.

Esposito, L. and Esposito, F. (1971). Foreign Competition and Domestic Industry Profitability. *Review of Economics and Statistics*, Vol. 53, 343-353.

Gaskins, D.W. (1971). Dynamic Limit Pricing: Optimal Pricing under Threat of Entry. *Journal of Economic Theory*, Vol. 3, 306-322.

Grubel, H.G. and Lloyd (1975). *Intra-industry Trade: the Theory and Measurement of International Trade in Differentiated Products*. London: Macmillan.

Hart, P. and Morgan, E. (1977). Market Structure and Economic Performance in the United Kingdom. *Journal of Industrial Economics*, Vol. XXV, 177-193.

Hicks, J.R. (1935). Annual Survey of Economic Theory: the Theory of Monopoly. *Econometrica*, Vol. 3, 12-16.

Jenny, F. and Weber, A. (1976). Profit Rates and Structural Variables in French Manufacturing Industries. *European Economic Review*, Vol. 7, 187-206.

Jones, J., Laudadio, L. and Percy, M. (1973). Market Structure and Profitability in Canadian Manufacturing Industry: Some Cross-Section Results. *Canadian Journal of Economics*, Vol. 6, 356-368.

Jones, J., Laudadio, L. and Percy, M. (1977). Profitability and Market Structure: A Cross-Section Comparison of Canadian and American Manufacturing Industry. *Journal of Industrial Economics*, Vol. XXV, 195-211.

Khalilzadeh-Shirazi, J. (1974). Market Structure and Price-Cost Margins in United Kingdom Manufacturing Industries. *Review of Economics and Statistics*, Vol. 56, 67-76.

Linder, S.B. (1961). *An Essay on Trade and Transformation*. New York: John Wiley & Sons.

Neumann, M., Böbel, I. and Haid, A. (1979). Profitability, Risk and Market Structure in West German Industries. *Journal of Industrial Economics*, Vol. 27, 227-242.

Pagoulatos, E. and Sorensen, R. (1976a). International Trade, International Investment and Industrial Profitability of U.S. Manufacturing. *Southern Economic Journal*, 425-433.

Pagoulatos, E. and Sorensen, R. (1976b). Foreign Trade, Concentration and Profitability in Open Economies. *European Economic Review*, Vol. 8, 255-267.

Spence, A.M. (1977). Entry, Capacity, Investment and Oligopolistic Pricing. *Bell Journal of Economics*, Vol. 8, 534-544.

FOOTNOTES

1. I should like to thank members of the Sheffield Industrial Economics Seminar Group for many helpful comments on an earlier version of this paper and also the Douglas Knoop Research Fund at Sheffield University for finance. The author remains responsible in full for the contents of the paper.

2. This ignores the problems of attaining the new equilibrium.

3. Subscripts to f and g represent partial derivatives, e.g.

$$f_D = \frac{\partial f}{\partial D}.$$

4. Most of the following studies include a number of other independent variables which are not reported here (e.g. the advertising to sales ratio).

5. A number of the above studies measure profitability as the rate of return on equity or total assets rather than the price-cost margin. No attempt is made here to distinguish between these concepts.

6. Note that these problems of non-competing imports and the inclusion of exports in the domestic concentration variable apply equally to all the studies mentioned above.

7. Since $DS = 1 - XS$, DS has been omitted from (R2).

8. Except where market power has resulted in, for instance, a high domestic price attracting imports even though comparative advantage has led to exports by domestic producers.

9. Grubel and Lloyd (1975) use the same function to measure the degree of intra-industry trade.

DISCUSSION : B.J. LOASBY

I propose to leave detailed technical questions for the general discussion, and to comment on some issues of principle.

There are half a dozen different kinds of theory of the firm and of industry. The most commonly used (as in this paper) is a structure-conduct-performance framework assuming profit maximisation; there have been some recent attempts to examine also the effects of performance on structure. Second favourites are managerial discretion models, especially growth-maximising models derived from Marris. Then come what are usually called behavioural theories, but which I prefer to call organisational theories, and among which I would place Mrs Penrose's theory of the growth of the firm. Alfred Marshall had a theory of the firm and the industry which has largely disappeared, but post-Marshallian theories have been put forward by Philip Andrews and George Richardson. Also neglected nowadays are Schumpeterian theories; and finally there are "Austrian" theories of the market process. I am not sure how to classify the models recently proposed by Harvey Leibenstein and by Burton Klein.

Now it is very noticeable that almost all econometric studies in industrial economics are related to one or other of the first two kinds of theory. I believe that the principal reason for this is that these are the only two kinds which focus on the conditions of equilibrium, conditions which can be related back to the initial data. All the others are theories of processes, in which equilibrium is either not defined or is a state of little interest, and in which the processes themselves, rather than the initial conditions, are used to explain the outcomes. Thus theories of the first two kinds not only conform to the general preference of economists for equilibrium theorising; they also usually have more modest data requirements, though as the author demonstrates in his paper there may nevertheless be considerable problems.

A model subjected to test in any category must include some maintained hypotheses - hypotheses which the testing procedure must assume to be true. Here firms in all industries are profit-maximisers, or at least equally keen on obtaining profits (no industry is particularly associated with growth maximisation) and equally successful in avoiding X-inefficiency. Every industry is a non-collusive oligopoly, operating at constant costs and producing (for much of the analysis) a homogeneous product. It is full time that someone using such a model tried to meet Andrews' criticism of the use of share-of-the-market demand curves in an equilibrium model which provides no logical basis either for customer preferences between firms or for barriers to entry.

In some respects the most dangerous maintained hypothesis is that the data relate to a state of equilibrium - or at least to states about equally close to equilibrium, either (as here) across industries or (as in the paper by Cowling and Waterson) over time. For, as is indicated in this paper, behaviour out of equilibrium may produce not merely different but even opposite results; for instance the efforts of firms to protect their market power by predatory pricing, based on the diversion of goods from export markets (footnote 3), would produce a relationship between power and profitability just the reverse of that postulated.

It is a great merit of this paper that it introduces international trade formally into models of industrial performance. Given the potential importance of current policy debates about import penetration and the export competitiveness of British industry, and the dubious analytical foundations for these debates, such a development is highly desirable. May I suggest that it would be theoretically preferable to incorporate foreign competition in both import and export markets into a redefined Herfindahl index? The underlying theory implies that it would make a difference whether an import share of, say, 30%, were contributed by one firm or ten.

However, the incorporation of foreign trade brings additional problems for the equilibrium assumption. The author notes the argument that export profits must be higher to compensate for greater risk. Now this argument requires export profits at times to be lower; and if the firms in an industry are exporting to the same markets, then the factors mentioned as the causes of export risk (exchange rate variations, government action) can affect a whole industry at one time. But the tests reported in this paper involve a much more general problem with the assumption of equilibrium. Although one can well appreciate the data reasons for choosing 1968, it was a special year. Aren't they all? Yes, but 1968 was especially special, particularly for British overseas trade. There was devaluation in November 1967, and a deflationary budget, incorporating large increases in indirect taxes, in the Spring of 1968. Obviously, there would be a good deal of adjustment taking place in that year, especially by firms trying to develop new export markets, or organising production to fulfil new orders. One thinks of the once-familiar "reverse J-curve" tracing out an 18-month path to equilibrium, and of what this implies for the relationship between export volumes and profitability during this period.

In the light of the difficulties of principle, which are characteristic of the field, and of the absence of much of the data which his theoretical model requires, Mr Lyons has done very well to get the results which he has. He has been quite open about the problems, especially about the ways in which his estimating equations fall short of the rigorous theoretical specifications which he would like them to have. This openness, as much as his achievements, should help to guide further progress towards the objectives which he sets out in his second paragraph.

University of Stirling Brian J Loasby

11. ON THE NATURE OF INDUSTRIAL MARKET POWER IN THE U.K.

Tim Hazledine

I. INTRODUCTION

Harry Johnson described Industrial Organisation as a 'peripheral' subject, 'on which the British have always been extremely weak'. On the face of it, there seems to be some justice in this. For one thing, Industrial Organisation has not achieved the sort of lively interaction between theory and measurement that has developed in other fields, such as the Demand for Money, the Consumption function, the determinants of investment, and so on, in which we can enjoy the sight of econometric models being quite tightly specified with respect to the definition and choice of variables to be included, the functional form, and the sign and even magnitude of coefficients to be expected, supposedly before any confrontation with the actual data.

In contrast, it is quite typical for Industrial Organisation papers to begin with a statement like 'economic theory tells us to include variables X, Y, and Z in our regression equation', with no elaboration of said 'theory', followed by a string of Ordinary Least Squares equations that show, implicitly or explicitly, evidence of a rather desperate search for the best 'fit' amongst a number of alternative specifications of functional form, databases, and explanatory variables.[1]

Furthermore, even after all this 'mining' of the data, the results achieved are usually rather poor, on the usual statistical criteria, at least by the standards of econometric work in other fields.

Yet, although the invocation of 'economic theory' in Industrial Organisation is rarely supported by explicit exposition, or even references to where such an exposition might be found, there does indeed exist a quite rich body of micro-economic theorising which could be called on to justify the proposition, which is central to this field, that there is a relationship between some measure(s) of the structure of a market, and the profits earned by the firms selling in that market.

In fact, there are two such bodies of theory - one dealing with oligopoly, the other with the threat of new entrants to an industry - and this is a part of the problem, though they both share, and are critically dependent on, a common basic assumption of the primacy of 'market price' as an instrument determining industry sales and market shares.

In this paper, I shall try to argue that this assumption is implausible and misleading; that it leads to a pre-occupation with the industry or 'market' that is unwarranted, and is largely responsible for the feebleness of the empirical results. In the next section we will examine Oligopoly theories, then, in section III, models of Barriers to Entry. In section IV, an alternative theory, based on a notion of market power as a *firm*-, not an *industry*-specific force, is sketched out and compared, in section V, against some empirical results on UK manufacturing. Section V summarises and concludes the paper.

II. OLIGOPOLY PRICING

There are two types of oligopoly models: those which allow collusion between sellers, and those which do not. The difficulty with maintaining a *collusive* cartel is supposedly the incentive each member has to cheat on the others by shading its price. Since, in general, the rewards from successful cheating are greater the smaller a seller is relative to the total market (because the perceived elasticity of demand is higher) and since, as Stigler has shown, the chances of cheating being detected are less the greater the number of sellers, it could be reasonable to propose that the margin a cartel can maintain between price and costs is related to some measure of the size distribution of sellers.

Models of *non-collusive* pricing have developed into a respectable branch of mathematical economic theory, beginning with Cournot in 1838. In these models, firms set prices (or quantities) independently; each maximising profits subject to some expectation as to how the other sellers will react - sub-species of these models being differentiated largely according to the particular 're-action rules' that they assume. Most are duopoly (two-seller) models, and find that the price will be set lower than its industry profit-maximising (monopolistic) level. Cowling and Waterson ingeniously extend the analysis to the general n-seller case, and obtain an expression for the price-cost margin as a function of, *inter alia*, the Hirschman (Herfindahl) measure of the size distribution of sellers.[2] The reason for this relationship is, as with collusive models, the fact that it becomes likely to be more profitable for a seller to cut price, the smaller its share of the total industry market; in this case because the smaller the seller, the smaller the reaction to its actions, and so the smaller the combined effect of action and reaction on the market price.

One rather obvious problem with these models is that the *ad hoc* reaction rules assumed in general turn out to be wrong *ex post*,[3] but no-one adjusts their behaviour to take account of this; another is their *a priori* ruling-out of the possibility of collusion.

Nevertheless, although the body of collusive and non-collusive oligopoly theory is awkward and not well-integrated, it does seem to cohere in its major qualitative prediction; namely that market power (i.e. the degree to which the monopoly price can be approached) is a characteristic of the *industry*, not the individual *firm*, and, in particular, is related to the size-distribution of sellers in the industry.

How does this proposition stand up against the available empirical evidence? The table in the Appendix summarizes the results of nine studies of profitability in UK manufacturing industries. Except for Cowling and Kelly, the authors all use cross-sectional data at the three-digit (minimum list heading) level of disaggregation. Coverage and the time period sampled vary somewhat between the studies. Row three of the table reports the significance levels found for concentration variables.[4]

As a whole, the results give little support to the hypothesis that seller market concentration is a significant determinant of profitability in the UK manufacturing sector. In the regressions in columns one to five, and nine, the concentration variable is 'significant' statistically only once, and then marginally.[5] Cowling and Waterson, do find their Herfindahl measure of concentration to be reasonably significant, but this may reflect no more than a simple correlation between the Herfindahl and the dependent variable.[6] Hart and Morgan found that the price-cost margin and the seller concentration ratio are, by themselves, correlated, but that when other explanatory variables are introduced concentration loses its significance, suggesting that it may be no more than a proxy for these factors, with not much independent ability to affect profitability.

In their study of food companies, Cowling and Kelly did achieve significant coefficients for concentration in a multi-variate regression, so it may be true that seller market structure is important in this particular sector of manufacturing. Be this as it may (there are alternative interpretations for concentration variables, to be mentioned in section IV below), the weight of the evidence seems to suggest that the central proposition of oligopoly theory is not valid for the UK manufacturing sector as a whole.

If so, where does the theory go wrong? The answer, I suggest, is that oligopoly models make too much both of the *difficulty* and of the *importance* of sellers co-ordinating their actions. Even without explicit collusion, there are a number of effective ways in which the firms in an industry can allow a co-ordinated industry price to emerge, as Scherer's survey illustrates (chapter 6). The acceptance of one of the firms as a 'price leader', for example, is a common phenomenon. Scherer's list of examples (p. 167) covers about 15 per cent of US industrial value added, and is not intended to be exhaustive.

Really, it is not very surprising that oligopolistic firms should be able to come up with ways to avoid frittering away their profits in unnecessary price competition, given that it is manifestly in their interest to do so.[7] Economists may have been mislead by their own difficulties in formally *modelling* price formation into assuming that firms find it just as hard to actually *do* it. Indeed, we seem to have made the problem hard in the wrong places. It is not that the oligopolists are supposed to have any difficulty in *knowing* what the joint profit-maximising price is, as might reasonably be thought an important real-world problem. On the contrary, demand and cost curves are typically assumed to be known and fixed. The problem is really not with price at all. It is with quantity; with *market shares*. Under the conditions of the market demand curve, any firm slightly under-cutting its rivals' price can sell as much as it wishes (within the limit of the total market demand). This extreme price responsiveness of market share gives each member of the cartel or collusive aggrement an incentive to try and cheat its colleagues by price-chiselling. All the oligopoly models can be seen as attempts to formulate assumptions about rivals' reactions which imply a stable distribution of market shares, to counter the inherent slipperiness of the oligopoly situation as it is initially set up.

Is, then, sharing the market really a basic problem limiting collusive success, given that the process of achieving price coordination does not in fact generally appear to be too difficult? Such evidence that is available suggests that it is not. For example, Atkin and Skinner, from a survey to which 205 'medium to large' UK companies responded, concluded that

> "pricing is an area of marketing which is totally neglected. Pricing as a marketing tool is rarely practised" (ii).

Only 17 percent of their respondents reported price to be 'vital' in overall marketing strategy (p. 74). To be consistent with the orthodox oligopoly model, 100 per cent should have so replied.

On reflection, I do not find this surprising. It may well be that 'marketing' - the improving or defending of market share - is typically far from a trivial matter of adjusting price, even when there is a relatively high substitutability between the products of different firms in the same industry (as, for example, in all the dominant firm-pricing industries cited by Scherer, above). There are many extremely difficult problems to be overcome - formulating a promotional and advertising strategy, establishing and maintaining distributive, wholesale and retail outlets, building up good-will and a reputation for reliability, maintaining supplies of output, financing expansion - by a successful marketing operation, even when 'the price is right'.

The implication from all this is, then, that the flaws in oligopoly theory can be traced to its too-unquestioning appropriation from microeconomics of the notion of the simple demand curve - the device making sales just a function of price. It seems, in reality, that selling, or marketing, is a difficult business involving the use of many instruments. Of these, price may even by the *least* popular, since price competition is a negative-sum game for the selling group as a whole. Good theories should take account of all this.

III. ENTRY THREAT MODELS

The second substantial group of industrial organisation models is concerned with the likelihood of new firms entering an industry, and with the proper response to this by the firms already in place behind the industry demand curve.

Interest in modelling the entry situation was, initially at least (that is, before mathematicising set in) nourished by the traditional and deeply felt belief in the strength of the forces of competition as an ultimate constraint on the exercise of monopoly power. Scherer writes that

> "It is (the) entry phenomenon, more than long-run substitution between different products, which prompted J.M. Clark, Sir Roy Harrod, P.W.S. Andrews, and others, to insist that the long-run demand curves confronting monopolists and oligopolistic groups tend to be highly elastic, approaching the horizontal" (pp. 220-1).

That is, monopoly profits are a short-run, transitory phenomenon. This doctrine has, of course, powerful laissez-faire implications, although the possibility remains of the competitive forces working sufficiently slowly to justify some public intervention to hurry along the process.

Formal modelling has proceeded along two paths, depending on whether entry is 'smooth' or 'lumpy'. When the long-run average cost curve is horizontal, so that firms can enter at any scale efficiently, the modeller's problem is basically just to explain why monopoly profits are not wiped out instantly. This is done by pre-supposing some 'friction' which prevents instantaneous entry, and assuming that the rate of entry is then (usually) a function of the excess of price over some 'normal' or perfectly competitive level. The analytical problem is simply to determine the most profitable way for existing firms to delay the inevitable competing-away of all their monopoly profits.

Even if its particular assumptions were valid (I shall argue below that they are not), it is difficult to argue that this literature has contributed insights sufficiently surprising or useful to justify the quite substantial resources of mathematical ability and journal pages that have been committed to it.

Of more interest are those models in which, due to some indivisibility such as a minimum efficient scale of production, entry is likely to take place either at some rate large enough to affect the demand curve facing existing firms, or not at all. This, the 'lumpy entry' situation, was studied first by Bain (1956) and Sylos (1962), and their work synthesized and extended in a famous paper by Modigliani (1958). These are comparative static models, yielding a price, to be charged indefinitely, which will optimally forestall entry.[8] In a survey paper, Bhagwati reports that

> "The premium that can be charged, consistent with the prevention of entry, varies directly with the minimum scale of the entrant's plant, and inversely with both the size of the total market, and price elasticity of industry demand" (pp. 306-7).

These conclusions, though not surprising, are certainly more interesting, and lead to more empirically testable hypotheses, than those of the 'smooth' entry theorists.

However, both groups of models share the basic assumption that it is the excess of price over its competitive level that induces entry. The rationale of this is that an excess price is a signal, in fact the only signal, received by potential entrants concerning the profitability of being in an industry. It is assumed that

> "The entrant is likely to read the current price policies of established firms as some sort of a 'statement of future intentions' regarding their policies after his entry has occurred" (Bain, p. 95; quoted by Scherer, p. 229).

I find this unconvincing (as does Scherer). Of all the important variables determining the profitability of an industry, price is possibly the least permanent. Price may be changed over-night, whereas other factors, such as the rate of technological advance, the efficiency of management, the rate of market growth, and some government policies, change only over years or decades. That is, of all the information that a potential entrant will amass concerning current conditions in an industry, that on *current* price is likely to be amongst the least valuable.

What *is* important is what will happen to price *after* entry occurs, and since price is an exceptionally flexible variable, there need be no particular connection between the pre- and post-entry prices that would be set by the existing firms. These firms need only *threaten* to lower prices after entry, and thus eliminate monopoly profits, if they desire to prevent entry. If their cost competitiveness, and/or control over marketing outlets, dominate those of the potential rival, the threat should be effective; if not, entry will occur, but in neither case is there any reason for the firms not to 'make hay while the sun shines', and charge what the market will bear in the short-run. Indeed, a price closer to the competitive level than could be sustained by market conditions might well be expected to *encourage* the ultimate form of entry - a takeover bid - since a firm charging such a price would be valued on the stock market lower than the earning power of its assets would justify. The only relevant empirical study that I know of, by Zimmerman and Honeycutt, did indeed find a negative relationship between the numberof entries and price-cost margins.

Spence has recently proposed a model in which excess capacity, not price, is the entry-limiting instrument. In fact, an excess capacity strategy *dominates* limit pricing as a barrier to entry, as Waterson has pointed out:

> "For fixed costs are no higher than under a static limit-pricing policy, yet output is at more profitable level" (p. 91).

This is because the limit-pricer must also carry the 'excess' capacity to meet the extra demand that its lower price generates, yet it never reaps the profits of a higher price enjoyed by the industry which uses excess capacity as a strategy.

Although the Spence model is undoubtedly an improvement on the price-limiting theory, we may ask, in the spirit of our objections to the latter, why should not the *threat* alone of adding to capacity be sufficient to deter entrants. Surely existing firms, with their greater experience, will be able to add new capacity at least as quickly as any newcomer could manage?

The entry-limiting models (including Spence's) share with oligopoly theory the same inherent weakness - an over-emphasis of the importance of price as a market-share controlling instrument. If the arguments made in the previous section are persuasive, then it must be inferred that 'entry', expecially on a large scale, is not a very sensible concept (except in the form of a takeover of existing assets), as it will just not usually be possible to enter a market suddenly by announcing the appropriate price - it takes time, resources and entrepeneurial flair to build up a market share.

How do entry models stand up to empirical testing? There are just a few relevant studies - it must be noted that in this field, the resources devoted to the production of theoretical models have been disproportionate to those committed to evaluating whether these theories have any base in reality. We have already noted the result of Zimmerman and Honeycutt, which certainly does not *support* any of the entry models. Orr found that past profit rates has no discernible influence on increases in the number of firms in Canadian manufacturing industries. Mueller, having divided 472 US firms into eight profitability-ranked groups, found that a significant proportion of the firms in the highest-profit group in 1949 were still there in 1972. My own work, reported below in section V, reveals no tendency for monopoly profits to be competed away over a fifteen year period.

These results seem to give no support at all to the small-scale or 'smooth' entry hypothesis of eventual complete competing-away of any outbreak of monopoly profits. The econometric evidence does not, however, allow us to assess the 'lumpy' on large-scale entry model, since those factors - scale economies, firm size relative to market size, buyer market power - which would influence an entry-limiting price, would also affect the profit-maximising price of, say, a monopolist or imperfect competitor who was quite unconcerned about any entry threat.

IV. TOWARDS A REALISTIC MODEL OF MARKET POWER

In the previous two sections it was argued that neither of the two currently dominant schools of industrial organisation theories of profitability survive testing of either the accuracy of their predictions or the plausibility of their assumptions; their failure was traced, in both cases, to a view of markets which attributes far more than seems empirically reasonable to the concept of market price as a prime mover of sales and market shares.

As well, we may note that the existence of *two* sets of theories leads to unresolved inconsistencies - oligopoly models ignore potential competitors, whereas the entry barriers literature focuses on these while assuming away all problems of coordination between existing sellers (such models always assume a monopolist, or a 'dominant firm').

Now, it might be expected, given the degree of intricacy achieved by orthodox oligopoly and entry threat models even with their quite restrictive assumptions, that building a fully comprehensive model to take into account all of the above criticisms would be a hopelessly difficult task.

So, no doubt, it would be, if we took over the traditional approach of formulating the problem in terms of resolving the interdependencies within a group of actual or potential competing sellers.

Perhaps, though, the reasons for the failure of oligopoly and entry models do themselves suggest that structure-performance modelling should proceed in a different direction, away from ever-more complicated horizontal co-ordination problems, and towards what turns out to be a much simpler framework for theorising. Consider the main objection raised in both sections II and III; that our present models make sales or market share a too-simple function of just price (along with, in more sophisticated variants, expenditure on advertising services), whereas firms themselves appear to find 'marketing' anything but trivial, in fact involving all sorts of thorny problems of product design, research and development, production engineering, inventory management, building up sales and distribution networks, public relations, obtaining and giving credit, and so on.

It is, I suggest, a short step from making lists of all the activities involved in selling goods, to recognising that they are not in perfectly elastic supply; that a firm cannot simply *buy* an increase in sales as assumed in traditional models, in which a reduction in price, or increase in the advertising budget, is sufficient to generate the desired change in quantity sold. Rather, the ability to produce and market output - market power - should be seen as a *property right* held by individual firms, in quantities varying according to the particular skills, luck, and histories of entrepreneurs and the organisations that they develop. That is, market power is basically a *firm-*, not an *industry-*specific attribute.

This concept is immediately attractive for its ability to confront the empirical realities invoked in the previous sections. The failure of industry-specific seller concentration variables to show much significance in profitability studies is no longer cause for concern. The durability of above-competitive profits is quite consistent with the idea of market power as a property right - as something *owned* and *controlled* in different quantities by different sellers. Furthermore, the persistent asymmetries and heterogeneities of observed industrial structures may fit better with a model in which the basic building blocks - firms - are expected to differ in significant respects, than with oligopoly and entry barrier models in which differences appear only at the industry level. Elsewhere (1978), I have attempted to build a formal model of price-setting based on a firm-specific concept of market power. This model has market power dependent on the size of a firm's 'territory' in product-characteristic space, and on the price at which the best alternative products (i.e. those at the borders of the territory) are available. Market power is definable for both sellers and buyers, and the actual price charged for each transaction is assumed to split the gains-from-trade determined by the relative size of each party's market power.

There is not space here to expound this model in more detail;[9] nor would it be particularly appropriate to do so, given that the industry-level data available for the empirical work reported below cannot provide a direct test of a firm-specific model. Indeed, even firm-level data of the sort suitable for econometric analysis may miss important nuances of the structure-conduct-performance relationship. Assembling a widely-based set of case-studies of particular firms and markets may be the only way to assess, for example, just how difficulties of coordination affect the price-setting behaviour of groups of firms.[10]

Be this as it may, it *is* nevertheless possible to suggest a number of measurable factors likely to influence profitability in a firm-specific model, some of which may survive aggregation to the industry level. An obvious proxy for the size of a firm's market 'territory' is its actual market share - the proportion of total industry sales that it supplies. If we make profitability an increasing function of market share in a firm-level model, and aggregate, industry profitability will be dependent on the distribution of market shares, which may be well enough proxied by one of the usual industry size-distribution indices such as the concentration ratio. The relationship will be diluted, however, if the market power of relatively high-market share firm is achieved at the expense of its smaller competitors, rather than being paid for by consumers and/or firms in other industries. This may help explain the feeble performance of concentration variables in U.K. industry-level studies that was noted above in section II. Using the firm-level data that is available in the U.S., Shepherd found that market share dominated concentration as a regressor in an equation explaining the rate of return on equity.[11]

A factor which *should* aggregate successfully to the industry level is the scale of operation required for efficient production, which may matter to profits if imperfections in capital markets increase the cost of financing projects as scale increases; thereby increasing the margin of price over costs that existing firms can charge without encouraging encroachment on their territory.

The propensity of a firm's customers to be affected by advertising messages should be related to the profits it can earn. Again, aggregation may be affected by external effects, though not necessarily so as to dilute the industry-level relationship, as when one firm's advertising efforts increase sales for the industry as a whole.

It was suggested above that profitability depends on the market power of *both* of the parties involved in each transaction. On the buyer side, important factors may be the degree of expertness of customers, and the size of their individual orders. I have no direct data on these, but they may be at least partly accounted for by noting the distribution of an industry's sales amongst various broad classes of customer - government, the export market, consumers, other firms. In the last case, when goods are bought for further processing and re-sale, the profits on the 'downstream' sales may tend to be filtered back to intermediate-goods suppliers.

A final easily measurable factor that is often assumed to be a dimension of market power is the rate of growth of demand recently experienced by an industry.

V. DATA AND ESTIMATION

The sample used was of 51 U.K. manufacturing industries at the level of aggregation of the 1963 Input-Output (I-O) tables. The data are from these tables, and from the 1954, 1958, 1963, 1968, and 1973 Censuses of Production, aggregated, where necessary, to be consistent with the I-O industry definitions.

The dependent profitability variable was calculated as the average over the five Census years of the ratio of Gross Profits (Net Output - Wages & Salaries) to a weighted sum of expenditures on capital accumulation, wages and salaries, and the value of end-year stocks. This requires some justification. A theoretically appropriate measure of the profitability of the firms in an industry is the ratio of the profits earned to the profits that the factor inputs committed to the industry would earn were the industry perfectly competitive (i.e. without market power). Many U.S. studies use the ratio of profits to the value of the firm's or industry's stock of fixed capital as the dependent profitability variable. This is appropriate if the relevant competitive rate of return is the same across the sample, and if fixed capital is the only input committed by capitalists to the productive process.

The present study departs from this definition of profitability in two ways. First, data on capital stock are, most unfortunately, not available in the U.K., and I was therefore forced to use as a proxy the flow of capital expenditures in each Census year, hoping that, with data averaged over five years, purely cyclical variations in expenditures would cancel out.

Secondly, I do not believe that fixed capital is the only input on which capitalists expect to earn a return. Tying-up funds in inventories has its opportunity cost, and managing and taking responsibility for a workforce ('meeting a payroll') are non-trivial tasks for which some return will be collected, proportional to the size of the workforce. That is, even under competitive conditions of free entry and exit, we should expect that two firms with capital stocks of similar value, but different-sized workforces, would earn different amounts of profit.

Having no precise *a priori* notion of what are the appropriate competitive rates of return with which to weight capital, inventories and workforce,[12] I carried out a search over a 'grid' of values, looking for the combination of weights which, in association with the explanatory market structure variables, generated a series of predicted values for Gross Profits (the numerator of the profitability variable, which is invariant to the weights) which correlated most closely with the actual values of Gross Profits of the industries in the sample. The best-fitting weights for investment, inventories, and wages and salaries, respectively, were 1.2, 0.2, and 0.2, although predictive power did not fall much over a quite wide range of alternative values (and neither the relative magnitude and significance of the coefficients of the explanatory variables), so long as all three were greater than zero.

The derivation of this profitability variable is discussed in detail in Hazledine (1978, Part III). It performed significantly better, in its ability to predict variations in Gross Profits across industries, than did the ratio of profits to sales or Gross Output that is suggested by oligopoly theory to be the proper dependent variable in the profitability-market structure regression.

The various industry-level market power proxies suggested in section IV were measured as follows:

Seller concentration (SCR) is the sum of the total sales of the five largest firms in each Minimum List Heading industry that is included in the I-O industry, as a percentage of total sales of all firms in the I-O industry.

The scale factor was simply proxied by the average Net Output of plants ('establishments') in each industry (NO/EST). The susceptability to advertising was measured by the ratio of advertising expenditures to total sales (ADVR)[13], and industry growth by the average of between-Census rates of growth of Gross Output (%DGO).

The I-O tables allowed calculation of the 1963 values of the proportion of industry sales made to consumers (BUYC), to the public sector (BUYP), to fixed capital formation (BUYK), to exports (BUYE), and to other firms as intermediate sales. The last named proportion was weighted by the *seller* concentration ratios of the buying industries to allow for their market power (BCRINT).

Results are shown for two of the most interesting specifications:[14]

$$(1)\quad AVPROF = \underset{(2.7)}{0.0167\ NO/EST} + \underset{(7.1)}{0.179\ ADVR} + \underset{(2.1)}{0.517\ \%DGO}$$

$$+ \underset{(5.6)}{0.0400\ BCRINT} - \underset{(-3.0)}{0.0441(BCRINT)^2} + \underset{(12.2)}{0.0136\ BUYC}$$

$$- \underset{(-0.9)}{0.0058\ BUYP} + \underset{(0.4)}{0.0013\ BUYK} + \underset{(3.8)}{0.0135\ BUYE}$$

$$R^2 = 0.733,\ \bar{R}^2 = 0.67$$

$$(2)\quad PROF\ 6873 = \underset{(2.2)}{0.322\ NO/EST} - \underset{(-1.9)}{0.0309\ (NO/EST)^2}$$

$$+ \underset{(1.0)}{0.0053\ ADVR} + \underset{(5.0)}{0.0457\ BCRINT}$$

$$- \underset{(-2.8)}{0.0519(BCRINT)^2} + \underset{(16.3)}{0.0110\ BUYC}$$

$$- \underset{(0.3)}{0.0024\ BUYP} + \underset{(0.9)}{0.0031\ BUYK} + \underset{(2.9)}{0.0130\ BUYE}$$

$$+ \underset{(3.9)}{0.785\ PROF5863}$$

$$R^2 = 0.733,\ \bar{R}^2 = 0.670$$

In (*1*), "AVPROF" is the average value of profitability calculated for each of the five Census years. The mean values of the variables are: 1.606 (AVPROF), 3.43 (NO/EST), 48.1 (NO/EST^2), 1.27 (ADVR), 0.187 (%DGO), 20.28 (BCRINT), 6.48 ($BCRINT^2$ - scaled), 34.60 (BUYC), 5.82 (BUYP), 8.76 (BUYK), 17.21 (BUYE).

Equation (*1*) shows regression coefficients with the expected signs, and, in some cases, with comfortably significant t-ratios (in brackets under each coefficient). When (*1*) was run with the concentration ratio instead of NO/EST, SCR had a positive coefficient with a t-ratio of 1.8. When both SCR and NO/EST were included, the latter retained its significance (t = 2.5), but the t-ratio of the SCR coefficient dropped to zero. Thus, the oligopoly model fails to be supported by my results, which are therefore in line with those of the other U.K. structure-performance studies surveyed in section II.

The most interesting variables are probably those measuring buyer-market structure. The values of the BCRINT coefficients imply that, over the relevant range, a 'piggyback effect' operates - profits earned by market power are shared with intermediate goods suppliers.[15] It is apparently more profitable, *ceteris paribus*, to sell to consumers, or in export markets, than to the public sector or in capital goods markets.

The overall explanatory power of regression (1) is considerably higher than that of any of the earlier studies listed in the Appendix. This seems to be due (a) to the use of averaged data which reduce cyclical 'noise', and (b) to the extensive specification of buyer-market structure variables.

Regression (2) looks for any tendency for monopoly profits to be competed away over time. The average of 1968 and 1973 profitability (PROF6873) is regressed on the set of market structure variables (with minor changes from (1)), plus the equivalent profitability variable for 1958-63 (PROF5863). Regression (2) gives no support to the proposition that an industry would earn lower profits, for a given set of market structure factors, the higher had been its profits in an earlier period, since the latter would have encouraged new entry. In fact, the coefficient on PROF5863 is *positive*, and is not significantly different from one, which would suggest that *all* market power in the earlier period is carried through.

V. *SUMMARY AND CONCLUSION*

In this paper I have tried to argue two propositions: *first*, that there *is* something in the industrial economy we can call 'market power' - a force responsible for *persistent* differences in profitability - and, *second*, that this market power is best, in general, seen as a firm not an industry-specific phenomenon.

I have criticised both of what I discern to be the main traditional sets of models. Neither seems to provide a plausible rationale for a *durable* market power-profitability relationship. In oligopoly theory, the reason given for prices not to tend to be set by the group of interdependent sellers at the joint-profit maximising (monopoly) level - namely, limited ability to coordinate pricing - is unconvincing. On the other hand, in the entry threat literature, market price is supposed inexorably to be whittled down to the competitive level when small-scale entry is possible, and to be set above the competitive price to the extent that economies of scale permit, when these are present, but not additionally to be affected by other market structure factors.

Furthermore, the two bodies of theories cannot consistently be considered together - oligopoly models consider only problems of coordination between existing sellers (that is, a group facing a fixed demand curve), whereas the entry literature brings in potential competitors, but assumes away all coordination problems by working with a 'dominant firm' or monopolist.

In both cases, the difficulties appear to be due to the assumption of homogeneity in the 'market' or industry, so that, with other attributes equal, market shares become very responsive to price. This leads to instability, with existing sellers being tempted to cheat each other by shading price, and new sellers always being on hand to enter a market and erode any monopoly profits.

I have suggested, in contrast, that the relevant number of characteristics of goods is typically rather large, and differs from seller to seller (and buyer to buyer) to the extent that it is hardly reasonable to suppose that such characteristics are in elastic supply. Rather, each firm's product characteristics are determined by its particular experience and skills, and can be thought of as a *property right* yielding profits, and not subject to arbitrary elimination by the actions of present or potential competitors, unless these can come up with a more valuable set of characteristics.

In support of these propositions, I reviewed the empirical studies on market structure and profitability in U.K. manufacturing industry, and introduced some results of my own. More work is needed, both in the development of the theory of firm-specific market power, and in testing it on a base of data compiled at the level of individual firms or product lines. The model should also provide a useful framework for case-studies of particular firms or industries, and for interpreting existing studies, such as those prepared by the U.K. Price Commission.

As for policy, the main implication, of course, is that this should focus on firm rather than industry factors such as concentration ratios. Policy-makers are in fact ahead of academic economists on this, at least in the U.K., when they make use of the criterion of the market share of a particular firm as an indicator of monopoly power (e.g. the Monopolies Commission). No simple index can be useful, though, since 'market power' as I have defined it can be due to a superior product as well as to, say, the monopolisation of sales outlets.

REFERENCES

Atkin, Bryan, and Skinner, Richard, (1975). *How British Industry Prices.* Industrial Market Research Ltd.

Bain, Joe S., (1956). *Barriers to New Competition.* Cambridge: Harvard University Press.

Bhagwati, Jagdish N. (1970). Oligopoly Theory, Entry Prevention, and Growth. *Oxford Economic Papers,* November.

Chamberlin, E.H. Duopoly: Value Where Sellers Are Few. *Quarterly Journal of Economics,* November 1929 (reprinted as chapter III in *The Theory of Monopolistic Competition.* Harvard, 1933).

Cowling, Keith, and Waterson, Michael (1976). Price-Cost Margins and Market Structure. *Economica,* August, pp. 267-74.

Cowling, Keith, Cable, John, Kelly, Michael and McGuinness, Tony (1975). *Advertising and Economic Behaviour.* London and Basingstoke: Macmillan.

Cowling, Keith, and Kelly, Michael (1975). Advertising and Price-Cost Margins. Chapter 7 in Cowling *et al.*

Cournot, Augustin (1963). *Researches into the Mathematical Principles of the Theory of Wealth,* translated by

N.T. Bacon. Homewood: Irwin, originally published in French in 1838.

Dixit, Avinash (1979). A Model of duopoly suggesting a theory of entry barriers. *Bell Journal of Economics*, Spring.

Hall, M. and Tideman, N. (1967). Measures of Concentration. *Journal of the American Statistical Association*, No. 62.

Hart, P.E. and Morgan, Eleanor (1977). Market Structure and Economic Performance in the United Kingdom. *Journal of Industrial Economics*, March, pp. 177-93.

Hazledine, Tim (1978). *Distribution, Efficiency and Market Power: A Study of the U.K. Manufacturing Sector, 1954-73*. Ph.D. Thesis, University of Warwick.

Hazledine, Tim (1979). Generalising from Case Studies: The 60 Reports of the U.K. Price Commission. Queen's University Discussion Paper No. 363; earlier version available as Warwick Economic Research Paper No. 147.

Hitiris, Theodore (1978). Effective Protection and Economic Performance in U.K. Manufacturing Industry, 1963 and 1968. *The Economic Journal*, March, pp. 107-20.

Holtermann, Sally E. (1973). Market Structure and Economic Performance in U.K. Manufacturing Industry. *Journal of Industrial Economics*, pp. 119-39.

Johnson, Harry (1974). Cambridge in the 1950s. *Encounter*, January.

Khalilzadeh-Shirazi, Javad (1974). Market Structure and Price-Cost Margins in United Kingdom Manufacturing Industries. *Review of Economics and Statistics*, February, pp. 67-76.

Lyons, Bruce (1979). Price-Cost Margins, Market Structure and International Trade; paper presented to the AUTE Annual Conference, Exeter, March 1979.

Lyons, Bruce and P.D. Kitchin (1979). Effective Protection

and Economic Performance in U.K. Manufacturing Industry, 1963 and 1968: A Comment. Mimeo.

Modigliani, Franco (1958). New Developments in the Oligopoly Front. *Journal of Political Economy*, June, pp. 215-32.

Mueller, Dennis C. (1977). The Persistence of Profits Above the Norm. *Economica*, November.

Orr, Dale (1974). The Determinants of Entry: A Study of the Canadian Manufacturing Industries. *Review of Economics and Statistics*, February, pp. 58-66.

Phillips, Almarin (1972). An Econometric Study of Price-Fixing Market Structure and Performance in British Industry in the Early 1950s. In Keith Cowling (ed.), *Market Structure and Corporate Behaviour*. London: Gray-Mills, pp. 175-92.

Scherer, F.M. (1970). *Industrial Market Structure and Economic Performance*. Chicago: Rand McNaly.

Schmalensee, Richard (1978). Entry Deterrence in the Ready-to-Eat Breakfast Cereal Industry. *Bell Journal of Economics*, Autumn.

Shepherd, W.G. (1972). Structure and Behaviour in British Industries, with U.S. Comparisons. *Journal of Industrial Economics*, November, pp. 35-54.

Spence, Michael (1977). Entry, capacity, investment and oligopolistic pricing. *Bell Journal of Economics*, Autumn, pp. 534-44.

Stigler, George (1964). A Theory of Oligopoly. *Journal of Political Economy*, February.

Sylos-Labini, Paolo (1962). *Oligopoly and Technical Progress*, (translated by Elizabeth Henderson). Cambridge: Harvard University Press.

Vanlommel, E., de Brabander, B. and Liebaers, D. (1977). Industrial Concentration in Belgium: Empirical Comparison of Alternative Seller Concentration Measures. *Journal of Industrial Economics*, September.

Waterson, Mike (1976). *Price-cost Margins and Market Structure.* Ph.D. Thesis, University of Warwick.

Zimmerman, D.L. and Honeycutt, T.C. (1977). The Industry Effects of Entry by Large Firms: An Empirical Note. *Industrial Organization Review*, Vol. 5, No. 1.

FOOTNOTES

1. Examples of vague appeals to the 'theory' are to be found in all of the first five studies surveyed in the Appendix (cf. Hazledine, 1978, p. 173). The 'Warwick' studies of Cowling and Waterson are notable exceptions to this methodology.

2. Although this index is usually named after Herfindahl, it seems that Hirschman thought of it first. Cf. A.O. Hirschman, The Paternity of an Index. *American Economic Review*, September 1964.

3. The exception is the Chamberlin proposition that each firm assumes that its price will be exactly matched by the other firms - this obviously leads to price being set at the monopoly level, regardless of the size distribution of sellers.

4. The particular form of concentration index used may not make much difference. Vanlommel *et al.*, found, for Belgium, that the four-firm concentration ratio seems 'to convey the same informational content' as both the Hirschman Index and an Entropy measure. Hall and Tideman found a correlation of 0.976 between the concentration ratio and the Hirschman Index for the U.S. Herfindahl Indices for *sales* (though not for *employment* - as used by Cowling and Waterson, Waterson, and Lyons) are not available for the U.K.

5. The recent study by Hitiris is not included in this survey, since the significance he finds for 'concentration' depends both on the inclusion of one outlying industry (Cement) and an incorrect method of calculating weighted concentration ratios. Cf. Lyons and Kitchin.

6. Cowling and Waterson do include two additional regressors, but both are insignificant. Waterson has

one other regressor in his equation.

7. This opinion is not without precedent. Cf. Chamberlin, for example.

8. The scope of 'optimisation' is rather restrictive, as Dixit points out, since it is not always profitable to absolutely exclude new entrants.

9. The idea of a 'product characteristic space' is due to Lancaster (1966). For an interesting recent application of the idea to pricing conduct in a particular industry, cf. Schmalensee (1978).

10. Since the AUTE conference, I have made an attempt at this, using the 60 studies of the U.K. Price Commission as a database. Cf. Hazledine (1979).

11. For more evidence on this, cf. pp. 282-5 in the recent edition of Scherer's book.

12. The weights will, in general, differ, since the 'capital' variable is a flow proxying a stock, end-year inventories is a stock variable, and wages and salaries a flow (wages and salaries are used rather than numbers of employees as a measure of the 'size' of the workforce).

13. This is a very crude specification (though apparently effective). Cf. the papers in the book of Cowling *et al.*, for a rather comprehensive analysis of the role of advertising in markets.

14. The experimentation involved in arriving at these regression specifications involved trying-out both linear and quadratic forms for some variables, and dropping three industries (Sugar, Mineral Oil Refining, Iron and Steel) for which there was extraneous evidence of unusual profitability experience due to non-market factors.

15. The idea of the 'piggyback' was introduced to me by Waterson.

APPENDIX: UK STRUCTURE-PROFITABILITY STUDIES: TABULATION OF RESULTS

	Shepherd	Phillips	Holtermann	Khalilzadeh-Shirazi	Hart and Morgan	Cowling and Kelly	Cowling and Waterson	Waterson	Lyons
Coverage	3-digit (22 small industries excluded)	71 3-digit (availability of CRs limits coverage)	113 MLH industries	60 MLH industries[1]	113 MLH industries	88 food companies	94 MLHs (changes in MLH descriptions limits coverage	51 input-output level industries[2]	118 MLH industries
Dependent variable	gross price cost margin 1958-63 average	gross margin 1951 (on gross output)	gross margin 1963 (on sales)	gross margin 1963 (on sales)	net margin 1968 (on net output)	gross margin (on sales) 5 year average 1964-69	ratio 1973-68 gross margins (on sales)	as for Cowling and Waterson 1968-73	gross margin 1968 (on sales
Concentration	SCR5, 1958-1963 average, adjusted for imports (+1.6)	SCR3, 1951 (+2.2)	SCR5, 1963 (-1.1)	SCR5, 1963 (+0.3)	- (dropped as insignificant) -	SCR4, 1963 (cf fn 4)	ratio 1963-1958 employment Herfindahls (+2.9)	ratio 1968-63 employment Herfindahls (+3.4)	employment Herfindahl (1.9)
Entry Barriers	sales, average 1958-63 (+2)	average employment size of plant 1951 (+2.2)	average employment size of largest plant (-1.0)	median plant net output/industry net output (+3.9)	median employment size (-1.5)	net assets, average 1965-69 (+0.1)	- -	- -	- -
Sales Growth	% change in sales, 1958-63 current prices (+2.0)	% change in gross output 1948-54 (-1.5)	% change in sales, 1958-63 current prices (+3.6)	% change in sales, 1958-63 current prices (+1.5)	% change in sales, 1963-68 current prices (+0.9)	- -	- -	- -	- -

	Shepherd	Phillips	Holtermann	Khalilzadeh Shirazi	Hart and Morgan	Cowling and Kelly	Cowling and Waterson	Waterson	Lyons
Advertising	-	advertising/ sales, 1948	advertising/ sales, 1963	advertising dummy 3/	advertising/ sales, 1968	advertising/ sales, average 1965-69	-	-	adverti- sing/ sales
	-	(+2.8)	(+5.9)	(+3.0)	(+4.1)	(+3.1)	-	-	(4.6)
Buyer Power	-	-	-	exports/ total output 1963	-	-	-	ratio 1968-73 constructed buyer Herfindahl (+2.5)	proportion of output exported (3.7)
	-	-	-	(+2.1)	-	-	-		
Capital Intensity	average 1958-63 capital expenditure/ output (-0.5)	-	asset value/ gross output	average 1969-70 net assets/sales	capital expenditure/ employment 1968	-	-	-	-
		-	(+2.1) average 1958-63 capital expenditure/ output 1963 (+4.1)	(+2.3)	(+6.0)	-	-	-	-
Other variables	-	SCR* advertising/ sales	-	imports/total output 1963	imports/ domestic sales 1968	additional advertising variables: total adv. exp. 1965-69 (t=+2.5) and the square of this (t=-1.8)	durable good dummy	-	proportion of domestic sales not imported
	-	(+1.5) 'effective price fixing dummy' (+1.3) Producer goods dummy (+1.0)	-	(-1.3)	(+0.2)		(+0.6) ratio 1968-73 prop'n union membership (+1.5)	-	(3.7) index of intra-industry trade (3.0)
$\bar{R}^2$ (R^2)	(0.114)	0.260	0.454	0.544	(0.462)	0.342	(0.096)	(0.267)	(0.312)

Footnotes to Table

(Numbers in brackets are the t-ratios of the estimates coefficients)

1. Excluded from the 119 industry MLH sample
   (a) milk, sugar (non-comparable price-cost margins)
   (b) industries with concentration ratios published for less than 80 per cent of their principal products
   (c) industries with specialization index less than 80 per cent
   (d) margarine and compound fats (an 'outlier')

2. (a) includes mining, construction
   (b) excludes seven industries (MLHs 211, 331, 390, 334, 338, 342 and 349, 362) with 'out of line' specialization and exclusiveness ratios. When not excluded 'results remain significant in many cases but the explanatory power is lower' (1975, p. 13).

3. Advertising dummy = 1 when advertising is one per cent or more of sales, zero otherwise.

4. Concentration included quadratically. Linear and squared coefficients had t-ratios of +3.1 and -2.8, respectively.

DISCUSSION: P.A. GEROSKI

I was delighted to come across this paper by Tim Hazledine for, while I do not agree with all of it, I found it stimulating and I believe that some of the questions he has raised and avenues he has explored will lead to important further developments.

Certainly one of the puzzles I have found in the recent Industrial Economics literature is why traditional structure-performance models don't appear to find support in U.K. samples when they have performed reasonably well elsewhere (see the Weiss survey, 1974). Why this is and what it might mean are important research issues and well worth our attention. Tim Hazledine's argument that tacit collusion is probably more ubiquitous than we imagine and that price may not be an important competitive tool is certainly one avenue to explore and it may be that there are important differences in American and U.K. business conduct which can explain the pattern of empirical findings. I think, however, that there are several other possible answers. One is to look more carefully at the null hypothesis and ask precisely what is implied by an insignificant co-efficient on a concentration variable in a profits regression. It has been argued (convincingly to my mind) that systematic under-statement of profits by profitable firms and other measure-ment problems bias regression results towards insignificance, so that while a positive co-efficient implies a relationship and probably understates it, a non-significant co-efficient will not necessarily imply that no relationship holds in reality. A second related avenue of enquiry relates to the empirical specification of the structure-performance models. With very few exceptions, research methodology involves a somewhat arbitrary subset of possible variables thrown together in a linear regression and estimated by O.L.S. Of the very many problems this raises, the simplest example is the introduction of the Comanor-Wilson proxy for minimum efficient scale which bears a tautological relation to concentration indices (Davies, 1980) and so may lead to unwarranted inferences about the role concentration plays. Omission of variables and simultaneous structures are other familiar problems.

Thus we have a problem of unusual results to explain and the alternatives of re-building our theories or devoting energy to more careful and complete econometric specification of our tests. Tim Hazledine has chosen the former path and has concentrated on firms and firm specific attributes, a path also being pursued by Shepherd (1972 and elsewhere) and others. However, while attention is focused on firms, these models are careful not to dismiss completely many important structural features of the industry or the conduct which occurs between rivalrous oligopolists producing similar products.

In this model, attention is focused on the firm's marketing skill and "this ability to produce and market output-market power" is seen as a property right. Using an analogy with spatial models, one then determines the sustainable mark-up of a firm by the "distance" it maintains in the relevant space from all sorts of potential rivals. The short sketch of the model that Tim presents leaves two questions open in my mind. First, while the model does banish some sort of concentration index from the forefront of the analysis and, indeed, an elastic view of actual and potential rivals can eliminate it altogether, nevertheless the predictions of the model seem more or less indistinguishable from more traditional models. One is still left with a similar list of potentially germane explanatory variables and, barring concentration, the ranking appears pretty similar. Furthermore, the banishing of concentration indices appears a little more apparent than real. Surely proximity and distance of substantial rivals will alter a firm's policies (price possibly aside) and careful measurement of this proximity in the relevant space is likely to yield some index very much like our traditional concentration ratios. That is, the behaviour of a firm with a large chunk of territory will differ from that of another large firm which has a smaller chunk and nearby neighbours with similar sized allotments.

My second question relates to the application of property rights to the analysis. As an expository device it probably has many virtues, but in the ill-defined space of product characteristics and in dealing with problems of the ability of a firm to market effectively, use of some particular characteristics or command over certain abilities are not really property rights for they are ill-defined and the process of exclusion is complicated. Thus, while it is certainly interesting to model firms as if they were trying to establish property rights in a relevant space, it seems to be unhelpful to think of a static equilibrium in which such rights are actually attained and immutably held.

Let me conclude with a few comments on the empirical results, comments which again may arise only from the relatively short sketch presented. The introduction of a new dependent variable (ratio of actual to competitive profits) is interesting but the claim that they perform better than price-cost margins is hard to accept. This is a tricky problem of comparing non-nested hypotheses, in this case being two dependent variables against the same independent variables. As is well known, comparison of corrected $\bar{R}^2$'s (especially when there is no constant in the equation) is not really appropriate for non-nested hypothesis testing, especially when trying to explain two different variables with different variability. Secondly, (as mentioned above) I am suspicious of the disappearance of concentration when some plant size variable is introduced. One has to be very careful that some summary of the plant size distribution is not conveying information about the distribution of firm sizes and so essentially adding no new information to that given by concentration indices. Finally, in line with a comment made above, I am not convinced that this particular test distinguishes the current model from the traditional alternative which is perfectly compatible with the introduction of buyer characteristic variables.

To sum up then, the current paper provides an interesting and thoughtful answer to some recent developments in structure-performance testing in the U.K. It is not the only answer one can give and only time and further research will tell what the answer really is. I would not like to leave you with the feeling that I have given a negative reaction to the path taken here. It seems to me well worth exploration and I await with interest further developments.

REFERENCES

Davies (1980). "Minimum Efficient Scale and Seller Concentration: An Empirical Problem". *Journal of Industrial Economics*, Vol. 28, pp. 287-301.

Shepherd (1972). "The Elements of Market Structure",

Review of Economics and Statistics.

Weiss (1974). "The Concentration-Profits Relationship and Anti-Trust" in Goldschmidt, H.m Mann, M. and Weston, J. (1974) *Industrial Concentration: The New Learning*, Little, Brawn and Company.

12. FACTORS AFFECTING THE GROWTH OF THE FIRM - THEORY AND PRACTICE

Aubrey Silberston

1. *THEORY*

Some results of our research on the growth of firms[1] have already been written up[2]. This paper draws on detailed case studies that we have made of some twenty firms in five British industries, although it does not refer to them in detail. Work is also being done in Germany along similar lines by Professor Kieser (of Mannheim) and his associates. The fact that the research was carried out by sociologists as well as economists has been explained elsewhere. We had to adopt a case study approach (supplemented by statistical data) partly because we wanted to throw light on organisational factors. We also wanted to investigate the reasons for strategic moves on the part of firms. We recognise the problems involved in interpreting businessmen's answers to questions on such issues, and we have been cautious in our interpretation of the evidence. But we think it better to try to discuss questions of this sort after studying individual firms instead of attempting to rely on some sort of aggregative statistical analysis.

A number of authors have contributed building blocks for a theory of the growth of the firm. Marris has produced the most complete theory, but other notable authors have been Chandler, Oliver Williamson, Cyert and March, Galbraith and Mueller, among others.

The Marris model of the firm is a steady state growth model, but it contains many features of interest to a study of the growth of actual firms. It is based on an assumption of the separation of ownership and control in the modern corporation (an assumption that we have already questioned in Nyman and Silberston (1978)). It is then argued that managers, who effectively control the large corporation, derive higher salaries and more prestige and power the larger the size of their firms. They aim therefore to maximise the rate of growth of their firms, subject to some minimum profit rate, and hence subject to some minimum stock-market valuation for their firm's shares. If this value is not reached, there is a danger that the firm will be taken over. This behaviour on the part of managers is contrasted with that of owners, who are alleged to be interested in maximising the present value of future profits (or rather of future dividends)[3]. High rates of growth imply high retention ratios, or the equivalent in terms of the balance between funds distributed and funds raised on the stock market[4].

The attainable rate of growth in the Marris model is constrained by two factors which tend to bring down the rate of profit once the rate of growth has passed a certain point. The first of these is the 'Penrose' effect (Penrose (1959)), which is based on the notion that a firm's speed of growth may in certain circumstances be inhibited by bottlenecks in management. At times there may be management slack, but rapid rates of growth and change are likely to cause managerial difficulties which tend to reduce efficiency and hence the rate of profit. The second constraining factor is that saturation may occur in particular markets if attempts are made to expand rapidly in them. The response to this on the part of firms wishing to grow fast, according to Marris, is to diversify into other markets, possibly involving different products. There are, however, likely to be difficulties about trying to diversify rapidly, since successively introduced new products will have declining appeal as the inventive resources of the firm are stretched. Penrose effects appear here also, therefore. A further problem with attempts to diversify is that the invasion of competitors' markets may cause serious problems of retaliation, but Marris himself does not make a great deal of this. Indeed, the comparative neglect of oligopolistic factors is one of the weaknesses of his model.

Mueller's life-cycle theory (Mueller 1972) is related to that of Marris. He emphasises the profitability of young growing firms and the loss of control and innovative ability in old, mature firms. The mature firm is run by managers anxious to maximise growth. They typically reinvest rather than distribute profits, but the marginal return on investment for such firms is low. This is why their stockholders (as opposed to stockholders in young firms) prefer dividends to retentions. Mature firms over-invest, so Mueller argues, and therefore misallocate the resources of the economy. Another consequence of their activities is that they help to raise overall concentration in the economy, and thus to concentrate political as well as economic power.

Then there are the views of Galbraith, particularly as expressed in 'The New Industrial State' (Galbraith (1967)), although these are related to size rather than to growth as such. Galbraith stresses the importance of capital investment and planning for the modern corporation. This is related to the importance of research and of the economies of large-scale technology. The manager of the large corporation needs to plan well ahead, and to this end manipulates the market so as to make it welcome the products that he chooses to put before it. He is also anxious to gain the co-operation of the State, in order further to safeguard the success of his corporation. As a result, the 'technostructure', as Galbraith calls it, comes to dominate not only the industrial sector but the State itself. Galbraith's main emphasis is on the importance of technocrats and large-scale technology, and on the ease with which the market can be manipulated by the large corporation. He also points out that large-scale technology necessitates a small number of firms in each market, so that oligopoly becomes an important feature of the industrial structure.

Turning to the more "managerial" models, Cyert and March (1963) have drawn attention to the conflicts within organisations that stem from the different roles that different members of management are called upon to play by virtue of their specialist appointments. Williamson (1970) has stressed the relationship between growth and the efficiency of the internal organisation of the firm. In particular he has stressed the superiority in large firms of the divisionalised or 'M' form of organisation over the centralised 'U' form. The fullest discussion of the relationship between internal organisation and those factors which affect size and growth is however contained in the classic works of Chandler (1962) and (1977). He stresses the way in which the growth of large American corporations has moved in cycles. Following the initial accumulation of resources, the need arises to use them more rationally than in the initial phase. Then follows a period of growth by diversification, which in its turn is again followed by a period of rationalisation. The periods of rationalisation throw up the need for a divisional forn of organisation, in order to decentralise decision-making. At the same time, the need is seen for a powerful headquarters organisation, to keep control of vital functions such as finance, and to lay stress on profit maximisation as the goal of the firm as a whole. Chandler observes that typically a new man at the top is needed for administrative change. He also stresses the importance of the changing market situation to the adjustments made within and by firms.

Chandler's observation that a new man at the top may be needed before administrative change can be brought about can be related to the importance that has sometimes been laid on the background, education, and characteristics of individual managers. I refer later to the question of ownership of different types, and its possible effect on firms' objectives and efficiency. Here, however, I am concerned with the importance of particular individuals to the success of the firms in which they work. Knight (1974) has drawn attention to this, and I am myself a strong believer in what might be called 'the great man theory' of the growth of firms. This is another theme that I discuss below.

2. *PRACTICE*

i) Introduction

There have been a good many empirical studies that have stemmed from writings on the theory of the growth of the firm. In particular, the implications of the separation of ownership from control have aroused a good deal of interest. Some doubt has been thrown on how far there is indeed such a separation (Nyman and Silberston (1978)) and we have suggested that in some 56 per cent of the top 250 British companies there is 'ownership' control in the sense that a small group of owners may have the power to change top management, and hence change company policy. We have also differentiated types of ownership by categories such as founders, families, other industrial companies and financial institutions[5]. We have suggested that financial institutions are likely to lay stress on profitability as an objective for the firms they control, especially on short and medium term profitability. We have not however investigated the effect on objectives of family and other types of ownership, an omission which I try to remedy below.

In Nyman & Silberston (1978) we gave a summary of other empirical work relating to ownership and its effect on performance. The only clear result of this work seems to be that owner-controlled companies have a higher rate of profit than management-controlled companies. But even this result is dubious, while Radice's finding (Radice (1971)) that owner-controlled companies have higher rates of growth also is contradicted by Holl (1975). As will be seen from what follows, I doubt whether any valid generalisations can be made on the basis of a crude distinction into 'owner' and 'management' controlled companies.

Before dealing with specific issues, I wish to emphasise a point made much more strongly by Chandler than by any of the other authors mentioned above. This is the importance of changes in the market situation to the structures and strategies that different firms adopt, and to their resulting performance. One would imagine that this would be a prominent feature of theories of the growth of the firm, but in fact the theories are surprisingly silent on the subject. The great importance of the market situation becomes apparant, however, as soon as one begins to study real firms. A number of aspects of the market are relevant to the position of any one firm. They include the state of the economy as a whole, the state of the relevant industry in relation to that of the economy, technical developments in that industry, and above all the intensity of competition facing the firm, from both domestic and foreign sources. All these aspects loom large in any practical consideration of the factors affecting the growth of firms.

ii) Ownership and objectives

The original family is still important, or was until recently, in several of our firms[6] (e.g. Lyons, Cadbury, Tesco, Associated Biscuit), and the original founders are still in control of two firms (Dixon & Mothercare). As it turned out, relatively few firms in our case studies are management controlled, although this latter category does include Unilever and I.C.I., both of which we studied in part.

All the firms we studied have been concerned with the need to grow in a growing market. All have wanted at least to keep their share of their markets, and their perceptions of likely changes in the nature and size of their markets have had an important influence on their decisions.

Some firms have wanted to grow, without acquisitions, in their existing lines. Others have grown by acquisitions in their existing fields. Several have looked to diversification - normally by acquisition - because they were worried about the lack of buoyancy of their original markets. Most have looked overseas, for expansion or for acquisition in their own lines, or for diversification (usually by acquisition), because the U.K. market was not showing fast enough growth.

The extent to which firms have gone mainly for profits or for expansion has differed over time[7]. At times of boom, mergers have accelerated, both for the economy generally and for our firms. In periods like the mid-1970's, when demand was low, our firms have, like others, acquired less and have concentrated on rationalisation and even on disposal. There has been much more emphasis on the need for profits in the 1970's, and especially on the need for adequate cash flow.

The choice between growth and profitability as objectives seems to have been largely a matter of timing. The aim in some sense has always been to maximise profits, or at least to earn good profits, but at different times different means have been seen as being appropriate to achieve this. When crises have occurred, however, the predominant emphasis has had to be on short-run profits.

There is no appreciable sign that where managers are in control they have been motivated by the effect of growth on their salaries and prestige[8]. The most dynamic firm in our food sample was probably Schweppes, which was management-controlled. Their growth motivation obviously owed much to the drive of Sir Frederic Hooper, formerly managing director, but an important factor in their policy was a need to protect success by growing larger and thus fending off takeover. Successful growth bred the need for further growth.

Unilever's growth drive was in the 1950's (as was the case with many other firms) to take advantage of growing markets. They realised later that there was not enough emphasis on profit, though their priorities changed partly because their markets changed, and became less buoyant.

Most family firms in our sample tried to expand, but not always successfully. This appears to have had little to do with type of objective as related to type of ownership. Objectives seemed to be much the same, but some firms were more successful in achieving them than others. One could argue that in the food industry, for example, the management of Unilever and Schweppes was simply better at achieving their objectives than that of the family dominated firms.

In the case of one food firm, however, Associated Biscuit, family control allowed unambitious targets to be set, and a policy of little rationalisation and little innovation to be pursued. Ownership protected a lack of efficiency. To some extent this may have been true of Lyons and Cadbury, where it is likely that outside influences would have led to greater pressure for success, or even takeover, if the family hold had not be so strong.

Batchelor is an interesting case of a drive for efficiency from the owning firm, in the shape of Unilever. Because of the drive from Unilever there was perhaps the 'purest' profit motivation of all, among our food firms, in the Batchelor case.

On the basis of our particular firms, it would seem that family domination is not as good for profitability and growth (except by merger) as management domination. This is the opposite conclusion from that of Radice, based on a statistical study of the relative performance of owner and management controlled firms. On further examination, however, it seems important to distinguish between the original founder of a family-owned firm and the succeeding family dynasty. The drive and efficiency of the founder may not be generally transmitted to his heirs or, as Marshall suspected, the heirs' circumstances may be such that there is no great pressure upon them to perform well in the business itself. If there is truth in this view, it is not enough to point to "ownership control". It is necessary to examine the identity of the generation concerned. Even this is not infallible, of course, since some families succeed in producing from time to time able heirs, with an exceptionally strong commitment to the family business. Such a process seems a good deal chancier, however, than the power of very large management-controlled firms such as Unilever to recruit and promote managers of outstanding ability.

iii) Mueller's Life-Cycle Thesis

All of the firms that we studied were "mature" in the Mueller sense, except for the two firms still controlled by their founders, Dixons & Mothercare. It is true that these two young firms have an outstanding record of growth and profitability - which is why we chose them - but there are other young firms which have done far less well, including many which went out of existence (by bankruptcy or merger) before they reached maturity. The mature firms in our sample have varied in their growth records. They have certainly not all been run by managers, as we have seen. Nor have they apparently taken maximum growth as their objective. On the other hand, there have been undoubted signs of lack of successful growth in many of our firms, especially perhaps in the family-dominated ones. Retention ratios have been high during certain periods (see below), and some "overinvestment" as Mueller argues, has undoubtedly occurred. Several of our firms have, however, had successful periods of investment and growth, and their differences in degree of success have been more obvious than their similarities.

On the basis of the firms we studied, leaving aside Dixons & Mothercare, there is some support for Mueller's hypothesis, but it seems to be limited support only. Perhaps Mueller's way of looking at firms is not very helpful when it comes to large firms. These have necessarily been long-established, and it is scarcely plausible to believe that all large firms have run out of steam. In any event, it must be remembered that large firms are made up of a number of subsidiary units. Some of these units or divisions will be "mature", while others will be young and growing. Within the large firm, therefore, there may co-exist examples of both young and old "firms", and it may not be easy to generalise about the "maturity" of the firms as a whole.

iv) Diversification and Growth

The Marris picture that firms diversify as they grow in size is to some extent true. But how far are the reasons for it those given by Marris, or indeed by Chandler?

Several steps are possible before diversification need be undertaken. First comes the possibility of expanding along with the market. Next, one can acquire firms in the same market in the same country. Then one can expand overseas if already established there, or by acquiring firms overseas. The possibility of taking all these steps, when it is felt that expansion in a firm's original product-line is likely to be profitable, puts off the time when diversification is needed.

When it does occur, diversification seems likely to be in a field related to the original field - for example, a move may take place from chocolates to chocolate biscuits, or from cocoa to tea. Many firms seem to have a notion of the area in which their experties lies, and diversify within that area. A true "conglomerate" would behave differently, but our particular firms are not on the whole like that, and neither are most firms in the U.K.[9]

Diversification is sometimes possible from a firm's own resources, but where it it outside the firm's usual line it is easier to merge. One obtains expertise in this way, together with a market share without having to fight for it. One problem with diversification is that if a firm is large in its existing lines, and acquires modestly, this gives it little effective diversification. Small acquisitions in diverse fields are quite common, but relatively large ones (for example Cadbury/Schweppes and Jeyes), are rarer. The larger the firm, the harder it is for it to diversify effectively.

Diversification may be used as a means of stepping up the firm's rate of growth, as Marris argued. But it may be desired simply to keep the firm's growth rate in line with the general growth of the economy, because demand for existing lines is dropping off relatively, e.g. chocolate confectionery in the case of Cadbury. Marris-type diversification could perhaps be called "aggressive" diversification. Some conglomerates certainly pursue diversification of this type, or have done in the past. Some of the retailers in our sample seem also to have behaved in this way, together with Schweppes in food. But for many of our firms diversification has certainly been mainly "defensive". It has been needed to safeguard the firm against relative decline. Similarly the overseas growth of many of our firms appears to have had such a motive. The endeavour has been primarily to sustain growth, rather than to step up its rate. In practice, however, "defensive" mergers have sometimes been on a large scale, and have therefore resulted in relative growth.

De-diversification - much less discussed - is in fact a common phenomenon. It is likely to follow a period of rapid growth, especially by acquisition. It can take the form of getting rid of parts of an acquired business, e.g. its interest in a particular country, or of getting rid of parts of the firm's original business. This is usually done for rationalisation and control reasons. But sometimes it is done simply to raise money, because the firm is short of cash - see, for example, the case of Lyons and the sale in 1976 of most of its U.K. hotels.

In the Marris model, the rate of profit falls after a certain point because, even with diversification, markets become saturated. If a firm can resort to acquisitions, however, it is not so easy for saturation of its markets to take place. The firm can grow almost indefinitely, provided it can cope with the management problems involved. These may be serious, however, and Marris argues that they too are likely to lead to a fall in the rate of profit, as 'Penrose' effects occur.

v) Management and Penrose effects

Edith Penrose (1959) stressed the fact that at times there are spare management resources which can be utilised to expand activities or to manage acquisitions. This enables managerial overheads to be spread. But when management becomes stretched, indigestion occurs, and growth must slow down to enable new managers to be trained, or old managers to assimilate previous growth.

These phenomena are clearly discernible in our firms. One apparent example of spare management resources being spread occurred when Schweppes took over Chivers. Spare management resources in Unilever also helped out Batchelors at difficult times for that firm.[10] On the other hand, numerous instances of management indigestion can be seen. They have occurred especially after periods of rapid expansion of acquisition, bringing a need for a quiet period thereafter. Diversification has been particularly associated with management problems, whether diversification has been internal or by acquisition. Sometimes the problem has been so great that de-diversification has had to be resorted to for this reason.

Particular problems arise with acquisitions. These bring in managers from outside the firm, probably with different styles and traditions. Even before an agreed merger the problems may begin to loom large, and many mergers are in fact not finally agreed because of problems such as deciding who is to be on the Board, etc.

After a merger, there may be great problems of assimilation. Differences in experience and attitudes may create what amounts to cultural shock. After a forced takeover in particular, the management atmosphere may be especially bad. It may, however, be easier to rationalise the resulting firm than after an agreed takeover. In the latter case, it may be difficult to get agreement on rationalisation, as was the case with Austin and Morris in B.M.C., or with Associated Biscuit in our sample.

The probability of management problems arising after acquisitions has gradually become better and better realised, particularly since the 1968 merger boom. There may be a brake on acquisitions now partly for this reason, as well as because of the overall state of the economy.

A good many managers in acquired firms leave after takeover, either because they dislike the new owners, or because their prospects of running their own firms have been blighted. This may have good as well as bad aspects. It allows managerial economies of scale to be grasped in the new merged firm, and may clear out dead wood. It may also release talent for other firms.

On the other hand, mergers may give a strong acquisition of managerial talent to the acquiring firm. Weinstock and G.E.C. is a famous example. L. Rose and Schweppes is an example from our case studies.[11] Sometimes this accession of management strength is anticipated, while at other times it may be an unexpected bonus.

How likely is it that taken-over firms will have good management? Marris foresees that firms which perform badly compared with their potential will be taken over, and Singh's work (Singh 1971) has given some confirmation of this. But this need not necessarily be so. A large firm may not find it difficult to take over a successful small firm (as Singh also showed) and it may want to do so if it has a choice between victims, because it creates fewer problems to take over success than failure (although it is more expensive). In addition, the small firm may be putting up strong opposition in the market. To take over the firm reduces competition as well as bringing with it good management (and perhaps a good product) which may be capable of greater things.

Acquisitions may give rise to management headaches, therefore, but may also help to give a new lease of life as regards quality of management. Perhaps this is the more likely to occur the smaller the size of the acquiring firm. Firms like Unilever are likely to have enough managerial talent already, but even they may need to take over specialised management if they wish to enter a new market.

vi) Retention ratio, growth and profitability

Marris argues that it is necessary to step up the retention ratio if a firm wishes to grow fast. Growth is likely to be associated, after a point, with a falling off in the rate of profit, and therefore a fall in the valuation ratio. This would be a handicap to a firm wishing to grow by takeover, although Marris does not stress this.

One solution for such a firm may appear to be to grow moderately, with a low retention ratio, in order to keep up its rate of profit, and hence its valuation ratio. Certainly, the valuation of its shares is very important to the takeover raider, both because it wants a high stock market rating if it wishes to exchange shares, and because it must try to convince the market that it can use the extra assets profitably if the takeover occurs. As we shall see shortly, however, this solution does not seem to be a very realistic one.

There has been much argument about how far dividends favourably affect the value of shares, other things equal, as against retentions. The weight of evidence now seems to be that distributions are better for share values (Edwards (1978)). It is interesting that those firms in our sample which were most anxious about their shareholders were keen on paying-out. For example, our most dynamic food firm, Schweppes, was also the food firm with the lowest retention ratio.[12]

The Marris picture is apparently confirmed by Unilever, with high retentions and (fairly) high growth, but contradicted by Schweppes - otherwise one of our most Marris-like firms. High retentions, however, may result from crisis, as well as from a desire to grow. Some family firms in our sample - such as Lyons and Cadbury - were forced at times to have high retentions because of cash problems. One of the paramount reasons for high retentions may well be a lack of liquidity (and probably of profitability), therefore. Another factor with family firms may be that there is less pressure for dividends, because members of families are not keen on high dividends because of their personal tax position. In so far as this is true, pressure to retain funds in a family controlled business, and to re-invest them, could lead to low profitability for investment at the margin, in the way that Mueller has suggested. This could be especially so when the apparently lower efficiency of some of these firms is taken into account.

It is clear from this brief discussion that the picture of the relationship between rate of growth, retention ratio and profit in the Marris model can be misleading outside his model. There is no necessary connection between a high retention ratio and a high rate of growth.[13] A high retention ratio may be forced on low profit firms. Conversely, high profits give resources for expansion or takeover, even when retentions are low. High profits lead to high share values, and hence to the possibility of raising funds externally and of exchanging shares for those of others.[14] For overseas expansion, a successful firm can provide expertise, and its reputation will enable it to rely on local money for most of the funds it needs. High profits are therefore a much better clue to high growth than are high retentions.[15]

Another point is that different firms may earn very different rates of profit at similar rates of growth. For any one firm the Marris relationship may hold, but there is no necessary reason for this to occur as between firms, since a faster growing firm may well have a higher rate of profit (instead of a lower rate of profit) than a slower growing firm. The key to success, in this as in other areas, is to do better than other firms whose circumstances and possibilities seem broadly similar.

To be fair to Marris, his is a long-run steady-state model, where retentions are, in effect, the only source of funds to finance growth. The Marris relationship can, however, be misleading if applied to a non-steady state world, where takeovers occur, and where big differences exist between the profitability and the entrepreneurial drive of different firms.

vii) Market changes and firm strategy

I referred earlier to a point stressed by Chandler - the importance of changes in the market situation to the structures and strategies that different firms adopt, and to their resulting performance. This is very evident in the firms that we studied.

Even in comparatively mature and stable industries, such as food manufacturing, great changes have taken place in the post-war period. Non-packaged and non-branded groceries have largely been replaced by pre-packed and branded lines. Frozen food has been introduced on a large scale, and there has been a growth of 'instant' beverages and 'instant' meals. Opportunities for product innovation have been numerous, in drinks as well as foods. At the industry level, there have been innovations in wholesaling and retailing, many of them associated with the growth of supermarkets and the development of 'own label' brands. Resale price maintenance has ended, and competition has increased - from U.S. and European firms, as well as from firms within the United Kingdom.

Individual food and drink firms have reacted in different ways. Mergers have been common, especially in brewing, and there has been much diversification. One reaction to increased foreign competition, and the comparatively slow-growing U.K. market, has been to expand overseas, as Lyons did, for example, at dramatic (and unfortunate) speed in the early 1970's. All the food firms we studied had to react to the changes that occurred in the market situation, but they differed both in the degree of innovation that they exhibited, as well as in the degree of success that they attained.

The firms that we studied in other industries found themselves in even faster-moving market situations. In retailing, the supermarket revolution was led by firms such as Tesco, and other firms that we looked at which helped to spark off changes in multiple retailing were Dixons and Mothercare. At the receiving end, so to speak, were department stores like Debenhams, forced by the pressures of competition to rationalise its activities and its property holdings. In engineering, one of our firms, Stone-Platt, was largely an innovator, while Vickers has had a chequered recent history, with slow-growing divisions as well as rapidly-growing and innovatory ones such as Howson-Algraphy. Of Baker Perkins it can perhaps be said that they have pursued a middle course between reacting to adverse market circumstances by small changes and by innovating. GEC has been notable for its rationalising activities. The chemical firms we looked at had to react to a great deal of change, and one of them (Albright & Wilson) found itself, like Lyons, in great difficulties after a bold overseas move.

If one can generalise about our sample of firms, it is clear that all of them, even in apparently stable industries, had to adjust to a great deal of external change. Some reacted in a comparatively passive way, while others were bolder. In some cases, parts of the same firm were passive while other parts were active. Boldness paid in some instances but in others was disastrous, or near-disastrous. Whatever the exact history, changes in th nature of markets had a profound effect on the strategies followed by our firms, and greatly preoccupied their managements. Many of the changes in internal structure that took place were sparked off by emergencies brought about by external events. In such circumstances, to concentrate on whether firms aim to maximise their profits or their rate of growth is not only to omit much relevant detail, but also to miss some of the primary forces which influence the strategies of individual firms.

viii) The "Great Man" and Firm Growth

It is obvious that individuals are important to the success of firms. The founder is clearly very important, as is evident in our sample, where we have Tesco, Mothercare and Dixons - all firms led now or until recently by their founders. In other firms there have been outstanding individuals, such as Sir Frederic Hooper in Schweppes, who were neither founders nor owners, while in other "family" firms there have been able family members, such as Adrian Cadbury. In all our firms, particular individuals have played a prominent part.

It could be argued that what has just been said is obvious - firms are collections of individuals, and it therefore follows that particular individuals have to hold the positions of power in them. What is being argued, however, goes well beyond this. Firstly, the "top" man (or woman), in the person of the chairman or managing director, is particularly influential in choosing people and formulating policies for the firm (see Nyman & Silberston (1978)). Secondly, the top man has a great deal of influence over the overall success of the firm. It is not true that it does not matter who is in charge of the firm, even when the firm is a very large one. In the case of Unilever, there have been a succession of able chairmen - all career managers. Would Unilever perhaps have been successful without any one outstanding figure? Management depth has ensured good leadership and able administration, with promotion on merit as the ethos of the firm. Nevertheless, it can be argued that differences in Unilever's performance over time have been attributable to changes in top leadership.

With smaller firms than Unilever, there is inevitably less depth of management, and particular chairmen or managing directors are more important. What certainly cannot be argued is that if A had not been chosen, then B would have emerged, and he would have performed in much the same way. If our studies show anything, it is that one man is very different from another, whether that man is a founder, a member of a founding family, or a manager with no ownership stake. That the founder is likely to be exceptional scarcely needs stressing - where would the Ford Motor Company be without Henry Ford? What is less readily recognised is that the success (or failure) of firms, however large, continues to depend on the ability of their leading individuals, long after the founder has departed. Among our firms, Hooper in Schweppes, Burney in Debenhams, Matthews in Vickers (not to speak of Weinstock in G.E.C.), have all had a great effect in helping their firms either to grow or to withstand difficult times. Other men in their place might have done well, but successful or not they would certainly - even with given external forces on their firms - have done different things, to a greater or lesser degree.

What the "great man" theory amounts to so far, therefore, is that particular chairmen or managing directors appear to have had great influences on the success or failure of their firms. Others in their place are likely to have behaved differently, with different outcomes. One can go further than this. Where a firm has done particularly well, compared with the average, this is not likely to be because of good luck (although luck may have played a part). It is because there has been an exceptional man at the top - a man for whom a replacement could not easily have been found and in whose absence the firm would have been less successful.

An objection that can be made to this line of approach is that if it were not firm A then it would be firm B that was successful. Clearly this is possible, especially in an easy market situation, with a growing demand for a known product. The more difficult the market situation, however, and the more innovatory the product, the less obvious is it that one firm would have succeeded if another had failed. In any event, firm A may be in one country and firm B in another. If one is concerned with the health of industry in a particular country, one cannot easily be satisfied with an "if not firm A, then firm B" approach.

An interesting feature of the "great man" is that he can give his firm indigestion. It is indeed typical to find his successor attempting to consolidate and to rationalise, especially if the "great man" had lost his grasp in his later years, and had failed to delegate sufficiently, or to make adequate preparation for his succession. This is a not uncommon phenomenon. The cycles of growth and consolidation that so many firms go through may thus be partly related to the successive qualities of the men in control of them, or to successive phases in the effectiveness of one man.

Do great men arrive at the head of their firms in a random manner or is there some process of selection at work?[16] Founders are of course a special case. They select themselves. Looked at before the event there is certainly a random element here, although after the event their special qualities may be very apparent. The situation is different with later generations. If a firm adopts the practice of automatically electing as Chairman the senior member of the family, it is a random matter whether any particular Chairman turns out to be good or bad. However, in firms where a member of the family becomes chairman, but is not necessarily the senior member, an important element of selection is introduced. Lyons and Cadbury, for example, in the mid-1960s, after their firms had run into difficulties, both chose comparatively junior family members to lead them. In other cases, chairmen or managing directors have been chosen for their abilities by outside institutions, as with Burney at Debenhams and Matthews at Vickers. In yet others, the top men have been selected internally, after a long period of testing and experience, as with all chairmen of Unilever and nearly all chairmen of I.C.I. It would be difficult to argue, in the light of this, that outstanding men normally reach the head of their firms in a random manner.

Finally, is everything that has been said so far about the "great man" simply tautologous? If a man is at the head of a successful firm is he therefore a great man by definition? The answer to this is clearly "no". His qualities must be judged by reference to the circumstances of his firm, both externally and internally. A "great man" is one who leads his firm to do well in difficult circumstances, or to do exceptionally well in normal circumstances. The more successful his firm is, as compared with other firms in similar circumstances, the "greater" the man at the top is likely to be. One cannot deny that luck enters into the story, but consistently good performance by a firm, as compared with similar firms, is very unlikely to be due simply to the exercise of its monopoly power.

It has been argued that this approach is deficient because the great man should be defined in relation to some testable intrinsic qualities rather than in this relative fashion. It would be very nice if this were possible, but a moment's thought will show it is not. Lord Nuffield, for example, was very successful for most of his life. What were his qualities? One can list them now, but could they have been listed in advance of his success? I suggest not. To be a successful entrepreneur demands a combination of qualities, and different combinations may prove to be successful in different circumstances or even in similar circumstances. But a forecast of success would be virtually impossible. Perhaps this can best be seen in another sphere - music. Could anyone have known in advance how wonderful a composer Mozart would be? It has even been suggested that his personality was incompatible with his achievement, and that in some mysterious way God must have been working through him. If Mozart could not have been predicted from the qualities he appeared to possess, could we do better in the case of a successful businessman?

I conclude that the comparative performance test is the only feasible one. Such a view of the great man may lack testable implications. It cannot, however, possibly lead to a denial that personal qualities are important for the success or failure of particular firms.

3. CONCLUSIONS

What can be said, following this review, of the various theories discussed at the beginning of this paper? Several comments have already been made, so that this concluding section will be brief.

Chandler stresses the growth pattern of firms, the growth of divisional forms of organisation, and the importance of the relationship of the headquarters and the divisions. Organisation is related to the particular stage of growth, and success depends on appropriate strategies as well as appropriate organisation. Chandler's picture of firm development has been borne out very much by our own study. How far our British firms pursue the same objectives as the U.S. firms investigated by Chandler, and how far their forms of organisation are as highly developed, are interesting questions, but they cannot be pursued at this stage.

The Marris model appears at first sight to have been contradicted at several points. In our firms (and more generally also) there is not much separation between ownership and control. In those of our firms run by professional management there does not seem - as far as one can judge these rather intangible things - to have been much of a desire for growth for reasons of personal income or power. Moreover, high growth has often been allied with low retention ratios, and low profitability with high retention ratios. Diversification has been for defensive as well as for aggressive reasons. Marris is right about Penrose effects, but even here growth can add to management strength if growth is by merger and mergers bring able managers with them. Marris has, however, identified many of the variables and relationships that appear to be important, and one must expect conclusions drawn from his model to become vulnerable once one departs from a steady-state world.

What of the "great man" theory of the growth of firms? Great men, or at least very able men, are needed at times of crisis, or to enable the firm to do well when its competitors are doing badly. A "great man" is of course often responsible for building up the firm in the first place. One of the troubles with great men, especially if they are founders, is that they often tend to rely on themselves and a few selected colleagues. They are in any event bound to be difficult to follow, but many tend to hang on too long and to make inadequate preparation for their succession. A firm run by managers might be more rationally organised, but such firms have their "stars" also, and these can cause similar problems to those which occur in owner-managed firms. The cycles of growth and consolidation that we have seen in most of our firms, whatever their ownership, can to some extent be attributed to the activities of outstanding men, and to the need for their successors to clear up and reorganise after they have gone.

None of this is to deny the great importance of market forces. It would however be misleading to say that firms have to act "within the constraints" of market forces. A multi-product firm can to some extent choose which market forces it confronts - by its choice of products and by its choice of markets. It can also modify market forces by introducing new products or new methods of selling, or by successfully competing with its rivals. For the firm, therefore, market forces are not "constraints", if by this we mean that the firm has no choice but to work within a given framework.

It is difficult to argue, looking at our firms, that their differing growth experiences reflect some random process, such as that suggested by Gibrat's law. Whatever can be said for Gibrat's law at the level of the economy as a whole, it cannot explain, except to a very small extent, why firm A is more successful than firm B. Here a great deal depends on the abilities of those in charge and the strategies that they follow.

The general state of the economy, together with market and other conditions in the industry concerned, are of course important. But it seems to be an attribute of successful firms that they are closely attuned to their environment, and react rapidly to changes in it. This is scarcely a random process. Chance may be a factor, but on the basis of the firms we have studied it appears to play a relatively minor role.

TABLE 1

The founding and control of firms co-operating with the Growth of Firms project

Company	*Rank in 1975 Times 1000 by turnover*	*Industry*	*Founder*
Albright & Wilson	124	Chemicals	Quaker
Associated Biscuits	187	Food	Quaker
Baker Perkins	359	Mech. Eng.	Quaker
British Home Stores	144	Retailing	American businessmen
Cadbury Schweppes	37	Food	Quaker (on Cadbury side)
Debenhams	105	Retailing	English drapers
Dixons Photographic	367	Retailing	Jewish
E.M.I.	64	Elec. Eng.	-
G.E.C.	12	Elec. Eng.	Jewish
I.C.I.	4	Chemicals	German, Jewish, Swedish, Swiss
I.T.T. Consumer Products	(Not ranked)	Elec. Eng.	American subsidiary
J. Lyons	58	Food	Jewish
Mothercare	363	Retailing	Iraqi Jewish
Sears Holdings	34	Retailing	Jewish
W.H. Smith	117	Retailing	English
Stone Platt	206	Mech. Eng.	Defensive Merger
Tesco	61	Retailing	Jewish
Unilever	5	Food	English: Nonconformist
Vickers	97	Mech. Eng.	Defensive Merger

Source: Nyman & Silberston (1978)

TABLE 2

Retention Ratios. Individual Firms in the Food Industry 1949-74.
%

	Lyons	*Associated Biscuit*	*Unilever*	*Cadbury*	*Schweppes*
1949-54	51.3	75.4	88.5	70.3	59.7
1955-59	54.2	76.5	82.1	71.7	55.7
1960-64	46.9	50.9	75.9	83.8	36.1
1965-69	45.5	53.6[2]	62.3	71.1[3]	41.1[3]
1970-74	62.7[1]	65.8	56.9	32.4[4]	
Average of years	51.7 (excl. 1974)	65.3 (excl. 1967)	73.7	74.2 (1949-1968)	49.1 (1949-68)
				28.2 (1969-74)	

1. 1970-73 only
2. Excluding 1967
3. 1965-68 only
4. 1969-74.

Note: The retention ratio is defined as retained profits as a proportion of retained profits plus dividends, net of income tax, on ordinary shares (Singh and Whittington (1968), p.237).

TABLE 3

Correlation coefficients between growth, profitability and retention ratio

(Years 1949-1975) where possible

	Multiple Correlation Coefficient (R)	*Partial Correlation Coefficient - Growth & retention ratio*	*Partial Correlation Coefficient - Growth & profitability*
All 18 firms	.3244*	.0232	.3105*
2 chemical firms	.3008*	.2530**	.0568
2 Elec. Eng. firms	.1186	-.0825	-.0650
5 food firms	.0434	-.0190	.0408
3 Mech. Eng. firms	.3601*	.2606*	.0983
6 retailing firms	.4947*	.1776**	.3127*
Associated Biscuits	.3892*	.3150	.1665
Cadbury (to 1968)	.5015*	-.1499	.3941**
Cadbury-Schweppes (from 1969)	.1745	-.0578	.1745
J. Lyons	.5252*	.3457**	-.5182*
Unilever	.7229*	.3703**	.7046*
Schweppes (to 1968)	.2439	-.2227	.1294

* Significant at 5% level

** Significant at 10% level

REFERENCES

Chandler, A.D. (1962). *Strategy and Structure.* Cambridge, Mass.: M.I.T. Press.

Chandler, A.D. (1977). *The Visible Hand.* Harvard University Press.

Cyert, R.M., and March, J.G. (1963). *A Behavioural Theory of the Firm.* Englewood Cliffs, N.J.: Prentice-Hall.

Edwards, J.S.S. (1978). Unpublished paper, Nuffield College, Oxford.

Francis, A. (1979). Families, firms & Finance Capital: the development of U.K. industrial firms with particular reference to their ownership and control. *Sociology, 14, 1, pp1 - 27.*

Francis, A. (1980). Company Objectives, Managerial Motivations and the Behaviour of Large Firms: An Empirical Test of the Theory of 'Managerial Capitalism'. *Cambridge Journal of Economics (forthcoming).*

Galbraith, J.K. (1967). *The New Industrial State.* London: Hamish Hamilton.

Heal, G.M., & Silberston, A. (1972). Alternative Managerial Objectives: An Exploratory Note. *Oxford Economic Papers, July.*

H.M.S.O. (1978). A Review of Monopolies and Mergers Policy. *Cmnd. 7198.*

Holl, P. (1975). Effect of Control Type on the Performance of the Firm in the U.K. *Journal of Industrial Economics, xxiii.*

Knight, A.W. (1974). *Private Enterprise and Public Intervention.* London: Allen & Unwin.

Marris, R.L. (1964). *The Economic Theory of Managerial Capitalism.* London: Macmillan.

Mueller, D.C. (1972). A Life Cycle Theory of the Firm. *Journal of Industrial Economics, July.*

Nyman, S. & Silberston, A. (1975). An Approach to the Study of the Growth of Firms. *Second Conference on Industrial Structure, Volume 11, Preprint Series 1/75-45.* International Institute of Management, Berlin.

Nyman, S. & Silberston, A. (1978). The Ownership and Control of Industry. *Oxford Economic Papers, March.*

Penrose, E.T. (1959). *The Theory of the Growth of the Firm.* Oxford: Blackwell.

Radice, H.K. (1971). Control Type, Profitability and Growth in Large Firms. *Economic Journal, 81.*

Silberston, A. (1972). Economies of Scale in Theory and Practice. *Economic Journal, March (Supplement).*

Silberston, A. & Nyman, S. (1978). The Theory of the growth of the firm - what can we learn from case studies? Paper given to *5th EARIE Meeting* - Nuremberg, September.

FOOTNOTES

1. Financed by the Social Science Research Council. The work is still in progress and this paper must be regarded as preliminary. I am grateful to Arthur Francis for helpful comments, and to Jeremy Turk - also to Richard Allard, the discussant of the paper, and an anonymous referee.
2. Nyman & Silberston (1975) & (1978), Silberston & Nyman (1978), and Francis (1979) & (1980).
3. See Heal and Silberston (1972) for an exposition of these relationships.
4. There is much discussion in Marris of gearing ratios and problems associated with them, but the basic steady state model can be looked at as one in which all funds are derived from retentions (Marris (1964)).
5. See also Francis (1979), who originally suggested these categories.
6. The firms we studied are listed in Table 1.
7. See Francis (1980) for a detailed discussion of the questions we put on these issues and the answers we received.
8. The great bulk of the income of our managers was derived from their salaries. These issues are being studied further.
9. See, for example, H.M.S.O. (1978) Annex D.
10. Large firms may not deliberately plan to have slack management, but may find it easier to squeeze out a few managers because they have a large number of managers in their employment.
11. The present Managing Director of Cadbury/Schweppes was with L. Rose, before Schweppes took it over.
12. The figures for our food firms are given in Table 2.
13. This statement is supported by Table 3 which sets out correlation coefficients between growth, profitability and retention ratios. Some of the values would be rather higher if time lags were introduced, but the differences are not great.
14. An important element in the ability to raise funds externally is the gearing (debt: equity) ratio. Low geared firms can have a reserve borrowing capacity which an imaginative management may use for growth.

15. The figures in Table 3 give only weak support to this view, but the conclusion in the text is based on wider evidence than is provided by the table.
16. This question was suggested by Richard Allard, the discussant of this paper.

DISCUSSION: RICHARD ALLARD

I found Aubrey Silberston's paper, and the previous material on which it is based, fascinating reading, and it is clear that the project from which it draws is already making a significant contribution to our understanding (or, perhaps more accurately, our awareness of lack of understanding) of the processes involved in the growth of firms.

My first comment concerns the relationship between performance and control type. The initial impression given by this paper is that no such relationship exists, but a second impression is that the greatest scope for discretionary behaviour by management occurs when managers also have a small but often central stake in the ownership of the firm. If this latter impression is correct, then it clearly supports Silberston's view that the simple dichotomy between owner controlled and manager controlled firms is far too simple to be useful.

The presumed tendency for a management controlled firm to behave in a non profit (or wealth) maximising fashion depends on the fact that the owners are unable to impose an appropriate set of incentives on the managers. As a consequence the managers are able to exercise a degree of control over the way in which the <u>potential</u> profits of the firm are divided between themselves (in such forms as excessive salaries, perks, a quiet life) and the owners. The extent of their control may be limited by such incentives as the owners are able to impose and by competition in the product markets or in the market for corporate control. But precisely the same analysis can be applied to the division between the majority of owners (perhaps 90% or 95%) and a management which incorporates a minority shareholding. In this case, however, the ability of the majority of shareholders to impose any form of discipline on management is likely to be signficantly reduced by the presence of probably the largest single organised group of shareholdings within the management. This same group of shareholdings is also likely to reduce the risk of unwanted takeover. The essential point is that even though the managers benefit from increased profits because of their shareholdings, it is nevertheless clearly in their interest to siphon off £100 of profits into £100 of managerial

managerial benefits, and their minority shareholding may increase their power to do so. Even if, as is likely to be the case, there is loss of wealth in translating profits into managerial benefits, a management with 10% ownership will still benefit as long as the £100 profits siphoned off results in at least £10 of managerial benefits (to the right managers).

The fact that managers have discretion over the level of profits does not mean that they will use it. They may obtain pleasure out of the attempt to maximise profits, or they may be concerned with the effect of the profitability of the business on the general status of the family (or other management minority shareholder such as a financial institution). But it is likely that some managements will use the available discretion, so that as the discretion increases we might expect both the average value of potential minus actual profits, and the variance of this value to increase.

If this line of argument is accepted, there is clearly need for further investigation into how the amount and form of any minority shareholding incorporated within the management affects the extent to which they are able to follow policies which fail to maximise the interests (generally wealth maximisation) of the majority of shareholders. However, my impression from the evidence presented in this paper is that the ordering with respect to the amount of discretion would be

control by management incorporating organised shareholding	>	control by management without minority shareholding	>	control by owners.

Although I am personally quite willing to be convinced that theories of the relation between control and performance based on a simple dichotomy between management and owner control do not have empirical support, the acceptance of such a null (no effect) hypothesis on the basis of the present study cannot carry too much statistical weight. With just 20 observations, and a great deal of the variance in behaviour being inexplicable by any purely economic model, only very strong relationships are likely to come through unscathed. (This is not, of course, in any way a criticism of the current study.)

There are two other points which I would like to mention more briefly. Silberston mentions that firms "have wanted at least to keep their share of their markets", which seems to suggest a very simple (short run) goal for management, of a "satisficing" kind. But do managers really mean when they answer in this way that they put a great deal of effort into improving performance if market share is below last years (or alternatively, are willing to sacrifice net wealth to increase market share), but not if market share is the same or higher than last years? An alternative is that they use market share, or the performance of comparable firms, as an arbitrary zero point on the scale they use to assess themselves by, with no suggestion that the extent of their efforts to improve their position on this scale is affected by whether they are currently scoring plus or minus.

Finally, I want to say a few words about "Great Men", and the process by which chairmen are selected. This topic is of importance both for theories of the growth of firms, especially those that are based on the Gibrat process, and for those aspects of government policy towards firms which are based on the quality of management. For the purpose of the Gibrat model, one could define the relevant time period as beginning with the selection of a new chairman, and continuing for as long as he remains in office. If we then supposed that all firms selected the quality of their next chairman at random from the same population of qualities, we would have something closely resembling a Gibrat process. In this context, Silberston is suggesting that the populations from which firms select the quality of their chairmen vary a great deal as between firms, and within firms over time. Thus we might suppose that firms such as Unilever always pick from a population with high mean and low variance, whilst a number of family firms pick from populations with low mean and high variance, until a crisis occurs, when they pick from a population with high mean and high variance. If this characterisation of the selection process is valid, and if most firms remain in a single category for a long time, then the relevance of models based on the simple Gibrat process might be very much reduced, except over such long periods of time (many generations of chairmen) to be uninteresting.

On the policy side, a conclusion that good management

begets good management (although I am not suggesting that Silberston would wish to support such a conclusion) would no doubt be welcomed by those wishing to promote the restructuring of industry. For that reason, if no other, any such conclusion should be subject to most careful scrutiny!

13. THE CAUSES OF SHIFTWORKING IN GREAT BRITAIN*

D. Bosworth, P. Dawkins and T. Westway

1. Introduction

Shiftworking has become an increasingly common feature of employment during the post-war period. The percentage of employees working shifts in manufacturing in Great Britain has been growing by about 1 percentage point per annum over the past 25 years. In certain industries, such as 'chemicals' and 'paper and board', shiftwork is now the dominant type of work pattern and, if present trends continue, this will be the case in more and more sectors of the economy in the future. Shiftworking, therefore, can no longer be treated as a rather obscure and insignificant feature of production and employment.

Interest in shiftworking has increased not only because of the higher levels of incidence, but also because it is associated with a number of policy issues that are of growing importance. An even more rapid rise in the extent of shiftworking, for example, has been suggested as a means of attaining a more intensive utilisation of capital, thus avoiding the major problems created by a low level of investment in industry and resulting, in particular, in higher levels of employment than would otherwise have been the case. While this policy option has mainly been investigated with the Third World countries in mind,[1] it has also been advocated as a means of avoiding the adverse employment consequences of slow growth and a lack of employment-creating investment in the face of rapid technological change in the

* We would like to thank members of the SSRC Labour Economics Study Group and our colleagues in the Department of Economics at Loughborough University and in the Manpower Research Group at Warwick University for helpful comments on earlier research that led to this paper. We would also like to acknowledge the *European Foundation for the Improvement of Living and Working Conditions*, which funded some of the preliminary research.

developed world.[2] At the same time, the underlying trends toward higher levels of shiftworking have themselves been the cause of some concern internationally, particularly insofar as they may be associated with adverse effects on health and on family and social life.[3] A further policy dimension arises out of the attempts by the Equal Opportunities Commission in the UK to harmonise the protective legislation for women as against men.[4]

This paper investigates the main influences on the incidence of shiftworking in the UK. The paper builds a theoretical framework that is helpful in establishing the set of variables that would appear to be important in determining the extent of shiftworking in industry. These variables are then used in an econometric model designed to explain the incidence of shiftworking in the manufacturing sector of the British economy. Section 2 outlines the theoretical framework that enables the more important influences on the incidence of shiftworking to be isolated. Section 3 discusses the sources of data that are used in this study and considers a number of measurement problems that arise. The equations estimated are reported in section 4, along with the results of the empirical tests of the model. Finally, section 5 draws some general conclusions from the work that we have undertaken.

2. *Factors Affecting the Incidence of Shiftworking*

2.1 A Theoretical Framework

The bulk of theoretical and empirical work in this area has focused on capital utilisation rather than shiftworking. At various times, capital utilisation has been treated as synonymous with the extent of overtime,[5] while, elsewhere, capital utilisation has been considered as synonymous with the intensity of shiftworking.[6] In practice, however, the relationship between capital utilisation, overtime and shiftworking is complex. The firm is clearly faced by some sort of trade-off between overtime and shiftwork and it is represented here by the least cost labour envelope, which describes the lowest cost of manning a process that is producing a given amount of output each period (e.g. day or week). Thus, the firm is assumed to minimise its costs subject to an output constraint.

This envelope is represented by the curve in Diagram (1). ALC denotes the minimum average labour cost per hour associated with various lengths of operating week (or day). Each point on ALC is associated with a particular work pattern (i.e. the least cost work pattern at that number of operating hours): H*, for example, may be associated with 'normal day plus overtime'; $\bar{H}$, on the other hand, is linked with a four crew-three shift system (each crew working 42 hours per week). The downward sloping part of ALC arises from the existence of certain fixed costs (i.e. those labour costs that are invariant with respect to the number of operating hours per week or per day) such as guaranteed minimum weekly pay. From the least cost labour envelope, the marginal labour cost of an extra operating hour can be calculated as the change in total labour cost caused by extending operating hours by one unit but maintaining output at the given level.

The second half of the picture is formed by the marginal capital savings curve, MCS, also shown in Diagram (1). Marginal capital savings are defined as the change in total capital costs caused by extending operations by one hour. The basic principle is easy to see where capital is perfectly divisible. Other things being equal: 90 machine tools operated for 42 hours per week are equivalent to 45 such machines operated for 84 hours or 30 operated for 126 hours per week.[8] Thus, the amount of money that the firm 'locks-up' in its capital stock, other things being equal, declines with the number of operating hours.

In this simple model where only labour costs and capital savings vary with the number of operating hours, equilibrium of the firm occurs where marginal labour costs are equal to marginal capital savings (i.e. at the intersection of MLC and MCS). Thus, in Diagram (1), the optimal degree of capital utilisation is H*/H and the cost minimising work pattern is shown by the system associated with the point on ALC at the number of hours H*. The theory outlined so far has been at the process level, but it can be extended to the plant, firm or industry by adopting a frequency distribution approach, whereby MLC and MCS in Diagram (1) can be treated as the curves associated with the modal values at that level of aggregation.[9]

Diagram (1) Optimal Operating Hours

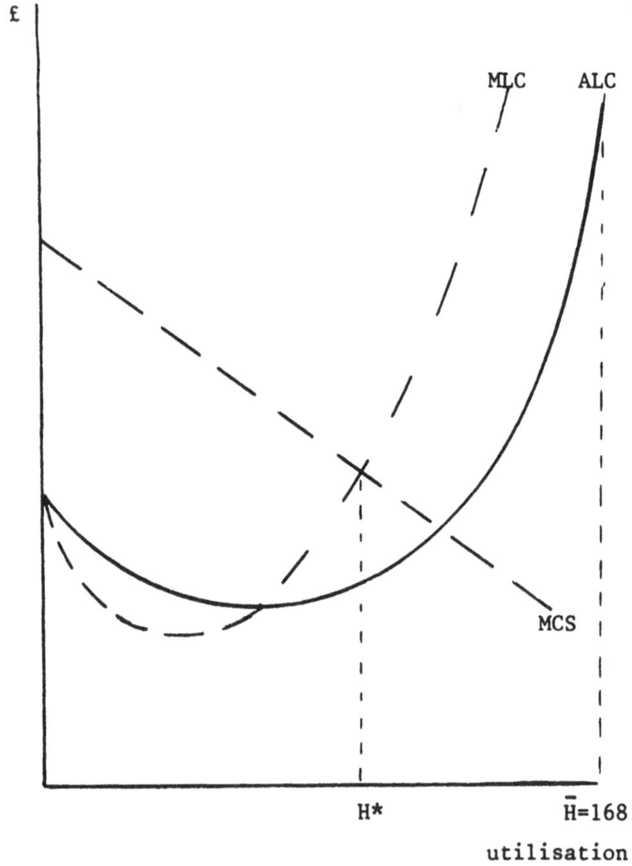

2.2 Factors Affecting the Choice of Work Pattern and Optimal Capital Utilisation

Given the theoretical framework outlined above, we can now investigate the various factors thought likely to influence the optimal level of capital utilisation and the associated choice of work pattern. These factors can be subdivided into those influencing labour costs and those influencing capital costs.

2.2.1 The Labour Costs

Basic Pay and the Shift Premium

The three most important elements of labour costs that determine the basic shape and position of the least cost labour envelope and therefore the shape and position of the MLC curve are basic pay, shift premia and overtime premia.[10] Overtime premia are important in determining at what point a given work pattern plus additional overtime becomes more costly than, and is therefore replaced by, a more intensive shift pattern with less overtime. Nevertheless, it is basic pay and the shift premia that determine the fundamental characteristics of the labour cost curves. The higher is basic pay relative to the absolute shift premium, the flatter is the labour cost envelope and the more attractive is shiftworking. The higher is the shift premium relative to basic pay, the steeper is the upward sloping part of the ALC and MLC curve and the less incentive there is to work shifts.

In considering what determines differences in labour costs between firms and therefore between industries, supply side characteristics should be analysed. Certain sub-groups can be expected to demand higher than average and other sub-groups lower than average remuneration for working shifts. In other words, there are a number of variables which are expected to affect the position of the MLC curve: (a) the ratio of manual to non-manual employees; (b) the ratio of male to female employees; (c) the ratio of employees with relatively high to those with relatively low financial commitments; (d) the provision of facilities supporting shiftwork in the locality; (e) the tradition of shiftworking in the area.

Manual and Non-Manual Workers

There are three possible reasons why this categorisation may affect the position of the MLC. The principal reason would seem to operate on the supply side: non-manual workers tend to be relatively more highly educated and this decreases their willingness to work the unsocial hours associated with shiftwork.[11] The second two reasons are more closely allied with the demand for shiftworkers. First, while the evidence about differences in labour productivity between day and night work is inconclusive, there does seem some reason for belieiving that the efficiency loss for white-collar workers is higher during unsocial hours of the day.[12] At any given shift premium, therefore, employers are likely to be more reluctant to employ non-manual employees on shiftwork than manual employees. Second, activities carried out by non-manual workers tend generally to be relatively less capital intensive and this tends to reduce the demand by firms for its non-manual employees to work shifts.

<u>Diagram (2) The Propensity to Work Shifts over the Life Cycle</u>

Propensity to work shifts

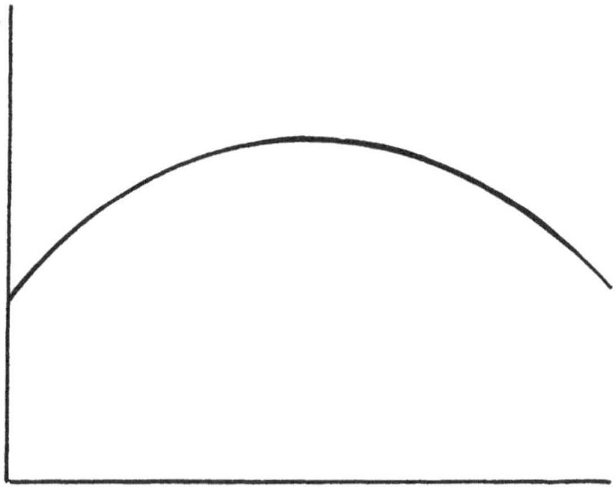

Age

Male and Female Employees

There would appear to be both legal and domestic constraints on the employment of women on shiftwork *visa vis* men.[13] The legal aspect appears to be a particularly important factor. Under British law, at present the employment of women on shifts between 6.00am and 10.00pm has to receive special authorisation from the Health and Safety Executive and the employment of women on night shifts has to be authorised by the Secretary of State for Employment. The percentage of women in total employment would therefore seem to be a potentially important variable.[14]

Financial Commitments of the Workers

It seems likely that the financial commitments of workers will influence their willingness to work shifts. While some work has been carried out relating the supply of shiftworkers to their tax codes,[15] a more accessible route is to relate the propensity to work shifts to the age of the employee.[16] It is argued that family responsibilities and financial commitments tend to reach a peak when the worker is middle-aged. In addition: younger workers attach greater importance to their social life and shiftwork tends to interfer more with their leisure activities than day work; older workers not only find their family and financial burdens declining but also find the potentially adverse health aspects of shiftwork relatively more important. Thus, the propensity to work shifts may be expected to bear something like a quadratio relationship to the age of employee, as shown in Diagram (2).

The Provision of Facilities supporting Shiftwork in the Locality

It is also thought that the propensity of an individual to supply himself to shiftwork depends partly on the facilities provided in the locality in which he is working. In particular it is thought that shiftworking may be more attractive in conurbations, where transport facilities are likely to be better for shiftworkers and entertainments more plentiful during abnormal leisure hours.

The Tradition of Shiftworking in the Area

It is also thought that people will have different propensities to work shifts depending upon the area of the country in which they live. There is a greater tradition of shiftworking in the Midlands and the North than in the South and East Anglia. The basic reason for this is the nature of the industry in these areas, which should be taken into account by the variables listed below as affecting the MCS curve. However, the higher incidence of shiftworking in certain areas has resulted in making this form of working more acceptable to workers, and again the amenities for shiftworkers are likely to be better in such areas.

2.2.2 Capital Costs

The shape of the MCS curve is determined principally by the ability to compensate for a smaller stock of capital by a higher level of capital utilisation. The principle is easily established as we argued in section 2.1 above.[17] Nevertheless, the precise nature of the MCS curve is potentially more complicated than the existing literature suggests. More intensive use may affect the efficiency of machines, either adversely or beneficially, depending on the process in question.[18] More importantly, the degree of utilisation can affect the life expectancy of machines and thereby the 'stock of capital services' still available from the machines. The greater the extent to which life expectancy is reduced by increased utilisation, the more steeply sloped the MCS curve becomes. At the present time our knowledge about the relationship between utilisation, 'wear and tear' and life expectancy is meagre.

The main influences affecting the position of the MCS curve are much more easily quantified. These factors can be summarised under the following headings: (a) The capital intensity of the production process; (b) the rate of technical obsolescence; (c) technical reasons for continuous operation; (d) plant/firm size; (e) the rate of interest.

Capital Intensity - The more capital intensive the process, other things being equal, the greater are the potential capital savings caused by increasing capital utilisation. It has been clear for some time that the more capital intensive the production process, the less serious is the problem of the rhythmically varying wage pattern and, other things being equal, the more intensively the capital will be utilised.[19]

Technical Obsolescence - A major attraction of shiftwork, giving rise to the capital savings, is that machines generally decline in value with the passage of time *even when they are not being used.*[20] In effect, the more rapid is the rate of technical obsolescence, the more quickly the firm must pay back its sunk costs and the higher the 'rental' or 'user cost' of capital and thus, under such conditions, the higher the level at which the MCS curve lies.

Technical Reasons for Continuous Operations - There are certain mechanical and chemical processes that take longer than a single shift (i.e. normal day working) to complete and, once started, are irreversible. Any mechanical or chemical processes where the nature of the output is *permanently fixed in an unacceptable form* by the failure to complete the required sequence of events is therefore associated with prohibitively high costs of shut-down. In effect, the MCS curve in this extreme case is vertical and lies at (or close to) 100 per cent utilisation. Certain industries stand out in this respect[21] and their influence might be accounted for by industry dummies, but we argue below that the relative size of standby electricity generating equipment is probably a more discerning variable.

Plant Size and Firm Size - Previous empirical work has consistently found a significant relationship between the extent of shiftworking and the size of the undertaking.[22] The principal explanation appears to be that small firms are less likely to adopt shiftworking because of "indivisibilities of management".[23] If supervision of production is only a part of a manager's job during the day time (i.e. there are other activities not associated with the day-to-day running of the production process), then, a move to shiftwork may involve the costly appointment of a specialist supervisor for the night period or a lack of supervision that leads to lower productivity and quality.

This argument can be interpreted as referring to the labour costs influences. However, we consider that it is at least as likely that the effect of plant size is through the indivisibility of capital. While in principle two shifts should facilitate the use of a capital stock half the size of that required on a normal day system, in a small plant the smallest possible units of capital may already be used on a normal day system, disallowing any capital savings from shiftworking.

Rate of Interest - The final influence on the position of the MCS is the rate of interest. The costlier it is to borrow funds (and, thereby, the higher the opportunity cost of using retained profits), the higher the capital savings from increased utilisation.

3. Data and Sources

The primary source of information used in this study is the DE *New Earnings Survey* (NES), which provides data on the incidence of shiftworking, shift premia, real basic pay (i.e. average earnings net of overtime and shift premia deflated by the retail price index[24]), the percentage of manual workers, the percentage of male workers, and the percentage working in the South and East Anglia in the labour force. While the NES dates back to 1968, information on shiftworking of the type described above has only been a regular, annual feature from 1973 onwards. Data for certain of the larger industry cells are published at MLH level, but the whole set of variables required for this study (especially to be compatible with other sources) are only consistently available at SIC Order level. As both the cross-sectional data for the manufacturing sector (14 observations) and the time series data for each industry (6 observations) are both inadequate to test the model described below, the decision was made to pool the data (giving 84 observations). In this instance, the benefits of a substantially larger sample appeared to considerably outweigh the potential statistical problems of pooled data Some *provisional* results are reported elsewhere[25] for a smaller pool of 56 observations (i.e. 14 industries and 4 years). The new and larger sample enable a check on those earlier results and the inclusion of certain time series variables (such as the interest rate) in the explanation of shiftworking.

As the incidence of shiftwork and, to a somewhat lesser extent, the percentage shift premia variables are central to the study, it is worth briefly outlining the more important data problems associated with them. The incidence of shiftworking is calculated as the ratio of shiftworkers to total employment. Because of the nature of the data shiftworkers are defined as workers receiving a shift premium. There may be, in practice, some shiftworkers who receive no shift premium (i.e. some of the day-workers on an alternating day and night system) at the time of the survey. A more important problem concerns the calculation of shift premia. While shift premia were available for manual males in all industries in all years, this was not the case for manual females, non-manual males and non-manual females. Nevertheless, there are good reasons to suppose that these will be very closely linked. In the derivation of a reduced form, the specification chosen eliminates the shift premium variable (rather than the incidence of shiftworking), but it appears in any simultaneous equations model of shiftworking.

Other data sources had to be found for the remaining variables. The average ages of employees in each industry and the percentage living in conurbations was calculated from data in the Census of Population (OPCS). This was only available for 1971 and appears in the regressions as a cross-sectional variable which does not change over time. This can be improved at a later stage when the new census of population data is published. Data on establishment size (i.e. the average number of employees per manufacturing unit) is published in the *Annual Abstract of Statistics* (CSO) and is available on an annual basis by SIC Order up to 1976. This is again an improvement on earlier work, which had to use interpolated values of establishment size based on 1968 and 1973 known values. Nevertheless, 1977 and 1978 values were not available at the time of this study, and several alternative estimates for 1977 and 1978 were tried, based on trends in size of manufacturing unit or simply using the last known observation (i.e. for 1976). The capital intensity of the firm was measured by the capital/labour ratio. Capital data was taken from CSO, *National Income and Expenditure, 1968-1978* at constant 1975 replacement cost and labour data from the DE, Annual Census of Employment, published in the *Annual Abstract of Statistics*. The capital stock data is published on the basis of more aggregate and somewhat inconsistent industry groups than the SIC Order data described above.[26] To avoid these problems, the rather more aggregate capital stock data was broken down from the 8 industries available using relative investment levels over the current year and previous two years and then re-aggregated to the 14 industry groups used in this study.[27] Firms that have a significant proportion of their processes which cannot be stopped at the end of shift will tend to install their own electricity generating capacity. Data from the CBI, *Survey of Energy Requirements, 1973,* indicated that a certain small group of industries stood out as having a high proportion of own-generating capacity. This was taken into account using a technological necessity dummy variable, taking a value of unity for these industries and zero elsewhere. Finally, the real rate of interest was constructed from data published by the CSO in *Economic Trends,* as MLR minus the rate of change in the retail price index.

4. *Regression Equations and Results*

4.1 *Limitations of the Model*

It has not been possible to formulate a 'complete' model of supply and demand as such a model would require a joint consideration of the supply of workers to normal day work and to shiftwork and also a joint consideration of industry's demands for workers on normal day and shiftwork. In order to arrive at a determinate model, therefore, at this stage, as a first approximation, each firm is assumed to be employing the optimal number of workers. In addition, the proportions of male and female, manual and non-manual workers are also determined exogenously. Attention therefore focuses on the process by which some proportion of the pool of employees in the industry end up as shiftworkers. In other words, what factors influence the supply of employees to shiftwork (rather than normal day work) and the demand by firms for shiftworkers (rather than normal day work).

4.2 *Supply and Demand Equations*

The discussion in section 2 highlighted a number of variables that, on theoretical grounds, can be expected to affect the supply of or demand for shiftworkers. Making use of this information, the demand for shiftworkers as a proportion of the total work force is represented by

$$\frac{SW}{L} = f\ (SP, BP, \frac{K}{L}, T, P, \frac{MN}{L}, MLR) \qquad (1)$$

where: *SW* is the number of shiftworkers; *L* is total employment; *SP* is the shift premium; *BP* denotes basic pay; $\frac{K}{L}$ is the capital/labour ratio; *T* the technological necessity dummy; *P* represents average plant size; $\frac{MN}{L}$ denotes the ratio of manual to all workers; and, finally, *MLR* is the minimum lending rate. On the supply side, the percentage of shiftworkers is represented by,

$$\frac{SW}{L} = g\ (SP, BP, \frac{M}{L}, \frac{MN}{L}, A, CON, AREA) \qquad (2)$$

where, in addition to the variables defined above: $\frac{M}{L}$ denotes the percentage of males in the work force, *A* denotes the average age of employees, *CON* denotes the percentage working in conurbations and *AREA* the percentage working in the South or East Anglia.

4.3 The Empirical Results

Data from 14 SIC orders for 1973-8 were used to give a pooled time series and cross-sectional sample of 84 observations. We had considerable reservations about using pooled data but the sample size was inadequate to use the time series or cross-sectional dimensions of the data separately. There were fears that the relatively low variability over time as opposed to cross-sectionally would increase the apparent fit of the model without adding to its explanatory power. Initial tests on the reduced form equations, however, showed that the addition of time dummies had a significant effect.[28] It should be stated that variations in the percentage of shiftworkers over time exceed 28 per cent in many industries and in some it was considerably greater than this.

A second problem was that the dependent variable, $\frac{SW}{L}$, is constrained to lie between 0 and 1. In order to overcome this difficulty and the additional problem of forecasting outside of the constrained range, the model was expressed in logit form. A clear case can thus be made for expressing the dependent variable in the form log $(\frac{SW}{L} / (1 - \frac{SW}{L}))$ (hereafter referred to as logit $\frac{SW}{L}$). This can be interpreted as the log of the odds of a person being a shiftworker. It was also decided to express $\frac{M}{L}$ and $\frac{MN}{L}$, the other variables expressed as probabilities, in this form and these are referred to as logit $\frac{M}{L}$ and logit $\frac{MN}{L}$. Age is specified quadratically to test the hypothesis that the propensity to work shifts peaks at about 40 years of age.

As both the supply and demand curves were over-identified, the parameters of the model were estimated using two stage least squares. The estimation procedure was based on an instrumental variable approach and thus invalidates the use of R^2 and hence its value is not reported. The demand for shiftworkers was specified as

$$logit \left(\frac{SW}{L}\right)_{it} = a+bSP_{it}+cBP_{it}+d\left(\frac{K}{L}\right)_{it}+eT_i+fP_{it}+g\ logit \left(\frac{MN}{L}\right)_{it} + hMLR_t \qquad (3)$$

and the supply of shiftworkers as

$$logit \left(\frac{SW}{L}\right)_{it} = +jSP_{it}+kBP_{it}+m\ logit \left(\frac{M}{L}\right)_{it}+n\ logit \left(\frac{MN}{L}\right)_{it} + pA_i+qA_i^2+r\ CON_i+s\ AREA_{it} \qquad (4)$$

where the variable names and expected parameter signs are given in Table (1). Subscripts i and t indicate where variables have been measured across industries and time respectively.

Table (1) - Variables, Variable Names and Expected signs

Name	Symbol	Demand Equation		Supply Equation	
		Coefficient	Expected Sign	Coefficient	Expected Sign
Percentage of shiftworkers	$\frac{SW}{L}$	dependent variable			
Constant		a		i	
Shift premium	SP	b	-	j	+
Basic Pay	BP	c	+	k	-
Capital intensity	$\frac{K}{L}$	d	+		
Technological necessity	T	e	+		
Plant size	P	f	+		
Proportion of male workers	$\frac{M}{L}$			m	+
Proportion of manual workers	$\frac{MN}{L}$	g	+	n	+
Interest rate	MLR	h	+		
Age	A			p	+
Age squared	A^2			q	-
Conurbation	CON			r	+
Area	$AREA$			s	-

The demand equation performed well with all variables possessing the correct sign. It was found, however, that when *MLR* was included its coefficient was insignificant and some of the other variables also became insignificant. It was thus omitted from the equation. Two stage least squares estimates of the demand and supply equations are given in Table (2) and three sets of these equations are reported. The plant size data, *P*, was unavailable for 1977 and 1978 and as a proxy for those years an average of the data for the previous years was taken for each individual group. To allow for the measurement errors that would occur dummy variables for 1977, D_{77}, and for 1978, D_{78}, were included. The addition of these dummies was statistically significant at the 1 per cent level ($F_{2,75} = 6.78$).

The supply equation, on the other hand, did not perform as well. The coefficient of *SP* possessed the wrong sign and logit *MN* was omitted as it was insignificant. Equation S1 in Table (2) gives the estimates for the coefficients of the remaining variables. As can be seen, several of these are also insignificant. (A dummy variable, D_{73}, is included for 1973 to allow for discrepancies in the *AREA* data for that year.) Omitting both of the regional variables, *AREA* and *CON* gave the results shown in Equation S4. As can be seen, the coefficients of *A* and A^2, powerful explanatory variables in the reduced form (Bosworth, Dawkins and Westaway, 1981), have become insignificant with 't' values of 1.13 and 1.09 respectively. However, when the supply equation was tested with *AREA* (plus its dummy) and *CON* included separately, the results given by Equations S2 and S3 are more acceptable in terms of the 't' values associated with the parameters, although they remain insignificant at the 5 per cent level. In terms of the standard error of the estimate there has been no improvement.

Table (2) Two Stage Least Squares Estimates of the Demand and Supply Equations

Dependent Variable Logit $\frac{SW}{L}$

(Absolute t values in parentheses)

	CONST.	SP	BP	$\frac{K}{L}$	T	P	D_{77}	D_{78}	logit $\frac{MN}{L}$	logit $\frac{M}{L}$	A	A^2	CON	AREA	D_{73}	Standard error of estimate
Equation D1	-9.31	-0.72 (3.79)	25.89 (5.15)	28.95 (2.25)	0.48 (2.53)	0.0041 (2.98)	-0.46 (1.91)	-0.66 (2.66)	0.99 (3.25)							0.7270
Equation S1	-1.71	-0.52 (2.81)	14.66 (2.66)							0.95 (4.69)	17.65 (1.65)	-0.22 (1.61)	1.48 (1.23)	-1.12 (0.86)	-0.12 (0.51)	0.7233
Equation D2	-9.40	-0.78 (4.15)	27.32 (5.50)	26.99 (2.13)	0.47 (2.52)	0.0043 (3.19)	-0.49 (2.07)	-0.70 (2.84)	0.97 (3.21)							0.7158
Equation S2	-370.06	-0.43 (2.81)	12.57 (2.57)							0.84 (4.60)	17.91 (1.69)	-0.22 (1.65)		-1.14 (1.58)	-0.19 (0.82)	0.7198
Equation D3	-9.28	-0.70 (3.62)	25.43 (4.97)	29.58 (2.27)	0.48 (2.53)	0.0041 (2.90)	-0.45 (1.85)	-0.65 (2.59)	1.00 (3.25)							0.7323
Equation S3	-308.09	-0.60 (3.91)	16.21 (3.22)							1.00 (5.33)	14.63 (1.46)	-0.18 (1.42)	1.96 (1.87)			0.722[illegible]
Equation D4	-9.55	-0.87 (4.51)	29.48 (5.84)	24.04 (1.91)	0.45 (2.48)	0.0047 (3.45)	-0.54 (2.30)	-0.75 (3.09)	0.93 (3.12)							0.7037
Equation S4	-239.39	-0.57 (4.01)	15.45 (3.25)							0.88 (4.95)	11.23 (1.13)	-0.13 (1.09)				0.7159

5. *Conclusions*

The empirical results show a strong relationship between the percentage of shiftworkers and the demand side variables. This then lends strong support to our model of the firm's decision about whether to use a shift system. This provides us with some confidence in the use of this model to undertake a more detailed analysis of the different types of work pattern that employers adopt with more detailed data that might become available. It also gives weight to the argument that the decision to work shifts is firmly based in economic and technological criteria and any moves to restrict shiftworking should thus be made with extreme caution. The evidence does not strongly support the supply side arguments although it is possible that through the period there has been an excess supply of shiftworkers so that the supply side variables have not influenced the quantity of shiftworkers actually employed. However, the supply equation does suggest a strong relationship between shiftworking and the percentage of male employees, supporting the hypothesis that family, social and legal constraints affect the propensity of women to work shifts. Also there is some support for the hypothesis that the willingness to work shifts changes over the life cycle of an employee, with the highest incidence of shiftwork occurring at an age of approximately 40. This is in line with our expectation that employees' financial commitments reach a maximum in the 35-45 age range.

REFERENCES

K. Alexander and J. Spraos, "Shiftworking: An Application of the Theory of the Firm", *Quarterly Journal of Economics*, 1956 (pp.603-612).

R.J. Ball and E.B.A. St. Cyr, "Short-Term Employment Functions in British Manufacturing Industry", *Review of Economic Studies*, Vol. 33, 1966.

D.L. Bosworth and P.J. Dawkins, *Some New Dimensions in Employment Theory and Policy*, Gower Press (1980a, forthcoming).

D.L. Bosworth and P.J. Dawkins, "Compensation for Workers' Disutility: Time of Day, Length of Shift and Other Features of Work Patterns", *Scottish Journal of Political Economy*, February, 1980b.

D.L. Bosworth, P.J. Dawkins and A.J. Westaway, "Explaining the Incidence of Shiftworking in Great Britain", *Economic Journal*, forthcoming (March 1981).

Central Statistical Office, *Economic Trends*, HMSO : London (annually).

Central Statistical Office, *National Income and Expenditure, 1966-1976*, HMSO: London (annually).

Central Statistical Office, *Annual Abstract of Statistics*, HMSO: London (annually).

Confederation of British Industries, *Survey of Energy Requirements, 1973* joint project with DTI, CBI: London 1974.

F.P. Cook, *Shiftwork*, Institute of Personnel Management: London, 1962

Department of Employment, *Gazette*, HMSO: London (monthly).

Department of Employment, *New Earnings Survey*, HMSO: London (annually).

Equal Opportunities Commission, *Health and Safety Legislation: Should We Distinguish Between Men and Women?*, EOC: Manchester March 1979.

European Commission, "Memorandum on Shiftwork", *EC Discussion Paper* V/1135/75-EN, 1977.

F. Fishwick and G. Harling, *Shiftwork in the Motor Industry*, NEDO: London, 1974.

T. Hazledine, "Employment and Output Functions for New Zealand Manufacturing Industries", *Journal of Industrial Economics*, 1974.

D. Heathfield, "Capital Utilisation", *Paper Presented to Conference on Capital*, University of Nantarre, Paris, 1976.

H. Hughes, R. Bautista, D. Lim, D. Morawetz and F. Thoumi, "Capital Utilisation in Manufacturing in Developing Countries", *World Bank Staff Working Paper No. 242*, 1976.

J. Hughes, "Shiftwork and the Shorter Week: Two Ways to Make Jobs", *Personnel Management*, May 1977.

I.L.O., "Working Paper on Night Work", *Tripartite Advisory Meeting on Night Work*, ILO: Geneva, 1978.

Industrial Society, *Survey of Shiftworking Practices*, The Industrial Society, Survey No. 194, London 1975.

L. Johansen, *Production Functions : An Integration of Micro and Macro, Short-Run and Long-Run Aspects*, North Holland Publishing Co : Amsterdam 1972.

R. Marris (assisted by D. MacLean and S. Berman), *The Economics of Capital Utilisation: A Report on Multiple Shiftwork*, Cambridge U.P., 1964.

R. Marris, *Multiple Shiftwork*, N.E.D.O., 1970.

M. Maurice, *Shiftwork: Economic Advantages and Social Costs*, ILO: Geneva, 1975.

P.E. Mott *et al., Shiftwork: The Social Psychological and Physical Consequences*, Ann Arbor, University of Michigan Press, 1965.

M.I. Nadiri and S. Rosen, "Inter-related Factor Demand Functions", *American Economic Review*. 1969.

National Board for Prices and Incomes (NBPI), Chairman A. Jones, *Hours of Work, Overtime and Shiftworking*, Report No. 161, Cmnd 4554, HMSO: London 1970.

S.D. Nollen, B.B. Eddy and V.H. Martin, *Permanent Part-Time Employment,* Praeger: New York, 1978.

Office of Population Censuses and Surveys, *Census of Population, 1971,* HMSO: London, 1973.

P.J. Sloane, "Economic Aspects of Shift and Night Work", *Paisley College Social Sciences Working Papers No. 25,* 1977.

J. Walker, *Human Aspects of Shiftwork*, Institute of Personnel Management, London, 1978.

G.C. Winston, "Capital Utilisation in Economic Development", *Economic Journal*, March 1971, pp.36-61.

G.C. Winston, "Capital Utilisation and Optimal Shiftwork", *Bangladesh Economic Review*, Vol. 11, April 1974, No. 2, pp.515-558.

G.C. Winston and T.O. McCoy, "Investment and the Optimal Idleness of Capital", *Review of Economic Studies,* Vol. 127, 1974.

FOOTNOTES

1. See, for example, Winston (1971; 1974) and Hughes *et al.* (1976).

2. See, for example, the idea of multiple part-time shiftwork patterns suggested by Nollen *et al.* (1978) and a discussion of the job-creating incidence of shiftworking by Hughes (1977).

3. Leading to suggestions for new legislation by the ILO (1978) and a draft directive of the EC (1977), as well as detailed investigations of shiftworking by the European Foundation for the Improvement of Living and Working Conditions, a quasi-autonomous EC body, EF (1978).
4. The consequences of the various options and the EOC's policy suggestions are outlined in EOC (1979). The UK policy appears to be one of removing the existing 'additional' protection given to women, while the EC would appear to prefer to tighten the legislation for men.
5. Nadiri and Rosen (1969) and Hazledine (1974).
6. Heathfield (1976).
7. This assumption underlies a good deal of the employment function and capital utilisation literature: see, for example, Ball and St Cyr (1966); Nadiri and Rosen (1969); Alexander and Spraos (1956); and Winston and McCoy (1974).
8. Cook (1962, p.8).
9. See the work of Johansen (1972) and its tentative application to this problem in Bosworth and Dawkins (1980a).
10. Overtime and shift premia both incorporate time of day and length of day dimensions. See Bosworth and Dawkins (1980b).
11. Mott *et al.* (1965, pp.27-30).
12. Walker (1978, p.52) discusses the productivity effect in jobs requiring vigilance and sustained attention, but there is no evidence that this is the sole domain of non-manual occupations.
13. For the strict legal position of women under the existing protective legislation, see Health and Safety Executive (1973), EOC (1978) and EOC (1979).
14. See Hughes *et al.* (1976).
15. Fishwick and Harling (1974, pp.23-28).
16. NBPI (1970, pp.63-64).
17. See Cook (1962) and Marris (1970) for a discussion of the underlying concept.
18. The general question of shut-down and start-up costs is discussed by Marris (1970, p.2). A specific example is that of the poor quality of output that is often obtained following a temporary shut-down of plant in the paper and board industry.

19. See, for example, Winston and McCoy (1974), who postulate a wage pattern which reaches a peak around midnight and a minimum point around mid-day.

20. Marris (1970, p.2.)

21. See NBPI (1970, p.71) and Marris (1970, p.1).

22. Sloane (1977, p.14), Maurice (1975, pp.21-22) and NBPI (1970, p.66) report some of the available evidence.

23. Marris (1964, pp.92-3) and Industrial Society (1975, p.2).

24. CSO, *Economic Trends*.

25. Bosworth, Dawkins and Westaway (1981).

26. The capital stock data is categorised by the old SIC Orders and thus involves some inconsistencies such as non-ferrous metals appearing in the engineering group.

27. A potentially more important problem of measurement, which could not be avoided in this study, concerns the fact that the simple ratio of capital per employee tends to understate capital intensity in those establishments and industries working higher than average amounts of shiftwork. This has also caused a divergence between actual and observed trends in capital intensity as shiftworking has grown secularly in the British manufacturing sector - see Bosworth and Dawkins (1980a).

28. Bosworth *et al* (1981).

*DISCUSSION: D.G. LESLIE**

The growth of shiftworking in the last 25 years in U.K. manufacturing industries, has aroused little comment amongst economists. This paper represents a useful first step to redress this imbalance - but it is only a first step and much more work is required before a satisfactory explanation emerges. The emphasis of the paper is to derive an empirically testable model to explain the incidence of shiftworking across industries and the empirical work is suggested by the theoretical part of the paper rather than rigorously implied by it. In some plants the number of hours per day that capital will be utilised is *technologically* determined and as such can only be of limited interest to economists. However, in many others the utilisation rate is an *economic* decision, influenced by ecônomic variables such as the size of the shift premium, capital intensity, etc. The authors control for the former type of industry through their technological necessity dummy and attempt to explain the latter.

It should be said at the outset that there is not necessarily a strong connection between the number of hours per day that a plant is utilised and the proportion of the workforce that is on shiftwork. According to the New Earnings Survey, the authors' data source, the shift premium and hence the numbers counted as being on shiftwork is defined as payment for 'shiftwork and for nightwork or weekend work, where these are not treated as overtime'. Thus, for example, in industry (1) a double day shift might predominate, with the plant utilised 16 hours a day, whereas in industry (2) a continuous three shift system might predominate, with the plant utilised 24 hours per day. The data will reveal roughly the same proportion of shiftworkers, but clearly there will be a large difference in the number of hours per day that each industry will operate. Also differences in the shift premium payment itself will to some extent reflect variations in the type of shift system operated. The paper implicitly makes a homogeneity assumption, namely that the type of shift system operated is the same across industries with the shift premium reflecting variations in payment for the same type of shiftwork. Related to this issue, I do not understand why the authors chose to aggregate both male and female workers in their study. It is well known that the labour supply behaviour of females differs greatly from males and at least one important source of heterogeneity could have been eliminated at the outset by considering each group separately.

In the theoretical part of the paper the authors seek to demonstrate that capital intensive technologies would be associated with long hours or multiple shifts. This can be shown more generally in the following way. Let the technology be represented by $Q = f(L, H, K)$ where Q is output, L is labour, H is hours of work and K represents capital. In order to focus in on capital intensity, let us simplify the technology to be $Q = H^{\beta} L \phi(k)$, i.e. it is assumed that the technology is homogeneous of degree one in capital and labour where k is the capital labour ratio and hence reflects capital intensity. Let the cost function be $rK + vL + g(H)\, H\, L$, where r represents the rental price of capital, v are fixed, purely man-related fringe costs and $g(H)$ is average hourly wage costs. To capture the idea of the *rhythmic* nature of wage costs throughout the day it is reasonable to suppose that the elasticity of average hourly wage costs $\eta(H)$ is a non-decreasing function of H. Cost minimisation reveals that

$$\frac{1}{\beta}\left(1 - \frac{k\,\phi'(k)}{\phi(k)}\right) = \frac{\dfrac{v}{H\,g(H)} + 1}{1 + \dfrac{H\,g'(H)}{g(H)}} \qquad (1)$$

or

$$\frac{1}{\beta}(1 - \alpha) = \frac{\dfrac{v}{Hg(H)} + 1}{1 + \eta(H)} \qquad (2)$$

α is the share of capital in value added and under competitive assumptions the larger α, the larger will be the capital intensity of the technology. Since $\eta(H)$ in non-decreasing in H it follows that capital intensive technologies will be associated with longer hours. For the 'fixed technology' case the result follows more directly, as might be imagined and it is this case which the authors discuss in their analysis. It should also be noted that when the technology is associated with multiple shifts the relevant capital labour ratio is labour employed per shift and not total employment.

Turning now to the empirical section of this paper, the authors propose a two equation equilibrium model. The authors specify a demand equation for shiftworkers and a supply equation for shiftworkers where the proportion of shiftworkers and the shift premium are the endogenous variables. The main worry with the results, as the authors readily admit, is the consistently negative coefficient associated with the shift premium in the supply equation which suggests that the authors are some way as yet from specifying the correct structure of the model. They argue that the poor fit of the supply equation may be due to persistent excess supply of shiftworkers over the period. However, if this is the maintained hypothesis, then it seems somewhat dubious to specify an *equilibrium model* at the outset.

Two final comments.

(1) The authors do not check the validity of the pooling procedure and this is something that could be done without much difficulty.

(2) The authors enter basic pay and the shift premium as *separate* variables in the supply and demand equations. It would seem to me that it is the *ratio* of the shift premium to basic pay that would influence the demand for and supply of shiftworkers. Indeed as it stands, with basic pay as a separate variable, their model implies that eventually there will be 100% shiftworking, given that real basic pay increases through time!

The authors tell me that they have access to a new data source which allows them to control for different types of shiftworking and which obviates the awkward necessity for pooling. This, I feel, will lead to a much more fruitful set of results. The authors are to be congratulated for attempting empirical work in a difficult area with more than the average set of data limitations.

FOOTNOTE

* Lecturer in Economics at the University of Manchester. I am extremely grateful to W. Peters for help in the preparation of this discussion, particularly in showing me the relationship between capital intensity and utilisation.

14. SHORT RUN GROWTH EFFECTS IN A MODEL OF COSTLY MIGRATION WITH BORROWING CONSTRAINTS : WILL RURAL DEVELOPMENT WORK?

S.M. Kanbur.

1 Introduction *

In the literature on migration in developing countries, a new orthodoxy seems to have established itself. This is the view that "rural development" (more specifically, an increase in rural incomes) must be the major policy instrument in tackling the "problem" of rural-urban migration. The best known proponent of this view concludes a recent paper as follows:

> "The above analysis leads us to reiterate once again a basic point which was made in our 1969 article and which now appears to be widely accepted in the migration and development literature, viz that any real attempt to tackle the widespread problem of excessive rural-urban migration in the context of rising urban unemployment will of necessity require concentrated efforts at narrowing the ubiquitous and, in most cases, growing imbalances between urban and rural "expected" incomes by holding the line on the growth of the former while focusing on rapidly raising the latter." (Todaro (1976))

This view also has its counterpart in the official and planning literature in developing countries, where rural development is increasingly put forward as a method of reducing migration to the towns.[1]

It is clear how such a conclusion can be drawn from models of this genre. To quote Thadani and Todaro (1979):

> "The mainstream economic theory in the explanation of rural-to-urban migration, the Todaro model, identifies 'expected' urban-rural real wage as the key determinant, where the 'expected' differential is determined by the interaction of two variables, the actual urban-rural wage differential and the probability of obtaining employment in the modern urban sector (Todaro, 1969, pp. 138-148)."

Thus, with costless migration, a given income ^{w}r in the rural sector, a given income ^{w}u in the urban sector and a probability p of finding an urban sector job, the rate of migration is hypothesised to be positively related to $p^{w}u - {}^{w}r$. It follows, then, that job creation in the urban sector, which increases p, will increase the rate of rural-urban migration. The same is true of an increase in ^{w}u, the modern sector wage. Hence, the conclusion emerges that it is rural development, as reflected in an increase in ^{w}r, which is necessary for the reduction of migration rates.

The object of this paper is to sound a note of caution about the efficacy of rural development as an instrument for reducing the rate of rural-urban migration. It will be argued that the short run effects of rural development are more complex than hitherto suggested by the literature and that policy makers may encounter an increased rate of migration, at least in the early stages of a rural development program. It is clear that to arrive at such a conclusion the model of this paper will have to depart from the assumptions of the Todaro model, since we have just seen that the latter produces a conclusion directly contrary to the one proposed in this paper. Our basic argument is stated simply - rural development will give rural people the resources with which to migrate, but a small amount of rural development may not provide sufficient incentive for some people to stay behind. The formalisation of this proposition follows closely its intuitive sense. Underlying the formalisation is a model of migration which concentrates on the rural environment of prospective migrants, in particular, their incomes and their capacity to borrow in order to finance the costs of migration. It has been argued by some that "the Todaro theory and its derivatives are urban oriented", and do not "analyse the individual decision to migrate on the premise that because decisions to migrate are made in the rural areas a theory of migration should emphasize the rural environment in which the decision is made" (Byerlee (1974)). The model put forward in this paper is an attempt at analysing migration from the rural perspective. A by-product of our approach is the formulation of a direct link between the distribution of income in the rural sector and the rate of migration from that sector.

The plan of the paper is as follows. The next section introduces the model. As was noted earlier, the assumptions behind the model are different from those of the Todaro model, and their empirical plausibility is an important factor in choosing between the two models. In order to preserve the continuity of the theoretical modelling, however, extensive use is made of footnotes to discuss the empirical evidence relating to the assumptions made, and these should be referred to. Section 3 considers the characterisation and effect of rural development on migration rates, and Section 4 concludes the paper.

2 A Model of Costly Migration with Borrowing Constraints

We concentrate on the migration decision of agents in the rural sector. There are two periods in the model, indexed 1 and 2. In period 1, the "pre-migration" period, rural income is given by w_1, and in period 2 (if the agent stays on in the rural sector) it is w_2. We suppose that

$$w_2 = w_2(w_1),\ w_2' > o,$$

so that those with higher incomes in the first period expect correspondingly high incomes in the second period (one simple form could be $w_2(w_1) = w_1$).

Migration is costly[2]. "Migration activity" is viewed as a production process which uses current rural sector income as input and produces expected urban sector income as output. Denoting this expected urban income by Ey, and the costs of migration by c, the "production function" for migration activity is assumed to be as depicted in Fig. 1.

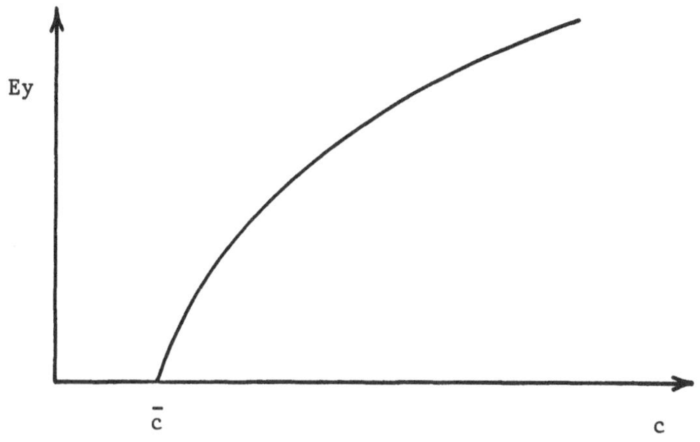

Figure 1

The interpretation is that there are certain fixed costs of migration. Beyond this, the expected income in the urban sector is a function of the amount spent on migration activity. The fixed costs may be transport costs[3], the costs of bribes and backhanders to achieve even entry into an urban labour queue, and/or (net) non-pecuniary costs of leaving the rural sector[4]. Over and above the fixed costs, by spending more (on job search, for example) the expected urban income can be increased[5,6] but there are diminishing returns to this expenditure[7].

As in the Todaro model, the agent is assumed to be risk neutral. Solely for convenience in exposition, discounting of the future is ignored. It is then clear that the only points relevant to the potential migrant are such that $Ey > c$ *i.e.* those above the 45° line, since migration activity is simply an input of "rural Rupees" for an output of "urban Rupees", and the two are not differentiated from each other. The migration decision is clearly relevant only to those for whom there exist such points above the 45° line, since for the others "migration efficiency" is so low that this activity does not make a profit. Fig. 2 illustrates these propositions. Also shown is the point of maximum gain from migration activity, (c^*, Ey^*). Clearly it is true that $\left.\frac{dEy}{dc}\right|_{c^*} = 1$.

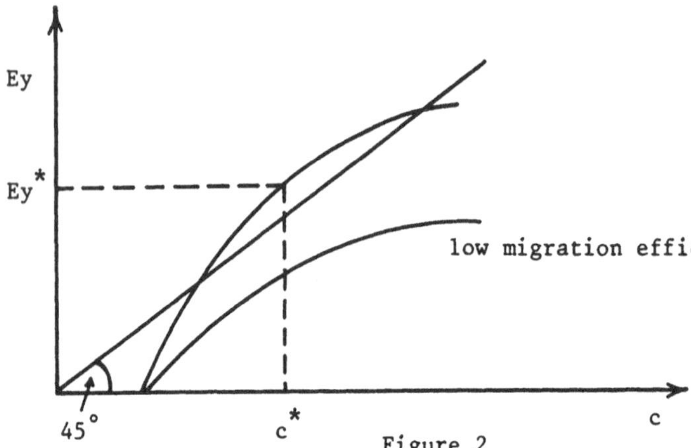

Figure 2

An important feature of the model will now be introduced. We assume that there is an imperfect capital market in the rural sector[8]. In particular, we make the polar assumption that there is no possibility at all of borrowing to finance migration expenditures[9,10]. It follows that migration takes place, if at all, at the end of the first period, when some income has been earned in order to finance the costs of migration[11].

If the agent migrates at the end of the first period after having spent c on the costs of migration, his net income over the two periods is given by

$$Ey(c) + w_1 - c.$$

If he decides not to migrate, his income over the two periods is given by

$$w_1 + w_2(w_1).$$

The choice between the two alternatives can be analysed in terms of the sign of the difference in returns between the two. Denoting G as this difference, it follows that

$$G = Ey(c) - c - w_2(w_1)$$

Remembering that all migration activity has to be financed out of current income (i.e. period 1 income), and that an unconstrained maximum of G with respect to c occurs at

$$G^* = Ey^* - c^* - w_2(w_1),$$

we get that for $w_1 > c^*$ migration takes place if $G^* > 0$. Defining $\bar{w}_1$ as the value of w_1 for which $G^* = 0$,

$$G^* \gtreqless 0 \iff w_1 \lesseqgtr \bar{w}_1 \quad \text{for } w_1 > c^*$$

where we have made use of the assumption that $w_2' > 0$. Thus for those with current incomes higher than c^* there is an incentive to migrate provided current incomes are not too high.

So much for those who can finance the optimum amount of migration activity. What about those with current incomes less than c*? For these people, migration may still be better than staying behind in the rural sector - it depends on how much migration activity they can finance, and on what rural income is due in the next period (both of these are related to the current income). But for those with low enough current incomes the migration activity that can be financed will not better the alternative of staying on in the rural sector. This is shown in Figure 3, which plots $Ey(c) - c$ against c, and $w_2(w_1)$ against w_1. We are assuming that the $w_2(w_1)$ curve has an intersection with the $Ey(c) - c$ curve, since otherwise there would be no migration and the problem would not exist. Obviously the point c_1 is such that

$$G \gtreqless 0 \iff w_1 \gtreqless c_1 \quad \text{for } w_1 < c^*$$

i.e. for those who cannot fully finance the optimum amount of migration expenditure, the maximum feasible amount still presents a better alternative if their incomes are above c_1. But for those with incomes below c_1, even the maximum feasible amount (which in this model is spending all the current income on migration activity[12]) is not good enough to better the prospect of staying on in the rural sector.

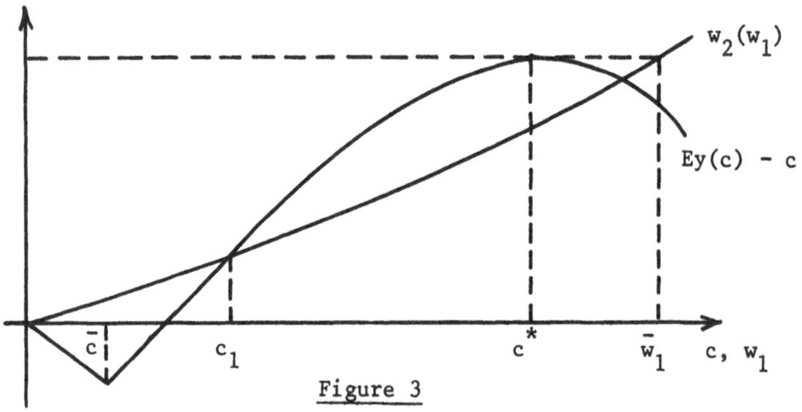

Figure 3

In Fig. 3 we have also indicated the point $\bar{w}_1$, the income level at which those who can finance the optimum amount of migration activity are just indifferent between migrating and not migrating. If we drew the curve $w_2(w_1)$ with both its intersections with the Ey - c curve to the left of c*, the point $\bar{w}_1$ would no longer be relevant. This role is taken over by $\bar{\bar{w}}_1$, the second point of intersection between the two curves. This is shown in Figure 4. Now all those with current incomes greater than $\bar{\bar{w}}_1$ whether they can finance c* or not, do not have the incentive to migrate. Whether the relevant point is $\bar{w}_1$ or $\bar{\bar{w}}_1$ is not important to our later argument. What is important is that there be a point such as this[13]. In what follows we use $\bar{w}_1$.

We thus have that current rural incomes can be characterised by three intervals[14].

(1) $w_1 \leqslant c_1$: At these income levels there is no gain from migration because incomes are not high enough to finance an adequate amount of migration activity.

(2) $\bar{w}_1 > w_1 > c_1$: These income levels provide both the resources <u>and</u> the incentive to migrate. They are high enough to finance an adequate amount of migration expenditure, but low enough to make migration the better alternative when compared to staying in the rural sector for both periods. In this range are some incomes at which the optimum amount of migration expenditure is not feasible - but the amount possible still dominates the non-migration alternative.

(3) $w_1 > \bar{w}_1$: These income levels can finance the optimum amount of migration activity, but they are so high that even this level of migration activity cannot better the current and future incomes in the rural sector.

Thus, remembering that the model is intended as a polar illustration of some tendencies neglected by the recent literature, we may characterise the above result as saying that since the poor do not have the <u>resources</u>, and the rich do not have the <u>incentive</u>, it is the middle income ranges from which migration rates are highest. Evidence relating to this theoretical finding is discussed in the footnote[15]. In the polar illustration of our model, the number of people in the range $\bar{w}_1 > w_1 > c_1$ reflects the "migration potential" of the rural sector. This migration potential will obviously depend crucially on the income distribution in the rural sector. The effect of rural development programs can now be analysed through their effect on the rural distribution of income and hence on migration rates.

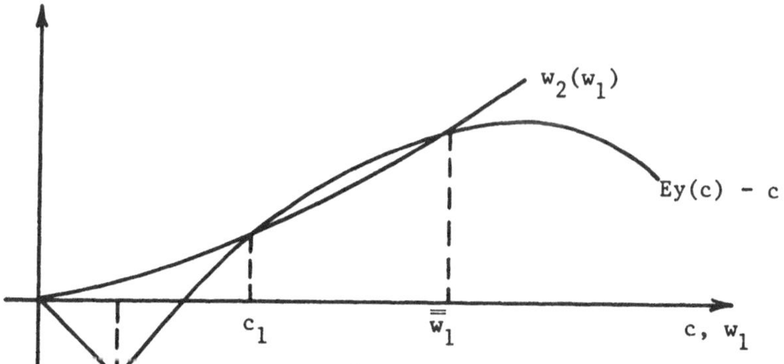

<u>Figure 4</u>

3 The Effect of "Rural Development"

Let the current income distribution of the rural sector be represented by its density function $f(w_1)$. Assuming that the Ey(c) function is the same for all, the rate of (potential) migration is given by

$$M = \int_{c_1}^{\bar{w}_1} f(w_1)\, dw_1 \tag{1}$$

Suppose that this rate of migration is considered to be "too high" and it is decided to initiate a program of "rural development". How should we characterise the effect of this rural development? In the context of our model the answer must obviously be - with respect to incomes in the rural sector[16]. The rural development program can affect both current period and expected future income in the rural sector. The effect of the latter in isolation is easily analysed. Suppose a program leaves current incomes unaltered but raises future expected income for all w_1, i.e. in Figure 3 the $w_2(w_1)$ curve rotates upwards. It can then be seen from the diagram that the migration range of incomes $(c_1, \bar{w}_1)$ is made smaller, thus reducing the migration rate for any given distribution of rural income.

However, now consider the case (arguably more plausible) where the rural development program affects the future expected income of an agent only through its effect on his current income (i.e. the $w_2(w_1)$ relationship remains unchanged). This is the case we concentrate on in this section. We will discuss two types of changes in the distribution of current rural income as the result of the program. First, we suppose that all current rural incomes are increased by an additive shift of size R. Second, we allow for an unequal distribution of the gains of rural development[17] by postulating a multiplicative increase of factor 1+R in all rural incomes. R can be thought of as the "intensity" of the rural development program.

The increase in rural incomes will remove some people from the migration range of incomes, but it will push others into this range. If the numbers of the former are greater than those of the latter, rural development will achieve its objective of reducing (the potential) rate of migration. In the additive case, the people who fall in the range $(c_1, \bar{w}_1)$ after a rural development program of intensity R are those people who were previously in the range $(c_1 - R, \bar{w}_1 - R)$. Define

$$I(R) = \int_{c_1 - R}^{\bar{w}_1 - R} f(w_1)\, dw_1 \qquad (2)$$

the post rural development migration rate. In the multiplicative case all those falling in the range $(c_1, \bar{w}_1)$ after the program of intensity R were previously in the range $\frac{c_1}{1+R}, \frac{w_1}{1+R}$, so that

$$I(R) = \int_{\frac{c_1}{1+R}}^{\frac{\bar{w}_1}{1+R}} f(w_1)\, dw_1 \qquad (3)$$

gives the post rural development migration rate in this case. Notice that in both cases $I(0) = M$, so that a question about the effects of a "small" amount of rural development can be translated into one about the sign of the derivative:

$$\left. \frac{dI(R)}{dR} \right|_{R=0} > 0$$

In general, however, the effects of the two types of programs of intensity R can be discussed in terms of the derivatives of (2) and (3) with respect to R, giving us:

$$\frac{dI(R)}{dR} \gtreqless 0 \quad <=> \quad \frac{f(c_1-R)}{f(\bar{w}_1-R)} \gtreqless 1 \tag{4}$$

$$\frac{dI(R)}{dR} \gtreqless 0 \quad <=> \quad \frac{f\left(\frac{c_1}{1+R}\right)}{f\left(\frac{\bar{w}_1}{1+R}\right)} \gtreqless \frac{\bar{w}_1}{c_1} \tag{5}$$

respectively: (4) and (5) can be used to get a complete characterisation of when rural development of the two types will and will not increase migration rates. These conditions can be investigated further for broad classes of income density. The results for the uniform, Pareto and lognormal densities are summarised in the accompanying Table. The uniform density case if the easiest. Here rural development of both types will either reduce migration rates or leave them unchanged. However, now consider a more plausible specification of the income distribution - the Pareto density. In this case there certainly exists a "large" amount of rural development which will reduce migration, but for both the additive and multiplicative cases it is seen that

$$\left.\frac{dI(R)}{dR}\right|_{R=0} > 0$$

i.e. a small amount of rural development will increase migration rates. This proposition is illustrated diagrammatically for the additive case in Figure 5.

Density / Type of increase in incomes	Uniform	Pareto
	$f(w_1) = \frac{1}{b-a}$, $a \leq w_1 \leq b$, $c_1 > a$	$f(w_1) = \frac{\alpha(w_1^*)^\alpha}{w_1^{\alpha+1}}$, $w_1 \geq w_1^*$, $c_1 > w^*$
Additive	$\frac{dI\ (R)}{dR} = 0$ for $0 < R < c_1 - a$ < 0 for $c_1 - a < R < w_1 - a$	$\frac{dI\ (R)}{dR} > 0$ for $0 \leq R < c_1 - w^*$ $= 0$ for $R = c_1 - w^*$ < 0 for $c_1 - w^* < R < \bar{w} - w^*$
Multiplicative	$\frac{dI\ (R)}{dR} < 0$ for $0 \leq R < \frac{\bar{w}_1 - a}{a}$	$\frac{dI\ (R)}{dR} > 0$ for $0 \leq R\ \frac{c_1 - w^*}{w^*}$ $= 0$ for $R = \frac{c_1 - w^*}{w^*}$ < 0 for $\frac{c_1 - w^*}{w^*} < R < \frac{\bar{w}_1 - w^*}{w^*}$

Density / Type of increase in incomes	Lognormal $f(w_1) \sim \Lambda(\mu,\sigma^2)$
Additive	$\frac{dI(R)}{dR} \gtreqless 0$ $\Leftrightarrow$ $\log(\bar{w}_1-R) + \log(c_1-R) \gtreqless 2(\mu-\sigma^2)$
Multiplicative	$\frac{dI(R)}{dR} \gtreqless 0$ $\Leftrightarrow$ $\log \bar{w}_1 + \log c_1 - 2\log(1+R) \gtreqless 2\mu$

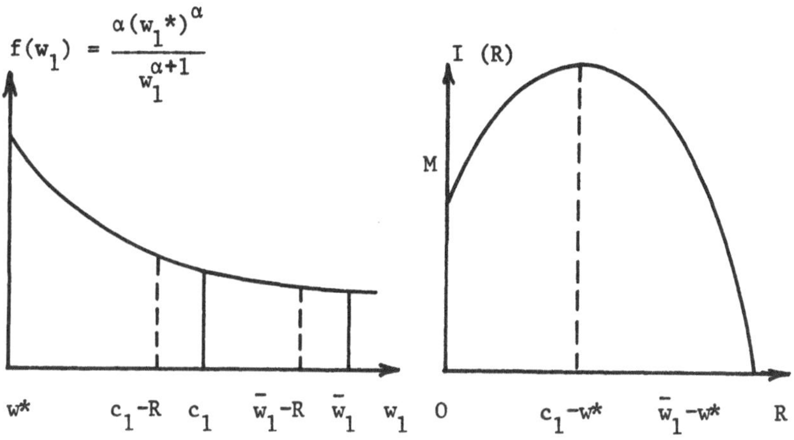

Figure 5

In the lognormal case it is seen again that there certainly exists a high enough intensity of rural development (of either type) which will reduce the migration rate. However, the effect of a "small" amount of rural development is less clear. From the table it can be inferred that

$$\left.\frac{dI(R)}{dR}\right|_{R=0} \gtreqless 0 \iff \log \bar{w}_1 + \log c_1 \gtreqless 2(\mu-\sigma^2) \qquad (6)$$

$$\left.\frac{dI(R)}{dR}\right|_{R=0} \gtreqless 0 \iff \log \bar{w}_1 + \log c_1 \gtreqless 2\mu \qquad (7)$$

for the additive and multiplicative cases respectively.

The effect of rural development on migration thus depends crucially on the income distribution parameters μ and σ^2. As a numerical illustration, suppose the mean of log-incomes is 4.61 and the variance of log-incomes is 0.20. These figures are taken from Robinson (1976), who bases them (roughly) on studies of South Korea and Turkey. Recalling the definitions of $\bar{w}_1$ and c_1 and denoting geometric mean income by μ^*, if we have the following ratios:

$$\frac{c_1}{\mu^*} = \frac{1}{4}, \quad \frac{\bar{w}_1}{\mu^*} = 5$$

then $\log \bar{w}_1 + \log c_1 = 9.44$, so that for both (6) and (7)

$$\left.\frac{dI(R)}{dR}\right|_{R=0} > 0.$$

Thus in this example a small amount of rural development will indeed increase migration rates. How intense must rural development be before this effect recedes, i.e. before increments in R stop increasing migration rates even further? Consider the multiplicative-lognormal case. From the relevant expression in the table and the numerical values used above, it can be shown that

$$\frac{dI(R)}{dR} < 0 \iff R > 0.12$$

i.e. rural development must be of the order of a 10% increase in current rural incomes before it stops increasing migration rates (see Figure 6). However, it should be emphasised that these figures are illustrative, and others in particular circumstances may give different results.

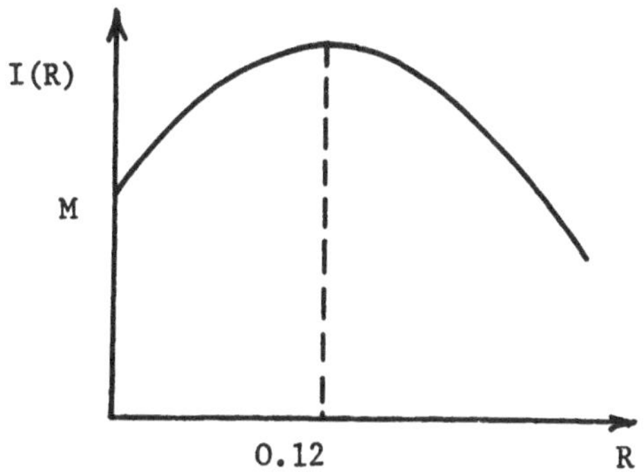

Figure 6

Finally, notice that from (6) and (7) we can make some inferences about the interactions between patterns of inequality and the impact of rural development on migration rates. Considering just the additive case, (6) tells us that for given $\bar{w}_1$ and c_1 the greater is σ^2 the more likely it is that small amounts of rural development will increase migration rates. However, comparing (6) and (7) we see that wherever the multiplicative case (which we have characterised as the more unequal pattern of rural development) increases migration rates, so will the additive case, but that there are some cases where the additive case increases migration rates but the multiplicative case does not[18]. Thus in this sense there appears to be a conflict between the equality increasing and migration reducing objectives of rural development.

In the previous section we identified a "migration range" of current rural incomes, where migration is feasible and desirable. The number of people in this range was referred to as the "migration potential" of the rural sector. In this section we have been looking at the effects of current income growth on this migration potential. A growth in incomes pushes some people into the migration range of incomes and pushes others out of this range. The net effect on the migration rate depends on the pattern of income growth and the pattern of income distribution in the rural sector. However, for broad classes of income growth and income distribution we have shown that the growth effects may be such as to increase migration rates.

At the beginning of this section we noted that if a rural development program left current incomes unaltered while shifting the $w_2(w_1)$ relationship upwards, then migration rates would be reduced. If the rural development program contains elements of increases in current incomes as well as shifts in the $w_2(w_1)$ relationship, then the two forces are pulling in opposite directions and the net effect on migration rates is ambiguous. Suffice it to say that the stronger is the current income growth component of a rural development program, the more likely it is that migration rates will increase.

4. Conclusions and Policy Implications

A natural way of thinking about the effect of increased rural incomes on migration is in terms of the "substitution effect" - the rural sector is made more attractive. This is the view which has been put forward in the recent literature. However, in this paper we have also been considering the "income effect" of an increase in rural incomes - people in the rural sector now have more money to spend on migration. Migration expenditure and the returns to this expenditure are a common theme in the literature on migration in a "human capital" framework (see Sjaastad (1962)), but have tended to be neglected in the literature on migration in developing countries. With a perfect capital market no special significance attaches to current incomes in the decision to migrate (except in so far as they influence expectations of future income). However, with imperfections in the capital market current incomes provide a source of finance for migration expenditures and hence we have the "income effect" of an increase in current incomes. With current incomes a major determinant of the migration decision, the income distribution comes to play an important part in determining rates of migration. In the previous section we have looked at changes in incomes as the result of postulated rural development programs, and argued that the income effects may be strong enough to actually increase migration rates.

The empirical plausibility of the assumptions behind the model has been argued extensively in the footnotes. The major methodological difference between this model and that of Todaro is that Todaro provides a well articulated concept of long run equilibrium, whereas the model of this paper (as indicated in the title) is essentially short run in that it does not take into account the effect of migration on urban sector opportunities. However, it is difficult to believe that the forces identified in this paper will disappear in a general equilibrium framework (although their effect may be lessened).

Finally, a comment on policy implications. Lest the results of this paper be used to justify a policy of no rural development, it is as well to point out that those who draw such a conclusion reveal a poor commitment to both rural development and the reduction of migration rates. The basic result of this paper is not that no amount of rural development will reduce migration, but that (in direct contrast to the Todaro literature) a small amount may not. If the object of policy should indeed be to reduce migration rates (and the full investigation of this claim is itself the subject for another paper), or if rural development is being "sold" to policy makers in terms of its effect on migration rates, then this paper has merely illuminated one aspect of the trade-off between these two. The observed choice then reveals the true commitment to rural development.

REFERENCES

Akerlof, G., 1970, The market for lemons: Qualitative uncertainty and the market mechanisms, Quarterly Journal of Economics

Benerjee, B. and Kanbur, S.M. 1978, On the Specification of Empirical Rural Urban Migration functions in Developing Countries: With an Application to Indian Data, Mineographed.

Barnum H.N. and Sabot R.H., 1976, Migration, education and urban surplus labour. The case of Tanzania, OECD, Paris.

Byerlee D., 1974, Rural-urban migration in Africa: Theory, policy and research implications, International Migration Review, Winter, 543-566.

Caldwell J.C., 1969, African rural-urban migration, Australian National University Press.

Chenery H., et al, 1974, Redistribution with Growth, Oxford University Press.

Connell J., et al, 1974, Migration from rural areas .... Institute for Development Studies, Discussion Paper 39.

David P.A., 1974, Fortune, risk, and the microeconomics of migration, in Reder and David (eds), Nations and households in economic growth, Essays in honour of Moses Abramovitz.

Ghatak S., 1975, Rural interest rates in the Indian economy, Journal of Development Studies, Vol.11, 190-201.

Herrick B., 1965, Urban migration and economic development in Chile, The M.I.T. Press.

Kanbur S.M., 1975, Background material on the Rural Industries Projects Study, Mimeo, Institute of Economic Growth, Delhi.

Phillips, D.G., 1959, Rural-to-urban migration in Iraq, Economic Development and Cultural Change, Vol.7, No.4.

Rao V.K.R.V. and Desai P.B., 1965, Greater Delhi: A Study in urbanisation, 1940-1957, Asia Publishing House.

Renu L.N. and Dhar P.N., 1968, in Decentralised development: A symposium, Vaikuntbhai Mehta Smarak Trust.

Robinson S., 1976, A note on the U hypothesis relating income inequality and economic development, American Economic Review, Vol. 66, 3, 437-440.

Sjaastad L.A., 1962, The costs and returns of human migration, Journal of Political Economy, Vol. 70 (supplement).

Stigler G., 1962, Information in the labour market, Journal of Political Economy, Vol. 70 (supplement).

Thadani, V.N. and Todaro, M.P., 1979, Female Migration in Developing Countries: A Framework for Analysis, Center for Policy Studies, Working Papers, No.47.

Todaro M.P., 1939, A model of labour migration and urban unemployment in less developed countries, American Economic Review, 59, 138-148.

Todaro M.P., 1976, Urban job expansion, induced migration and rising unemployment, Journal of Development Economics, 3, 211-225

FOOTNOTES

* These ideas were conceived while I was visiting the Institute of Economic Growth, Delhi, and were put forward in an intuitive and suggestive fashion in Kanbur (1975). I am grateful to Dr D.B. Gupta, Professor N.H. Stern and Professor J.E. Stiglitz for their help and encouragement. I am especially indebted to Biswait Banerjee. Our joint empirical work, Banerjee and Kanbur (1978), has given me further confidence in the theoretical ideas in this paper.

1. See, for example, Renu and Dhar (1968): "The Rural Industries Planning Committee worked out a scheme of projects for intensive development of industries in rural areas which were aimed to (i) enlarge employment opportunities, (ii) diversify rural occupations, (iii) raise income and living standards of rural communities, and (iv) halt the exodus to urban centres."

2. This aspect of migration, obscured in the recent literature, was given much importance only a decade or so ago. See Sjaastad (1962).

3. Obviously transport costs will vary considerably between countries and even between regions within a country, depending on geography, whether a well developed transport system is in operation, whether it is subsidised by the government, etc. But transport costs are in the nature of fixed costs, and although different from one case to another, they can be considerable. As Caldwell (1969) notes in his study of migration in Ghana, "Travelling to the town costs money. A major anomaly in Ghana is that relative distances mean that it costs comparatively little from the richer south and a considerable amount from the poorer north. Lorry fares alone can absorb £2 or more per person for a journey from the further flung parts of the Upper Region to Accra, an amount representing almost one tenth of the annual national income per head there, and a considerably greater fraction of cash incomes."

4. In the sociological and empirical literature these have been studied under the general heading of "adjustment problems" of migrants. See Phillips (1959) and Caldwell (1969).

5. The involvement of potential migrants in "pre-migrational" activity has been noted in the empirical literature. This can mean taking up jobs or acquiring skills (which has an opportunity cost of current income foregone) which would improve their chances of getting an urban sector job. The acquiring of education (which also has an opportunity cost) would also seem to be an important input into migration activity since the urban sector prospects are better for educated migrants. See Barnum and Sabot (1976) and Caldwell (1969).

6. Job search in the urban sector is also a costly process from the point of view of the prospective migrant in the rural sector. Although he may be lucky and get a job straight away, there is evidence that some migrants may suffer long periods of unemployment (Herrick (1965)), or underemployment. Although the costs of job search for a single migrant may be thought of as being lower because of the assistance of relatives in the town, (Caldwell (1969)), when viewed as a problem of household maximisation these costs remain unaltered.

7. There does not seem to be any direct evidence which can be brought to bear on the hypothesis of diminishing returns to migration expenditures beyond the fixed costs $\bar{c}$. However, a theoretical justification can be given for diminishing returns in the fixed sample search framework of Stigler (1962). Suppose there is a distribution of wage offers in the urban sector, with a cumulative distribution F(x). In a fixed sample framework the agent can sample randomly and select the maximum wage offer in his sample. The distribution function of the maximum wage in a sample of size n is $[F(x)]^n$. The expected wage with a sample of size n is thus

$$Ey(n) = \int_0^{\bar{x}} x d\{F(x)\}^n$$

Integrating by parts and using the same formula for a sample of size n+1, we see that the incremental gains from search are given by

$$Ey(n+1) - Ey(n) + \int_{0}^{\bar{x}} \{F(x)\}^{n}\{1-F(x)\}\, dx,$$

which is a decreasing function of n. Assuming a cost $\hat{c}$ per draw and writing $c = n\hat{c}$ we get the suggested shape for Ey(c)

8. There is a large theoretical and empirical literature on the imperfections of rural credit markets in developing countries. On a theoretical level Akerlof (1970) has provided an explanation for such imperfections in the presence of "qualitative uncertainty". Empirical and institutional investigations usually attribute high interest rates and borrowing constraints to difficulties associated with lending in the rural sector, and there is evidence that interest rates and borrowing difficulties are less for higher incomes. See Ghatak (1975) and the references cited there.

9. Some direct evidence on the amount of migration expenditure financed through borrowing is given by Caldwell (1969) - Table 5:10 on p.135. In the urban survey, in response to the question "When you first came to Accra how did you get enough money to be able to do it?", only 6% responded that they had borrowed the money commercially, whereas 48% had used their own money and 36% had received grants from relatives. The reason for such a small amount of borrowing is to be found in the next question, addressed to those who had borrowed - "Did you pay it all back?", 47% responded "No", and this figure is obviously likely to be an understatement.

10. Another type of evidence which may give some indication of the extent to which borrowing figures in migration finance is available in Rao and Desai's (1965) Study of Delhi. The evidence relates to the

sources of funds for investment in the small establishments sector, the point being that we would expect migrants to have a disproportionately large representation in this sector. Rao and Desai note that "Further inquiry about the source from which the moneys required for the investments were obtained indicates that the bulk of capital has been provided by the proprietors from their own resources. The number of units reported to have resorted to borrowing is only 391, or 7.5% of the total sample ..." (pp. 407-408). Of non-refugee migrant units, 5.5% had resorted to borrowing, while 3.4% of the total investment had been raised by borrowing. Although not conclusive (since it refers to total investment and not the initial outlay), this evidence does tend to provide support for our assumption that borrowing for migration finance is limited.

11. A comment is perhaps required on the interpretation of the timing of migration. The first period is a "pre-migration" period in the sense that it is used for job search etc., and to generate income to finance the costs of migration. The structure of a two period model does not allow us to consider in greater detail the possibility of migrating "before" the end of the first period - if, for example, the migrant is lucky and finds a job early on. For this a continuous time model is required and takes us beyond the scope of the present paper.

12. Such a result is likely to occur where the structure of the model combines the choice of a continuous variable (in this case migration expenditure) with a discrete decision (to migrate or not). We could, for example, have specified that at most a given fraction of current income could be spent on migration. This device has been used by David (1974), for example. However, the basic structure of the model remains the same - over some range the whole amount allotted to migration expenditure will actually be spent. The use of this device in our case would simply complicate notation without altering the structure of the argument except in a superficial way.

13. Also, the way the $w_2(w_1)$ relationship is depicted in Figures 3 and 4 assumed that $w_2'' > 0$. But this is not important. We could just as well have $w_2'' < 0$. What is important is the assumption that $w_2' > 0$ (since this gives two points of intersection), and this assumption, we have argued, is reasonable.

14. It should be noted that the particular form of the Ey(c) curve shown in Figure 1 is not the only one which will give this result. The important feature in Figure 1 is the local non-concavity generated by the fixed costs of migration. However, one can depict the Ey(c) curve with an initial interval of increasing returns and get equivalent results:-

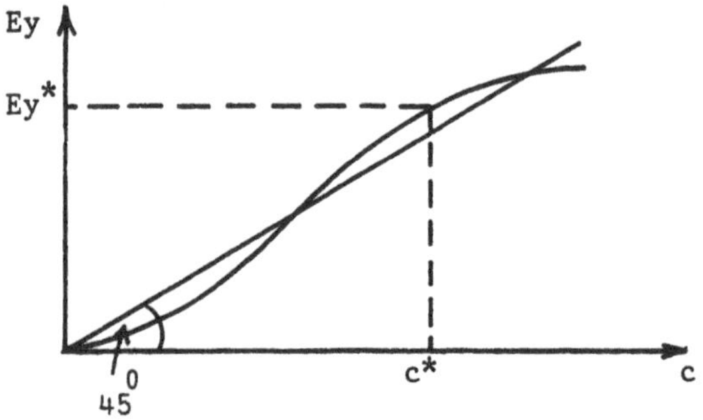

Figure 1'

15. To bring direct econometric evidence to bear on this conclusion is problematic. Most econometric studies of migration are highly aggregative and not designed to test the micro predictions of this model. However, what this prediction does tell us is that since migration rates are likely to first rise and then fall with income a simple regression equation test where the coefficient of the income term can only be positive or negative for the whole range of incomes, will be an inadequate test. Indeed, such specification error may be part of the explanation of the poor performance of many econometric models of migration. However, recent empirical work by Banerjee and Kanbur (1978),

a study of aggregative inter-state rural-urban migration flows in India, does indeed confirm that migration rates first rise and then fall as origin income increases.

Another source of evidence, which seems more useful from our point of view, is micro survey data. Caldwell (1969) did find that of the three classifications of economic status - average, above average and below average - migration propensities were highest in the above average group. But the classification may not have been fine enough to bring out the decline in migration rates at high levels of income. Another source of micro level data are the Village Studies compiled by the Institute for Development Studies, Sussex (1974). Although the evidence presented by these studies is certainly varied, there is some suggestion that in a number of cases the sort of effects predicted by our model were in operation. In some villages "the poorest people may be handicapped by the lack of money, connections in town or knowledge from undertaking migration. Epstein found that the poorest caste, the A.K.S., in two Mysore villages, did not seek work in towns, although they would have liked to, since they lacked the links with prominent people in town and faced severe competition from the higher caste men who were preferred" Again, "Yeshwant found that in 4 Tamil Nadu villages the Harijans were the group least likely to migrate (because of their lack of education, finance and information on the availability of jobs); the most migrant group were the small cultivators and agricultural workers about the middle of the economic scale, while landowners were intermediate", (p 1.8, emphasis added).

16. Of course there are other aspects of "rural development", such as the extension of health and welfare services or educational facilities in rural areas. However, in this paper only the effects on current future income are being considered. By rural development programs we have in mind such things as irrigation projects, the building of feeder road

systems, and the setting up of industrial projects as envisaged in Renu and Dhar (1968).

17. See Chenery et al (1974), Ch.VI, especially the discussion on the "leakages" of benefits from rural development program.

18. This will be the case even when "equal cost" comparisons are being made between the two types of rural development.

15. ESTIMATION OF CROSS SECTION PRODUCTION FUNCTIONS UNDER STRUCTURAL CHANGE IN INDIAN AGRICULTURE

A. Parikh and P.K. Trivedi

1. INTRODUCTION[1]

Recent literature on the theory and estimation of production function has stressed the distinctions between several different concepts of it, e.g. *ex ante* vs. *ex post*, long run vs. short run, micro vs. macro and so forth.[2] There is also an increased awareness of the difficulties associated with estimating the production function as a technique relationship and a greater attempt at interpreting at least the econometric production functions as technique-cum-behavioural relationships. In this paper we shall be interested principally in the estimation of this latter type of relationship even though, for convenience, we frequently use the terminology which, strictly speaking, applies only to the technique relation. The main objective of the paper is to provide 'improved' estimates of a cross section produnction function for four major crops grown in Andhra Pradesh, India. The unit of observation is a district and we exploit both cross section and time series data. There are several motives underlying our investigation. Firstly, we think that the approach sometimes referred to as "planning from above", which involves a central planning agency issuing directives and guidelines as well as allocating resources to lower level units, requires the kind of quantitative information we aim to obtain from our econometric investigation, see Gadgil (1964). However, our study is confined only to one state whereas for comparative purposes we require similar estimates for other states also.[3] Another separate motive underlying this study is to obtain estimates of a 'long run' relationship between outputs and some inputs. The interest in this type of relationship arises because a number of interesting economic hypotheses regarding irrigation and chemical fertilizer inputs require a comparison between short run and long run estimates. For example, it is often argued that the long run response of output to increased irrigation is greater than the short run response because the effect of increased availability of irrigation water is to facilitate multiple cropping, reduce uncertainty, encourage adoption of modern practices and generally change behaviour in a way which leads to a greater output response. If it is the case that this takes time, we should expect the long run responses to exceed the short run ones. In this paper we proceed on the assumption that cross section data, with the district serving as the unit of observation, are more likely to reveal the long run relationship whereas time series data for districts are more likely to reveal the short run relationship. Elsewhere, see Parikh and Trivedi (1979), we have made an extensive study of the district level time series relationship and we shall draw upon the estimates provided there when making comparisons.

In any exercise such as ours it is necessary to allow for structural change in general and technical change in particular. We shall argue that there are a number of reasons for expecting parameters of our relationship to vary over time. Both random and systematic variation is to be expected and hence these must be properly taken into account in the estimation of the long run relationship. We shall propose using an econometric framework which allows for parameter variation to some extent. Questions concerning parameter variation are raised in the light of general awareness that agricultural producers in Andhra Pradesh have experimented with improved and high yielding varieties (especially of rice)[4] and that even where only the traditional varieties are grown the agricultural practices may have changed.

The rest of the paper is organised as follows. In section 2 we provide a brief description of the data used, the specification adopted and the limitations of that specification. In section 3 we discuss our choice of a scheme for parameter variation and outline the Bayesian estimation procedure that we have used. Section 4 contains various estimates which are used in the next two sections for three main purposes - to throw light on the aforementioned hypotheses, to assess the claim that the Bayesian estimates provide an improvement on the ordinary least squares estimates and to also assess whether cross section estimates provided by us do actually pertain to the long run. Finally we attempt to form a view of the nature of structural change affecting agricultural production of rice.

2. DATA AND SPECIFICATION

2.1 Data

Data on output and inputs for the production of rice, tobacco, groundnuts and sugarcane in twenty districts of Andhra Pradesh have been used. These four are the major crops. The data period is 1959-60 through 1974-75. These data were collected by Dr. D. Brown until 1968-69 and subsequently extended to 1974-75 by Dr. S.K. Raheja at the Institute of Agricultural Research Statistics.

Ordinarily when estimating a production function an exhaustive list of well-defined inputs must be specified. Unfortunately such is not the case in the present study. In the brief description we provide below we shall stress the limitation of the data partly because these limitations have some bearing on our choice of estimation procedure.

Output is measured in physical units (metric tonnes) without explicitly taking account of quality variations.

Both irrigated and unirrigated area measures are somewhat rough, the main problem being one of aggregation of a heterogeneous input. In India the smaller holdings are better irrigated, as noted by Hanumantha Rao (1965). This is because irrigated holdings may get relatively more fragmented or are leased out in small plots to tenants by landowners to maximize their return. We also have some evidence (Bhardwaj, 1974) that inputs per acre are considerably higher in irrigated holdings as compared with unirrigated holdings. This *a priori* information tends to indicate that irrigated area is a very heterogeneous input and does not bear solely the water input but a combination of several inputs which can not be completely satisfactorily quantified in terms of acres of land. Irrigated acreage takes no account of intensity, frequency, timing or quality of irrigation as we would want to do in production function estimation.[5] The unirrigated area measure is also crude since it fails to take account of variation in soil types both within and between districts.

The data on chemical fertilizers were not available by crop use and were expressed as the aggregate units of nitrogen, phosphorus and potash used. We use the sum of the three as a single input.[6] Not only the quantity but also the timing and composition of fertilizer used can be important in determining crop response.

Data on rainfall were collected from the Indian Meteorological Department, New Delhi. Rainfall was recorded at each of the centres and if there were three or four centres in a district, an average over those centres was used to obtain districtwise actual rainfall during that year. The inclusion of rainfall variable is justified by treating it as an indicator of availability of water in water scarce agriculture. We have treated rainfall as a proxy for weather index. The normal index of weather consists of rainfall, humidity, temperature and other components. Such an index is not available, and therefore rainfall variable is a surrogate or proxy for weather.

We have no information on human and bullock labour and although these might be important inputs in traditional agriculture, we were not able to obtain this data. However, some of the Farm Management studies have found that the bullock labour coefficient was not significantly different from zero (Government of India, 1958). In subsistence agriculture, family labour may have been used to a significant extent. The proportion of hired labour on small sized farms may be very small. But in the absence of any disaggregated information, we have to treat it as an omitted factor.

Omission of relevant inputs from the relationship will lead to biasses in estimation. However, a number of uses to which we put our estimates actually involve relative magnitudes. Hence it is the relative bias of the two estimates being compared which is important.

2.2 *Specification*

The specified cross sectional relationship is as follows:

$$Y_{ijt} = A_{jt}\, I_{ijt}^{\alpha_{jt}}\, UI_{ijt}^{\beta_{jt}}\, F_{ijt}^{\gamma_{jt}}\, R_{it}^{\lambda_{jt}}\, \varepsilon_{it}$$

i = 1,2...20, districts
j = 1,...4, crops,
t = 1,2...16, time periods,

where Y_{ijt} is the output of crop j (metric tonnes) in district i at time t,

A_{jt} is the constant for crop j at each point of time t,

I_{ijt} is the irrigated area for crop j in district i at time t,

UI_{ijt} is the unirrigated area for crop j in district i at time t, derived as a difference between the total area and irrigated area under crop j at each point of time

F_{ijt} is the chemical fertilizers used for crop j in district i at time t (Total nutrients in tonnes = Nitrogen + Phosphorus + Potash)

R_{it} is the rainfall for district i at time t (millimetres)

and ε_{ijt} is the unobserved error for crop j in district i at time t.

A_{jt}, α_{jt}, β_{jt}, γ_{jt} and λ_{jt} are parameters to be estimated.

2.3 *Limitations of the Chosen Functional Form*

The choice of the log-linear relationship was partly based on grounds of computational convenience, especially in the context of the Bayesian estimation technique where the theory and computer programmes are only available for handling linear models. Partly, however, this choice was also influenced by previous work on cross section production functions where the Cobb-Douglas form has been found to provide a good fit to the data, see, for example, Bardhan (1973) and Nath (1974). We did not try a linear form because our data on inputs and outputs have a large range and a degree of curvilinearity can be expected. This issue is probably best handled using model comparison criteria.[7] The choice of the Cobb-Douglas framework imposes one probably serious limitation on the study. As explained earlier we wish to study the question of structural change in this paper. It is natural to entertain the possibility that structural change affects the elasticity of substitution between inputs, but the choice of the Cobb-Douglas form constrains the elasticity to unity. Quadratic or the trans-log form would be free from this difficulty but only at the expense of introducing additional parameters in the model. See Berndt and Christenson (1973). Given that we have at most twenty cross section observations, precise estimation of a large number of parameters is not possible and this too forces us back to the Cobb-Douglas form. (We did not consider Kmenta-type approximation to the C.E.S. form, see Kmenta (1967), for the same reasons as apply to the trans-log form.)

The Cobb-Douglas production function assumes unitary elasticity of substitution but on *a priori* grounds, one would expect that irrigation and fertilizers would be complementary inputs. The problem of complementary inputs is econometrically very difficult to tackle from the available aggregate information. Hardly any empirical studies are available on this issue and Parikh (1969) using Slutsky-Hicks-Allen-Schultz (SHAS) definition[8] of complementarity (making use of limited cross section statewise data on consumption of fertilizers and water charges) shows that irrigation and fertilizers turn out to be substitutes instead of complements. Parikh (1969) argues that SHAS complementarity would not be symmetric since irrigation precedes the use of chemical fertilizers. This is because if price of chemical fertilizers increases, farmers are unlikely to reduce the irrigated area under a given crop.

One could regard the term $\log A_{jt} + \lambda_{jt} \log R_{it}$ as a rainfall dependent constant term in the production function for a given crop. A possible interpretation is that availability of water increases or decreases efficiency at each point of time and for each district. This implies that rainfall shifts the constant term of the Cobb-Douglas production function but does not affect other elasticity coefficients. Once again, the use of the trans-log production function would be more appropriate for explaining the role of water, including the interaction between rainfall and various sources of irrigation, e.g. tanks, wells, canals. The latter may also affect the elasticities of output with respect to irrigated and unirrigated areas.

The stochastic disturbance in our specification will be assumed to be log-normally distributed. This standard and convenient specification also suffers from several limitations such as those discussed by Just and Pope (1978). Once again, however, relaxing this assumption would involve other difficulties which cannot be satisfactorily handled within our chosen econometric framework.

3. *THE NATURE OF THE CROSS SECTION PRODUCTION FUNCTION*

3.1 Long run vs. short run

We have already indicated that the connection between the relation we study in this paper and a production function, defined as a technique relation, is not clear cut. But we *are* after the analogue of the long run production function. We now consider the conditions which would be favourable to the estimation of the long run function. We assume that these conditions are the same for the long run technique relation as for our analogous relationship. Johansen (1975) distinguishes the *ex ante* production function from the *ex post* one and lists three conditions which are favourable to the estimation of the long run *ex ante* relation from cross section data. These are (i) the farms are established on the basis of the same technological information, (ii) all observations correspond to full capacity utilization and (iii) the spread in the observations makes the estimation possible.[9] We are aware of the possibility of embodied technical change having affected our relationship. This comes through as a result of adoption of new varieties, termed 'varietal change' henceforth. If this change proceeded smoothly then the identification of the long run relation is aided. However, we have no firm information to suggest that this is indeed so.[10] Johansen's second condition is not easy to interpret in the context of traditional agriculture for which the notion of full capacity utilization is hard to define at all precisely. Within individual districts farms are unlikely to be of similar or optimal size. Large and small farms probably coexist and, as has been pointed out by, for example, Bardhan (1973), Bhardwaj (1974) and H. Rao (1965), small farms are typically more intensively cultivated than large farms. Clearly the district-level data conceals inefficient farms. Thus it is quite unrealistic to expect our data to reveal the *ex ante* micro relationship. Finally, the condition of sufficient spread in observations is more likely to be satisfied in our cross section rather than the time series data because between district variability is very much greater than within district variability over about fourteen years for which we have data. In conclusion the results of this paper probably reveal an *ex post* macro relationship between some inputs and outputs and not an *ex ante* micro relationship. The *ex post* relationship is likely to reflect behavioural elements rather than purely technical ones. Its primary use may be as a common long run descriptive relationship.

The long run production function of economic theory is the envelope relationship. The long run relationship that we seek to estimate is of course not the envelope relationship. It is long run in the sense that it abstracts from the effects of high-frequency movements in the explanatory variables and from all short run dynamics.

3.2 Sources of Parameter Variation

In the agricultural situation the output response is likely to exhibit randomness arising from the omission of a large number of factors which affect parameters of the production function. For example, there may be no satisfactory way of allowing for variations in weather patterns, soil fertility, pest infestation, agricultural practices and so forth. We would therefore expect the parameters of the cross section relation to display variability over time. In addition such variability may be amplified by the process of aggregation across units which are not completely homogeneous[11] and by the 'mis-measurement' of heterogeneous inputs that we have already referred to. Note also that we cannot expect the effects of such 'mis-measurement' on values of parameters to be constant through time. A number of authors, e.g. Zellner and Swamy, have argued that the parameter variation induced by such factors is random such that an appropriate estimation technique can be devised to yield estimates of the level of the response and the variation around that level. But some forces behind parameter variation may induce *systematic* changes in the *level* and we shall now briefly discuss these.

Structural change ordinarily comes through changes in behavioural parameters, changes in technique relations and changes in the institutional set up. The first and the third can be interrelated. For example, changes in pattern of land holding, tenurial relationships and so forth could actually change the attitudes of farmers and also their actual behaviour. The estimated relationship of this paper could also reflect the effects of learning-by-doing, especially in relation to the application of fertilizers and the use of new and improved varieties of seed. Technical change affecting production could take the form of increased availability, knowledge and adoption of new and improved varieties of seeds, new input combinations and changes in input ratios as compared with the traditional varieties. *A priori* information, see, for example, Gupta *et al* (1973), suggests that the kind of structural changes we have just referred to may have affected rice production in particular. However, the available information is somewhat incomplete. Because of lack of experience with newer varieties, especially regarding their maturation periods, there has been much experimentation with different varieties and the final outcome is uncertain. An econometric implication may be that the kind of parameter variation scheme we consider may not adequately allow for structural change. Note that we are discussing structural change which is superimposed on 'normal' parameter variation and, given the latter, the former may be rather difficult to identify. We shall rely largely on the outcome of predictive tests to form a judgement on this issue. It is clear, however, that the notion of a long run relationship becomes quite fuzzy once these types of structural change are allowed for. (Some readers may prefer to think of structural change as the change that affects only the traditional varieties and technical change as the change associated with the adoption of new and improved varieties. In this terminology we are dealing with structural-cum-technical change.)

4. ESTIMATION

In addition to ordinary least squares applied to each year for which cross section observations are available, the previously mentioned Bayesian technique was also used. Lindley and Smith (1972) and Smith (1973) are the basic references. Novick *et.al.* (1972) provide an application (in psychology). The Bayesian technique is based on a hierarchical linear model with the following structure:

$$y_t = X_t\beta_t + u_t \qquad t = 1,\ldots T \qquad (2)$$

$$u_t \sim N(O,\sigma_t^2 I_n) \qquad (3)$$

$$\beta_t = \overline{\beta} + v_t \qquad t = 1,\ldots T \qquad (4)$$

$$v_t \sim N(O,\Sigma) \qquad (5)$$

$$\overline{\beta} = \beta^{\dagger} + w_t \qquad t = 1,\ldots T \qquad (6)$$

$$w_t \sim N(O,\Phi) \qquad (7)$$

Here y_t and u_t are (nxl) vectors, X_t is (nxk) matrix, β_t is (kxl) vector, n denotes the number of cross section observations, T the number of cross sections. u, v and w are unobservable random disturbances, and β_t(t=1,...T), $\overline{\beta}$ and β^* are unknown parameters, and σ_t^2,(t=1,...T), Σ and Φ are unknown variance matrices. (2)-(3) define the data generation process and (4)-(5) represent the *a priori* belief that the regression parameters for each cross section are drawn from a *common* normal population. This is the exchangeability - between - regressions assumption in the Lindley and Smith terminology and $\overline{\beta}$ and Σ are hyperparameters. (6)-(7) represent a second stage prior which reflects "beliefs about beliefs". If ignorance about the parameters is confined to the second stage, this can be represented by $\Phi^{-1} \to 0$. Expressions (2)-(5), possibly without the normality assumption at (5), also define the random coefficient regression model such as that of Swamy (1970, 1971) and there are similarities between the Bayesian estimation procedure and that of Swamy, see Smith (1973) and Parikh and Trivedi (1979) for a brief comparison.

Our objective in applying the Bayesian technique is to exploit the prior information embodied in the exchangeability assumption at (4)-(5). The details of the full estimation procedure are contained in Lindley and Smith (1972), Smith (1973) and we have used a slightly different approach in obtaining estimates of σ_t^2 and Σ. In the rest of this section we simply focus on the salient features of the resulting estimates and on some of the problems of estimation.

If, for expository purposes, we assume (i) σ_t^2 and Σ are given, and (ii) $\Phi^{-1} \rightarrow 0$, then it can be shown that the mean of the posterior distribution of β_t is a matrix-weighted average of the least squares estimator $b_t = (X_t'X_t)^{-1}X_t'y_t$ and the estimator for $\bar{\beta}$, say $\bar{b}$, where the latter is obtained by pooling all the data for T cross sections, the pooling having been made possible by the exchangeability assumption at (4)-(5). In other words, the Bayesian technique for estimating β_t involves shrinkage of b_t in the direction of $\bar{b}$, the extent of the shrinkage depending upon the relative sample precision. Thus the Bayesian technique uses more information (in fact all information) in estimating β_t than is the case for the least squares estimator. Consequently we expect the resultant estimates to yield better predictions on the mean square error sense. When variances are not known and estimated values are substituted, the resultant Bayesian estimator will have a lower expected mean square error and, given imprecise variance estimates, the potential improvement may not be realised in each and every prediction situation. The method is not without its own accompanying problems. Their discussion is, however, somewhat technical and can be obtained from the authors. We have not taken explicitly the random coefficient approach to estimation and investigators who prefer to work in the sampling theory framework are referred to Hsiao (1975) and Swamy and Mehta (1977). A simple basic exposition can be found in Maddala (1977). In another paper, (Parikh and Trivedi, 1979) have carefully examined the connection between the random coefficient regression (RCR) model and our own model. It is clear from that analysis that depending upon how one approaches the estimation of unknown variances, one could obtain results very similar to ours by that method. Our estimation approach is not purely Bayesian but empirical Bayesian, because unknown parameters in prior distribution are estimated and not simply imposed.

As a result the estimation method end up being very similar to maximum likelihood.

5. RESULTS

5.1 Alternative sets of estimates

The basic Cobb-Douglas specification was estimated in the following ways for each of the four crops:

1. Using OLS year by year.

2. Using the Bayesian technique.

3. Using averaged cross section data with averaging done over all the years.

4. Using averaged time series data with the averaging done over all the districts.

Our primary interest is in the results obtained by methods 1 and 2; but the 'macro' time series and cross section estimates obtained by methods 3 and 4 respectively, define state level relationships which we shall also use later for certain comparative purposes. Method 3 smoothes out intertemporal variation in the data. This may be a sensible thing to do if we wish to smooth out the influence of transitory factors that induce additional sampling variation in the estimates. The smoothing may also be justified if the smoothed data are subject to a lesser degree to measurement errors. But if the cross section estimates are indeed varying over time, then smoothing data prior to estimation deprives us of an opportunity of studying the variation. Method 4 involved smoothing data over districts and considerations and reservations similar to those just mentioned apply here also. The estimators used in methods 3 and 4 will be denoted by

$$b_3 = (\overline{X}_t'\overline{X}_t)^{-1}\overline{X}_t'\overline{y}_t \qquad (8)$$

and

$$b_4 = (\overline{X}_i'\overline{X}_i)^{-1}\overline{X}_i'\overline{y}_i \qquad (9)$$

We identify b_3 with long run macro estimates and b_4 with short run macro estimates.[12]

The Bayesian estimates for β_t are, in our view, the 'improved' estimates of parameters in a given year. The Bayesian estimates of $\bar{\beta}$ is a smoothed estimate of the parameters in a representative year (the notion of a representative year is blurred in presence of structural change). b_3 is an estimate of the long run relationship based on smoothed cross section data but assuming away the possibility of intertemporal parameter variation. Finally b_4 is a time-series aggregative estimate.[13,14]

5.2 *Year to year variations in elasticities*

In Tables 1 to 4 we have given Bayes and least squares point estimates year by year from 1959-60 through 1974-75 for each crop. The OLS estimates have quite large associated standard errors. If the usual t-test is carried out at the conventional 5 per cent significance level, many of the coefficients will be judged to be insignificantly different from zero. On the other hand, despite year to year fluctuations many of them remain consistently positive, as we expect on *a priori* grounds; this suggests that the large standard errors reflect the inherent variability of the coefficients. The Bayes point estimates do actually have the expected sign in more cases than the OLS estimates. This is partly the result of shrinkage towards the coefficients' mean vector. The posterior mean vector and the associated variances are also given in each table. These show that pooling has resulted in the mean vector being estimated with a considerable increase in precision. For convenience, in subsequent discussion we direct attention at the posterior mean (see $\bar{b}$ in Section 4) rather than year by year estimates. In the case of rice the results show that the irrigated area is the most important input with a coefficient approaching 0.9. This is because rice is largely grown on irrigated land. For sugarcane, the other wet season crop, irrigated area also remains the most important input. For tobacco and groundnuts unirrigated area is relatively the more important input, especially for groundnuts. This is easy to understand in view of the role of groundnuts as a 'dry season' crop. The posterior mean estimates of the fertilizer elasticity has the highest value of 0.36 for tobacco; the remaining values are 0.18 for rice, 0.10 for groundnuts and 0.06 for sugarcane. As previously explained these are probably rather distorted by mismeasurement of this particular input. Whereas our use of the total fertilizer usage variable leads to an overstatement of this input for every crop and district, at the same time we have probably understated the relative variation in consumption of chemical fertilizers. It is hard to say in what direction the coefficients have been distorted. On the basis of the recommended dosages we would expect that most of the chemical fertilizers would have been used in sugarcane and rice production - for the former the recommended dosages are 5 to 6 times those for rice. The low elasticity obtained for sugarcane is therefore rather implausible. Also note that these coefficients do vary a great deal. Finally, we note that the coefficient of the rainfall variable shows a very mixed pattern. Where much of the total area is under irrigation, as in the case of sugarcane and rice, we may not expect the coefficient to be significant. However, in all four cases the posterior variance is large compared with the mean so that the variable appears overall to have negligible additional explanatory power.

5.3 Estimation of marginal productivity

Estimates of marginal physical production (MPP) around the geometric means of inputs and outputs are given in Table 5. Comparisons of productivity of a given input across crops or between pairs of inputs can be made in value terms. This we can attempt only for the chemical fertilizers variable. But first consider the results on marginal physical products alone. The estimates given in Table 5 show considerable variation in the marginal productivity, especially that of the fertilizers. By definition this variation reflects the joint effects of variations in the estimated elasticities and of the ratio of output to input. Where a very small amount of one particular input is used, of course the marginal productivity comes out very high. (In this situation we would also expect that the difference between marginal value product and the price of input would be high also.) In the case of rice, marginal physical productivity of irrigated area varies between 0.723 to 1.593 tonnes; for groundnuts, marginal product of irrigated area varies between 0.69 to 4.97 tonnes while that of unirrigated area the variation is from 0.31 to 0.92 tonnes. Thus the marginal productivity of irrigated area is about 3-5 times that of unirrigated area. In the case of tobacco this ratio is of the order to 6 to 10.

A comparison of the marginal value product (MVP) with the input price (P) can be made for the fertilizer input. The calculations have been made for rice using the prices given in Table 5. Such calculations are apt to be somewhat unreliable given variation in output price during any one year. MPP is also a 'gross' concept since a number of relevant inputs have been omitted and because complementarity with included inputs is ignored. Ignoring these difficulties and basing the ratio of fertilizer to output price in the range of 3 to 4, MVP/P comes out in the range 1.75 to 2.30.[15]

5.4 Long run vs. short run

It was stated earlier that we are after a long run relationship. There arises the question whether we have succeeded in doing so. We attempt to answer this in two ways. First we check the consistency between our cross section estimates and time series estimates. If it is indeed true that the time series estimates reflect short run output responses to input variations then we should expect at least some of the responses to be smaller and we shall check to see if this is so. Second we devise a predictive test which compares predictions from 'short run' and 'long run' relationships.

In Table 6 below are given the estimates of elasticity of output with respect to irrigated area, unirrigated area and fertilizers and rainfall obtained from both cross section and time series data. The Bayesian point estimates for each year in the sample are averaged to yield the estimate of posterior mean (BAY posterior mean) crop by crop. The associated posterior variance is also given. The OLS estimates using averaged cross section data, see the definition of b_3 above in (9), and averaged time series data, see the definition of b_4 above in (9), are also given. In the table these appear in respectively, OLS (Aggregated) row and TS and CS columns. The Bayesian time series estimates are obtained by estimating and averaging *districtwise* cropwise relationships within the framework of the hierarchical prior model described in section 4.

The difference between the time series and cross section elasticity estimates for irrigated area tend to be either small, as in the case of groundnuts and sugarcane, or they go the 'wrong' way, as in the case of rice and tobacco. That is, they are inconsistent with our *a priori* expectation that the long run output response to irrigated acreage will exceed the short run response, see section 1. With respect to unirrigated area there is a slight tendency for the long run elasticity to exceed the short run one. In the case of fertilizers also it seems generally true that the elasticity estimated from cross section data is larger than from time series data, but this difference is sizeable only in the case of rice and sugarcane crops. Overall then, the evidence for the cross section estimates reflecting long run behaviour is somewhat mixed and a further verification seems desirable.

The long run technical relationship between inputs and a given level of output represents an envelope of various short run technical relationships. That is, a given bundle of inputs will produce a larger output if combined according to the long run technical relation than would be the case if they were combined in accordance with the technical relationship described by any short run production function. (The long run function of micro theory would have this property.) Now the relation between the short run technique relationship and the average time series production function on one hand, and between the theoretical long run production function (i.e. the envelope) and the average cross section relationship on the other is quite tenuous. Nevertheless, in the absence of significant structural change, the following seems plausible. Suppose we predict the output of crops, district by district, for specified time periods, using the actually observed input combinations for those districts and using cross section production function estimates. Next we note that the actual observed output for each district and time period represents a point on or around the district's short run production function. If the cross section estimates do reflect the long run relationship, we should expect that the use of cross section estimates will lead to, on average, an over-prediction of actual output.

To verify these somewhat intuitive notions we used the following sets of cross section estimates to make predictions for all districts and crops using the input data for 1970-71, 1971-72, 1972-73 and 1973-74:

(i) Bayes point estimates for the 1968-69 cross section, obtained using cross section data for the ten years 1959-60 through 1968-69, denoted by BAY-68/69;

(ii) OLS point estimates for 1968-69, denoted by OLS-68/69;

(iii) Bayes posterior mean estimates, denoted by BAY-PM, derived from the ten year data as in (i) above.

(iv) OLS estimates based on averaged ("smoothed") cross-section data, denoted by OLS-MACRO.

The results based on estimates for ten years are not reported here to save space.

Our choice of the estimation period ensures that the exercise reported below remains a genuine "outside sample period" prediction exercise.[16] The prediction errors obtained were examined for their sign; the sum of squared prediction errors was also calculated. These estimates are given in Table 7 below. In the case of tobacco, groundnuts and sugarcane, but not of rice, there was a broad tendency for the cross section estimates to over-predict the district output levels and the extent of over-prediction was the greatest when OLS-MACRO estimates were used. The results for rice will be examined separately. One possible explanation for the broad tendency of the results is that the predictions are based on biased estimates. The Bayes estimates are biased; the OLS estimates could also reflect aggregation bias. However, this cannot convincingly explain why the biases should typically lead to overprediction. In general, it is difficult to say anything about the direction of biases due to aggregation. The second alternative explanation, that the cross section estimates reflect misspecification bias is also not convincing because it would be difficult to establish that misspecification would lead to over-prediction. The third explanation that a relation analogous to the long run relationship has been estimated therefore seems more plausible.

In the case of rice prediction errors were not generally positive. As discussed in section 3, there is *a priori* information to suggest that the short run production relation may have shifted. Successful adoption of new high-yielding varieties could move the short run function in such a way that an envelope-type relationship based entirely on previous estimates may no longer apply. If the shift of the short run relationship were sufficiently great then we might even observe negative prediction errors for these districts. We have observed this tendency for several districts, and this leads us to conclude that there is evidence of technical change of the kind mentioned in section 3 at least in the case of rice. (Using BAY posterior mean systematic overprediction was observed in only 6 out of 20 districts.)

For the W. Godavari district, the OLS-MACRO had a lower mean square error than any of the other estimates for rice and tobacco crops. For sugarcane and groundnuts, BAY-PM estimates had lower mean square errors. For the crops where structural change seems to have occurred, the long run production relationship has a better predictive power than the corresponding short run relation. In general, for tobacco and groundnuts, there was very little possibility of technical change since both are grown under dry conditions. For tobacco, the substitution of irrigated area for unirrigated area was a possibility but this does not seem to have happened during the periods 1970-71 to 1973-74. Once again, our macro estimates tend to overpredict a great deal more than BAY-PM or BAY 1968-69 estimates. The mean square prediction errors are higher for tobacco and groundnuts for almost every single district. The possibility that irrigated area is substituted for unirrigated area strongly exists for W. Godavari, which is an important tobacco growing district.

There is also a possibility that overpredictions from cross-section relations will depend upon the size of the district since it is an "average" relationship. Districts which are lower than average size in terms of output might have overpredictions while districts smaller than average size will have more underpredictions. This, however, does not seem to be the case since most of the districts show overpredictions with respect to sugarcane, groundnut and tobacco.

6. EVALUATION OF POINT ESTIMATES

In this section we attempt to assess our claim that the Bayes point estimates constitute an improvement on the OLS estimates. As stated earlier, if the Bayesian specification of the model is appropriate then they should lead to improved prediction. Improvement here is meant in the prediction mean square error sense. We shall attempt a cross-validatory exercise to check whether the potential of the Bayes technique is actually realised.

The prediction errors based on Bayesian and OLS estimates are likely to be affected by several factors (a) misspecification of the model[17]; (b) technical change, especially varietal change, and (c) the change in relationship among explanatory variables during the post-sample period. Had we had no technical change and no misspecification, we could have identified the realised gains of using prior information in the estimation. Since such an ideal situation is not obtained, and the structural change and collinearity[18] probably get confounded in OLS estimation, we ask the question whether the Bayesian estimates produce lower prediction mean square errors than OLS estimates.

6.1 In-Sample Prediction Performance

Our first set of predictions were made using the OLS and the Bayesian point estimates for 1968-69 and the posterior mean estimates obtained by averaging over all years for which we had estimates, see Tables 1 to 4. Predictions were generated for every year except 1968-69 and mean square prediction error computed year by year. As expected the prediction mean-square error for every year was lower than that of OLS when BAY 68-69 estimates were used and was generally lower than that of OLS when BAY-PM estimates were used. The Bayesian estimates are of course based on information about all years whereas the OLS ones are not and so the better prediction performance of the Bayes method is not surprising. To save space we have not included here the detailed results of this exercise.

6.2 Outside Sample Period Prediction Performance

On a cropwise basis predictions were generated and the mean square error of prediction errors calculated for between four and six years using the following three sets of estimates obtained from the results pertaining to the first ten years' data: (i) BAY-PM, (ii) OLS-MEAN and (iii) OLS-68/69. BAY-PM is used because it makes a suitable allowance for the variability of the parameters. OLS-MEAN can also be thought to produce a similar smoothing effect, but without any theoretical justification. OLS-68/69 is the last year in the ten year data period so it seems worthwhile comparing its performance with that of other estimates.

Table 8 contains the mean square errors obtained. BAY-PM and OLS-MEAN have a very similar prediction performance in all cases. In four years out of four in the case of rice, in four years out of five in the case of tobacco and in five years out of six in the case of groundnuts, BAY-PM and OLS-MEAN have smaller prediction mean square error than OLS 68/69. In the case of sugarcane OLS 68/69 has the smaller prediction mean square error in two years and the larger in the other two. Overall, however, the evidence seems to be that smoothing and averaging of coefficients leads to improved prediction performance. In the Bayesian framework smoothing and averaging is justified by the assumption of exchangeability between regressions and therefore we might say that the use of this prior information assumption is the cause of this improvement. The fact that the OLS-MEAN and BAY-PM turn out to be rather close is interesting but cannot be expected to be a feature of all data sets.

7. CONCLUSIONS

We have not found strong evidence in support of the hypothesis that the long run (cross section) elasticity of output with respect to irrigated land is larger than the same short run (time series) elasticity. For two of the four crops,viz: groundnuts and tobacco, this seems to be the case but for rice the latter exceeds the former and for sugarcane the two are much the same. A similar comparison for fertilisers shows that there is stronger evidence that the long run output elasticity with respect to fertilizers exceeds the short run elasticity. Using our preferred Bayes estimates we find that the long run elasticity can be almost three times the short run elasticity.

Our calculations confirm our *a priori* expectations that the marginal productivity of inputs varies substantially from year to year. In comparing the marginal productivity of irrigated and unirrigated land we find that this differential is very large for tobacco where the ratio is of the order of five, but typically much smaller for groundnuts. Given that most of the area under rice and sugarcane is irrigated we have not carried out such a comparison in those two cases.

We have found some evidence which suggests that rice production in Andhra Pradesh has undergone significant structural change. This evidence from cross section data is consistent with similar evidence from district level-time series data which we have presented in Parikh and Trivedi (1979). The nature of the structural change is probably technical-behavioural, arising from a more wide-spread adoption of new and high-yielding varieties of rice such as Jaya, CO-29 and Mashori.[19]

On the methodological side we feel that *a priori* reasoning and post model evaluations support the use of the Bayes estimation technique. However, much of the improvement in prediction results from the Bayes posterior mean estimates smoothing out the fluctuations in cross section estimates from year to year. Other methods of estimation which have this feature, such as certain variants of the random coefficient regression model, should also do well in a prediction exercise.

The policy suggestions for "planning from above" are important to Indian planners. It is obvious that irrigated area is a very important input but we also find overall that marginal value productivity for irrigated area is considerably greater than that of chemical fertilizers and the explanation for this may lie in the scope offered by irrigation for multiple cropping, intensive cultivation and changes in cropping pattern. Fertilizers seem to have very high marginal productivity when they are used under irrigated conditions. For the tobacco crop, unirrigated area and irrigated area both have high marginal value productivity but this of course does not imply that all land may be allocated to tobacco, since there are constraints such as soil fertility which affect allocation of land to alternative crops. Note also that the MVP concept and its empirical implementation does not fully take into consideration the qualitative and technical requirements for crop cultivation. Moreover, the differences in costs of cultivation between crops are ignored and therefore instead of marginal profitability, we are dealing with marginal value products.

REFERENCES

Aigner, D.J. & S. Goldfeld (1974). Estimation and Prediction from Aggregate Data when Aggregates are Measured more Accurately than their Components, *Econometrica*, Vol. 42, 113-134.

Aigner, D.J. & S.F. Chu (1968). On Estimating the Industry Production Function, *American Economic Review*, Vol. 58, 826-839.

Bardhan, P.K. (1973). Size, Productivity and Returns to Scale: An Analysis of Farm Level Data in Indian Agriculture, *Journal of Political Economy*, 1370-1386.

Berndt, E.R. & L.R. Christensen (1973). The Translog Function and the Substitution of Equipment Structures and Labour in U.S. Manufacturing, 1939-1968, *Journal of Econometrics*, Vol. 1, 81-113.

Bhardwaj, K. (1974). *Production Conditions in Indian Agriculture*, Department of Applied Economics, Cambridge University Press, Cambridge.

Bliss, C.J. & N.S. Stern (1980). *Palanpur: Studies in the Economy of an Indian Village*, O.U.P. 1980, forthcoming.

Brown, D.D. (1971). *Agricultural Development in India's Districts*, Harvard University Press, Cambridge, Massachusetts.

Farrell, M.J. (1957). The Measurement of Productive Efficiency, *Journal of Royal Statistical Society*, Series A, 120(3), 253-81.

Gadgil, D.R. (1964). *Planning and Economic Policy in India*, Gokhale Institute of Politics and Economics, Poona, Orient & Longman Ltd.

Government of India (1960). *Studies in Economics of Farm Management In Punjab*. Directorate of Economics and Statistics, Ministry of Food and Agriculture.

Grunfeld, Y. & Z. Grilliches (1960). Is Aggregation Necessarily Bad?, *Review of Economics and Statistics*, 42, 1-13.

Gupta, S.A., Banerjee, A.K., Malhotra, P.C. & M. Rajagopalan (1973). A Study on High Yielding Varieties of Rice in Andhra Pradesh, *Agricultural Situation in India*, Vol. 28, 1, 17-21.

Hanumantha Rao, C.H. (1965). *Agricultural Production Functions, Costs and Returns in India*, Asia Publishing House, Bombay.

Hoch, I. (1962). Estimation of Production Function Parameters Combining Time-Series and Cross-Section Data, *Econometrica*, Vol. 30, 34-53.

Hsiao, C. (1975). Some Estimation Methods for a Random Coefficient Model, *Econometrica*, Vol. 43, 305-326.

Just, R.E. & R.D. Pope (1978). Stochastic Specification of Production Functions and Economic Implications, *Journal of Econometrics*, Vol. 7, 67-86.

Johansen, L. (1975). *Production Functions: An Integration of Micro and Macro Short-Run and Long-Run Aspects*, North Holland Publishing Company, Amsterdam.

Lindley, D.V. & A.F.M. Smith (1972). Bayes Estimates for the Linear Model, *Journal of Royal Statistical Society*, Series A, 1-41.

Kmenta, J. (1967). On Estimation of CES Production Function, *International Economic Review*, 8, 180-192.

Kuh, E. (1959). The Validity of Cross-Sectionally Estimated Behaviour Equations in Time-Series Application, *Econometrica*, 27, 197-214.

Maddala, G.S. *Econometrics*, McGraw Hill, New York, pp. 400-403.

Mellor, J.W. (1962). Increasing Agricultural Production in Early Stages of Economic Development: Relationships, Problems and Prospects, *Indian Journal of Agricultural Economics*, 17(2), 29-46.

Minhas, B.S., Parikh, K.S. & T.N. Srinivasan (1974). Towards the Structure of a Production Function for Wheat Yields with Dated Inputs of Irrigated Water, *Water Resources Research*, 10, 383-393.

Moore, C.V. (1961). A General Framework for Estimating the Production Function for Crops Using Irrigation Water, *Journal of Farm Economics*, 43(4), 876-888.

Nath, S.K. (1974). Estimating the Seasonal Marginal Product of Labour in Agriculture, *Oxford Economic Papers*, Vol. 26, 375-387.

Novick, M.R., Jackson, P.M., Thayer, D.T. & N.S. Cole (1972). Estimating Multiple Regressions in m Groups: A Cross-Validation Study, *British Journal of Mathematical and Statistical Psychology*, 35, 33-50.

Parikh, A. (1969). Complementarity between Irrigation and Fertilizers in Indian Agriculture, *Indian Journal of Agricultural Economics*, 24(3).

Parikh, A. & P. Trivedi (1979). Estimation of Returns to Inputs in Indian Agriculture, *A.N.U. Discussion Paper*, May 1979.

Pesaran, M.H. & A. Deaton (1978). Testing Non-Nested Nonlinear Regression Models, *Econometrica*, 46, 677-694.

Samuelson, P.A. (1974). Complementarity: An Essay on the 40th Anniversary of the Hicks-Allen Revolution in Demand Theory, *Journal of Economic Literature*, XII, 4, 1255-1289.

Sato, K. (1975). *Production Function and Aggregation*, North-Holland, Amsterdam.

Smith, A.F.M. (1973). A General Bayesian Linear Model, *Journal of Royal Statistical Society*, Series B, 35(1), 67-75.

Swamy, P.A.V.B. (1970). Efficient Inference in a Random Coefficient Regression Model, *Econometrica*, Vol. 38, 311-323.

Swamy, P.A.V.B. (1971). *Statistical Inference in a Random Coefficient Regression Model*, Springer-Verlag.

Swamy, P.A.V.B. & J.S. Mehta (1977). Estimation of Linear Models with Time and Cross-Sectionally Varying Coefficients, *Journal of the American Statistical Association*, Vol. 72, 890-898.

Zellner, A. (1969). On the Aggregation Problem: A New Approach to a Troublesome Problem in Fox, K.A. *et.al.* (editors): *Economic Models Estimation and Risk Programming*. Essays in Honours of G. Tintner, New York: Springer-Verlag 1969.

FOOTNOTES

1. The authors wish to thank Mrs. Susan Bailey for very able research assistance at the University of East Anglia, Norwich, Dr. T. Fearn for providing the computer program and Dr. S.K. Raheja for making some of the data available. The paper was completed during the second author's visit to the Department of Economics, University of Southampton. Houblon Norman Fund award enabled the first author to spend six months at the Indian Planning Commission, New Delhi, during which period data for this study was completed.

2. See, for example, Johansen (1975) and Sato (1975).

3. As data are available to support such investigations this is not, in principle, a difficulty.

4. See Gupta *et. al.* (1973).

5. The problem of aggregation in respect of this variable is substantial and has several dimensions. See, for example, Moore (1961), Minhas, Parikh and Sriniviasan (1974) on the issue of water requirements for sustaining life and growth of plants. See also Rao (1965) on the relation between the size of holding and quality of irrigation. These studies help one to appreciate that irrigated area is a very heterogeneous input. Bardhan (1973) uses expenditure on irrigation in his study, and this could be a better measure for some purposes. However he, like Mellor (1962), regards irrigation as land-augmenting technical change which improves land productivity, reduces uncertainty and facilitates double cropping.

6. Approximate methods might be used to allocate the total fertilisers used for individual crops using information on recommended dosage for irrigated and unirrigated area. However, there is no reason to believe that the recommended dosages based on responses in agricultural research stations correspond to actual practice. There is some evidence that actual usage falls far short of recommended dosage. See, for example, Bliss and Stern (1980), Ch. 8.

7. These would involve a comparison of, for example, linear vs. log-linear models. See for example, Pesaran and Deaton (1978). Even when parameter variation is not considered, the non-nestedness of the rival models involves application of somewhat complicated and numerically exacting methods which are still somewhat underdeveloped.

8. Samuelson (1974) suggests six alternative definitions and suggests "money metric utility approach" which is somewhat similar to Edgeworth-Pareto introspective cardinal utility approach.

9. In *ex post* production function estimation a possibility of simultaneous equations bias exists due to demand for inputs and supply of output being dependent upon some common stochastic factors. See Hoch (1962).

10. If this condition is not satisfied one could attempt to fit a frontier production function by either the Aigner-Chu's or Farrell's method. Such an exercise would need to be based on micro information. See Aigner and Chu (1968) and Farrell (1957).

11. Zellner (1962) and Swamy (1971) have elaborated this point in a different context.

12. These estimators yield unbiased but not efficient estimates. For a discussion of their properties and for the appropriate formulae for standard errors of b_3 and b_4, see Swamy (1971).

    Consider the simple model

    $$y_{it} = \beta_t x_{it} + u_{it} \qquad i = 1,\ldots n \; ; \; t = 1,\ldots T$$

    $$\beta_t = \overline{\beta} + \varepsilon_t$$

    Combining the two equations and summing over i we obtain

    $$\Sigma y_{it} = \Sigma(\overline{\beta} + \varepsilon_t)x_{it} + \Sigma u_{it}$$

    $$= \overline{\beta}\,\Sigma x_{it} + (\Sigma x_{it}\varepsilon_t + \Sigma u_{it}).$$

    From this last equation we can see that it is possible to estimate $\overline{\beta}$ from smoothed data. But, in general, the stochastic specifications in the smoothed and unsmoothed cases must be different.

13. In Parikh and Trivedi (1979) we give estimate for the representative district also.

14. If the data on inputs are subject to considerable measurement error, and if the measurement error is such that summation over time periods or over districts leads to an aggregate measure that is subject to a smaller measurement error, then the bias from this source alone may be smaller in the case of the aggregative estimates. If, in addition, there are no interdistrict or intertemporal parameter differences, least squares on aggregated data will yield unbiased estimates of district - or yearwise relationships.

But in presence of such parameter differences aggregated data will yield biased estimates of district-level and yearwise relationships. See Aigner and Goldfeld (1974), and Grunfeld and Griliches (1960).

15. The margin by which this exceeds unity is a matter for considerable discussion. Bliss and Stern (1980) attempt to explain this by appealing to the farmer's uncertainty of the crop response to input variations.

16. The point estimates based on this ten year period are also required for a further cross-validatory check to be undertaken in the next section.

17. The model can be misspecified if the error structure is not correct. There are omitted variables which means that we are dealing basically with an under-specified equation. The functional form which we have used is Cobb-Douglas and this is rather restrictive.

18. Different collinear structures between sample and post-sample period could produce large prediction errors in the absence of any structural change when OLS estimates are used. Structural change is interpreted as change in coefficients which is not random but systematic or evolutionary.

19. A more thorough quantitative investigation of the nature of structural change is strongly recommended.

TABLE 1

RICE: CROSS SECTION OLS AND BAY ESTIMATES

Year	Method of Estimation	Intercept	Irrigated Area	Fertilisers	Rainfall	Common Residual Variance
1959-60	OLS	1.0101	0.8773	0.1198	-0.0232	0.02122
	BAY	0.9198	0.8895	0.1121	-0.0238	
1960-61	OLS	-0.7441	0.9937	0.0947	0.0514	0.06368
	BAY	-0.1510	0.9675	0.1141	-0.0122	
1961-62	OLS	1.5409	0.8407	0.1713	-0.0826	0.03118
	BAY	0.9977	0.8660	0.1359	-0.0123	
1962-63	OLS	1.1082	0.8404	0.1292	0.0036	0.07278
	BAY	1.0480	0.8538	0.1326	-0.0142	
1963-64	OLS	1.5071	0.8473	0.1086	-0.0361	0.02145
	BAY	1.3195	0.8584	0.1133	-0.0335	
1964-65	OLS	0.5435	0.8251	0.0814	0.1901	0.02572
	BAY	1.0256	0.8298	0.1072	0.0786	
1965-66	OLS	0.8954	0.6992	0.3496	0.0055	0.04705
	BAY	0.3967	0.7657	0.2681	0.0629	
1966-67	OLS	-0.1689	0.3337	0.4879	0.6105	0.04589
	BAY	-0.2176	0.5114	0.3774	0.4513	
1967-68	OLS	-3.2093	0.5867	0.5028	0.5868	0.06641
	BAY	-1.9167	0.6365	0.4158	0.4234	
1968-69	OLS	4.6644	0.9691	0.0630	-0.7107	0.04612
	BAY	3.3708	0.9877	0.0576	-0.5371	
1970-71	OLS	-0.3575	0.9005	0.1597	0.0518	0.02758
	BAY	0.1334	0.9082	0.1569	-0.0270	
1971-72	OLS	-0.7768	1.1202	0.0858	-0.1548	0.02645
	BAY	-0.5310	1.0924	0.0917	-0.1524	
1972-73	OLS	-2.1654	0.9336	0.2932	0.0931	0.10231
	BAY	-1.9324	0.9162	0.2692	0.1225	
1973-74	OLS	-1.7732	0.8308	0.2728	0.2648	0.02871
	BAY	-1.0945	0.8228	0.2496	0.2091	
Posterior means		0.2406	0.8504	0.1858	0.0382	0.04306
Estimates of Variances of Posterior Means		0.5173	0.0041	0.0024	0.0125	
Modal Variances		5.3026	0.0471	0.0277	0.1362	

TABLE 2

GROUNDNUTS: CROSS SECTION OLS AND BAY ESTIMATES

Year	Method of Estimation	Irrigated Area	Unirrigated Area	Chemical Fertilisers	Rainfall	Common Residual Variance
1959-60	OLS	0.14855	0.69571	0.17447	-0.40227	0.0680
	BAY	0.13299	0.69774	0.14336	-0.37126	
1960-61	OLS	0.17530	0.73383	0.18379	-0.14845	0.12971
	BAY	0.12379	0.80208	0.16814	0.22801	
1961-62	OLS	0.08757	0.63821	0.05957	-0.40617	0.13537
	BAY	0.09314	0.66362	0.06765	-0.31393	
1962-63	OLS	0.03206	0.91456	0.18197	0.47014	0.07530
	BAY	0.04984	0.89631	0.15820	0.41968	
1963-64	OLS	0.09371	0.84493	0.07378	-0.13219	0.07270
	BAY	0.08909	0.84051	0.07968	-0.07105	
1964-65	OLS	0.02969	0.92258	0.10055	0.35672	0.10013
	BAY	0.05460	0.90010	0.10989	0.25656	
1965-66	OLS	0.11883	0.92789	-0.22456	0.11574	0.61584
	BAY	0.09683	0.94073	-0.06408	0.14371	
1966-67	OLS	0.13363	0.23034	0.15166	-0.29495	1.58757
	BAY	0.15184	0.24302	0.13022	-0.46371	
1967-68	OLS	0.04113	1.03800	0.25204	0.99089	0.0887
	BAY	0.05736	0.97738	0.14608	0.61891	
1968-69	OLS	0.03948	0.92296	0.17992	0.26097	0.14223
	BAY	0.05762	0.90676	0.14248	0.28478	
1969-70	OLS	0.09070	0.85988	0.08597	0.24029	0.14894
	BAY	0.08661	0.85327	0.09314	0.22110	
1970-71	OLS	0.03031	0.93231	0.18519	-0.53732	0.12062
	BAY	0.05075	0.91236	0.12549	-0.22669	
1971-72	OLS	0.04083	0.94294	0.23592	1.47240	0.15638
	BAY	0.06480	0.91607	0.17343	1.03070	
1972-73	OLS	0.11241	0.85891	0.01015	1.00400	0.16223
	BAY	0.08966	0.87237	0.08816	0.82545	
1973-74	OLS	0.19160	0.53236	-0.22398	-1.22130	0.24762
	BAY	0.13854	0.57413	-0.00941	-0.92016	
1974-75	OLS	0.04364	0.69224	-0.06771	-2.14680	0.18572
	BAY	0.08903	0.65675	0.02256	-1.24230	
Posterior Means		0.09815	0.79082	0.09844	0.02624	0.22154
Estimates of Variances of Posterior Means		0.00042	0.00494	0.00298	0.07252	
Modal Variances		0.00389	0.06730	0.02418	0.86601	

TABLE 3

TOBACCO: CROSS SECTION OLS AND BAY ESTIMATES

Year	Method of Estimation	Elasticity Coefficients with Respect to: Irrigated Area	Unirrigated Area	Chemical Fertilisers	Rainfall	Common Residual Variance
1959-60	OLS	0.28275	0.72856	-0.06837	0.10525	0.44927
	BAY	0.24781	0.76509	0.01958	0.03824	
1960-61	OLS	0.36944	0.63392	0.09930	0.72007	0.34830
	BAY	0.31463	0.64039	0.18609	0.08903	
1961-62	OLS	0.25303	0.91944	0.14887	-0.95790	0.12378
	BAY	0.23382	0.87187	0.14058	-0.71257	
1962-63	OLS	0.21800	0.86467	0.22805	-0.64565	0.12863
	BAY	0.20754	0.83940	0.19986	-0.52336	
1963-64	OLS	0.12645	0.78515	0.18799	-0.25616	0.08866
	BAY	0.14886	0.76475	0.22076	-0.19767	
1964-65	OLS	0.09809	0.73718	0.31220	0.07945	0.07680
	BAY	0.13511	0.72809	0.29422	-0.09933	
1965-66	OLS	0.16042	0.75287	0.23777	-0.37499	0.1163
	BAY	0.17288	0.74034	0.25680	-0.30611	
1966-67	OLS	0.32226	0.43838	0.45525	-1.85680	0.41724
	BAY	0.27072	0.45337	0.52764	-1.15500	
1967-68	OLS	0.01391	0.39479	0.82518	-0.08216	1.92507
	BAY	0.07144	0.40371	0.79232	-0.18746	
1968-69	OLS	0.13617	0.90492	0.02400	-0.20555	0.04402
	BAY	0.15894	0.86750	0.08434	-0.19276	
1970-71	OLS	0.10242	0.79341	0.25797	0.10984	0.31776
	BAY	0.12439	0.78380	0.24956	-0.01532	
1971-72	OLS	0.20479	0.47495	0.41738	0.70636	0.43352
	BAY	0.20737	0.51774	0.42445	0.17284	
1972-73	OLS	0.27581	0.25135	0.80631	-0.36141	1.10077
	BAY	0.26246	0.26348	0.79135	-0.33841	
1973-74	OLS	0.16161	0.21211	1.28110	-0.43434	1.03015
	BAY	0.18402	0.23004	1.02080	-0.61704	
1974-75	OLS	0.14604	0.81918	0.34751	-0.04774	0.11552
	BAY	0.15888	0.80614	0.23761	-0.19280	
Posterior Means		0.19326	0.64505	0.36307	-0.28251	0.39063
Estimates of Variances of Posterior Means		0.00115	0.00660	0.01479	0.06176	
Modal Variances		0.01214	0.08806	0.17852	0.53307	

* All Variables were measured from their means. Constant can be obtained by using estimated regression coefficients.

TABLE 4

SUGARCANE: CROSS SECTION OLS AND BAY ESTIMATES

Year	Method of Estimation	Elasticity Coefficients with Respect to: Area	Chemical Fertilisers	Rainfall	Common Residual Variance
1959-60	OLS	0.98500	0.04036	0.06885	0.01775
	BAY	0.98809	0.04850	0.05425	
1960-61	OLS	0.98184	0.09757	-0.10171	0.02560
	BAY	0.98984	0.07748	-0.02275	
1961-62	OLS	1.00520	0.01048	0.06970	0.00418
	BAY	0.99833	0.03224	0.02111	
1962-63	OLS	0.98805	0.01949	0.16816	0.02974
	BAY	0.98891	0.03618	0.10990	
1963-64	OLS	0.99222	0.04799	-0.01774	0.00407
	BAY	0.99459	0.05138	-0.00917	
1964-65	OLS	0.99825	0.05493	-0.11777	0.01016
	BAY	0.99950	0.05342	-0.06378	
1966-67	OLS	0.99182	0.03430	0.07314	0.02815
	BAY	0.99155	0.04562	0.05201	
1968-69	OLS	0.98681	0.07024	0.16194	0.00470
	BAY	0.98778	0.06578	0.09773	
1969-70	OLS	0.98489	0.05543	0.03227	0.00382
	BAY	0.98944	0.05620	0.03161	
1970-71	OLS	0.99345	0.11759	-0.12087	0.01440
	BAY	0.99447	0.08686	-0.06707	
1971-72	OLS	1.01710	0.10510	0.11315	0.02197
	BAY	1.00530	0.07733	0.02160	
1972-73	OLS	0.97629	0.11851	0.03714	0.01874
	BAY	0.98311	0.09466	0.04109	
1973-74	OLS	1.02610	0.08348	-0.24185	0.00579
	BAY	1.01690	0.07037	-0.19587	
1974-75	OLS	1.03300	-0.02234	-0.36032	0.01984
	BAY	1.02410	0.02451	-0.21869	
Posterior Means		0.99656	0.05861	-0.01057	0.01276
Estimates of Variances of Posterior Means		0.00005	0.00024	0.00271	
Modal Variances		0.00040	0.00184	0.02519	

TABLE 5

MARGINAL PHYSICAL PRODUCTIVITY OF INPUTS AT MEAN VALUES BY CROPS

Year/ Crop	RICE Irri- gated Area	RICE Ferti- lisers	GROUNDNUT Irri- gated Area	GROUNDNUT Unirri- gated Area	GROUNDNUT Ferti- lisers	TOBACCO Irri- gated Area	TOBACCO Unirri- gated Area	TOBACCO Ferti- lisers	SUGARCANE Irri- gated Area	SUGARCANE Ferti- lisers
1959-60	1.151	15.497	4.97	0.56	1.48	1.928	0.775	0.054	8.248	0.323
1960-61	1.257	12.982	3.12	0.62	1.42	1.605	0.628	0.181	8.649	0.594
1961-62	1.218	16.998	2.55	0.59	0.67	2.179	0.674	0.135	8.339	0.194
1962-63	1.109	9.185	1.42	0.71	0.92	1.991	0.633	0.113	8.853	0.098
1963-64	1.217	6.248	1.76	0.68	0.38	3.447	0.828	0.177	8.621	0.197
1964-65	1.309	5.333	1.09	0.80	0.52	2.416	0.917	0.177	8.389	0.237
1965-66	1.019	12.178	1.51	0.78	Negative	2.785	0.809	0.124	-	-
1966-67	0.723	13.552	1.23	0.31	0.45	4.657	0.864	0.256	7.566	0.118
1967-68	0.908	9.761	0.84	0.85	0.48	1.617	0.589	0.316	-	-
1968-69	1.186	0.669	0.73	0.77	0.29	2.663	0.901	0.023	7.475	0.136
1969-70	-	-	1.27	0.79	0.23	-	-	-	7.010	0.093
1970-71	1.256	2.396	1.107	0.92	0.28	3.459	0.614	0.049	7.412	0.125
1971-72	1.593	1.255	0.73	0.83	0.48	5.575	0.622	0.115	8.311	0.119
1972-73	1.296	4.227	1.66	0.66	0.19	8.007	0.374	0.183	7.184	0.164
1973-74	1.413	5.371	1.22	0.83	Negative	10.830	0.449	0.312	7.665	0.142
1974-75	-	-	1.04	0.68	0.07	8.822	0.807	0.063	7.635	0.035
Mean	1.182	6.965	0.69	0.71	0.52	3.768	0.764	0.175	7.924	0.160
Marginal Value Product	655.0	3860.0	781.2	803.7	588.6	14455.5	2931.0	671.3	981.4	18.0
Assumed Price of Crop (per ton) Average price of 65-69	554.20		1132.10			3836.40			112.50	

TABLE 6

BAY Posterior Mean, Its Variance, OLS Estimates from Aggregate Data

Crop	Elasticity with respect to	Irrigated Area		Unirrigated Area		Fertilizers		Rainfall	
		TS[1]	CS[2]	TS	CS	TS	CS	TS	CS
Sugarcane	BAY	0.9856	0.9965	-	-	-0.0498	0.0586	0.0081	-0.0106
	Variance	(0.0012)	(0.00005)	-	-	(0.00057)	(0.0002)	(0.00255)	(0.0027)
	OLS (Mean)	1.0055	0.9907	-	-	0.05345	0.0548	0.00132	0.0266
	OLS (Aggregated)	0.9320	0.9956	-	-	-0.0492	0.0661	-0.0486	-0.0235
Groundnuts	BAY	0.1248	0.0892	0.6636	0.7908	0.0741	0.0984	0.1554	0.0262
	Variance	(0.0014)	(0.0004)	(0.0176)	(0.0049)	(0.0039)	(0.0029)	(0.0135)	(0.0725)
	OLS (Mean)	0.1589	0.0899	0.6548	0.07867	0.0642	0.1133	0.1453	0.0810
	OLS (Aggregated)	0.3461	0.0818	0.6004	0.8957	-0.0132	0.0895	0.4954	0.5056
Tobacco	BAY	0.1185	0.1932	0.6326	0.6450	0.1749	0.3630	0.0976	-0.2821
	Variance	(0.0051)	(0.0011)	(0.0236)	(0.0066)	(0.0061)	(0.0148)	(0.0348)	(0.0617)
	OLS (Mean)	0.1272	0.1979	0.6563	0.7159	0.1930	0.2450	0.1954	-0.3474
	OLS (Aggregated)	0.0900	0.2351	0.1130	0.6746	0.3386	0.3158	0.0980	-0.6771
Rice	BAY	1.0159	0.8504	-	-	0.0654	0.1858	0.1653	0.0382
	Variance	(0.0040)	(0.0041)	-	-	(0.00056)	(0.0024)	(0.0097)	(0.0125)
	OLS (Mean)	1.1563	0.9490	-	-	0.0474	0.0829	0.1417	-0.0178
	OLS (Aggregated)	1.6121	0.8637	-	-	0.0186	0.1682	-0.2472	-0.2129

(1) Time Series
(2) Cross Section

TABLE 7
TIME SERIES PREDICTIONS FROM CROSS SECTION EQUATIONS

Mean Square Prediction Errors

Name of District	BAY 68-69 R^1	BAY 68-69 T^2	BAY 68-69 G^3	BAY 68-69 S^4	OLS 68-69 R^1	OLS 68-69 T^2	OLS 68-69 G^3	OLS 68-69 S^4
Srikakulam	0.264	4.59	0.091*	0.028	0.036	4.69	0.095*	0.047
Vishakhapatnam	0.664	0.146	0.319	-	0.0287	0.193	0.346	-
E. Godavari	0.084*	0.164	0.0129	0.036*	0.025*	0.125	0.0228	0.637*
W. Godavari	0.630*	6.44*	0.544	0.010*	0.051*	6.54*	0.622	0.007
Krishna	0.659*	0.081	0.114	0.031	0.064*	0.090	0.114	0.051
Guntur	0.491	0.176	0.0992	0.022	0.066	0.130	0.130	0.020
Nellore	0.935	0.083	0.6016	0.030	0.224	0.0768	0.0567	0.010
Kurnool	0.192	0.029*	4.165*	0.041	0.273	0.0419*	4.19*	0.029
Anantpur	0.262	0.275	-	0.013	0.125	0.337	-	0.007
Cudappa	0.531	-	0.2939	0.032	0.166	-	0.353	0.018
Chitoor	1.11	-	0.2418	0.034*	0.264	-	0.272*	0.036*
Hyderabad	0.99	3.96	0.1516	0.146	0.527	4.309	0.148	0.109
Nizamabad	0.798	1.82	0.3843	0.0922*	0.778	1.884	0.376	0.085*
Medak	2.56	0.976	0.5643	0.1576	2.98	1.114	0.669	0.123
Mehbobnagar	1.438	1.17	0.9426	0.0676	0.424	1.316	0.942	0.078
Nalgonda	0.393	1.86	0.5442	-	0.095	1.977	0.537	-
Warangal	2.71	0.54	0.6993	-	0.221	0.560	0.736	-
Khamman	0.126	0.156	0.3395	-	0.725	0.149	0.371	-
Karimnagar	2.44	0.423	0.0379	0.666	0.800	0.477	0.0396	0.612
Adilabad	-	0.538	0.3277	-	-	0.583	0.379	-

1.2.3.4. R = Rice, T = Tobacco, G = Groundnut, S = Sugarcane

* indicates that district is an important producer for this crop.

TABLE 7 CONTINUED

Name of District	BAY - PM				OLS - MACRO			
	R	T	G	S	R	T	G	S
Srikakulam	0.155	3.51	0.052*	0.039	0.075	3.18	0.191*	0.0553
Vishakhapatnam	0.129	0.242	0.45	-	0.182	0.32	0.268	-
E. Godavari	0.061*	0.389	0.014	0.035*	0.074*	0.62	0.0207	0.0398*
W. Godavari	0.082*	5.20*	0.348	0.007*	0.038*	4.91*	0.627	0.0095
Krishna	0.069*	0.126	0.048	0.039	0.229*	0.24	0.191	0.0636
Guntur	0.092	0.366	0.044	0.019	0.125	0.457	0.197	0.0220
Nellore	0.083	0.150	0.449	0.016	0.164	0.288	0.380	0.103
Kurnool	0.106	0.030	3.06*	0.030	0.092	0.103	3.96*	0.329
Anantpur	0.013	0.190*	-	0.007	0.022	0.265*	-	0.0110
Cudappa	0.167	-	0.230	0.020	0.146	-	0.516	0.0193
Chitoor	0.081	-	0.170*	0.028	0.062	-	0.439*	0.0472
Hyderabad	0.112	2.73	0.254	0.1132	0.339	2.27	0.119	0.110
Nizamabad	0.133	1.74	0.329	0.0848*	0.372	1.42	0.534	0.090*
Medak	1.411	0.62	0.418	0.1414	1.944	0.52	0.750	0.112
Mehbobnagar	0.140	0.86	1.05	0.060	0.291	0.84	1.53	0.095
Nalgonda	0.045	1.77	0.441	-	0.0231	2.10	0.266	-
Warangal	0.148	0.60	0.797	-	0.130	0.89	0.557	-
Khamman	0.299	0.349	0.323	-	0.625	0.64	0.427	-
Karimnagar	0.225	0.641	0.030	0.600	0.300	1.09	0.163	0.64
Adilabad	-	0.56	0.408	-	-	0.91	0.350	-

R = Rice T = Tobacco G = Groundnut S = Sugarcane

* indicates that district is an important producer of this crop.

TABLE 8

MEAN SQUARE PREDICTION ERRORS FOR BAY AND OLS ESTIMATES[1]

Year/ Crop	RICE			GROUNDNUT			TOBACCO			SUGARCANE		
	BAY[2]	OLS[3]	OLS_{68-69}	BAY[2]	OLS[3]	OLS_{68-69}	BAY[2]	OLS[3]	OLS_{68-69}	BAY[2]	OLS[3]	OLS_{68-69}
1969-70	-	-	-	0.1183	0.1187	0.1203	-	-	-	-	-	-
1970-71	0.0238	0.0256	0.0505	0.1471	0.1464	0.1143	0.3011	0.2991	0.2709	0.0214	0.0212	0.0153
1971-72	0.0768	0.0800	0.1094	0.1901	0.1902	0.1682	0.4557	0.4666	0.7682	0.0171	0.0169	0.0206
1972-73	0.1213	0.1210	0.2373	0.1943	0.1944	0.1901	2.1855	2.1904	3.6338	0.0149	0.0144	0.0168
1973-74	0.0311	0.0334	0.3683	0.3261	0.3264	0.4625	2.2117	2.2250	3.6836	0.0273	0.0270	0.0211
1974-75	-	-	-	0.2946	0.2948	0.4126	0.1258	0.1245	0.1026	-	-	-
Average Mean Square Error	0.0632	0.0649	0.1914	0.2117	0.2118	0.2446	1.0559	1.0590	1.6918	0.0202	0.0199	0.0185

1) Data for first 10 years are used to derive the estimators and estimated parameters are used for predicting the output for years 1969-70 to 1974-75.

2) BAY estimates are mean of modes based on 10 years' results.

3) OLS estimates are mean of OLS estimates based on 10 years' data.

DISCUSSION : P.N. JUNANKAR

This is an interesting exercise in Bayesian econometrics. The authors have done a competent and comprehensive job in estimating Cobb-Douglas production functions using cross-section/time-series data for Indian Agriculture. Their aim is to obtain "improved" estimates of production functions to aid "planning from above", to compare short and long-run elasticities and to study structural/technical change. My comments are structured as follows: I summarise their paper in Section 1; in Section 2, I comment on the underlying economic theory, on their data and measurement of variables, and on their econometric results. (I shall not comment on the *general* methodological comparison of Bayesian and Classical methods in Econometrics).[1]

Section 1

The authors use a standard Cobb-Douglas production function which they estimate using a time-series of a cross-section of data. Their econometric estimation is based on Lindley and Smith (1972) which uses a "hierarchical linear model". Their basic *a priori* assumption is that "the regression parameters for each cross-section are drawn from a *common* normal population." This is referred to as the "exchangeability assumption". Their production function has irrigated and unirrigated area, fertilisers and rainfall as inputs (the latter, clearly, is an exogenous variable). Their results are very mixed. Except for irrigated area and unirrigated area, the other parameter estimates are badly defined. They also find that short-run and long-run elasticities do not conform to their prior expectations, although prediction tests suggest that cross-section (long-run?) equations over-predict compared with time-series estimates. For rice production, under-prediction is explained by technical change. Their estimates of marginal physical products (MPPs) suggest that irrigated area has a much higher MPP than unirrigated area; the marginal value products of fertilisers are in excess of the input price. Overall, they argue their results justify the use of Bayesian estimation methods even though they are computationally more involved.

Section 2

(*a*) *Theory* The authors attempt to estimate a long-run *ex post* macro production function by using a time-series of a cross-section of data. Thus, given a *technological* production function and assuming certain behaviour on the part of the economic agents we *may* identify the production function or we may obtain some hybrid relation. Without worrying about problems of aggregation, it is clear that an estimated production function assumes that all the 'districts' face the *same* technological conditions and that differences in input combinations are due to *either* differences in input prices (assuming cost minimising/profit maximising behaviour) *or* due to some arbitrary distribution of technical efficiencies. (Differences in fixed endowments will also suffice.) Although the authors are aware of the problem of simultaneity (footnote, p. 11) they ignore the problem. Similarly, they mention the problem of a 'frontier' production function but proceed to ignore it. Would it be possible for the authors to estimate profit functions allowing (and testing) for differences in technological and economic efficiency? (See Yotopoulos & Lau (I973), Junankar (I980)).

(*b*) *Data* The authors are aware of the limitations of their data but feel the exercise is valid inspite of it. For anyone who has fitted production functions for Indian Agriculture the absence of human and bullock labour is surprising! They justify ignoring bullock labour by referring to some studies that found it non-significant using *Classical* statistics methods! Of course since the data do not exist for these variables they can do only one of two things: ignore the variables or not carry out the estimation. They believe that in a comparison of "relative magnitudes" (p. 6) it does not matter. This is a *non-sequitur*. For comparing short and long run elasticities omitted variables do matter if their relative importance is changing over time. Similarly, omitted variables would have differing importance for different crops. Even when comparing two estimation methods (especially in small samples) differences in the estimates may arise due to variations in the omitted factors. Their measure of fertilisers is admittedly crude: a simple aggregate of the *weights* of different chemical fertilisers (potassium, nitrogen, phosphorus) - again variations in the *mix* over time and over districts at different times would bias the results in some unknown way. Why did they not use price indices to weight those fertilisers? They raise the important question about the *timing* of fertiliser and rainfall although data limitations prevent them from doing anything about it.

(*c*) *Results* Since the "proof of the pudding is in the eating" let us see to what extent their Bayesian estimation provides valuable/better information. If we treat the estimates as that of a technological production function then it appears that in 1971/72 and 1972/73 there were increasing returns to scale for rice (ignoring the Rainfall variable which often has an incorrect sign). If there are increasing returns to scale, what behaviour is assumed for economic agents? (There are other crops which appear to have increasing returns).

The estimates of marginal productivities presented in Table 5 are interesting. The 'large' variation in the MPPs from year to year suggest some dramatic changes in input combination (if we are estimating a production function) or are they due to omitted factors? The estimates of marginal value products (MVPs) for the *same* input for different crops suggest non-maximising behaviour. The MVP for fertiliser used in rice production is over 200 times that in sugarcane production and over 5 times that in tobacco production (a cash crop). Although similar differences in MVP's exist for land, one could argue that land is not suitalbe for different crops. If the estimates are meant to reflect "behavioural relationships" it is difficult to explain such huge differences in MVPs for different crops.

The most interesting part of their paper is comparing short and long run estimates by looking at predictions within and outside the sample space. However, after several comparisons, the authors conclude "that the OLS-Mean and BAY-PM turn out to be rather close is interesting but cannot be expected to be a feature of all data sets." (p. 28). It seems to me that instead of comparing Bayesian estimates with OLS estimates the authors should have compared their results with a random coefficients model or at least with an OLS estimate using pooled data with a time trend/dummy.

Section 3

The authors have provided an interesting econometric exercise in estimating production functions. Given that their results are not uniformly better than OLS estimates, it seems they will not convince the majority of the practitioners in the field. To what extent their results are sensitive to the specified functional form or to the specification and measurement of variables, or due to heteroscedasticity, is difficult to gauge. To non-Bayesians like myself, I would prefer to see estimation subject to restrictions imposed by economic theory and statistical tests of hypotheses.

REFERENCES

Lindley, D.V. and Smith, A.F.M. (I972) "Bayes Estimates for the Linear Model" *Journal of the Royal Statistical Society, Series B*

Yotopoulos, P.A. & Lau, L.J. (I973) "A Test for Relative Economic Efficiency: Some Further Results", *Amerian Economic Review*, March

Junankar, P.N. (I980) "Tests of the Profit Maximisation Hypotheses: A Study of Indian Agriculture" *Journal of Development Studies*, January

FOOTNOTES

1. These comments are as they were presented at the A.U.T.E. conference in Durham 26*th*-28*th* March, I980

16. THIRD WORLD INDUSTRIALISATION AND THE STRUCTURE OF THE WORLD ECONOMY

Ajit Singh

I. Introduction[1]

Two long-term phenomena in the world economy have increasingly become the focus of public attention: industrialisation in the third world, and what has come to be called 'de-industrialisation' in the advanced countries. Although economists tend to be wary of relating the two, many policy-makers, government, business and trade union officials in the advanced countries and in their international organisations regard these long-run tendencies as organically connected.

The third world has made rapid industrial progress during the last two decades; nevertheless, its share of world industrial production only increased from a mere 6% or so in 1960 to 9% in 1977.[2] There is, however, a group of third world countries - the so-called newly industrialising countries (NICs)[3] - which have been particularly successful in creating their own industrial capacities and capabilities. These countries are now providing actual and potential competition for the older industrial nations, not just in labour-intensive products, but also in a range of capital-intensive industries like steel and shipbuilding. The crude steel output of the developing countries increased from 2% of world steel production in 1950 to approximately 11% in 1977. Further, at a time of severe recession in the industry and despite a warning from EEC Industries Commissioner Davignon,[4] the third world countries are planning to triple their steel production by 1985 (which would raise their share of world output to 15%).[5] As President Giscard d'Estaing explains: "There have always been low wages in the world. What is new is that these countries have access to the same technologies as we have".

Overall between 1970 and 1976, manufacturing exports from the third world to the developed market economy (mainly the OECD) countries grew in volume terms at a rate of 14% a year. This growth was more than twice as fast as that of imports of manufactures into the OECD countries from the rest of the world (including their intra-trade), and four times as fast as the growth of their manufacturing output. Consequently, during this period, the developing countries' share of the total manufactured imports of the OECD countries, although still small, increased by 50%, from 4.9 to 7.3%.[6] Over the long term, it is the declared intention of the third world nations to change the structure of the world economy so that it is no longer divided into countries which are mainly producers and exporters of food and raw materials and those which are mainly producers and exporters of manufactures. In pursuance of this goal, the third world countries adopted in 1975 the Lima declaration, according to which they aim to increase their share of world industrial output to 25% by the year 2000.[7]

In the advanced industrial countries, there has been increasing concern in recent years with the phenomenon known as 'de-industrialisation', which in its popular conception is associated with a long-run decline in industrial employment. In addition, apart from the effects of the post-1973 recession, because of demographic and social factors leading to an increase in the size of the labour force, many of these countries are currently experiencing large-scale unemployment, the highest since the second world war. Consequently, there has been growing pressure, particularly from trade unions, for protection directed against the third world and other competitor countries. In one form or another, protective measures are being increasingly imposed on third world manufactures.[8] As Commissioner Davignon comments in relation to steel: "If market forces were allowed free play, about one-third of Europe's steel industry would disappear." The Commission and the OECD have therefore set up a permanent steel committee with third world participation - essentially a cartel - to provide a non-market solution to the steel crisis. Similar measures are being taken, both in Western Europe and in the United States, in a host of other industries.

The main purpose of this paper is to explore the nature of the relationship between industrialisation in the third world and 'de-industrialisation' in the advanced countries. The order of discussion is as follows. The following two sections examine various aspects of third-world industrialisation: its necessity, its comparative structural characteristics, the Lima target and its implications. The question of 'de-industrialisation' in the advanced countries, and the conceptual issues it raises, are considered in section IV. In the light of that discussion, the relationship between third world industrialisation and de-industrialisation is examined in section V. Finally, section VI briefly discusses policy options for third world industrial development, in the current context of a possible slow-down in the long-term growth of advanced countries.

II. The necessity of third world industrialisation

There are good economic reasons why the third world countries should regard rapid industrialisation as being essential for raising the standards of living of their people and for changing the current unequal structure of the world economy.[9] A wide range of historical and cross-section studies indicate that manufacturing industry plays a leading role in economic development in the specific sense that a 1% increase in gross domestic product is normally associated with a more than 1% increase in value added in manufacturing. (See, for example, Chenery (1960), Kaldor (1967), Chenery and Taylor (1968), Paige (1961), Kuznets (1971), Cripps and Tarling (1973), Chenery and Syrquin (1975), UNCTAD (1978b).) Further, there is evidence that the growth elasticity of manufacturing is greater the lower a country's per capita income. Table 1 reports the results of a recent comprehensive UNIDO (1979a) study based on data from nearly 100 developing and developed countries over the period 1960-75. The table gives pooled cross-section and time-series estimates of the growth elasticities of manufacturing for various groups of countries, distinguished by their size and certain other characteristics.[10] These estimates suggest that at the average levels of per capita incomes in the third world countries, the value of this elasticity is about 1.5.[11]

There is a systematic body of economic reasoning which not only explains why manufacturing industry should expand at a faster rate than the economy as a whole during the course of economic development, but would also assign strategic causal significance to manufacturing in raising the overall rate of growth of productivity in the economy. Very briefly,[12] first, at the simplest level, as the income elasticity of demand for manufacturing is considerably

Table 1: Estimates[a] of the elasticities of manufacturing value added with respect to GDP for 98 countries in six groups (based on pooled time-series for 1960 - 1975)

Country[b] sample	Manufacturing elasticity			Per capita GDP (1970 US dollars)		
	Maximum	Minimum	Mean	Minimum	Maximum	Mean
L_h	1.59	0.99	1.23	467	5349	1990
L_1	2.13	1.47	1.81	58	670	192
SI	1.85	1.31	1.59	42	1326	221
S2P	1.42	1.02	1.16	102	3460	952
S2I	1.66	1.14	1.35	159	4517	1142
CP	1.62	1.08	1.30	227	2099	841

a The estimates are based on the following regression equation

$$ln\ v_{it} = \alpha_i + \beta_1\ ln\ y_{it} + \beta_2\ (ln\ y_{it})^2 + U_{it}$$

where v is per capita manufacturing value added

y is per capita GDP

i is country subscript

t refers to the year

U represents the disturbance term.

b L_h: large high income countries; L_1: large low income; SI: small low income; S2P: small with primary orientation; S2I: small with industrial orientation; CP: centrally planned economies.

For further details see Note 10.

Source: UNIDO (1979a).

greater than that for food and for agricultural products, manufacturing can be expected to grow relatively faster. Secondly, following the classic work of Allyn Young (1928) (and of course before that, of Adam Smith and other classical economists), the economists with a structural approach to economic growth argue that manufacturing is subject to increasing returns, both in the static and, more importantly, in the dynamic sense of Kaldor. Because of these favourable demand elasticities and the dynamic economies of scale, manufacturing industry not only grows more quickly than other sectors, but its growth is normally associated with increased employment. In agriculture, on the other hand, where there is usually considerable disguised unemployment, expansion of productivity and output is usually connected with a reduction in the labour force employed. The expansion of manufacturing industry thus helps raise the rate of growth of productivity in agriculture in two ways: (a) by absorbing redundant labour, and (b) by providing modern industrial inputs, which incidentally raise both land and labour productivity. Thirdly, it is argued that the expansion of manufacturing industry also increases the pace of technical change and helps raise productivity growth in sectors other than agriculture.[13]

In recent years, there has been a growing debate in the third world countries and in the international development agencies (the World Bank, ILO, etc.) on the so-called 'basic needs' approach to development. The third world nations have been strongly urged to modify their development policies and goals in such a way so as to meet as quickly as possible the basic needs - food, shelter, clothing - of their poorest people. The ILO (1976), which first put forward the concept of basic needs, has estimated that if these minimal needs of the poorest 20% of the third world population are to be satisfied by the end of the century, national incomes in the third world countries should on average grow at a rate of 7 to 8% per annum. This calculation allows for the feasible redistributions of incomes within these countries. If such a goal for the required rate of economic growth to remove absolute poverty were accepted, it would entail, in terms of the elasticity estimates in Table 1, an expansion of manufacturing industry in the third world of over 10% per annum.[14] By past standards, the latter figure implies very fast industrialisation of these economies. (See further section III.)

The structural approach to the process of economic growth not only stresses the key role of manufacturing but it also suggests that within manufacturing, capital goods industries need to grow at a faster rate than consumer goods industries. Again, both historical and cross-section studies of industrial development confirm that the growth elasticity of producer goods industries is usually considerably greater than that of consumer goods industries: i.e. an x% increase in GDP is associated with kx%, and k′x%, increases in the production of capital goods and consumer good respectively where k is greater than k′; the value of k normally tends to be well above 1.5.

Table 2 reports cross-section estimates of the elasticities for various branches of manufacturing industry, based separately on data from two groups of 'large' (population greater than 20 million) and small countries respectively. As in the case of Table 1, both developed and developing economies are included in the two samples; the underlying regression equations are based on statistics for the year 1970.

The table shows that in general growth elasticities have a much greater value than the size elasticities. For large countries, the latter are in fact usually negative; for small countries, they are more often positive, but still relatively quite small.[15] However, for both large and small economies the growth elasticity for consumer products - food, drink, tobacco - is usually around 1, whilst for machinery, transport equipment, iron and steel, it is substantially higher.[16] The reasons for this phenomenon again lie partly in demand conditions and partly in production conditions, but, more importantly, in the inter-action of the two. It is argued that in capital goods industries, such as engineering and machinery equipment, there is greater scope for dynamic economies and technological change. Further, as Kaldor (1967) has observed: "The expansion of capacity in the investment goods sector feeds upon itself, by increasing the growth rate of demand for its own output, thereby providing both the incentives and the means for its own further expansion. The establishment of an investment goods sector thus provides for a built-in element of acceleration in the rate of growth of demand for manufactured goods" (p. 30).

Table 2: Growth and size elasticities in selected individual manufacturing industries for two country groups[a]

Industry	Large countries		Small countries with modest resources	
	Growth	Size	Growth	Size
Food Products	1.07	-0.11	0.54	-0.45
Beverages	1.15	-0.62	0.53	-0.25
Tobacco	0.65	-0.12	1.38	0.29
Textiles	1.02	-0.04	0.99	0.63
Clothing	1.55	-0.59	1.05	-0.20
Leather & fur products	1.15	-0.28	0.96	0.43
Footwear	1.14	-0.57	0.70	-0.29
Industrial Chemicals	1.67	0.18	1.44	-0.01
Iron and Steel	1.81	0.27	2.09	-0.04
Non-ferrous metals	1.44	0.09	1.23	-0.07
Metal products excl. machinery	1.48	-0.15	1.36	0.20
Non-electrical machinery	2.05	0.40	1.98	0.44
Electrical machinery	1.77	0.11	2.28	0.10
Transport equipment	1.86	0.25	1.60	-0.52
Prof. & scientif. equipm., photogr. & optic. goods	2.10	0.40	1.50	0.26

a Elasticity estimates are based on the following cross-section equation:

$$\ell n\ (v/N) = \beta_0 + \beta_1 \quad \ell n\ Y + \beta_2 \quad \ell n\ N$$

where v is value added (in millions of 1970 US dollars),

Y is per capita GDP and

N is population (in millions). Data for 1970 for 25 large and 34 small countries were used in the analysis.

Source: UNIDO (1979a).

III. *The development of industry in the third world: past achievement and future target*

Table 3 provides a broad overview of the comparative structural characteristics of industrial development in the third world during the last two decades. Over the period 1960-75, manufacturing[17] production in the third world countries grew at an appreciably faster rate than in the developed market economies (mainly OECD countries), and also somewhat faster than the world average. Consequently, the third world's share in world manufacturing production increased from 6.9% in 1960 to 8.6% in 1975. However, the figures for the whole period 1960-75 conceal the fact that there was a trend increase in industrial growth in the developing countries in the second half of that period, and a trend decline in developed market economies over the same sub-period. Up to 1968, manufacturing output was growing at much the same rate in the two groups of countries; the third world's share in world industrial production remained exactly the same in 1968 as it was in 1960. However, since 1968, the third world's industrial growth has been twice as fast as that in the western countries. The post-1973 world recession seems to have had little effect on overall industrial growth in the developing countries. Provisional figures indicate that by 1977 the third world's share in world industrial production had improved further, to 9%. Table 3 also shows that the East European centrally planned economies have throughout grown appreciably faster than either the third world or the developed market economy countries; their share in world industrial production increased from about 18% in 1960 to approximately 28% in 1975.[18]

An important consequence of industrial development in the third world countries during the past two decades has been a significant change in the structure of their economies. The share of manufacturing industry in their GDP has increased from an average of about 15% in 1960 to about 19% in 1975. Further, disaggregated data for the individual industrial branches shows that industrial development in the third world has been widely based. The third world's share has increased in most industrial groups.[19] Over the period 1960 to 1976, the developing countries increased their share of world output of heavy industry from 4.9% to 6.2%, and of light industries from 11.8 to 12.4%. Because of the relatively faster development

Table 3: The growth[a] of manufacturing output (volume), employment and productivity in developing, developed market economy and centrally planned economy countries, 1960-75, 1968-75 (% p.a.)

	1960 - 1975			1968 - 1975		
	Output	Employment	Productivity	Output	Employment	Productivity
Developing countries	7.4	4.9	2.4	9.1	7.0	2.0
Developed market economies	5.7	0.9	4.8	4.1	0.4	3.7
Centrally planned economies	10.0	3.4	6.4	10.7	2.6	7.9
World average[b]	7.1	2.8	4.2	6.5	2.9	3.5

a Based on regression on time

b Based on statistics from 85 developing countries and 35 developed countries (28 developed market economies and 7 centrally-planned economies). China, North Korea, Vietnam, Albania and Mongolia are not included.

Source: UNIDO (1979a).

of heavy industry, by 1976 it accounted for just over half of the total manufacturing production of the developing countries, compared with 37% in 1960.[20]

Turning to employment in industry, there are two points which deserve notice. Firstly, contrary to the common assertion that industry does not create employment, industrial employment in the developing countries has increased at a rate of approximately 5% per annum during the period 1960-75.[21] This is considerably greater than the rate of growth of population in these countries, although it is somewhat lower than the rate of urbanisation. Secondly, Table 3 indicates that in the developed market economies, unlike the developing countries, there has been a trend decline in the growth of industrial employment since the middle 1960s. More importantly, in the latter group of countries, there is evidence of a marked change in the previously observed relationship between growth of output and employment. Whereas up to the mid-1960s the elasticity of manufacturing employment with respect to manufacturing output was approximately 0.5, since then the value of this elasticity has fallen substantially. (See further Kaldor (1975), Singh (1977a); see also section IV.) However, in the developing countries, there does not appear to be any such structural break in the relationships between these variables. A 1% increase in industrial output continues to be associated on average with an 0.7 to 0.8% growth in industrial employment in these economies.

Due to the greater value of the employment elasticity in the developing countries than in the developed market economies, the latter have recorded a higher rate of growth of productivity, despite their lower rate of expansion of manufacturing production. (See Table 3.) This must inevitably further widen the gap in the levels of industrial productivity between the two groups of countries. Nevertheless, since the third world countries suffer from widespread under-utilisation of labour, and there is a relatively larger gap between the levels of productivity in manufacturing and other sectors in these economies, industrial development would have helped to reduce the differences in GDP per capita between the developing and the developed countries.

Although over the last two decades the third world

countries have on the whole a reasonable record of achievement in the expansion of industrial output and employment, this will not be at all adequate if they are to reach their declared aim - the Lima target of 25% of world manufacturing production by the year 2000. The United Nations Industrial Development Organisation (UNIDO) have recently carried out an elaborate statistical exercise to analyse the implications of the Lima target. The results are summarised in Table 4. These suggest that if the developed (both the market and the centrally planned economies) and the developing countries continued to grow at their 'historic' rate (i.e. those implied by the actual growth rates over the period 1960-75 - see notes to Table 4), the third world's share of world manufacturing output in the year 2000 would be only 13.9% - slightly more than half the Lima target.[22] However, if the economies of developed countries were to grow on average at a rate one percentage point below their historic rates, i.e. at 4.6%, and the developing countries were similarly to grow about two percentage points faster over the next two decades (the 'high growth' assumption in Table 4), the latter's share of world industrial output would approximate that implied by the Lima target.

There are three observations which are pertinent to the above analysis. First, neither of the two assumptions made in the 'high growth' scenario are necessarily unrealistic. There are a number of forces which could easily cause a reduction of one percentage point or more in the future trend growth rates of advanced countries. (See further sections IV and VI.) As Table 3 showed, such a decline in the growth of manufacturing production in the advanced countries did occur during 1968-1975; there was also similarly a trend increase in industrial growth in the third world countries over this period. In fact, if the trends observed during the second subperiod, 1968-75, rather than the whole period, 1960-75, were to continue in the future, the third world countries would easily meet the Lima target before the year 2000.

Secondly, whatever the merits of the Lima target as a suitable goal for the third world countries to set themselves, manufacturing in these countries needs to grow at the rate suggested by the 'high growth' scenario in Table 4 (at about 10% per annum) for quite another reason. The analysis in section II, based on rather different premises, indicated that such a rate of industrial growth was required if the

Table 4: Growth rates of GDP and manufacturing value added for the developed and developing countries: actual (1960-75) and projected (1975-2000) on two different assumptions

	Actual 1960 - 1975		Projected, 1975 - 2000: Historical[a]		Projected, 1975 - 2000: High Growth[b]	
Economic grouping	GDP	MVA	GDP	MVA[c]	GDP	MVA[c]
Developed countries	4.9	6.0	5.6	5.7	4.6	4.9
Developing countries	5.7	7.4	6.8	8.0	8.2	10.1

a It is assumed that GDP grows at historical rates. This assumption implies that the resultant averages for 1975-2000 will exceed the corresponding figures for 1960-1975, since countries with high historical rates of growth (e.g. Japan and the centrally planned economies) become more important in the calculation of the average for each economic grouping.

b It is assumed that in developed countries, GDP grows at 1% below the historical average for each country; for developing countries, it is assumed to grow at 2% above the historical average for all countries except those with exceptional growth, which are assumed to grow at the same rates as their historical averages.

c Manufacturing value added. Derived from equations based on assumptions about growth in GDP.

Source: UNIDO (1979a)

Note: All figures are based on 1970 prices and are averages for each economic grouping.

third world countries were to eradicate absolute poverty and to meet the basic minimal needs of their poorest people by the year 2000. If economic expansion in the advanced economies were to slow down substantially in the next decade or so, the third world would obviously be able to meet the Lima target at a much lower rate of industrial growth than 10%. However, in such circumstances, although the Lima target would be achieved, the minimal basic needs of the people in the third world would not be met even over the next generation.

Thirdly, the figures in Table 4, coupled with the estimates of the relative rates of increase in the population in the developing and the developed countries, suggest that, even if the Lima target were to be met by the year 2000, per capita value added in manufacturing in the third world countries would be less than 15% of that in the developed countries. However, by then, the structure of the third world economies would have altered fundamentally; manufacturing's share in GDP in these countries would be similar to that in the rich countries.

Finally, it should be noted that the above discussion has been at an aggregate level for the third world as a whole. There are of course very great differences in performance and industrial potential between these countries. However, the purpose of the analysis is not to predict or to suggest industrial growth paths for particular countries, but to draw attention to certain long-term trends in the world economy and to examine their implications. It is useful to the extent that it gives a broad picture of the kind of adjustments which may be required.

IV. *De-industrialisation in advanced countries: conceptual issues*

In the popular conception, 'de-industrialisation' is associated with a long-term decline in industrial employment and increasing overall unemployment in the economy. It will, therefore, be useful to examine the long-term movements of manufacturing employment and output, as well as unemployment, in industrial economies. Table 5 shows that, considered in terms of the share of manufacturing employment in total employment, several of these countries could be regarded as 'de-industrialising' since the middle 1960s. Between 1960

Table 5: The proportion of manufacturing employment in total employment in advanced industrial countries [a] 1950 - 1975 (%)

	UK	Japan	Italy	Belgium	France	Germany	Netherlands	Sweden	USA [b]
1950	34.7	-	-	32.7	-	-	30.2	-	34.4
1955	35.9	18.3	22.8	33.1	26.8	-	30.2	-	35.3
1960	35.8	21.3	26.6	33.5	27.9	34.7	28.6	32.1 [c]	33.6
1965	35.0	24.3	28.9	33.9	28.3	36.3	28.2	32.4	32.8
1970	34.7	27.0	31.7	32.7	27.8	37.4	26.2	27.6	32.3
1971	34.0	27.0	32.0	32.3	28.0	37.0	25.7	27.3	31.9
1972	32.9	27.0	32.1	31.9	28.0	36.6	25.1	27.1	31.2
1973	32.3	27.4	32.2	31.8	27.9	36.1	24.1	27.5	31.6
1974	32.3	27.2	32.6	31.5	28.1	36.6	24.5	28.3	31.0
1975	30.9	25.8	32.6	30.1	27.9	35.9	24.0	28.0	29.0

a The series presented is an estimated reference series which makes allowance for discontinuities in official labour statistics, due to changes in industrial classification, methods of collection, etc. In some cases, particularly the UK, there are substantial differences between this series and the published inconsistent one.

b Industrial employment.

c For 1961; 1960 not available.

Source: Brown and Sheriff (1979); based on OECD *Manpower Statistics* and *Labour Force Statistics*

and 1975, the proportion of the labour force employed in industry fell appreciably in the UK, the Netherlands, Belgium, Sweden and the US. The trend decline in manufacturing employment appears to have accelerated towards the late 1960s in most of these economies. For example, in the UK in 1976, there were 1.1 million fewer workers employed in manufacturing than in the comparable year 1969; during the seven-year period, the proportion of the UK labour force employed in manufacturing fell from 34.7. to 30.1%.[23]

However, Table 6, which shows the share of manufacturing output (measured at constant prices) in total output, indicates a rather different pattern. There does not appear to be any long-term decline in the output share (similar to that observed for employment) in any of the countries, including the UK. In the UK (as well as in some of the other countries), the share did fall in the recession years 1974 and 1975, but at the cyclical peak in 1973 it was similar to that at the earlier peaks. If manufacturing output is measured at current prices, there is, indeed, a trend decline in manufacturing's share in virtually every industrial country.[24] This is not surprising; as productivity rises faster in manufacturing than in other sectors (particularly services), prices of manufactured goods would be expected to increase relatively more slowly.

To the extent that manufacturing plays a causal role in economic growth, as suggested in section II, it could be argued that the statistics of manufacturing's share in the economy (in Tables 5 and 6) cannot accurately portray the relative decline of manufacturing industry. A lower rate of growth of manufacturing output or employment may by itself lead to lower overall economic growth, without significantly altering the ratio between manufacturing and total output. It is, therefore, more appropriate to consider 'de-industrialisation' in terms of any long-term changes in the rates of growth of output and employment in manufacturing, rather than in terms of these ratios. Such evidence has been examined in Singh (1977a); however, it reveals even more starkly a pattern similar to that outlined above. There was not only a trend decline in the rate of growth of the manufacturing labour force in every country after about the middle 1960s, but some registered an actual fall in manufacturing employment for the first time since early 1950s. These tendencies became more pronounced in the late

Table 6: Manufacturing output as a proportion of GDP at 1963 prices, in advanced countries,[a] 1950-75 (%)

	1950	1955	1960	1965	1970	1973	1974	1975
UK	29.3	30.6	31.0	31.1	31.7	31.5	30.6	29.1
Canada	25.1	24.7	24.2	27.1	26.4	27.1	26.8	25.5
Japan	n/a	22.2	31.7[e]	34.7[e]	41.9	41.8	40.9	35.5
France	32.6	33.3	35.0	36.2	38.0	39.6	39.4	36.0
W. Germany	31.0[b]	37.2	39.9	42.6	44.5	44.6	44.5	43.2
Italy	17.9[c]	22.6	25.5	27.6	31.2	32.0	n/a	n/a
Belgium	n/a	n/a	26.0	27.3	30.3	31.7	31.5	30.0
Netherlands[d]	32.7	33.8	36.6	38.4	41.7	42.3	42.1	41.0
Sweden	25.2	25.6	27.7	29.8	31.9	32.5	32.6	33.8
USA	28.2	28.9	27.4	29.3	27.9	29.2	28.1	26.0

a GDP at market prices, except for Italy and Canada, where at factor cost.

b Excludes the Saar and West Berlin, also mining and quarrying.

c For 1951.

d Manufacturing here refers to manufacturing plus construction, mining and quarrying and gas, electricity and water. In 1970 manufacturing output comprised 74.7% of all four categories. From 1970 the production value of crude petroleum and natural gas is included in manufacturing output.

e This figure is not consistent with the series for 1970-75.

Source: Brown and Sheriff (1979); based on OECD, *National Accounts of OECD Countries* and *Industrial Production: Historical Statistics* (for France and Japan).

1960s and early 1970s, even before the slow-down in the growth of the world economy following the oil price rise of 1973. However, as far as the growth of manufacturing output (in constant prices) is concerned, there is little evidence of a trend decline in any of the countries until the 1973 peak.

As was mentioned in section II, there is thus evidence of a structural change in the relationship between growth rates of output and employment in the industrial countries since the mid-1960s. One plausible explanation is that this was due to the liberalisation of world trade and increased international competition, as well as the worldwide merger movement.[25] These factors led to rationalisation within the manufacturing sector in each country, resulting in increases in output and productivity, despite the absolute or relative decrease in employment. On this argument, this would have been a once-for-all effect, if the post-1973 world recession had not been super-imposed on it. Table 7 shows that the overall rates of unemployment in the industrial countries have been historically high since 1970. However, this can be only partly due to the observed structural changes in the relationship between growth of output, employment and productivity. Quite apart from the post-1973 slow-down in economic growth, increases in the labour force arising from demographic and social factors (the coming of age of the generation of the 'baby boom' and the rise in participation rates of married women) are also in part responsible for these high rates.

I have argued elsewhere (Singh, 1977a), that, for an open industrial economy, the popular notions of de-industrialisation described above are analytically unsatisfactory. This is for the simple reason that a decline in the proportion of manufacturing employment, or even output, or a deceleration in their rate of growth, may reflect no more than a normal adjustment of the economy to changing domestic and world market conditions, leading to the expansion of some sectors and contraction of others. I have, therefore, suggested that the question whether de-industrialisation in this sense implies any structural maladjustment of the economy can only properly be considered in terms of the interactions of the economy with the rest of the world, i.e. in terms of its overall trading and payments position in the world economy. The structural characteristics of the domestic economy alone are not adequate for such an

Table 7: Unemployment rates in selected industrial market economy countries, 1960-1976[a]

Country	1960-67	1968-70	1971-76	1971	1972	1973	1974	1975	1976
United States	4.9	3.9	6.2	5.7	5.4	4.7	5.4	5.8	7.7
Canada	5.1	5.1	6.3	6.3	6.3	5.6	5.4	7.1	7.2
Japan	1.3	1.1	1.5	1.2	1.4	1.3	1.4	1.9	2.0
Germany (Fed. Rep. of)	0.8	0.8	2.4	0.7	0.9	1.0	2.2	4.8	4.7
France	1.3	2.0	3.2	2.6	2.7	2.6	2.8	4.0	4.2
Italy	3.3	3.3	3.3	3.1	3.6	3.4	2.9	3.3	3.7
United Kingdom	1.5	2.1	3.3	2.9	3.2	2.3	2.1	3.9	5.4
Netherlands	1.0	1.5	3.2	1.4	2.4	2.4	3.0	4.7	5.1
Belgium	2.1	2.6[b]	3.1	1.7	2.2	2.2	2.4	4.5	5.8
Denmark	1.4[c]	0.9[d]	3.1	1.1	0.9	0.9	3.5	6.0	6.1
Norway	1.0	1.0	1.4	- /	1.0	0.8	0.7	1.3	1.3
Sweden	1.6[e]	1.9	2.2	2.5	2.7	2.5	2.0	1.6	1.6
Australia	1.5[f]	1.5	3.0[g]	1.6 /	2.2	1.9	2.2	4.4	4.4

a National definitions.
b Average rate for 1968 and 1969.
c Average rate for 1960, 1965 and 1967.
d Average rate for 1969 and 1970.
e Average rate for 1962-1967.
f Average rate for 1964-1967.
g Average rate for 1972-1976.

/ denotes a discontinuity in the series

Source: Mukherjee (1978), based on OECD: *Labour Force Statistics*; OECD *Economic Outlook*.

assessment.

In the specific case of the UK economy, whose historical evolution has been such that it is a net importer of food and raw materials, which have largely to be paid for by exports of manufactures, I have proposed the following definition of the optimum size and structure of manufacturing industry. Given the normal levels of the other components of the balance of payments, an efficient manufacturing sector is one which not only satisfies consumer demand at least resource cost, but also yields sufficient net exports (currently as well as potentially) to pay for the country's import requirements at socially acceptable levels of output, employment and the exchange rate.[26] The latter restrictions are important, since at low enough levels of output and employment, or more arguably at a sufficiently low exchange rate, almost any manufacturing sector may be able to meet this criterion of efficiency. (The exchange rate should be regarded here as an indicator of the acceptable levels of inflation and inequality of income distribution.) It is also necessary to emphasise the significance of the qualification that, to be efficient, the manufacturing sector must be able to fulfil the above requirements not merely currently, but also in the long run. For instance, a windfall gain to the balance of payments (e.g. from North Sea oil) may put it temporarily into surplus (at desired levels of output, employment, etc.), although manufacturing industry may be incapable of ensuring this when 'normal' conditions return.[27]

Considered in these terms, there is a large body of empirical evidence which suggests that UK manufacturing industry is characterised by long-term structural disequilibrium, which is becoming more acute over time. (See Singh, 1977a, b; Blackaby, 1979.) Industry is losing ground in both home and foreign markets and is increasingly unable to achieve a current account balance at full employment, despite cost and price competitiveness (achieved by currency depreciation).[28] It is because of this long-term disequilibrium that de-industrialisation (in the popular sense of a fall in manufacturing employment) is a matter of grave concern for the UK economy.

It is important to observe that in terms of the above conception not all industrial countries are likely to be in the same situation as the UK. Table 8 examines the

Table 8: Export performance, export-price competitiveness and efficiency wages: UK and other advanced countries - 1964-77

	U.S.	Japan	Germany	France	Italy	UK
Share in world exports of Manufactures (%)						
1964	21.5	8.1	19.3	8.7	6.3	14.4
1970	18.5	11.7	19.8	8.7	7.2	10.8
1974	17.2	14.5	21.7	9.3	6.7	8.8
1977	15.9	15.4	20.8	9.9	7.4	9.3
Export unit values of Manufactures ($US) (annual % change)						
1964-74	5.4	7.5	7.2	5.9	5.1	5.6
1970-74	8.2	16.0	14.5	12.8	11.4	11.2
1970-77	11.0	14.5	16.3	15.7	15.3	14.2
Wage costs per unit of output ($US) (annual % change)						
1964-74	2.1	8.6	8.3	4.2	7.0	5.2
1970-74	3.1	19.1	14.4	11.6	11.2	9.7
1970-77	8.0	23.7	19.3	15.6	14.7	13.7

Source: Ray (1976); Brown and Sheriff (1979), and OECD (1978).

relative export performance of the leading economies during the period 1964-1977. It shows that some countries, notably Japan, have been improving their share of world exports; others like France have been more or less holding their own. However, the US like the UK has been losing its share of world markets in manufacturing, despite the lowest relative increases in wage costs and export prices. There is some empirical evidence that the US industrial economy could now well be in a position of long-term disequilibrium of the kind which has been characteristic of the UK economy (see CEPG (1979 and section V below).[29]

The foregoing discussion of the concept of 'de-industrialisation' for an open industrial economy also provides a useful framework within which to analyse the general question of the relationship between 'de-industrialisation' in the advanced countries and the industrialisation of the third world. Two central issues are raised. First, to what extent if any is a particular industrial country or a group of these countries in long-run disequilibrium in the sense that their economies are prevented by their balance of payments situation from achieving (say) full employment? Secondly, if they are so constrained, to what extent could this be ascribed to competition from third world manufactures? It should, however, be observed that in principle, even if industrialisation of the third world does not impose a balance-of-payments constraint on the rich countries, it could harm their economic development in another way. It could lead to a change in the structure of these economies, say towards services - a specialisation which may be unfavourable from the point of view of the future growth of productivity. This argument is of course similar to that used in the past by the developing countries themselves - that trade with the rich countries had pushed them into 'unfavourable' patterns of production, for which the terms of trade moved against them in the long run, and for which growth potential was low.

V. *Third world industrialisation and de-industrialisation in advanced countries*

Tables 9 and 10 summarise some of the main features of third world exports of manufactures to the advanced countries. Firstly, Table 9 (p.178) indicates that, although still very small, the third world's share in all developed country markets has increased appreciably, particularly during the last ten years. Statistics on the relative growth rates (not shown in Table 9) suggest that, in the developed market economies as a whole, imports of manufactures from the third world increased at much the same rate in the 1960s as the former's imports from the rest of the world (chiefly, their intra-trade). However, since 1970 third world imports have been increasing at more than twice the rate of the latter[30] (UNCTAD, 1978a).

Secondly, Table 10 indicates that the expansion in third world manufactured exports has been fairly widely based; it has not been confined to traditional products, such as food, textiles, leather and footwear, and furniture.[31] There was, for example, an impressive increase in the exports of engineering and metal products. Between 1970 and 1976, the developing countries' share of total imports of the developed market economies for this category of products increased by more than two and a half times; by 1976 it had become the second largest dollar earner among the third world's non-petroleum manufactured exports.[32] There was similarly fast growth in the third world's share of the developed economies' imports of iron and steel.

Finally, it is important to note that the third world exports of manufactures are highly concentrated in a small group of countries. In 1976, the 12 leading exporters of manufactures (excluding petroleum products and unwrought non-ferrous metals) accounted for 83% of total developing countries' exports to the developed market economies. (See UNCTAD (1978a); see also Note 3, p.191.)

Table 9: Developing market economies' share of manufactured exports in major markets - 1961-1978 (%)

	1961	1965	1969	1973	1978
EEC 9 market	4	5	6	5	7
US market	11	12	12	16	17
Japan and other developed market economies	4	4	4	6	7
OPEC market	3	5	7	8	7
Other developing market economies	4	5	8	10	11

CEPG (1979) For definitions of the country groups and products, see CEPG (1979), Appendix A.

Table 10: Imports by product group of manufactures by 21 developed market-economy countries from developing countries and territories (DC) and from the world, 1970-1976

Product group	Imports from DC (million dollars)	Annual average percentage change 1970-76		DC percentage share	
	1976	DC	World	1970	1976
Food Products	2140	18	16	16.6	18.3
Drink and Tobacco products	226	1	15	10.2	4.8
Wood products and furniture	1999	22	19	12.5	14.2
Rubber products	127	29	20	1.5	2.3
Leather and footwear	1581	31	21	13.3	22.1
Textiles	3091	21	16	11.6	14.8
Clothing	6431	34	24	22.9	37.2
Chemicals	1303	19	20	3.2	3.0
Pulp, paper and board	230	32	17	0.7	1.5
Non-metallic mineral products	205	22	17	2.3	2.9
Iron and steel	989	22	14	2.8	4.3
Worked non-ferrous metals	398	16	13	5.4	6.3
Road motor vehicles	251	48	21	0.2	0.5
Other engineering and metal products	5764	39	18	1.7	4.6
Miscellaneous light manufactures	2409	20	19	10.4	11.1
Total	27145	26	18	4.9	7.3

Source: Adapted from UNCTAD (1978a).

Note: For descriptions of the countries and products see UNCTAD (1978a), Annex. The countries included under DC above are different from the list of developing countries in Tables 1 - 4.

As for the impact of third world exports on output and employment in the industrial countries, there is a large body of empirical studies on these issues, dating back to the early 1960s. This research has recently been reviewed in UNIDO (1979c). These studies have normally been carried out at a fairly high level of product disaggregation. It will be useful to examine briefly the methodology and the conclusions of the most important of the recent studies (e.g. Frank (1977) for the US, Cable (1978) and Foreign and Commonwealth Office (1979) for the UK). The following model is used for analysing the effects of trade on industrial employment in all three studies

$$dE = \frac{1}{P_t}\,(dD + dX - dM - E_{t+1}\,dP) \quad (1)$$

[33]

where E = Employment
D = Home demand (volume)
X = Exports (volume)
M = Imports (volume)
P = Productivity per worker year
t, $t+1$ are the time periods being considered and
d indicates the change between t and $t+1$.

In other words, given the level of productivity, the model ascribes changes in employment between any two periods to the growth of home demand, to the growth of exports and of imports; the last term indicates the effect of changes in productivity. It is thus a comparative static model, in which the variables on the right-hand side act independently and their effects on employment are additive.

For both the UK and the US, the application of the model yields two kinds of conclusions.[34] First, relative to the growth of productivity and changes in home demand, trade (with both the developed and the developing countries) has a small effect on reducing manufacturing employment. Secondly, the effect of trade with the less developed countries on aggregate unemployment in the two economies has been (absolutely) negligible. For example, the Foreign and Commonwealth Office (1979) estimated that between 1970 and 1977, increased imports of manufactures (SITC categories 5 - 8) into the UK from 23 newly industrialising countries is 'unlikely to have displaced more than 2 per cent of the 1970 labour force of the industries concerned'. However, over the same period, the increase in UK manufactured exports to the less developed countries is thought to have led to an increase in employment of a similar order of magnitude. Thus it is concluded: 'Any net displacement [of labour, due to trade with the less developed countries] appears to have been quite small' (p.25).

In general for the developed countries, empirical studies indicate that, taking into account both the negative effects of increased third world imports and the positive effects of the resulting increased exports (arising from the high import propensity of the developing countries), the net impact on employment is slightly negative. This is because imports tend to replace labour in the labour-intensive industries, and exports generally accrue to the more capital-intensive industries (e.g. machinery) whose products are imported by the developing nations. However, although the overall employment effects are regarded as being very small, it is recognised that they would nevertheless pose important adjustment problems in the advanced countries, since they tend to be concentrated in particular regions and confined to particular categories of workers (e.g. women). (UNIDO, 1979c.)

The above conclusions seem reasonable enough, but unfortunately there are serious reservations concerning the model (equation (1)) on which they are based. First, as noted earlier, it is an additive model, which precludes any interaction amongst the independent variables. Thus increases in productivity, in terms of the model, always lead to a reduction in employment, which is clearly unsatisfactory. It is more reasonable to envisage the growth of productivity leading to a reduction in domestic prices and thereby interacting with all the other variables - for example reducing the level of imports from what it otherwise would have been, increasing domestic demand, and on account of both these factors increasing domestic output and employment. Secondly, the model does not consider the competitive effects of imports on the home country's export market in third world countries. Thirdly, and most importantly, equation (1) is singularly inappropriate for analysing the effects of trade in a balance of payments-constrained economy such as that of the UK. In such an economy, an increase in trade imbalance has a multiple effect on the level of domestic demand and output and hence on unemployment. These effects manifest themselves at the level of the economy as a whole and not simply as indirect microeconomic effects of the kind which are often allowed for in the empirical studies. Apart from the direct and indirect impact at the microeconomic level, the deterioration of the trade balance in a particular industry means that unless there is an equal improvement of the balance in another industry, the government (through fiscal and monetary policies) is forced to run the economy at a lower level of output and employment than it otherwise would.

In view of the above difficulties, an alternative approach to examining the impact of third world industrial exports on the advanced countries, which fits in with the earlier analysis of de-industrialisation, seems more useful. In recent contributions, Cripps (1978) and CEPG (1979) have argued that because of long-term structural features which cause adverse and probably cumulative time trends in imports and exports, some advanced countries are in long-term disequilibrium in the sense discussed in section IV, i.e. they are balance-of-payments constrained; others however are not.[35] The second group (which would include Japan and West Germany) may choose price stability rather than full employment, but they are not prevented by balance-of-payments reasons from achieving the latter.[36] On the other hand, it is an underlying assumption of this approach that countries like the US and UK, which are balance-of-payments constrained, are unable to correct the disequilibrium by exchange rate depreciation for all the reasons discussed in the recent literature. (See Featherstone, Moore and Rhodes, 1977; Blackaby, 1979.) They are therefore forced to have low rates of growth of output and employment and therefore investment, which in a free trading system could in fact worsen the initial disequilibrium. (Singh, 1977a.)

The impact of third world manufactured exports on the industrial countries may therefore be studied at two levels. The first is the extent, if any, to which these flows contribute to increasing the imbalances in the international trading system as a whole. Since third world countries have a high propensity to import, their exports to the advanced countries should at first sight cause no disturbance to the system as a whole. However, if trade flows are such that the bulk of third world exports (say) go to balance-of-payments-constrained countries such as the UK, and their imports come from an unconstrained country such as Japan, this would obviously exacerbate the existing imbalances and reduce world trade, output and employment from what they otherwise would be. Although there is not sufficient research on this topic, there is evidence that the third world's trade in manufactures is to some degree a source of imbalance in the international system. (For example, there is a trend increase in Japan's share of third world markets. See CEPG, 1979, Appendix A.)[37]

Secondly, within this framework one could consider the effects on individual countries. For example, previous studies have shown that the main cause of the UK's disequilibrium is trade in finished manufactures with the other advanced nations and not with the third world. Whereas the trade balance in manufactures with other industrial countries has been deteriorating over the last decade or more, with the developing countries it has actually improved. (Woodward, 1977; Singh, 1977b.) The Foreign and Commonwealth Office's (1979) comprehensive study of manufacturing trade between the UK and the newly industrialising countries also provides interesting information bearing on this issue. In 1977, the NICs accounted for 10% of total UK imports of finished manufactures, whilst Japan accounted for 7.7%. (See Table 11.) However, the UK's trade balance with Japan has been increasingly going into deficit, whilst with the NICs there has been a growing surplus. In 1977, the surplus from NICs amounted to about 30% of the total UK surplus on finished manufactures (see Table 12). There is, therefore, a prima facie case for arguing that, despite the fast pace of industrialisation in the NICs and a large increase in their manufactured exports to the UK, the UK's trade with the NICs is leading to an increase in domestic output and employment rather than a reduction.[38] It is trade with the Japanese, by contributing to a further tightening of the balance of payments constraint, which is causing losses in jobs and production. It could well be the case that in the other balance-of-payments-constrained countries, manufacturing trade with the third world has become disequilibriating. Nevertheless, it is likely in general to be a far smaller source of disequilibrium than trade with Japan and other industrial countries.

Thus, quite apart from the effects of the rise in oil prices, imbalances in trade in manufactures are, indeed, an important cause of the slow growth of output, and hence

Table 11: UK imports of finished manufactures (SITC 7 and 8) - percentage coming from NICs, Japan and other countries

Year	From:	NICs	Japan	Others
1963		11.3	2.4	86.3
1964		10.2	2.5	87.2
1965		8.1	2.7	89.4
1966		8.4	2.9	88.6
1967		8.2	3.3	88.5
1968		8.1	2.9	89.0
1969		8.3	2.2	89.5
1970		8.2	3.0	88.7
1971		9.4	4.2	86.4
1972		9.4	6.6	83.9
1973		10.1	7.2	82.7
1974		10.1	7.0	82.9
1975		9.8	6.7	83.5
1976		10.5	6.9	82.6
1977		9.9	7.7	82.4

Source: Foreign and Commonwealth Office (1979).

Table 12: Evolution of UK trade balances in finished manufactures (SITC 7 and 8) with NICs, Japan and other countries, 1963-1977, selected years

(at current prices - $ million, exports f.o.b., imports c.i.f.)

	1963	1964	1968	1969	1973	1974	1976	1977
Balance with:								
NICS								
Exports	360.0	353.7	478.4	552.8	971.7	1254.0	1913.3	2387.4
Imports	73.5	85.6	134.1	152.7	465.7	560.0	925.6	1129.4
Balance	+286.4	+268.1	+344.3	+400.1	+506.0	+694.0	+987.6	+1258.0
Japan								
Exports	21.9	30.7	44.5	60.4	96.2	127.6	147.6	203.7
Imports	15.6	21.2	47.4	40.3	334.3	390.4	613.5	869.4
Balance	+6.3	+9.5	-2.9	+20.0	-238.2	-262.8	-465.9	-665.7
Others								
Exports	1747.9	1308.3	2672.1	3078.8	4856.0	6158.4	10443.3	12856.8
Imports	561.1	729.8	1471.3	1642.0	3831.6	4599.5	7313.5	9356.7
Balance	+1186.8	+1078.5	1200.9	+1436.8	+1024.5	+1559.0	+3129.8	+3500.1
World								
Exports	2129.8	2192.8	3195.1	3692.0	5924.0	7540.1	12504.1	15447.9
Imports	650.3	836.6	1652.8	1835.1	4631.6	5549.6	8852.6	11355.5
Balance	+1479.5	+1356.1	+1542.2	+1856.9	+1292.3	+1990.5	+3651.5	+4092.5

Source: Foreign and Commonwealth Office (1979)

of an increase in unemployment in many of the developed countries. However, these imbalances are essentially due to trade amongst the industrial countries themselves rather than their trade with the third world.[39]

VI. Prospects for third world industrialisation

Despite the slow-down in the expansion of the world economy, the third world countries are in principle in a better position to push ahead with industrialisation than they were a couple of decades ago. A number of them now have the necessary infrastructure, a level of development of key industries, technical and scientific skills and, more importantly, the crucial framework for the further development of these skills, to be able to sustain much higher levels of industrial development. Although 'technology' is still a handicap and will remain so for a long time, it is much less of a disadvantage, and the third world's absorptive capacity is very much higher, than even a decade ago.

In general, the major constraint on future industrial development in the market economy countries of the third world is likely to be the rate of growth of demand, rather than the supply-side factors. This is for two reasons. First, up to now in many of these countries, increased supply resulting from industrialisation has been able to replace imports from the developed countries. This process has probably already reached its limit in some countries; in several others it may shortly do so, if industrial development continues at the same rate as in the past.

Secondly, it is unlikely that the industrial countries will continue to absorb the growth of manufactured exports from the third world at the same rate as in the past. This is partly because for a variety of reasons (disequilibria due to the inadequacies of the international trading and monetary system, or possibly longer-term factors associated with the Kuznets or Kondratrief cycles etc.), the advanced market economies may be entering a period of low long-term growth. Consequently, world trade is likely to grow more slowly than in the past. Further there is growing resistance from trade unions to third world imports, which is bound to affect public policy. Third world countries are certainly right to fight for greater access to developed markets, so as to redress the existing imbalance in world trade, whereby they are forced to export mainly raw materials and commodities and import manufactures. They should also use any bargaining power which they derive from being net importers of manufactures to gain better treatment for their manufactured exports. Nevertheless, in the existing climate, these efforts may not lead to practical results.

The analysis of section V suggests that a better third world strategy for many newly industrialising countries may well be for them to enter into long-term trading arrangements with the 'weaker' industrial countries (e.g. the UK, the US and Italy).[40] The NICs could agree to import capital equipment from these countries, rather than from Japan or Germany, in return for their acceptance of third world manufactured exports. In view of the recession in the capital goods industries in these countries, such a course of action may not only be mutually beneficial to the groups of countries involved,[41] but paradoxically may also be an equilibriating force for the international trading system.

However, in the long term, accelerated industrialisation in the third world requires a relatively much faster expansion of internal demand, individually and collectively, in these countries than has been the case hitherto. This in turn emphasises the need for appropriate strategies towards the development of agriculture and, more importantly, towards the more equitable distribution of the benefits of economic development. If the third world countries adopted sensible policies in these spheres, this would also make possible greater trade between them and thus further encourage their industrial development.

REFERENCES

Barraclough, G. (1978). The Struggle for the Third World, and Waiting for the New Order. *New York Review of Books*, 26 October and 9 November.

Blackaby, F.T. (ed.) (1979). *De-industrialisation*. London: Heinemann.

Brown, C.J.F. and Sheriff, T.D. (1979). De-industrialisation, a background paper, in Blackaby (1979).

Cable, V. (1977). British protectionism and ldc imports. *ODI Review*.

Cairncross, A. (1979). What is de-industrialisation? in Blackaby (1979).

CEPG (1979). *Economic Policy Review*, 5, Cambridge, Department of Applied Economics.

Chenery, H. (1960). Patterns of industrial growth. *American Economic Review*, Vol. 50, No. 4, September.

Chenery, H. and Taylor, L. (1968). Development patterns: among countries and over time. *Review of Economics and Statistics*, Vol. 50, No. 4, November.

Cornwall, J. (1976). Diffusion, convergence and Kaldor's laws. *Economic Journal*, June.

Cripps, T.F. (1978). Causes of growth and recession in world trade. *Economic Policy Review*, No. 4, Cambridge, Department of Applied Economics.

Cripps, T.F. and Tarling, R.J. (1973). *Growth in advanced capitalist economies*. Cambridge: CUP.

Fetherston, M., Moore, B. and Rhodes, J. (1977). Manufacturing export shares and cost-competitiveness of advanced industrial countries. *Economic Policy Review*, No. 3, Cambridge, Department of Applied Economics.

Foreign and Commonwealth Office (1979). The newly industrialising countries and the adjustment problem. London, January.

Frank, Ch. R., Jr. (1977). *Foreign Trade and Domestic Aid*. Washington, D.C.: Brookings Institution.

Godley, W. and Gudgin, G. (1979). International trade and output as a system. Department of Applied Economics, Cambridge, *mimeo*.

Gomulka, S. (1971). *Inventive activity, diffusion and stages of economic growth*. Aarhus: Institute of Economics.

Hughes, A. and Singh, A. (1979). Mergers, concentration and competition in advanced capitalist economies: an international perspective. Forthcoming in *Causes and Effects of Mergers: A Comparative International Study of Seven Nations.*

ILO (1976). *Employment, Growth and basic needs: a one-world problem.* Geneva: International Labour Office.

Kaldor, N. (1967). *Strategic Factors in Economic Development.* Ithaca: Cornell UP.

Kaldor, N. (1975). Economic Growth and the Verdoorn Law: a comment on Mr. Rowthorn's article. *Economic Journal*, December.

Kuznets, S. (1971). *Economic Growth of Nations*, Cambridge, Mass.: Harvard UP.

Lydall, H.F. (1975). *Trade and Employment.* Geneva: International Labour Office.

Leontieff, W. *et al.* (1977). *The Future of the World Economy.* New York: Oxford University Press.

Mukherjee, S. (1978). *Restructuring of industrial economies and trade with developing countries.* Geneva: International Labour Office.

Nayyar, D. (1978). Transnational corporations and manufacturing exports from poor countries. *Economic Journal*, March.

OECD (1978). *Economic Outlook, Occasional Studies*, Paris, July.

Paige, D. (1961). Economic growth: the past hundred years. *National Institute Economic Review*, July.

Ray, C.F. (1976). Labour costs in OECD countries, 1964-75. *National Institute Economic Review*, November.

Rowthorn, R.E. (1975a). What remains of Kaldor's Law. *Economic Journal*, March.

Rowthorn, R.E. (1975b). A reply to Lord Kaldor's comment. *Economic Journal*, December.

Singh, A. (1977a). UK industry and the world economy: a case of de-industrialisation? *Cambridge Journal of Economics*, Vol. 1, No. 2, June.

Singh, A. (1977b). The structural transformation of British industry: an alternative view. Department of Applied Economics, Cambridge, *mimeo*.

Singh, A. (1979a). North Sea oil and the reconstruction of UK industry, in Blackaby (1979).

Singh, A. (1979b). The basic needs approach to development versus the new international economic order: the significance of third world industrialisation. *World Development*, June.

Singh, A. (1980). UK industry and the less developed countries: a long term structural analysis of trade and its impact on the UK economy. Department of Applied Economics, Cambridge, *mimeo*.

Singh, A. and Bienefeld, M. (1977). Industry and urban economy in Tanzania. Background paper for the ILO/JASPA Employment Advisory Mission to Tanzania, *mimeo*.

Stewart, F. (1977). *Technology and Employment*. London.

UNCTAD (1978a). Recent trends and developments in trade in manufactures and semi-manufactures of developing countries and territories, 1977 review. Report by the UNCTAD Secretariat, Geneva, *mimeo*.

UNCTAD (1978b). *Restructuring of world industry: new dimensions for trade co-operation*. New York: United Nations.

UNCTAD (1978c). Growing protectionism and the standstill on trade barriers against imports from developing countries. Geneva, TD/B/C.2/194, 21 March.

UNCTAD (1978d). The role of transnational corporations in the marketing and distribution of exports and imports of developing countries. (TD/B/C.2/197), 16 March.

UNIDO (1975). *Lima Declaration of plan of action on Industrial Development and co-operation.* Vienna: United Nations Industrial Development Organisation.

UNIDO (1979a). *World Industry since 1960: Progress and Prospects.* New York.

UNIDO (1979b). Industrialisation and social objectives of development: some elements of complementarity. *Industry and Development*, No. 4.

UNIDO (1979c). The impact of trade with developing countries on employment in developed countries. Global and Conceptual Studies Section, International Centre for Industrial Studies Vienna.

Winter, L.A. (1979). *The Main Determinants of UK Visible Exports and their Prices.* Ph.D. dissertation. Cambridge: forthcoming as *Projecting Exports*, Cambridge University Press.

Woodward, V. (1976). Government policy and the structure of the economy. Cambridge, Department of Applied Economics, *mimeo.*

Young, A. (1928). Increasing returns and economic progress. *Economic Journal*, December.

FOOTNOTES

1. An earlier version of this paper was presented at the 1979 conference of the Association of University Teachers of Economics, held in Exeter. I am grateful to Jo Bradley, Francis Cripps, David Currie, Graeme Dorrance, John Eatwell, Barry Moore, John Rhodes, Bob Rowthorn and an anonymous referee for helpful discussions or comments on the original draft; the usual caveat applies.

2. See further section III below.

3. A recent Foreign and Commonwealth Office (1979) study included the following in its list of newly industrialising countries: Hong Kong, India, S. Korea, Taiwan, Singapore, Malaysia, Pakistan, Iran, Phillipines, Thailand, Brazil, Argentina, Mexico, Spain, Portugal, Israel, Malta,

Yugoslavia, Greece, Turkey, Poland, Romania and Hungary. However, some of these would not normally be regarded as being third world countries (e.g. Poland, Hungary). The OECD's list of NICs in another recent study is somewhat different. Nevertheless, all such lists usually include Hong Kong, S. Korea, Singapore, Mexico, Brazil, India, Yugoslavia and Taiwan, which between them account for more than 70% of total third world exports of manufactures to the advanced market economy countries. See further section V.

4. Davignon told the developing countries "to stop getting into manufacturing facilities, primarily steel, that provide competition for the rich world". Quoted in Barraclough (1978).

5. These estimates do not include China; their source is the UNIDO report on the steel industry, quoted in *Financial Times*, 7 December 1978.

6. See further section V.

7. See UNIDO (1975).

8. For a detailed account of these measures, see UNCTAD (1978c).

9. For an earlier version of this argument, see Singh (1979b).

10. The number of countries in the 6 country groups identified in Table 1 is as follows:

    L_H 11; L_P 13; S_1 18; S_{2P} 19; S_{2I} 28 and CP 9.

    The stratification of the countries into the various groups was determined by means of cluster analysis using the following criteria: (a) size; (b) resource endowment and (c) production orientation towards primary or manufacturing development. The number of pooled time-series and cross section observations for the period 1960-75 for the respective groups were 176, 208, 288, 304, 448 and 144. The regression equation given in Table 1 provided a very satisfactory fit in each of the country groups, as measured by R^2 and the standard error of the estimates.

11. A broadly similar estimate of the growth elasticity for manufacturing for a typical developing country was obtained by UNCTAD (1978b) in a cross-section study for 1970 of over 50 developing and developed market economy countries. The elasticities were estimated from the following regression equation:

$$log\ v = \beta_0 + \beta_1\ log\ y\ \beta_2(log\ y)^2 + \beta_3\ log\ N$$

where v is value added per capita in manufacturing, y is per capita GDP and N is the size of the population.
See further Singh (1979b)

12. In the context of this paper, this must necessarily be a brief outline of a vast subject. Apart from the references given earlier in the text, see further Gomulka (1971), Kaldor (1975), Rowthorn (1975a, b), Cornwall (1976).

13. Arguments analogous to those in the text have been put forward by Kaldor and others in stressing the structural importance of the manufacturing sector in the growth of overall productivity in the advanced countries. More specifically, first, Cripps and Tarling (1973), in their analysis of the growth process in advanced industrial countries during 1950-70, found confirmation of Kaldor's hypothesis that the 'faster the overall rate of growth, the greater is the excess of the rate of growth of manufacturing production over the rate of growth of economy as a whole'. Secondly, even for advanced countries, where the scope for surplus labour in agriculture may be thought to be much less than in the developing countries, there was evidence that the faster the growth of industrial production and the faster the decline in non-industrial employment, the greater the increase in the growth of productivity in the economy as a whole. The following cross-section relationships for the periods 1950-65 and 1965-75 respectively were observed for these countries:

1950-65

$$p_{GDP} = 1.7 + \underset{(.06)}{0.54}\ q_{ind} - \underset{(.202)}{0.81}\ e_{Ni} \qquad R^2 = 0.81$$

<u>1965-75</u>

$$P_{GDP} = 1.15 + 0.64\, q_{ind} - 0.87\, e_{n.i} \qquad R^2 = .96$$
$$(.06) \qquad (0.12)$$

P_{GDP} is the productivity growth in the economy as a whole
q_{ind} is the rate of growth of industrial production, and
$e_{n.i}$ of that of non-industrial employment.

See further Cripps and Tarling (1973), Kaldor (1975), Rowthorn (1975a,b).

14. For a fuller discussion of the relationship between the satisfaction of basic needs and industrialisation, see Singh (1979b).

15. The results for other types of small economies - i.e. those with abundant resources - are not reported in Table 2. Although the latter reveal somewhat different coefficients for the size elasticities, in general they also show substantially greater values of growth elasticities for producer goods than for the consumer goods industries. See further UNIDO (1979a).

16. These elasticities reflect 'average' experience (being derived from a regression equation). They therefore do not mean that every country has to develop its own steel industry; however, this analysis does suggest the importance of the development of capital goods industries for a country to achieve fast economic growth. A similar conclusion is reached by Leontieff (1977).

17. All the figures quoted in this section, unless otherwise indicated, refer to manufacturing, i.e. ISIC Major Division 3. The words 'manufacturing' and 'industry' are used interchangeably in the text.

18. China is not included in any of the groupings in Table 3. According to UNIDO (1979a) estimates, the inclusion of China would lead to the following percentage shares of the various groups in world manufacturing value added in 1975:

developing countries 8.27; developed market economies 58.70; centrally planned economies (excl. China) 28.06; China 4.96.

19. See UNCTAD (1978a), UNIDO (1979b), UNIDO (1979a).

20. The source of the statistics in this paragraph is UNIDO (1979b).

21. It is important to emphasise that the industrial statistics in Table 3 exclude 'small' firms - in the third world countries, usually firms employing less than 5 or 10 workers. Such firms in the so-called informal sector may account for a fairly large proportion of manufacturing employment, although not of manufacturing output. Expansion of manufacturing output and employment in the formal sector may sometimes be at the expense of the informal sector, but it need not necessarily be so. It could also help to increase the output and employment of small firms.

22. Table 4 shows only the projected growth rates under two different assumptions; it does not show the implied shares of the two groups of countries in world manufacturing production.

23. The latest EEC statistics indicate that even in France, Germany and Italy - the three countries in Table 5 which do not show any long-term trend decline in the proportion of manufacturing employment - there has occurred, between 1974 and 1978, a significant reduction in industry's share in the total labour force. (*Economist*, 15-21 Sept. 1979). However, the latter period is too short to draw any conclusions with respect to long-term changes in the trend.

24. See Singh (1977a); Brown and Sheriff (1979).

25. See Hughes and Singh (1980) for a fuller discussion.

26. For a detailed justification of this definition, see Singh (1977a, 1979b). It should be noted that this conception of an efficient manufacturing sector does not in any way deny the structural importance of manufacturing in the process of economic growth, in the sense discussed in section II. The long-term balance-

of-payments considerations further strengthen the case for the development of successful manufacturing industry.

27. For a discussion of the implications of this conception of de-industrialisation, see also Cairncross (1979), Singh (1979a).

28. For a detailed analysis of the evidence leading to this conclusion, the reader is referred to the references cited in the text.

29. It should be noted that Table 8 provides statistics only on export performance. The fact that a country is losing (or increasing) its share of the world exports of manufactures does not by itself show whether or not it is in long-term disequilibrium in the sense discussed in relation to the UK economy. To establish the latter proposition, it is necessary to study inter alia the behaviour of imports, the movements in the other components of the balance of payments, as well as current and prospective changes in the structure of domestic production.

30. Between 1970 and 1976, the developing countries' exports of manufactures to developed market-economy countries increased in volume terms at a rate of about 14% per annum.

31. The definitions of the country groups (developed and developing) in this table are somewhat different than in Table 9. See UNCTAD (1978a) Annex and CEPG (1979), Appendix A.

32. The subsidiaries of the US multinationals have played a leading role in such exports. See UNCTAD (1978d), Nayyar (1978). As for the overall evaluation of the role of multinationals in promoting economic development in the developing countries, there is a vast literature. This subject must, however, lie outside the scope of the present paper.

33. The equation is derived from the following two identities:

$$O = D + X - M$$

and $P = O/E$

where O is gross output and the other symbols are as in the text.

34. Frank's (1977) study for the US covers the period 1963-71, and examines the effects of changes in trade on 207 'import-competing' industries at the five-digit level. These industries accounted for 46% of total manufacturing output and 40% of manufacturing employment in the US in 1971. Cable (1978) examined the effects of changes in trade over the period 1970-75 on four main product groups, where competition from third world imports has been regarded as being particularly severe - footwear, clothing, cotton textile fabrics and textile yarns. The Foreign and Commonwealth Office (1979) is a more wide-ranging enquiry, which examines in detail the UK's trade over the period 1970-77 with the 23 most important (in terms of UK trade) newly industrialising countries.

35. For a detailed description of the world trading system in these terms, and of the underlying analytical model, see CEPG (1979), Chapter I and Appendix I. The adverse long-term time trend terms in the import and export functions for manufactures have for example been observed in a number of econometric studies for the UK economy. See among others, Fetherston, Moore and Rhodes (1977) and Winter (1979).

36. This is not to say that even Japan or W. Germany may not sometimes be forced by a short-term worsening of the trade balance (due to, say, a large increase in the oil bill) to take immediate remedial action, as indeed they have done in the past. The argument in the text refers to the long-established structural trends. For example, in Japan, excluding fuels, the current account balance has risen rapidly and consistently from $ 1.4 billion in 1960 to $ 36.7 billion in 1977 (at constant 1975 prices for manufactures). See further Gudgin and Godley (1979); CEPG (1979).

37. Lydall's (1975) major study was also concerned with the impact of increased manufactured exports from the developing countries on the developed countries as a whole. However, he assumed 'a balanced increase in trade' between the two groups and did not consider the

imbalances which, despite the overall balance, this may create in the individual developed countries.

38. For a fuller examination of these issues and for a disaggregated analysis of the UK's manufacturing trade with the third world countries, see Singh (1980).

39. In this paper, the 'Club of Rome' type issues concerning the future of the world economy have not been considered - i.e. whether the present rate of growth of the world economy is sustainable given the foreseeable availabilities of raw materials. A proper treatment of these questions would require a great deal of space and take us too far afield from the main theme of this paper. There are, however, two relevant considerations which arise from the earlier analysis and to which I should like to draw attention. First, Table 4, on the implications of the Lima target, suggests that even if the third world countries were able to meet the target (of 25% of world manufacturing production), by the year 2000, the overall rate of growth of the world economy during the next two decades would be somewhat lower than what it was in the twenty years preceding the oil price rise of 1973. Secondly, Table 3 (on the growth of manufacturing production in the various groups of countries between 1960-1975) shows that there has already been a fundamental relocation of world industry during this period which has not harmed industrial development in the old industrial countries. The share of the centrally planned economies of Eastern Europe in world manufacturing increased from 18% to 28%; it would be difficult to argue that this was at the expense of the Western industrial economies.

40. 'Weaker' in the sense of being balance-of-payments constrained. However, in relation to Italy, see the interesting recent paper by G. De Vivo and M. Pivetti in the *Cambridge Journal of Economics*, March 1980.

41. With respect to the UK, it could be argued that the third world countries would in that case be purchasing machinery and equipment which is not the most modern. This may, however, be an advantage rather than a disadvantage at the level of economic development at which many third world countries presently are. See further Stewart (1977); UNIDO (1979a); Singh and Bienefeld (1977).